BY THE GRACE OF THE GODS 2

Story:	Art:	Character Design:
Roy	**Ranran**	**Ririnra**

Translation: Sheldon Drzka
Lettering: Elena Pizarro
Cover Design: Andrea Miller
Editor: Tania Biswas

BY THE GRACE OF THE GODS Volume 2
© Roy
© 2018 Ranran / SQUARE ENIX CO., LTD.
First published in Japan in 2018 by SQUARE ENIX CO., LTD.
English translation rights arranged with
SQUARE ENIX CO., LTD. and SQUARE ENIX, INC.
English translation © 2021 by SQUARE ENIX CO., LTD.

ISBN: 978-1-64609-081-5

Library of Congress Cataloging-in-Publication
Data is on file with the publisher.

Printed in the U.S.A.
First printing, May 2021
10 9 8 7 6 5 4 3 2 1

SQUARE ENIX
MANGA & BOOKS
www.square-enix-books.com

⟩ THE FIRST CAMP ⟨

The duke's entourage, Ryoma in tow, departed from the Forest of Gana. During the early part of their journey, however, a landslide forced them to set up camp for a night.

"Squad 3! All is well!"

"Good work! Squad 4 will take over the watch now!"

As the sun set on the encampment, there was a changing of the guard keeping watch over the duke and his family.

Ryoma was outside of his assigned tent, absentmindedly watching the switch.

Five figures approached him.

"Oh, Ryoma. What are you doing there?"

"Ah! Welcome back."

It was the current duke, Reinhart, who had addressed Ryoma. He returned the boy's reflexive response with a smile. Reinhart was accompanied by his wife, Elise; their daughter, Eliaria; the previous duke, Reinbach; and the family butler, Sebas. They all spoke to Ryoma in turn.

"Oh, did you come out to meet us?"

"We're back, Ryoma."

"Aren't you cold just standing there?"

"The rain might have stopped, but the sun has gone down, after all"

"Thank you. I'm not cold. The smell after the rain makes me feel at peace."

Still unaccustomed to conversations with others after spending years in solitude, Ryoma often gave short answers. Thanks to his self-sufficient lifestyle in the forest, the chilly evening air was no problem for him. Back before he became proficient with magic, starting a fire with fire magic was all Ryoma could do to stay warm.

His current situation weighed on him more than the cold. It wasn't exactly an issue, but he did feel uncomfortable being around so many people after three years.

"Are you all right?"

"You don't have to stand out here. You can go inside."

The duke and his family looked worried about Ryoma, who they thought distrusted other human beings. Ryoma picked up on this but didn't agree with the assessment.

Even in his past life, Ryoma wasn't very good at being sociable. Now in his reincarnated form, three years of living as he liked in the forest had soothed his soul, despite work fatigue typically making him feel antisocial. That's why he had been interested in leaving the forest and hadn't turned down the invitation of his current companions.

"I just can't relax. I'm fine. Sorry to make you worry. You're good people."

While Ryoma had been standing there, several guards had spoken to him. Some wanted help removing debris from the road, while others thanked him for using barrier magic to assist in setting up camp. He didn't sense fear from any of them.

It was true that the duke and his family had personally brought Ryoma along, but he was a child without any parents who had been living alone in the forest. It wouldn't have been wrong to write him off as a homeless waif, and yet all the guards were kind to him. Ryoma even thought it odd that none of them seemed the least bit suspicious.

On top of that, Ryoma was responsible for his own security and meals in the forest, but now the family's guards and their maids provided all that. As for food, plenty had been prepared for the journey and stored with Sebas's space magic, so there was no need to hunt. Now Ryoma had a lot of time on his hands.

"That's partly because we notified the guards beforehand, but I suppose it's that you don't look much like a waif to begin with, Ryoma. Your appearance is clean, and though you're not exactly a chatterbox, you seem to have a fair grasp of manners and etiquette."

"True. Besides, you haven't been acting fishy at all. And of course, you saved the life of our man Hughes. To the guards, you saved one of their own. There isn't a fellow in this outfit who would feel indiscriminate hostility toward a child like that. It may be difficult, but going forward, you should accept it for what it is."

"That's right. And if you have too much free time, you should do something to take your mind off your worries."

"If you are interested in board games, Master Ryoma, I have several stored in my Item Box."

"Um, Ryoma, if you don't mind, I'd like to ask you something about slimes..."

"Oh, uh...then why don't we go inside?"

Ryoma sensed the consideration of the five and was slightly bewildered by it, but he went along anyway.

The six of them walked several paces to a large tent and went inside. They sat at a table and were immediately served a hot drink by the two maids.

"Ahhh... That warms me up," Eliaria said after taking a big gulp.

Going by the eagerness with which the adults also partook of their beverages, Ryoma guessed they'd all grown chilled from being outside. At the same time, he wondered what the whole family had being doing outside in the first place.

"We were addressing all our guards."

"A third of them had just finished their training before embarking on this journey with us, so they're new at this. Even though they work for us, there aren't many chances to speak to them directly. So we took this opportunity to talk to them, learn their names and faces, give them a bit of liquor, and just show our general appreciation."

Listening to Reinhart's explanation reminded Ryoma of the company he had worked for in his past life.

The young company president would suddenly drop in on Ryoma's department, with no rhyme or reason, only to exercise his authority. If he spoke to you, you would have to stop what you were doing. And the longer he talked, the further behind you would fall in your work. When he couldn't answer the president's questions to the man's satisfaction, Ryoma would be subjected to a meaningless lecture. Preparedness, ambition, spirit... In a scolding voice, the president once forced his new employee to listen to a nebulous idealistic treatise that made him wither in his seat. Ryoma had searched for scraps of wisdom in his boss's diatribe, but though the speech was long, it was light on content, and the main points were vague.

It had proven an excruciating waste of time.

"The light in your eyes has suddenly gone out... Are you all right?"

"Oh! I'm fine. I was just recalling something that happened in my village."

Ryoma immediately sought to change the subject.

However, three years of isolation had done nothing to improve on his already poor conversational skills, so...

"Ryoma, the chief of your village must have been an odd duck, indeed…"

"Mm. Truly a bad example. It's fine to speak with one of your retinue, but you mustn't interfere with their work. It's even worse if you browbeat them while exposing your own incompetence. I never want to see you become like that, Eliaria."

"I won't, Grandfather!"

So they wouldn't think he was dissembling, Ryoma had told them more or less what he had been thinking back on, though couched in terms of something that had happened in his "old village."

Reinbach, picking up on Ryoma's desire to change the subject, mercifully did so.

"Ah, well. By the way, Elia, didn't you want to ask Ryoma something?"

"Oh, that's right! May I ask you a question about raising slimes?"

Ryoma was quick to respond.

"Sure! Anything."

He could easily become discouraged by suddenly reminiscing about his past life, but he could just as easily regain his equilibrium.

This was especially true when the topic turned to slimes, with Ryoma growing more talkative.

"It's about what I should feed my slime…"

Eliaria had admired Ryoma's cleaner slimes, and she took his advice in the Forest of Gana, choosing a slime that would likely evolve into a cleaner slime and making a Taming Contract with it. Naturally, her plan afterward was to do everything she could to encourage her slime to evolve into cleaner slime.

"Um… Cleaner slime food is human sebum and stuff like that, right? Is mine alone enough? I would hate to have it go hungry because my body isn't producing enough oils."

"I think it should be fine. Just so long as you're raising the one slime… When I had my first slime, it took six months for it to evolve. As long as you're feeding it something, there's no problem. But if you're really worried…you could always feed it something else."

Eliaria harbored reservations about that answer.

"May I? You told me that what slimes eat has an effect on their evolution, but if you give it something else, could it evolve into something else?"

"If you feed it a lot every day, there's nothing to worry about."

As examples, Ryoma brought up sticky slime and poison slime. These two kinds had preferences for green caterpillars and poisonous plants respectively, but they would also eat meat from animals Ryoma had hunted. Through a myriad of experiments, Ryoma had learned that if you gave your slime a regular diet of its favorites and corresponding food, there was very little chance that the course of its evolution would change.

"So…I think it's a good idea to feed your slime mainly food that suits its taste while supplementing its nutrition with other foodstuffs. You chose your slime with the idea that it would become cleaner slime, milady, so if you give it what it prefers every day, it's highly unlikely that it would evolve into anything other than that.

If you're going to give it something else, tallow would be good, if possible. It's the fat from animals. Before my slimes evolved into cleaner slimes, it seemed that went down easier than meat."

"Oh, really?! We can buy tallow somewhere, can't we, Father?"

"There are products that use tallow and shops that deal in it as an ingredient. I'm sure if I put in an order with the Merchants' Guild, it would be readily obtainable."

"...I see. So you can buy it in town..."

For Ryoma, who had lived a self-sufficient life in the woods, obtaining tallow would've involved him hunting down an animal and removing the fat himself.

Eliaria was pleased to hear the tips on feeding, and Ryoma warmed to his subject. Eventually, the conversation turned to the topic of whether or not slimes evolve unconsciously.

"...First of all, a slime is a monster that doesn't need much food, so even if it does without for a while, it won't starve to death right away. If food is truly scarce, it will go out in search of its own. Anyway, I'm sure you wouldn't let it starve."

"Thank you, Ryoma. That's a load off my mind."

"Glad to hear it."

"One more thing... I'd like to hear more about post-evolution cleaner slimes. I don't think my father knows much about them either."

"As far as cleaner slimes go... I think I told you just about all there is to know. Other than it's a slime that prefers to eat sebum and dirt..."

After a moment, Ryoma shared an idea he had been mulling in his head.

"...I think maybe...slimes evolved into cleaner slimes to have a symbiotic relationship with humans."

"A symbiotic relationship?"

"Er... I remember hearing a long time ago that evolution is 'the phenomenon of a living being's characteristics changing over generations' and that the purpose of evolution is for the living being to adapt to its environment... The changes may be unintended, but in nature, if a creature can't find something to eat or can't protect itself, it won't be able to survive and procreate. That's why living beings in the wild continue to evolve to keep up with their surroundings."

After checking to see that she understood his explanation, Ryoma continued.

"In the case of the slimes, when each one begins to evolve, the process takes less than a night, but I think the goal is the same."

Sticky slime evolved sticky solution to capture prey.

Poison slime evolved the ability to eat poisonous things and protect itself with poison.

Acid slime, like poison slime, evolved to absorb hard bones and to defend itself.

Scavenger slime evolved the ability to eat anything, particularly things that are inedible.

Through evolution, slimes were able to procure food more easily and, depending on the type, acquired methods of self-defense.

Ryoma thought that these were the results of the slimes changing themselves and that they did it for survival.

"There are a great many ways to survive and cases of symbiotic relationships, which I mentioned before, in the world... There are numerous creatures out there that live in the same environments as other creatures, and they both benefit by cooperating with one another. That's what my grandmother told me."

On Earth, there were remora that clung to large sharks, eating parasites and excrement. Another example was clownfish that lived among sea anemones.

"There certainly are many monsters that employ such a mode of life."

"Indeed. Mailfish, for example."

Ryoma was relieved.

They'd understood what he was trying to say, and this world also had creatures that coexisted with one another.

"So I suspect cleaner slime have also achieved that kind of evolution."

Whether or not they fed on sebum or filth, cleaner slimes didn't have the capacity to hunt the people or animals that produced those things. Cleaner slimes were no different than regular slimes when it came to fighting ability.

There were of course rare cases of illogical evolution, where the objective failed or was lost sight of.

However, by virtue of human patronage, cleaner slimes gained the ability to be useful to people by cleaning their bodies.

Ryoma thought that counted as a relationship.

"To sum it all up, I think it's possible that cleaner slimes evolved to be able to coexist with humans. I guess that's the only other thing I didn't tell you."

"Interesting."

"That does sound like it could be a possibility."

While the adults were talking about it, Eliaria pondered Ryoma's words.

Eventually, a radiant smile lit up her face.

"Slimes that can coexist with people... Ryoma! Now I'm looking forward to this little one's evolution even more!"

"That's great..."

Seeing her so pleased made Ryoma feel warm inside too.

"I can't wait for it to evolve."

"Ah... If you prepare a lot of food for it, a slime will evolve faster. I did an experiment on that, so I'm positive."

"Oh! Then if I bathe several times a day, it may evolve that much quicker."

"Elia, taking too many baths isn't good for your health."

"It would use up a lot of water and firewood as well."

"...True..."

Eliaria gave up on the idea.

As the daughter of a duke, she was privileged, but within limits. Her parents made sure of that.

Ryoma was charmed by the sight of the girl reluctantly letting go of her wasteful idea.

"How about a way that's not unhealthy or wasteful?"

Ryoma already had a plan. From an Item Box, he took out an approximately two-liter container marked "Magic Recovery Medicine, Economy Size."

§

One hour later...

One more large tent had just been set up in a corner of the encampment.

It was meant for meetings, with enough room to accommodate several adults, though no floor had been laid.

Soldiers on their breaks were lined up at the entrance to the tent, with a few milling about to maintain the line.

A young soldier walked up to another who was standing at the end of the queue.

"Hello. I heard we could wash up inside. Is this where we get in line?"

"Yes. According to the soldiers who've already come out, they've got a huge tub of hot water that you can bathe in. You know the child that His Grace picked up in the forest?"

"The boy who was helping us clear away debris this afternoon?"

"Aye. Apparently, he and the young mistress wanted to show their appreciation to us for guarding them."

"Ain't that grand?! I never expected soldiers like us to get rewarded like that."

It must have been a boring wait. The man in front of the last two joined the conversation. He looked at the young soldier.

"Mm? Why are you empty-handed? What about your clothes?"

"Huh? I heard we could just come as we are."

"Oh, that's if you're just going to wash your body. Look over there."

The young man followed his comrade's gaze to Ryoma, who had used earth magic to erect a large platform, atop which cleaner slimes were lined up. Two maids joined him, accepting clothes from a number of soldiers.

"Apparently, the slimes on that platform eat people's sweat and grime. The duke's staff are using them to clean our clothes. And it only takes 'em a few seconds."

"You've got gear you've been wearing since yesterday, right? Take them over there. That way, after you get cleaned up, you'll be able to wear fresh clothes for a day.

Also, that stone wall with the door is a toilet. There're slimes down the hole that eat what we drop, so it doesn't stink. Now no one's gotta hold their breath when they go. And they said we're free to use it."

"...You wouldn't think we were on the march."

"Just don't get spoiled. All this ain't a regular feature."

"Yeah, usually, unless we reach a town or river, we gotta keep wearing our clothes as is, no matter how sweaty or foul they get."

"I-I see! I'll keep that in mind."

"Well, we're gettin' treated this time around by the young miss and the kid, so take advantage!"

"Right! I'll go get my clothes!"

The young soldier ran off, and the conversation continued between the other two men.

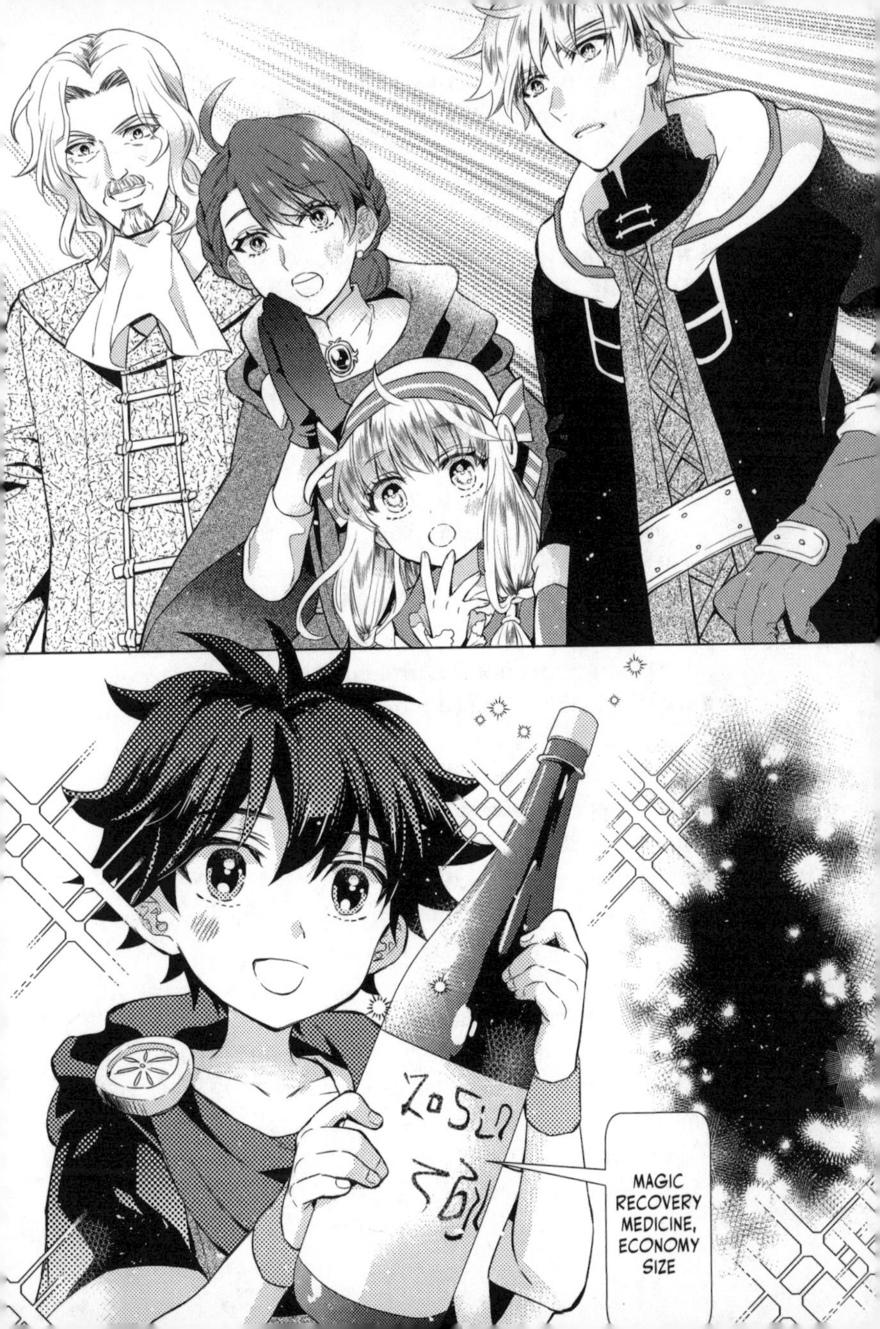
MAGIC RECOVERY MEDICINE, ECONOMY SIZE

Another pair of men emerged from the rear of the tent, satisfied smiles on their faces.

"Milady?! Are you around?"

"Oh, come over here, you two."

"Hughes! There are new recruits here who are still learning, so please set a good example."

"Oh, what's the harm, Camil? So how's it going, milady?"

"You never listen..."

"It's going very well. And this is so much fun!"

Out back of the tent, Eliaria, the duke's daughter, was using fire magic under the direction of butler Sebas. She was keeping the fire going to heat the cauldron connected to the giant hot-water tub in the tent.

"I get to be useful to everyone with my magic, and my slime is pleased about it too!"

She looked affectionately at the hollow next to the cauldron. Ryoma had made a deep hole connected to a sloping channel that he'd dug from within the tent. The used hot water would be dumped into the channel and flow right into the hole.

"Ryoma, I'm impressed with this idea of yours, putting a large hot-water vessel inside a tent and then turning it into a steam bath with the steam from the hot water and barrier magic. On top of that, collecting the used hot water for milady's slime to consume on the one hand...and even giving your own slimes a feast on the other."

"I overhead them talking over there. They love it."

"Really? That makes me so happy!"

"It's not like we forced them to use it and certainly no one's complaining about a place where they get to bathe and warm up. Also, milady, this is from Ryoma."

Camil gave her a bottle.

"Oh, the one from before."

"A homemade magic recovery potion, I take it."

"Milady, you haven't talked to him about your magical energy?"

"No, I…just haven't found the right time…"

"It seems he has an enormous amount of magical energy too, and you know what he's like. You should go ahead and ask him about it."

"Hughes…"

With a word, Camil restrained Hughes from further addressing Eliaria's anxiety.

Of course, Hughes meant well, but it wasn't his place.

"Mm, well, you'll know when you're ready, li'l miss."

"Thank you for worrying about me."

"Sure. Anyway, we gave you the potion, so we'll be on our way."

"Oh, where are you going?"

"The place we put the fallen trees this afternoon. Ryoma wants us to pick any red fruit we find growing on them."

"Over there, y'all. Check it out!"

Hughes was pointing at Ryoma in the distance, accepting some kind of sweet from a soldier.

"More 'n' more of us are showing him our thanks. He says he wants to repay our kindness too. I don't really get it, but he said if he sets traps using the red fruit as a lure, we may be able to capture tasty birds for tomorrow's breakfast. What did he call them, again? 'Swallows'?"

"Fruit birds. He said they resemble a bird called a 'swallow.'"

"I've never heard they were edible."

"He said they're so small and weak that their meat goes bad soon after they die, so you have to capture them alive if you're going to eat them. That's why it's not commonly known. But Ryoma can catch them alive by using sticky slimes."

"He also said they're so delicious that it's worth all the effort. He especially wants you to try it, milady."

"Oh! I'm looking forward to it. But for now, I'll keep doing my best here."

"Yes, keep up the good work, milady."

"Thank you!"

Full of more spirit than ever, Eliaria returned to the job of boiling the water.

"Milady, please make a fire for this cauldron next."

"All right."

Eliaria was skilled at fire magic, and no ordinary person had even a fraction of the magical energy she possessed. Ryoma didn't know that yet, but as it happened, she was the right person in the right place for the job.

Powerful flames borne of her seemingly inexhaustible magic quickly got the water bubbling, which gave the soldiers a few minutes of comfort and eventually became nutrition for her familiar. She had a complex about the amount of magical energy she had versus her ability to control it, but in fact, she was secretly pleased when her magic was useful to people.

As Hughes suggested, making up her mind to tackle the issue plaguing her was for another day...

However, perhaps this experience would become a small help when that time eventually came.

But most importantly...

"...... ♪"

Deep down in the hollow, Eliaria's slime silently continued to drink the soldiers' used bathwater as it flowed down the channel, consuming a huge quantity of nutrients and bringing it ever closer to its long-awaited evolution.

THE END

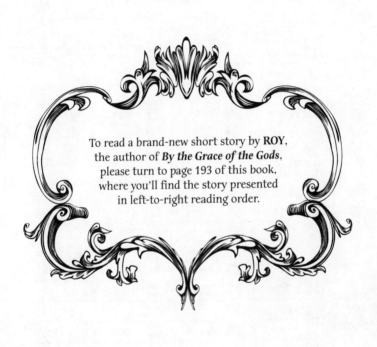

To read a brand-new short story by **ROY**,
the author of *By the Grace of the Gods*,
please turn to page 193 of this book,
where you'll find the story presented
in left-to-right reading order.

RYOMA TAKEBAYASHI

NAME	RYOMA TAKEBAYASHI (SEX: MALE • AGE: 11 • SPECIES: HUMAN)
STRENGTH	11,052 (AVERAGE FOR ADULT MALE: 1,000)
MAGIC	198,000 (NORMAL MAGIC-USER: 1,000-5,000)
TITLES	ASCENDANT • GRADUATE FROM AN UNFORTUNATE LIFE • GOD OF WAR'S APPRENTICE • BELOVED CHILD OF THE GODS
GUARDIANS	GAIN THE CREATOR • KUFO, GOD OF LIFE • LULUTIA, GODDESS OF LOVE • TEKUN, GOD OF WINE

EVERYDAY SKILLS

HOUSEKEEPING	10	ETIQUETTE	7	PERFORMANCE	3	SINGING	3
CALCULATION	5						

COMBAT SKILLS

UNARMED	7	SWORD	7	DAGGER	6	CONCEALED WEAPONS	7
SPEAR	4	BOW & ARROW	6	STAFF	6	CHAIN WEAPONS	4
THROWING WEAPONS	7	STEALTH	7	TRAPPING	6	BODY CONTROL	6
ENERGY MEDITATION	5						

MAGIC SKILLS

TAMING	2	BARRIER	2	HEALING	1	ALCHEMY	2
FIRE	3	WATER	3	WIND	2	EARTH	4
NEUTRAL	3	LIGHTNING	1	ICE	2	POISON	2
WOOD	3	LIGHT	2	DARK	1	SPACE	3
MAGIC DETECTION	3	MAGIC CONTROL	4	MAGIC RECOVERY	2		

CRAFTING SKILLS

MEDICINE	6	METALWORK	1	BUILDING	3	WOODWORK	3
SCULPTURE	4	PAINTING	4				

RESISTANCE SKILLS

PHYSICAL PAIN RESIST	8	MENTAL PAIN RESIST	9	HEALTH	7
STENCH RESISTANCE	3				

SPECIAL SKILLS

LIFE BOOST	3	SUPER-RECOVER	3	STAMINA BOOST	6	FOCUS	5
SURVIVAL ARTS	5	ORACLE	3				

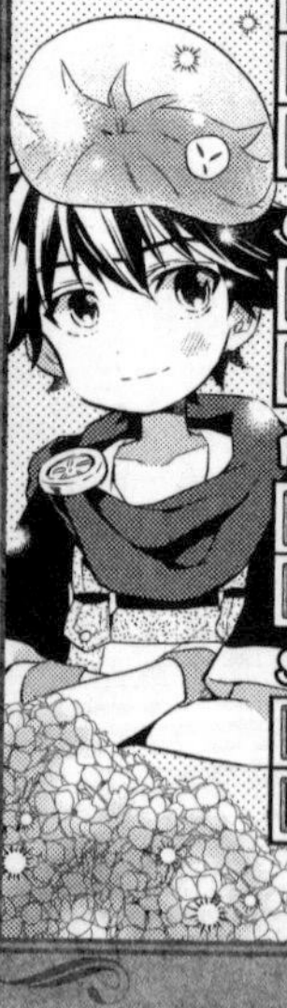

CURRENT STATS

Tabuchi's Journal

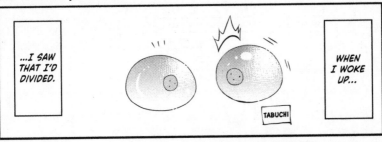

WHEN I WOKE UP...
...I SAW THAT I'D DIVIDED.
TABUCHI
WHY DOES IT LOOK EXACTLY LIKE ME?
OF COURSE.
GLOOM
?
HE WON'T BE ABLE TO TELL WHICH ONE I AM NOW.
HUH?? YOU'VE DIVIDED!
GREAT JOB, TABUCHI-KUN!
HUH?!
HE CAN STILL TELL ME APART!!
TABUCHI IS BESIDE HIMSELF WITH JOY~!
ALL RIGHT, I'LL DO A TAMING CONTRACT WITH YOU TOO!!
RYOMA REALIZED RIGHT AWAY BECAUSE HE DIDN'T YET HAVE A CONTRACT WITH THE NEWLY DIVIDED SLIME.
GOOD LUCK, TABUCHI!!

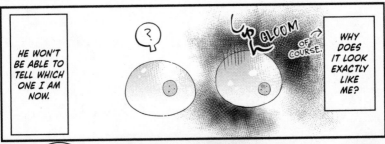

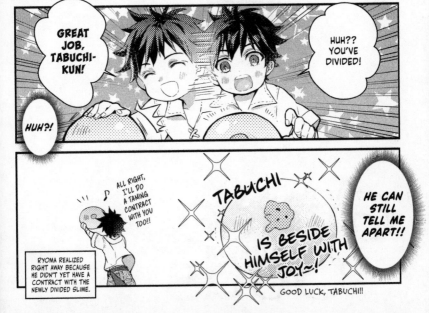

BY THE
GRACE
OF THE
GODS

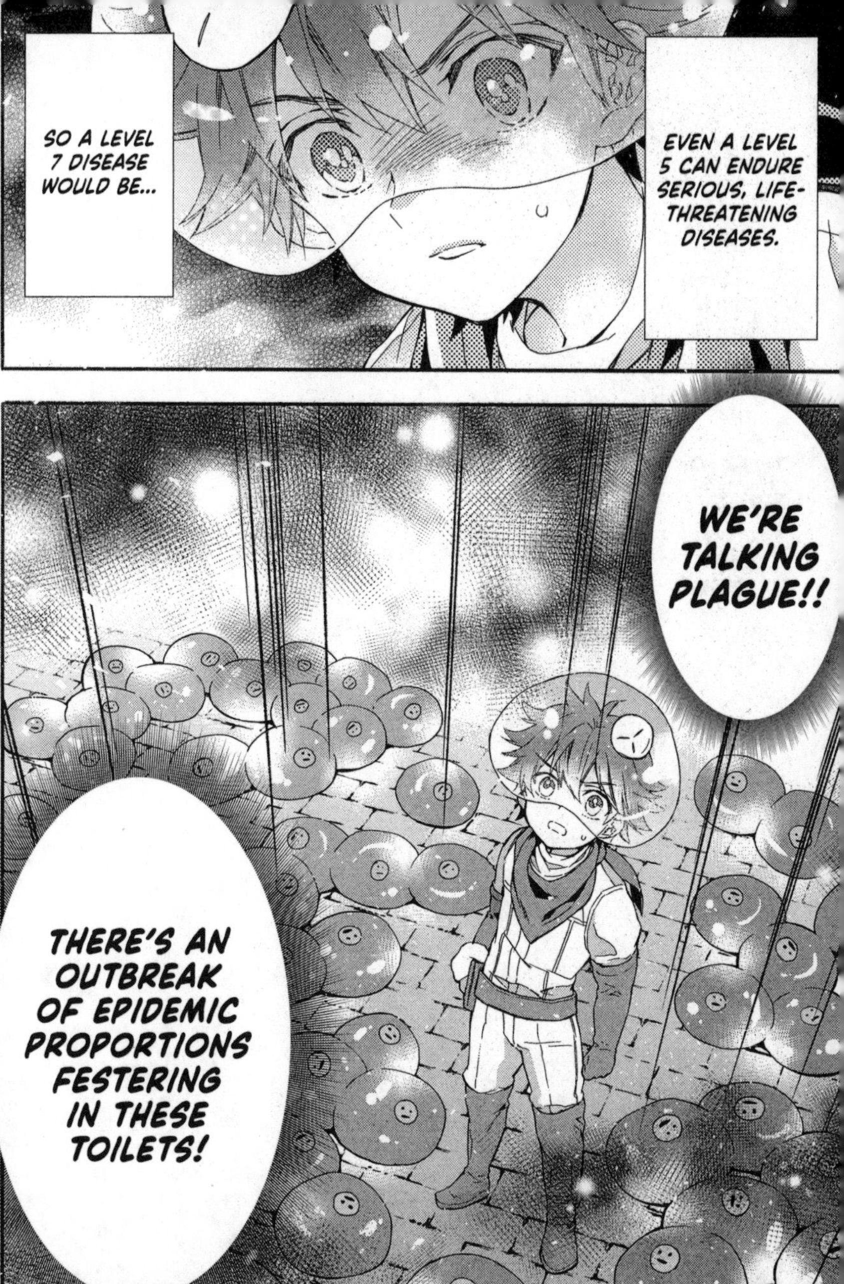
EVEN A LEVEL 5 CAN ENDURE SERIOUS, LIFE-THREATENING DISEASES.
SO A LEVEL 7 DISEASE WOULD BE...
WE'RE TALKING PLAGUE!!
THERE'S AN OUTBREAK OF EPIDEMIC PROPORTIONS FESTERING IN THESE TOILETS!

BY THE GRACE OF THE GODS Volume 2: The End

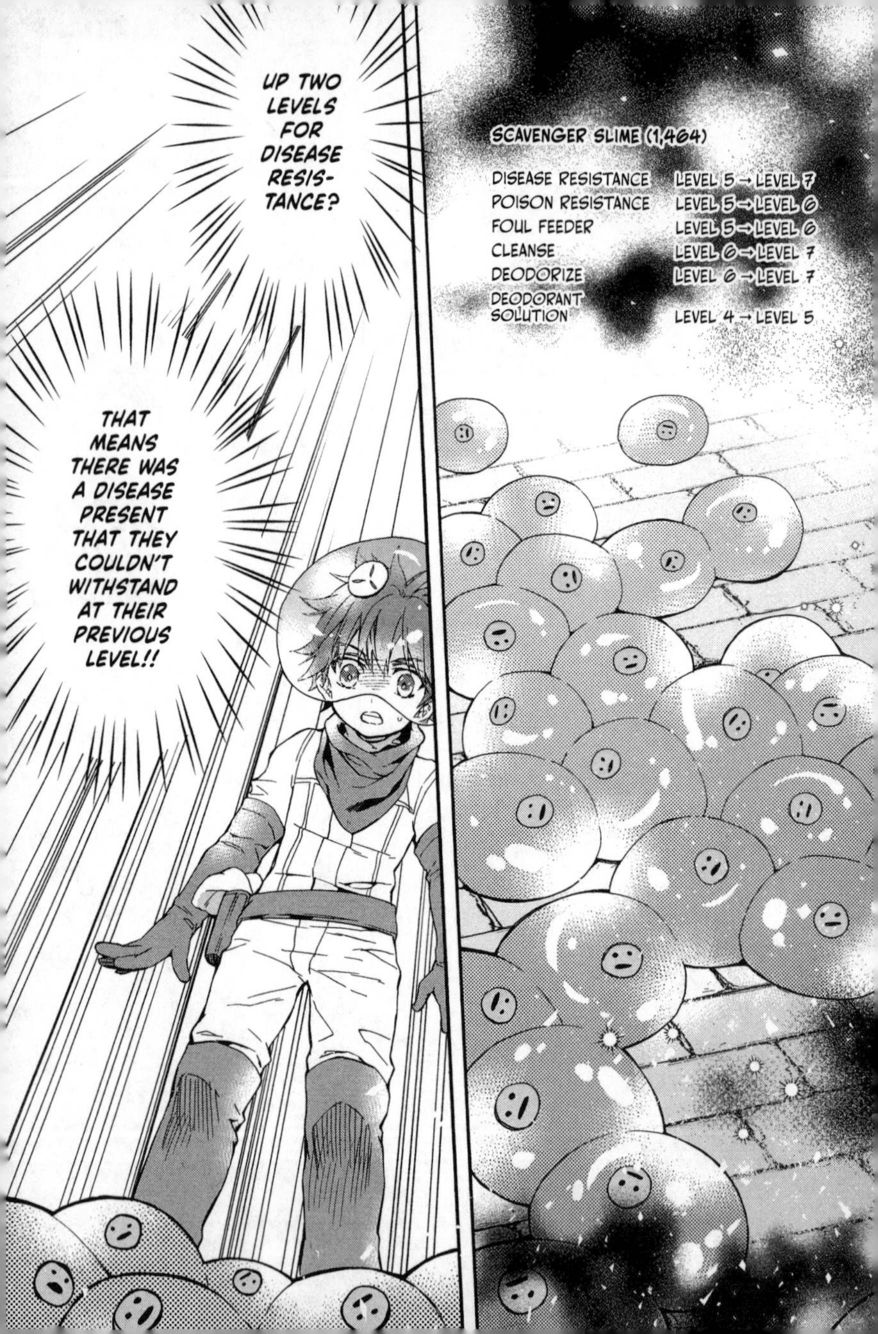
SCAVENGER SLIME (1,464)
DISEASE RESISTANCE LEVEL 5 → LEVEL 7
POISON RESISTANCE LEVEL 5 → LEVEL 6
FOUL FEEDER LEVEL 5 → LEVEL 6
CLEANSE LEVEL 6 → LEVEL 7
DEODORIZE LEVEL 6 → LEVEL 7
DEODORANT SOLUTION LEVEL 4 → LEVEL 5
UP TWO LEVELS FOR DISEASE RESISTANCE?
THAT MEANS THERE WAS A DISEASE PRESENT THAT THEY COULDN'T WITHSTAND AT THEIR PREVIOUS LEVEL!!

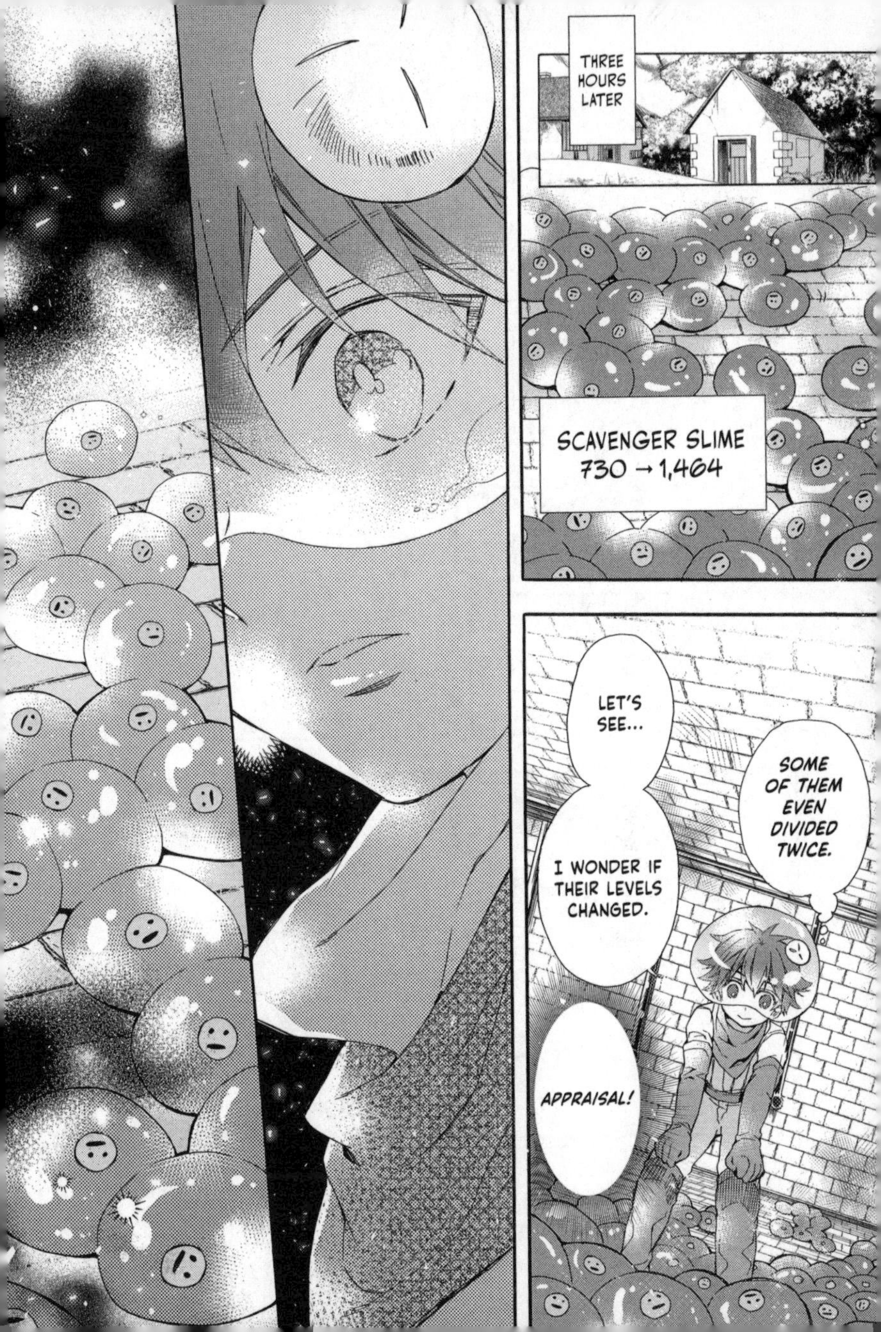
THREE HOURS LATER
SCAVENGER SLIME
730 → 1,464
SOME OF THEM EVEN DIVIDED TWICE.
LET'S SEE...
I WONDER IF THEIR LEVELS CHANGED.
APPRAISAL!

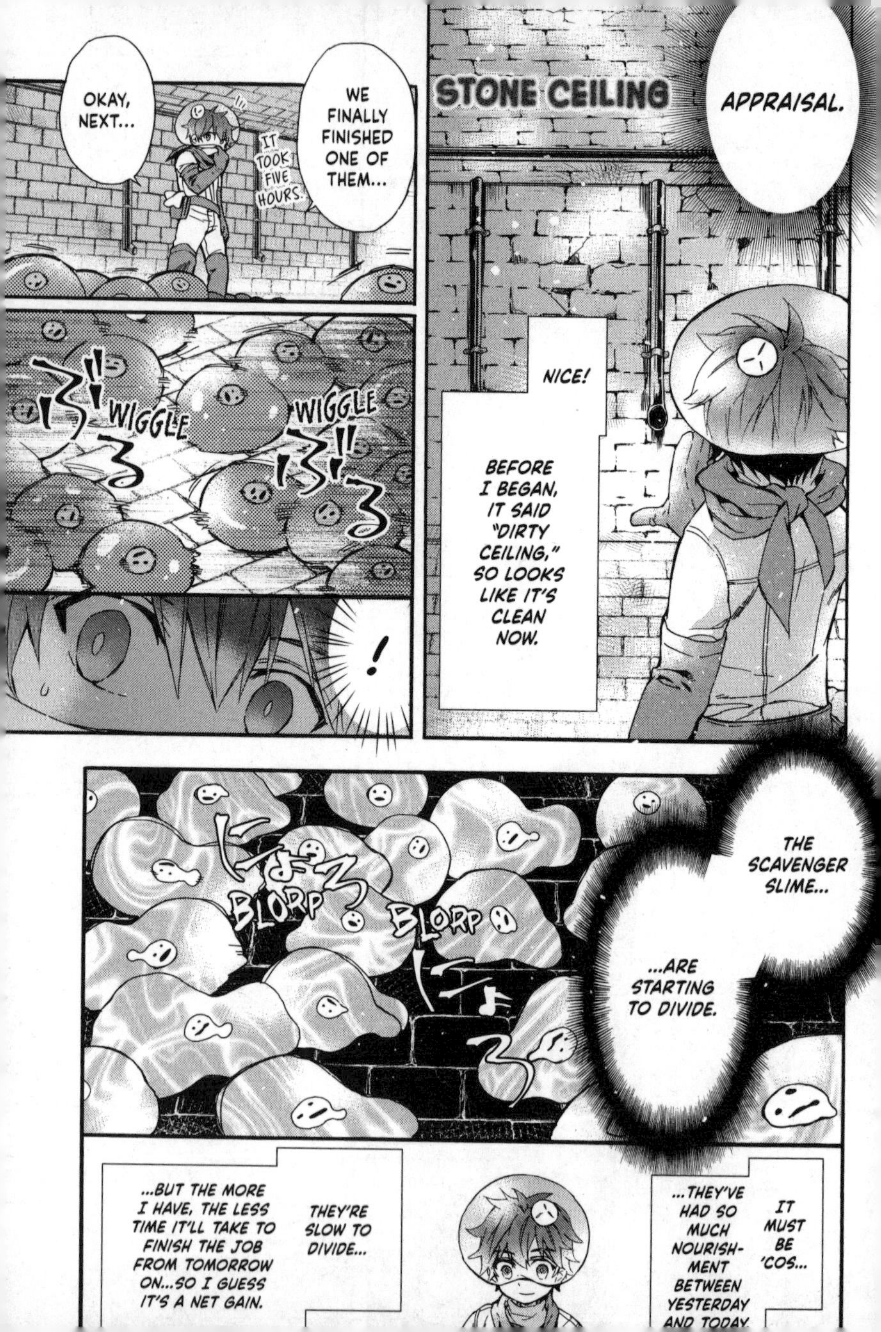

APPRAISAL.
STONE CEILING
NICE!
BEFORE I BEGAN, IT SAID "DIRTY CEILING," SO LOOKS LIKE IT'S CLEAN NOW.
WE FINALLY FINISHED ONE OF THEM...
IT TOOK FIVE HOURS.
OKAY, NEXT...
WIGGLE
WIGGLE
!
THE SCAVENGER SLIME...
...ARE STARTING TO DIVIDE.
BLORP
BLORP
IT MUST BE 'COS...
...THEY'VE HAD SO MUCH NOURISHMENT BETWEEN YESTERDAY AND TODAY
THEY'RE SLOW TO DIVIDE...
...BUT THE MORE I HAVE, THE LESS TIME IT'LL TAKE TO FINISH THE JOB FROM TOMORROW ON...SO I GUESS IT'S A NET GAIN.

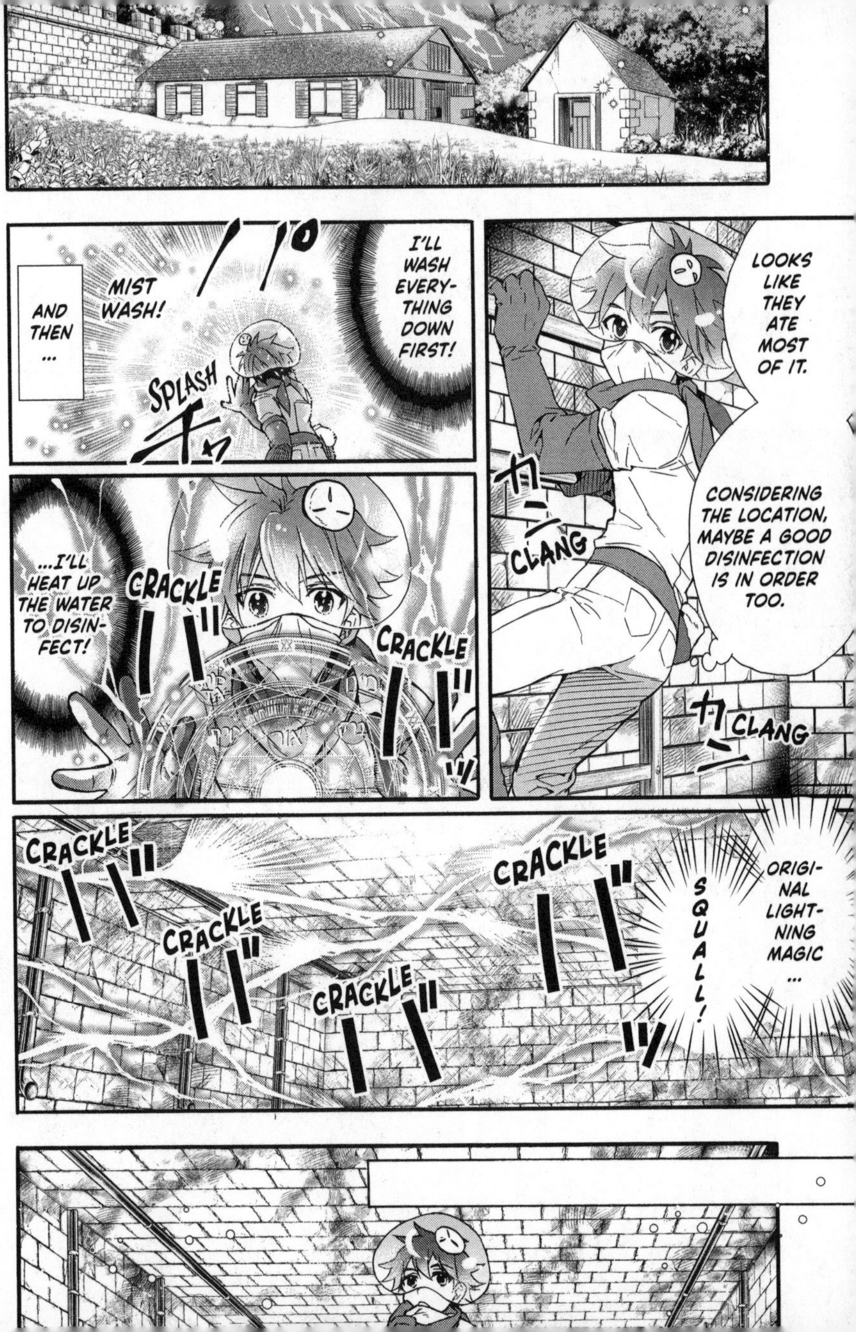

LOOKS LIKE THEY ATE MOST OF IT.
CLANG
CONSIDERING THE LOCATION, MAYBE A GOOD DISINFECTION IS IN ORDER TOO.
CLANG
I'LL WASH EVERYTHING DOWN FIRST!
MIST WASH!
AND THEN...
SPLASH
...I'LL HEAT UP THE WATER TO DISINFECT!
CRACKLE
CRACKLE
ORIGINAL LIGHTNING MAGIC...
SQUALL!
CRACKLE
CRACKLE
CRACKLE
CRACKLE

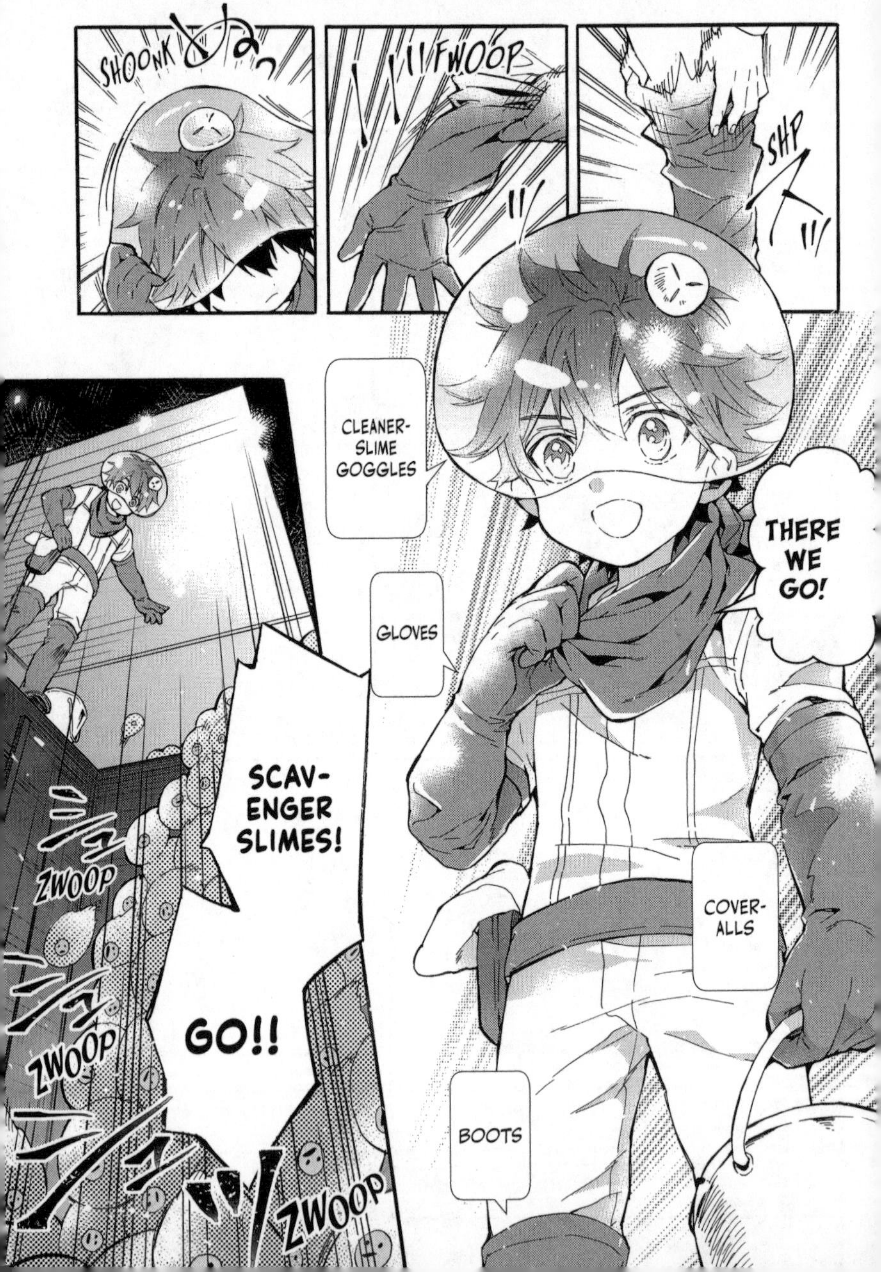
SHP
FWOOP
SHOONK
THERE WE GO!
CLEANER-SLIME GOGGLES
GLOVES
COVER-ALLS
BOOTS
SCAV-ENGER SLIMES!
GO!!
ZWOOP
ZWOOP
ZWOOP

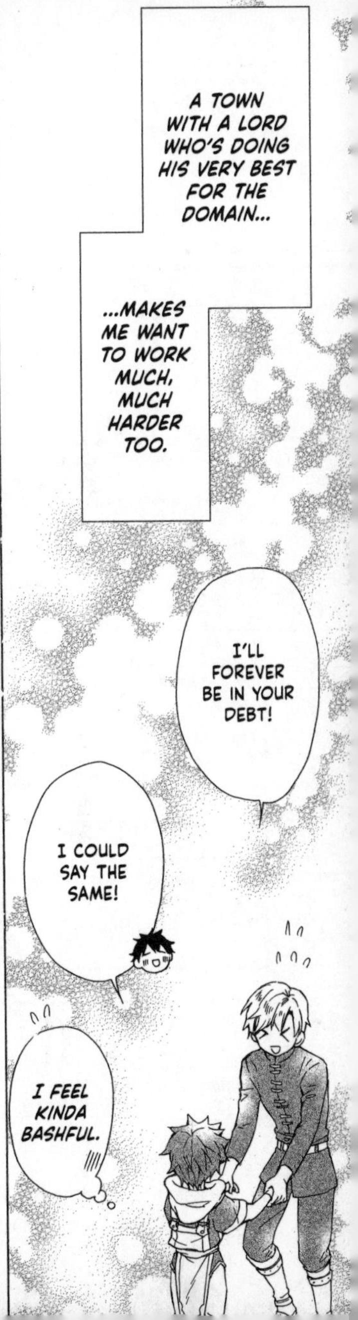
A TOWN WITH A LORD WHO'S DOING HIS VERY BEST FOR THE DOMAIN...
...MAKES ME WANT TO WORK MUCH, MUCH HARDER TOO.
I'LL FOREVER BE IN YOUR DEBT!
I COULD SAY THE SAME!
I FEEL KINDA BASHFUL.
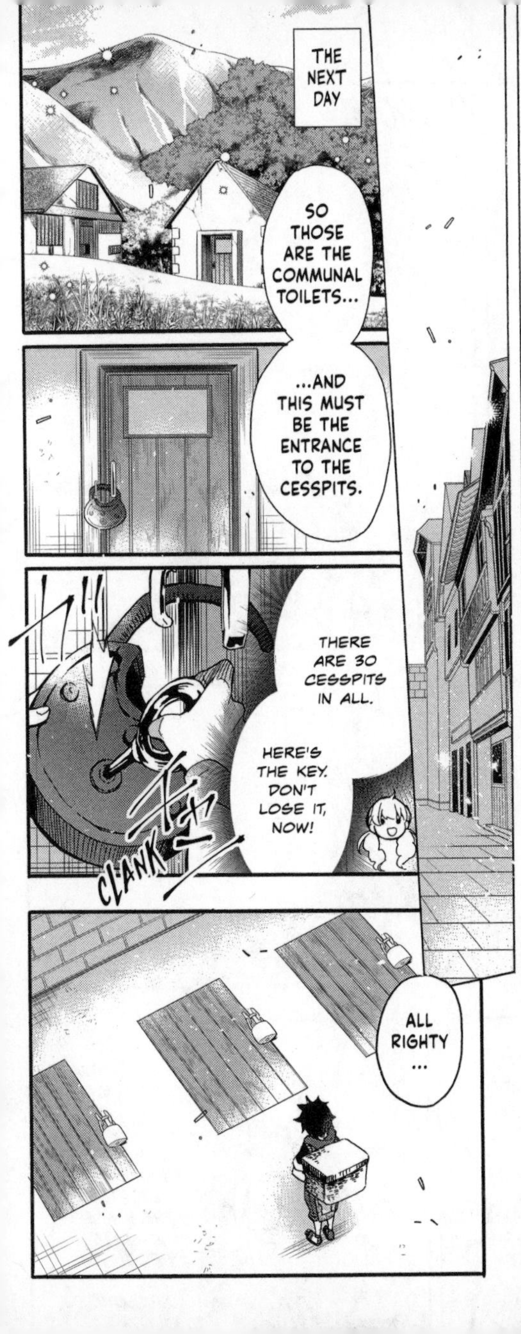
THE NEXT DAY
SO THOSE ARE THE COMMUNAL TOILETS...
...AND THIS MUST BE THE ENTRANCE TO THE CESSPITS.
THERE ARE 30 CESSPITS IN ALL.
HERE'S THE KEY. DON'T LOSE IT, NOW!
CLANK
ALL RIGHTY...

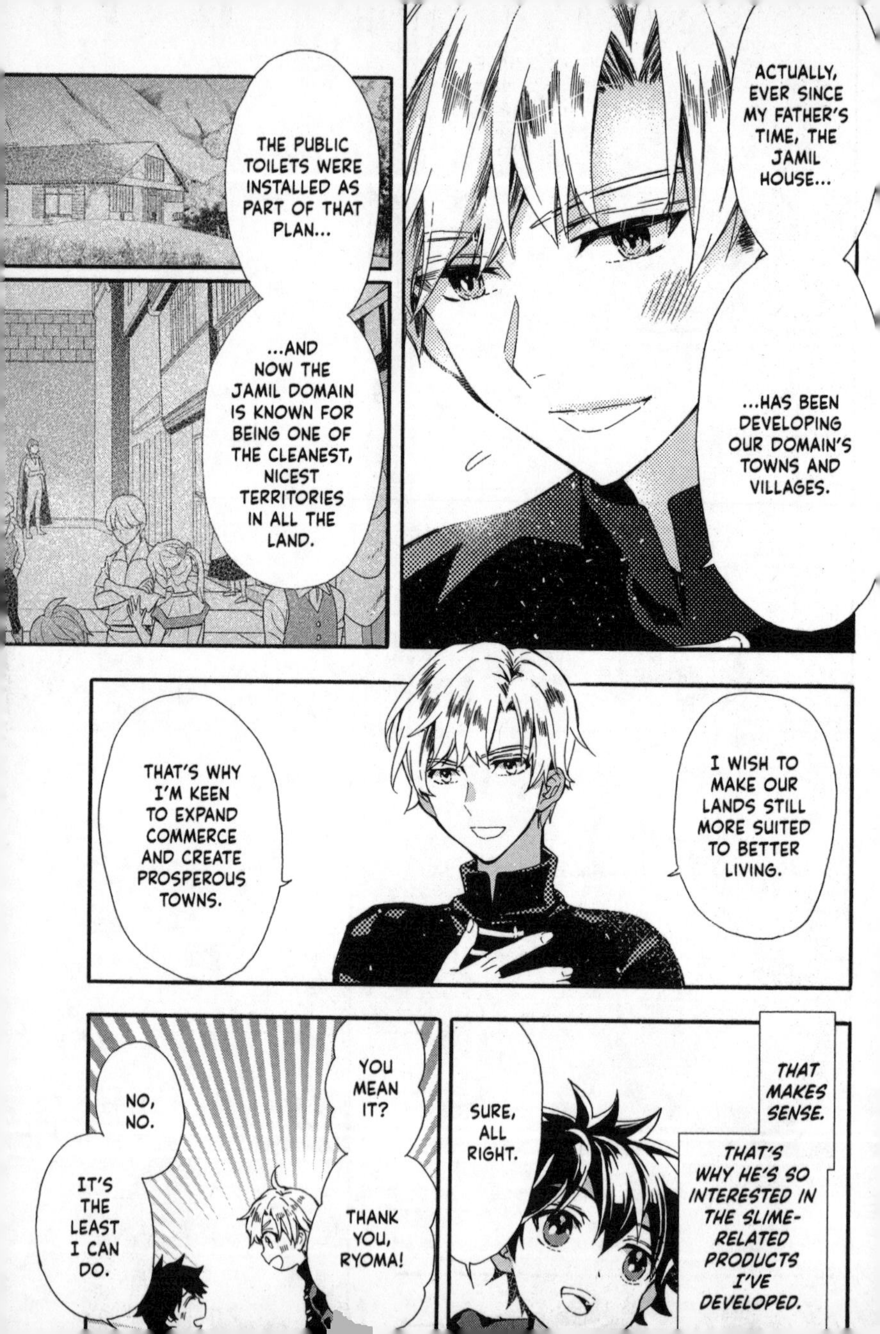
ACTUALLY, EVER SINCE MY FATHER'S TIME, THE JAMIL HOUSE...
...HAS BEEN DEVELOPING OUR DOMAIN'S TOWNS AND VILLAGES.
THE PUBLIC TOILETS WERE INSTALLED AS PART OF THAT PLAN...
...AND NOW THE JAMIL DOMAIN IS KNOWN FOR BEING ONE OF THE CLEANEST, NICEST TERRITORIES IN ALL THE LAND.
I WISH TO MAKE OUR LANDS STILL MORE SUITED TO BETTER LIVING.
THAT'S WHY I'M KEEN TO EXPAND COMMERCE AND CREATE PROSPEROUS TOWNS.
THAT MAKES SENSE.
THAT'S WHY HE'S SO INTERESTED IN THE SLIME-RELATED PRODUCTS I'VE DEVELOPED.
SURE, ALL RIGHT.
YOU MEAN IT?
THANK YOU, RYOMA!
NO, NO.
IT'S THE LEAST I CAN DO.

IT'S THREAD I MADE BY COMBINING THE STICKY AND HARDENING SOLUTIONS FROM STICKY SLIMES.

STICKY SOLUTION	HARDENING SOLUTION	USE
3	7	SEWING
4	6	
5	5	TRAPS
6	4	HUNTING

STRENGTH

THE STRENGTH CHANGES ACCORDING TO THE RATIO OF THE TWO SOLUTIONS.

OH, THAT...

WHAT IS THIS ...?

I'VE NEVER SEEN THREAD LIKE THIS BEFORE.

IT'S SO TOUGH, YET SILKY.

HUH?

NO, NO, YOU CAN HAVE IT.

YOU'RE ALWAYS HELPING ME OUT...

ME TOO...

CAN I BUY SOME FROM YOU?

THIS IS THE FIRST TIME I'VE SEEN SUCH SOFT, BEAUTIFUL THREAD!

THREAD?

HUUUUH?

LET'S ...

...MARKET THAT TOO!

RYOMA...

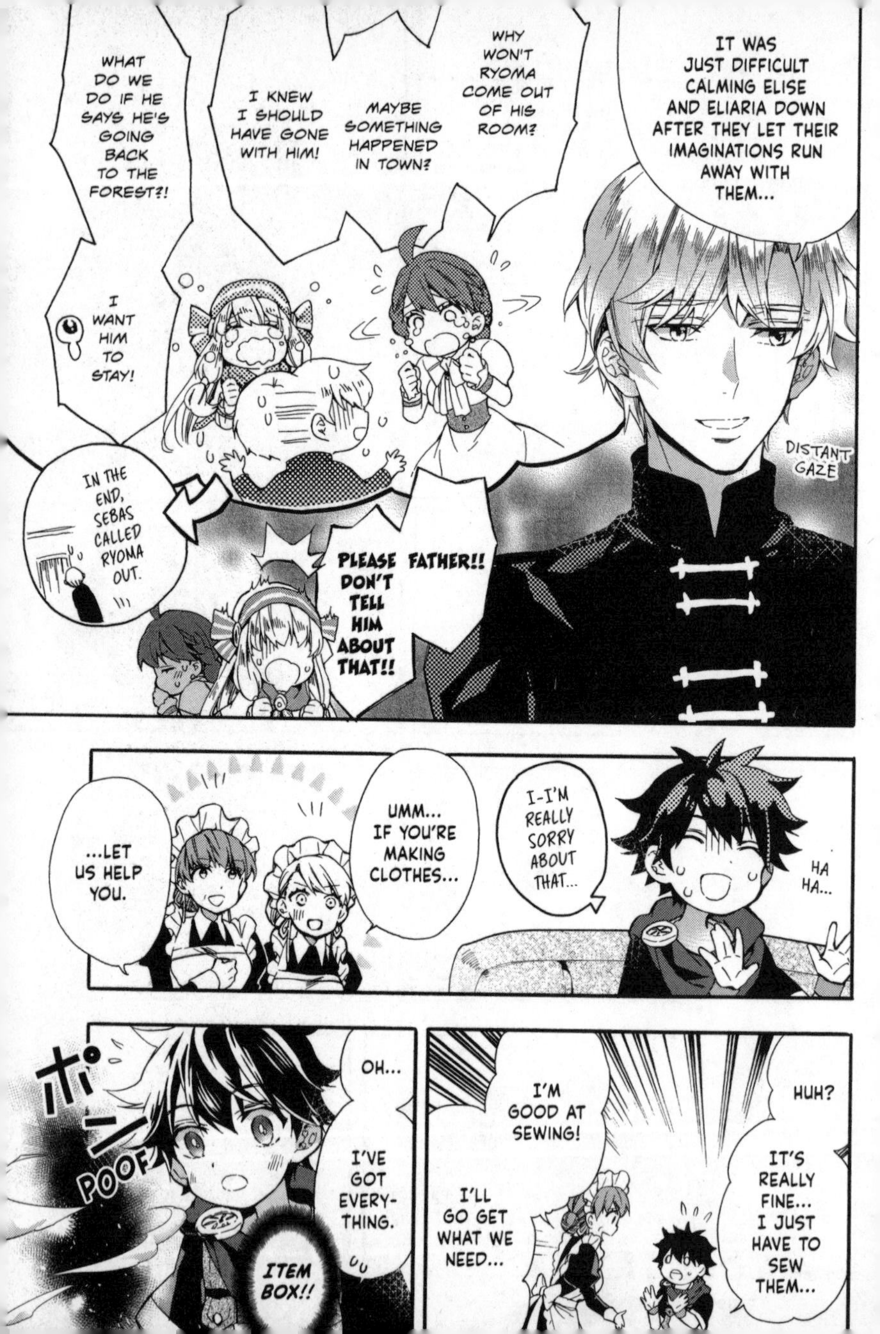
IT WAS JUST DIFFICULT CALMING ELISE AND ELIARIA DOWN AFTER THEY LET THEIR IMAGINATIONS RUN AWAY WITH THEM...
WHY WON'T RYOMA COME OUT OF HIS ROOM?
MAYBE SOMETHING HAPPENED IN TOWN?
I KNEW I SHOULD HAVE GONE WITH HIM!
WHAT DO WE DO IF HE SAYS HE'S GOING BACK TO THE FOREST?!
I WANT HIM TO STAY!
DISTANT GAZE
PLEASE FATHER!! DON'T TELL HIM ABOUT THAT!!
IN THE END, SEBAS CALLED RYOMA OUT.
HA HA...
I-I'M REALLY SORRY ABOUT THAT...
UMM... IF YOU'RE MAKING CLOTHES...
...LET US HELP YOU.
HUH?
IT'S REALLY FINE... I JUST HAVE TO SEW THEM...
I'M GOOD AT SEWING!
I'LL GO GET WHAT WE NEED...
OH...
I'VE GOT EVERY-THING.
ポーン
POOF
ITEM BOX!!

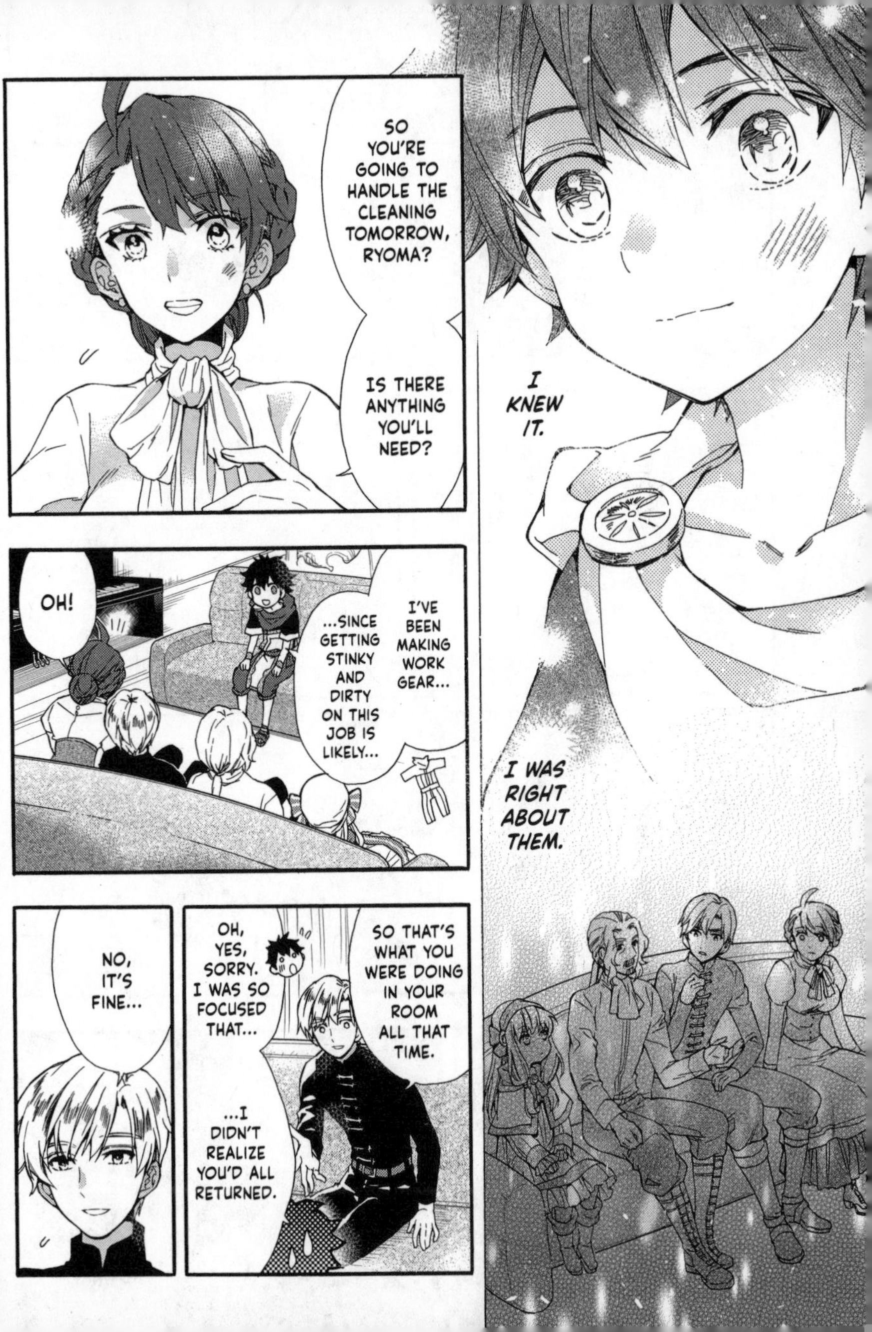
I KNEW IT.
I WAS RIGHT ABOUT THEM.
SO YOU'RE GOING TO HANDLE THE CLEANING TOMORROW, RYOMA?
IS THERE ANYTHING YOU'LL NEED?
I'VE BEEN MAKING WORK GEAR...
...SINCE GETTING STINKY AND DIRTY ON THIS JOB IS LIKELY...
OH!
SO THAT'S WHAT YOU WERE DOING IN YOUR ROOM ALL THAT TIME.
OH, YES, SORRY. I WAS SO FOCUSED THAT...
...I DIDN'T REALIZE YOU'D ALL RETURNED.
NO, IT'S FINE...

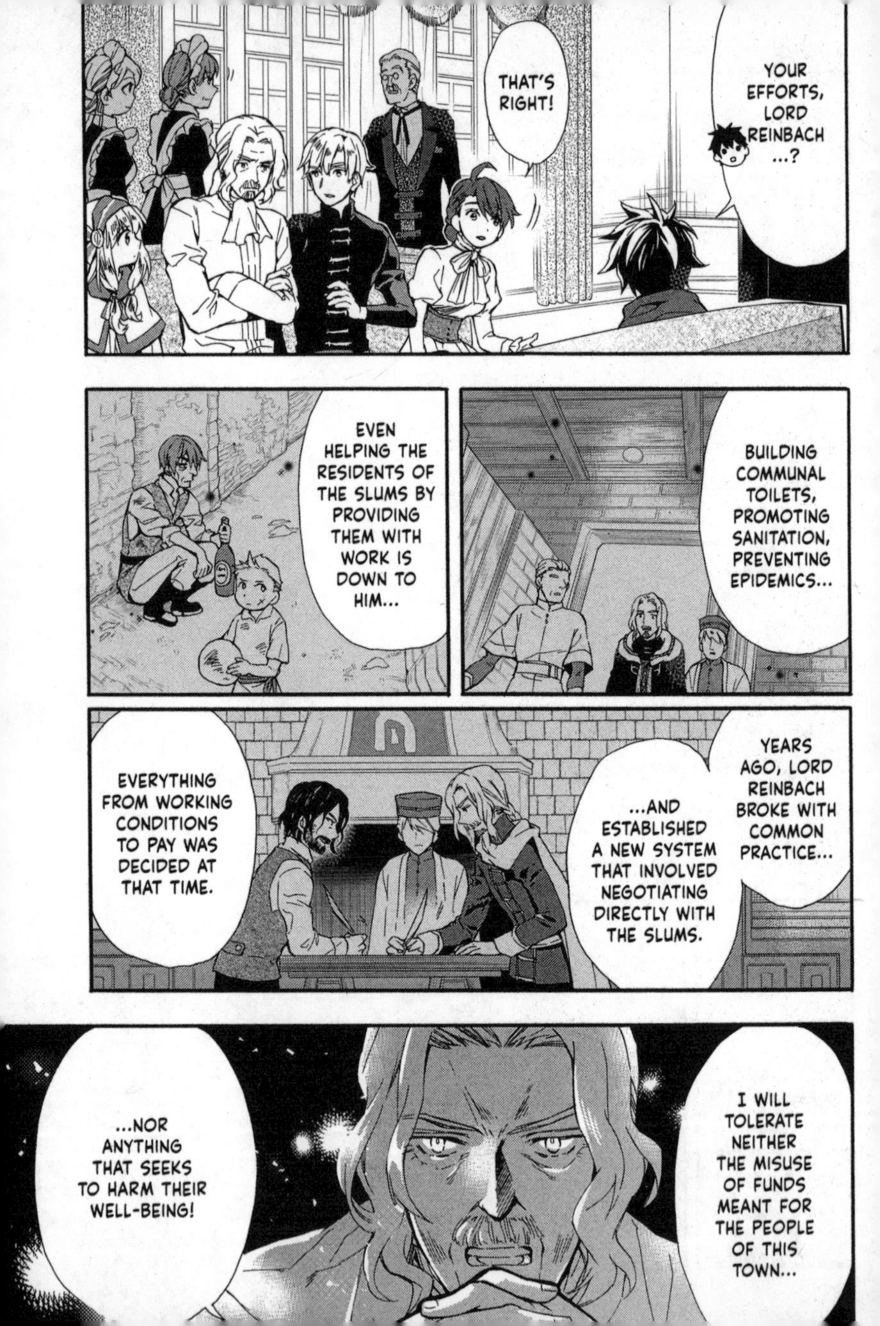
YOUR EFFORTS, LORD REINBACH ...?
THAT'S RIGHT!
BUILDING COMMUNAL TOILETS, PROMOTING SANITATION, PREVENTING EPIDEMICS...
EVEN HELPING THE RESIDENTS OF THE SLUMS BY PROVIDING THEM WITH WORK IS DOWN TO HIM...
YEARS AGO, LORD REINBACH BROKE WITH COMMON PRACTICE...
...AND ESTABLISHED A NEW SYSTEM THAT INVOLVED NEGOTIATING DIRECTLY WITH THE SLUMS.
EVERYTHING FROM WORKING CONDITIONS TO PAY WAS DECIDED AT THAT TIME.
I WILL TOLERATE NEITHER THE MISUSE OF FUNDS MEANT FOR THE PEOPLE OF THIS TOWN...
...NOR ANYTHING THAT SEEKS TO HARM THEIR WELL-BEING!

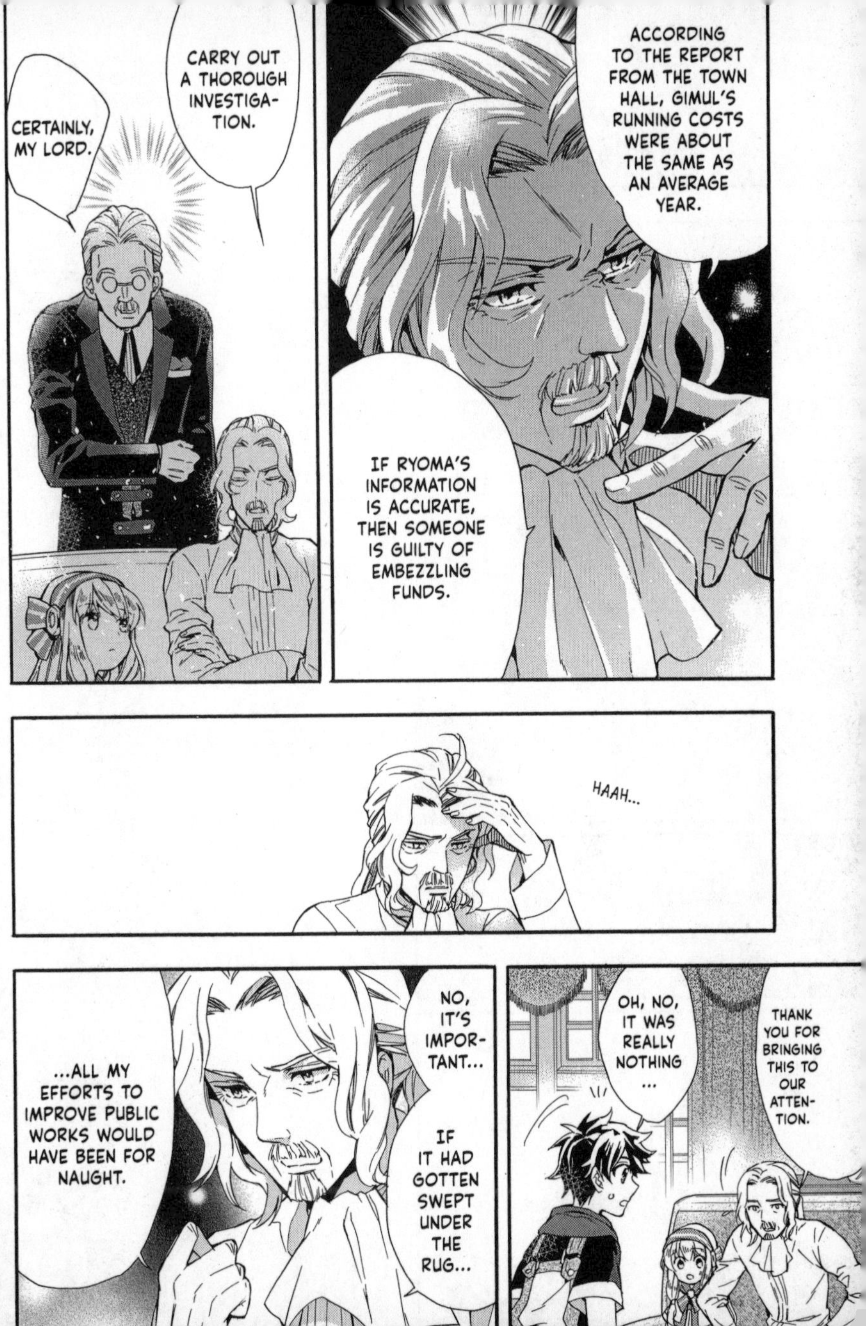
ACCORDING TO THE REPORT FROM THE TOWN HALL, GIMUL'S RUNNING COSTS WERE ABOUT THE SAME AS AN AVERAGE YEAR.
IF RYOMA'S INFORMATION IS ACCURATE, THEN SOMEONE IS GUILTY OF EMBEZZLING FUNDS.
CARRY OUT A THOROUGH INVESTIGATION.
CERTAINLY, MY LORD.
HAAH...
THANK YOU FOR BRINGING THIS TO OUR ATTENTION.
OH, NO, IT WAS REALLY NOTHING...
NO, IT'S IMPORTANT...
IF IT HAD GOTTEN SWEPT UNDER THE RUG...
...ALL MY EFFORTS TO IMPROVE PUBLIC WORKS WOULD HAVE BEEN FOR NAUGHT.

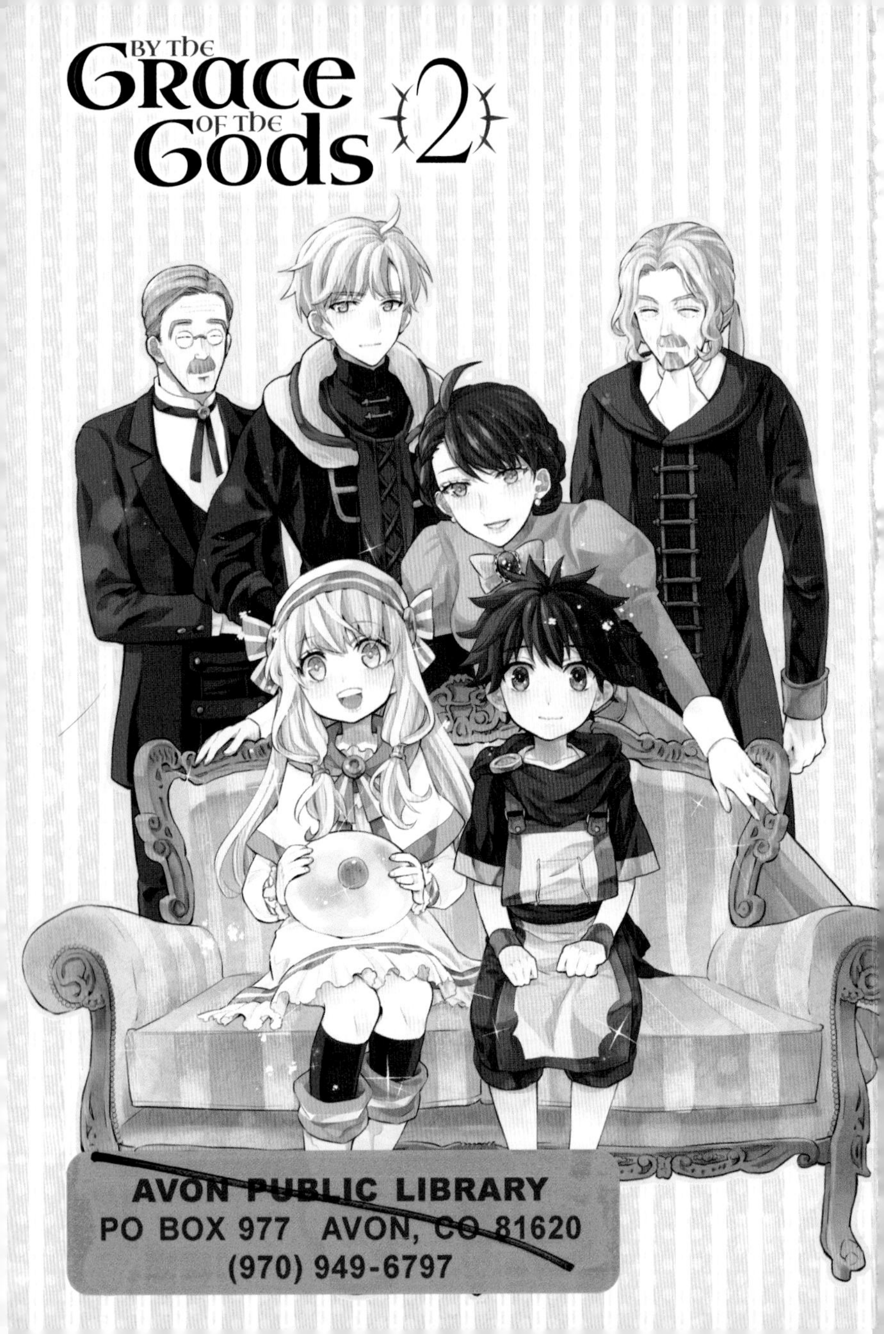
BY THE
GRACE
OF THE
GODS
2

CONTENTS

❴2❵

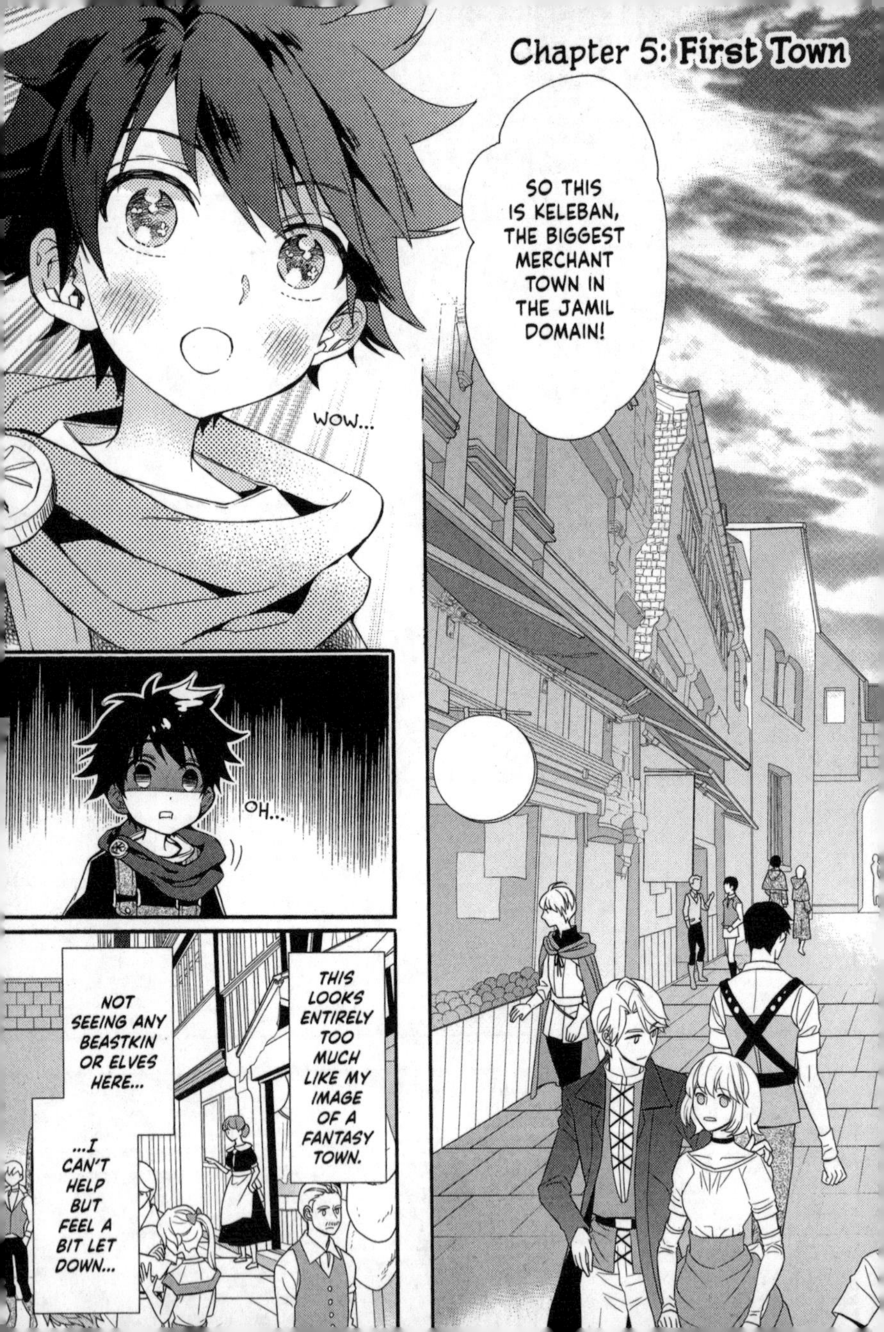
Chapter 5: First Town
SO THIS IS KELEBAN, THE BIGGEST MERCHANT TOWN IN THE JAMIL DOMAIN!
WOW...
OH...
THIS LOOKS ENTIRELY TOO MUCH LIKE MY IMAGE OF A FANTASY TOWN.
NOT SEEING ANY BEASTKIN OR ELVES HERE...
...I CAN'T HELP BUT FEEL A BIT LET DOWN...

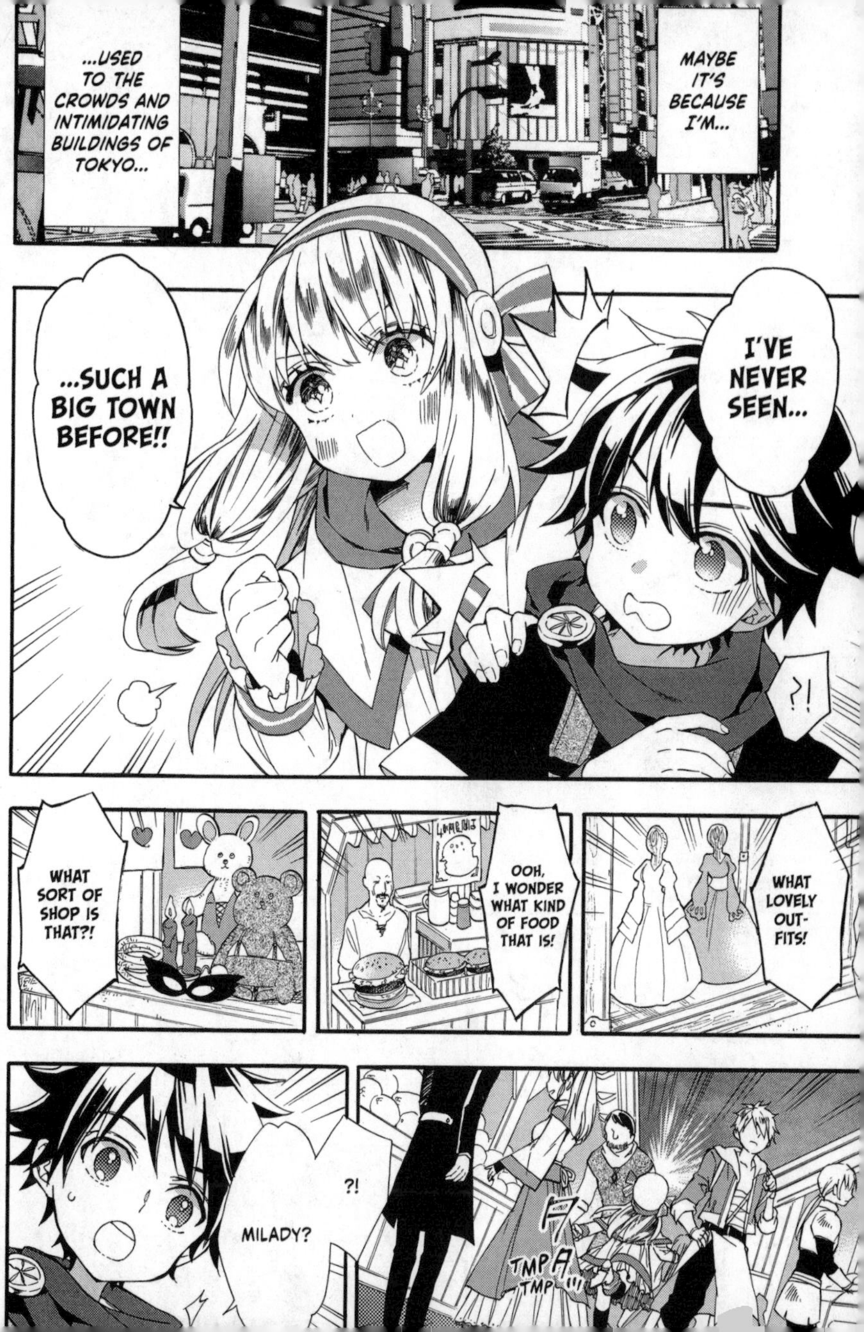
MAYBE IT'S BECAUSE I'M...
...USED TO THE CROWDS AND INTIMIDATING BUILDINGS OF TOKYO...
I'VE NEVER SEEN...
...SUCH A BIG TOWN BEFORE!!
?!
WHAT LOVELY OUT-FITS!
OOH, I WONDER WHAT KIND OF FOOD THAT IS!
WHAT SORT OF SHOP IS THAT?!
TMP TMP
?!
MILADY?

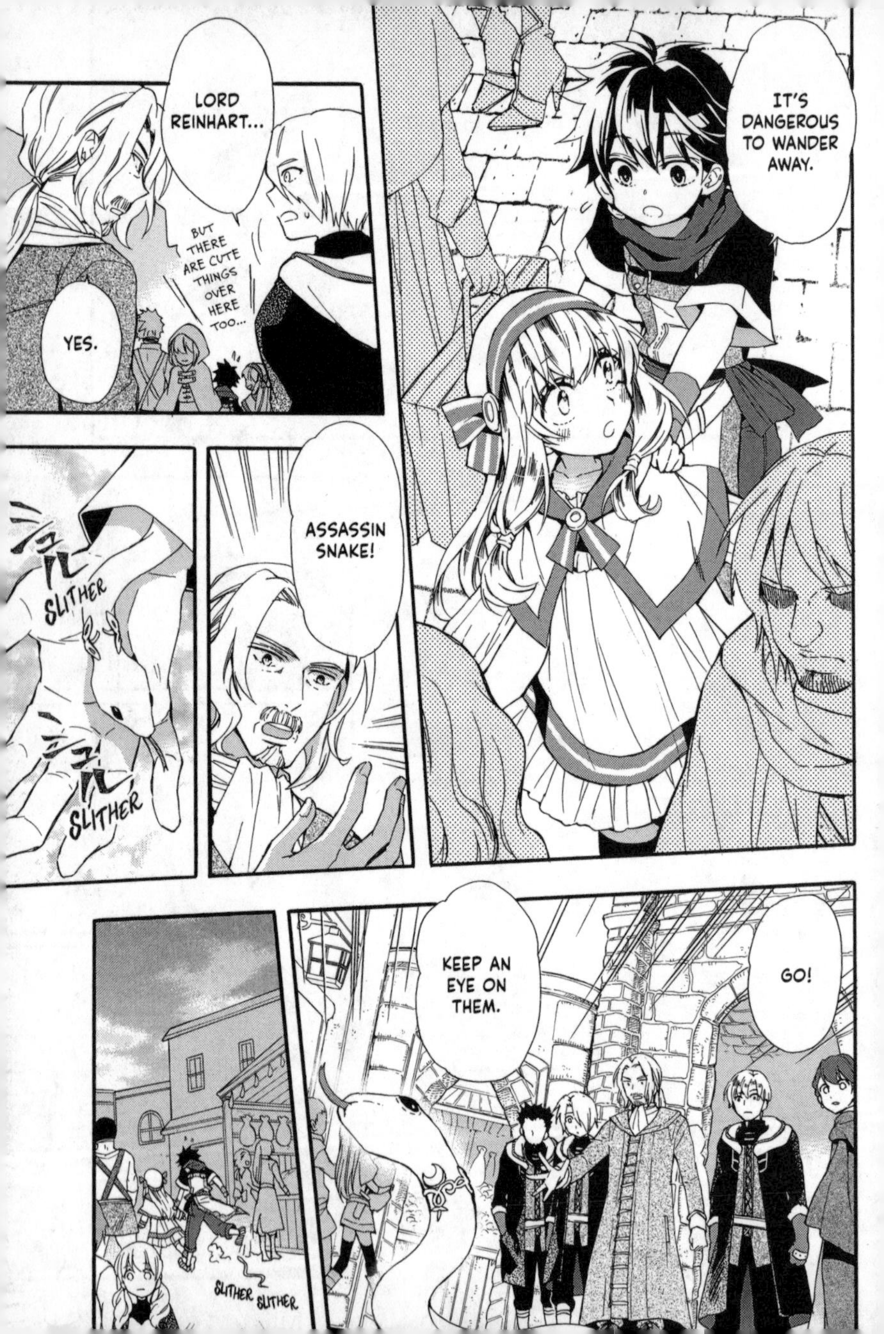
IT'S DANGEROUS TO WANDER AWAY.
LORD REINHART...
BUT THERE ARE CUTE THINGS OVER HERE TOO...
YES.
ASSASSIN SNAKE!
SLITHER
SLITHER
GO!
KEEP AN EYE ON THEM.
SLITHER SLITHER

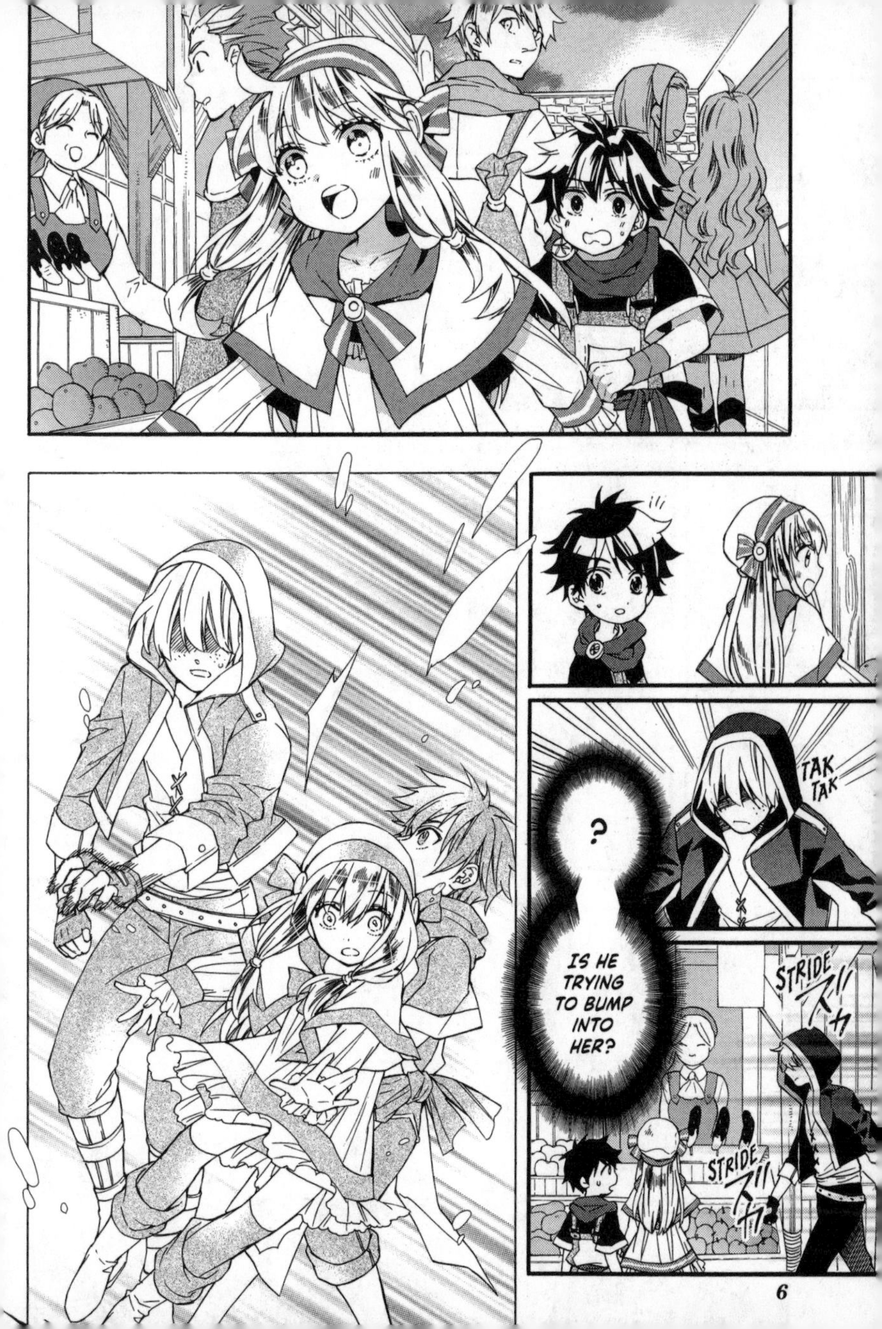
?
TAK TAK
IS HE TRYING TO BUMP INTO HER?
STRIDE
STRIDE

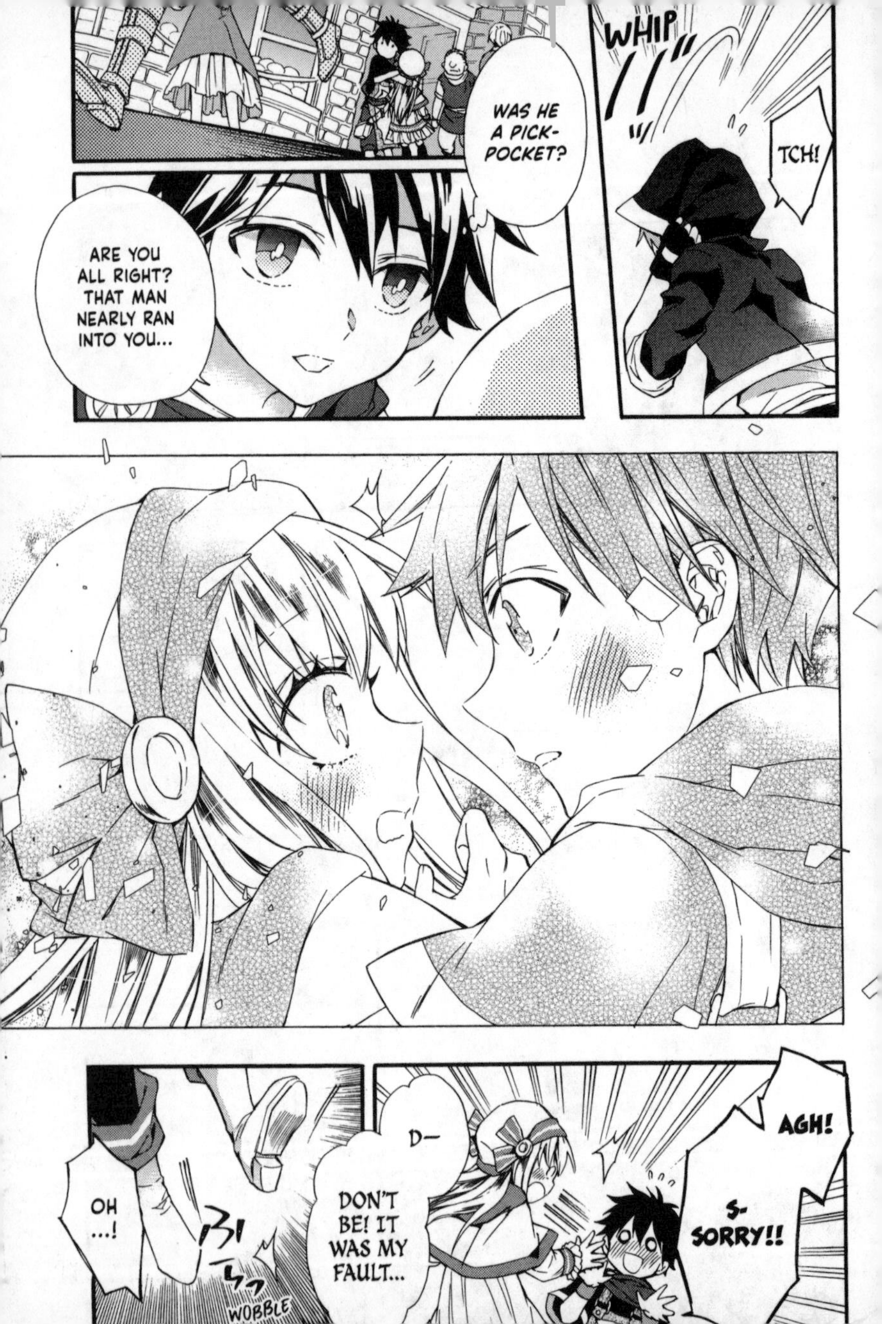
WHIP
TCH!
WAS HE A PICK-POCKET?
ARE YOU ALL RIGHT? THAT MAN NEARLY RAN INTO YOU...
AGH!
D—
S-SORRY!!
DON'T BE! IT WAS MY FAULT...
OH ...!
WOBBLE

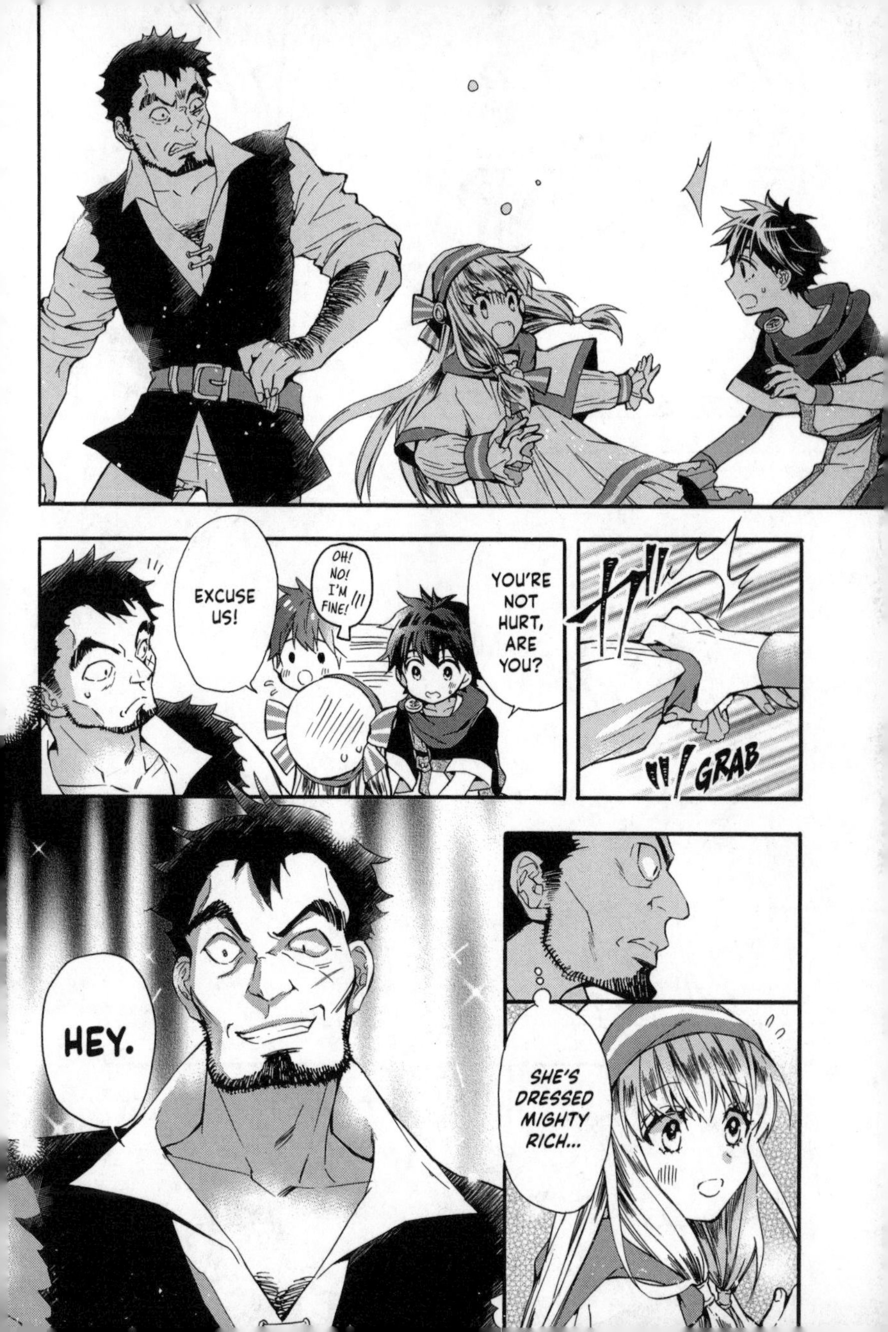
GRAB
YOU'RE NOT HURT, ARE YOU?
OH! NO! I'M FINE!
EXCUSE US!
SHE'S DRESSED MIGHTY RICH...
HEY.

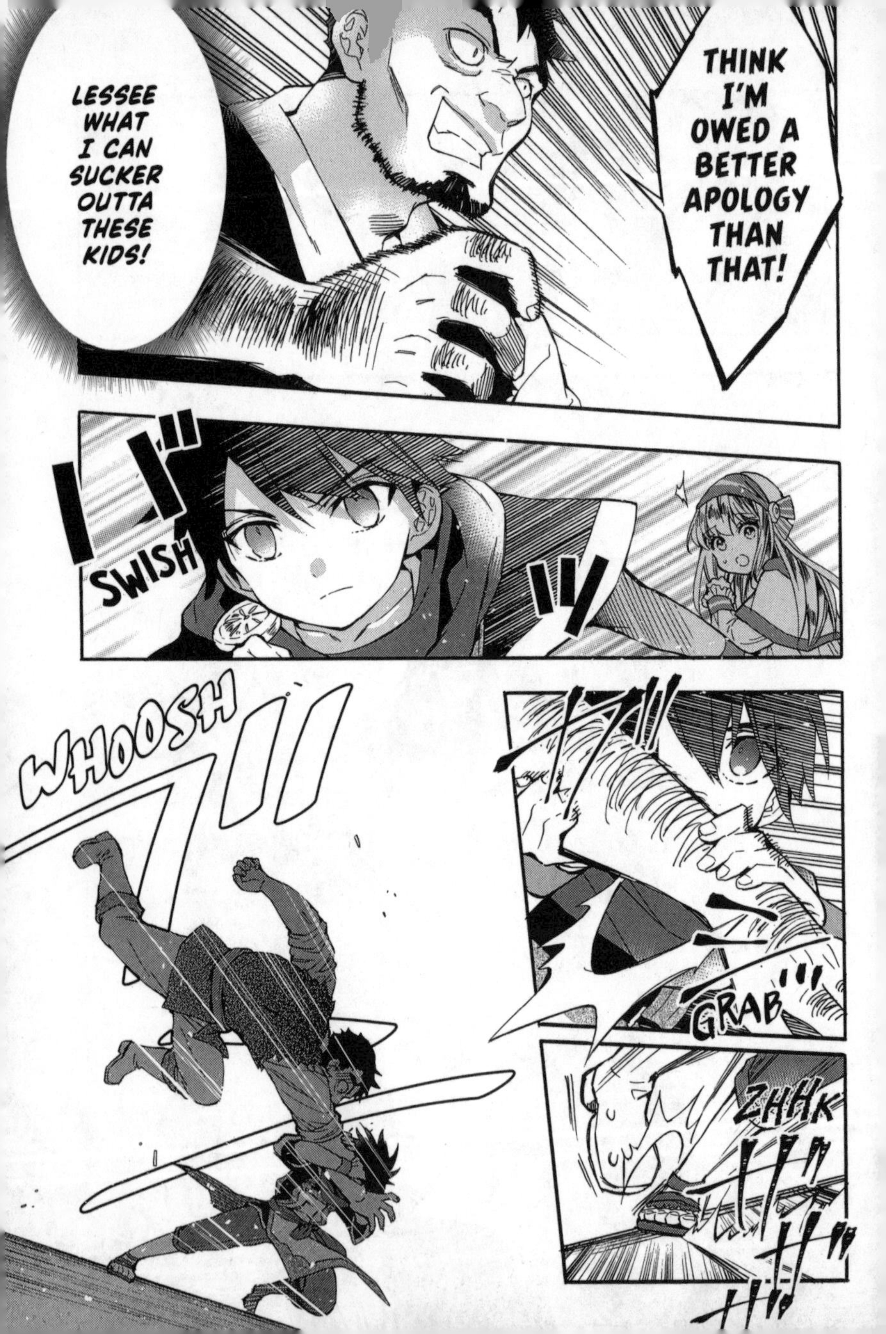
THINK I'M OWED A BETTER APOLOGY THAN THAT!
LESSEE WHAT I CAN SUCKER OUTTA THESE KIDS!
SWISH
GRAB
ZHHK
WHOOSH

WHOA!

WHIIIZ

I'M SORRY!!

I...

SHALL WE GO?

YES.

INN

OWIE, OWIE, OW...

NO, NOT AT ALL.

REALLY!?

DIDN'T IT LEAVE YOU WINDED, RYOMA?

THE CARRIAGE RIDE...

ARE YOU ALL RIGHT ...?

YES, MY FEET ARE JUST A LITTLE TIRED.

PLUS, THIS WAS MY FIRST LONG CARRIAGE TRIP...

JUST ME, HUH? EVEN THOUGH WE'RE THE SAME AGE...

WELL...

...THAT'S NORMAL FOR YOUR FIRST BIG JOURNEY, MILADY.

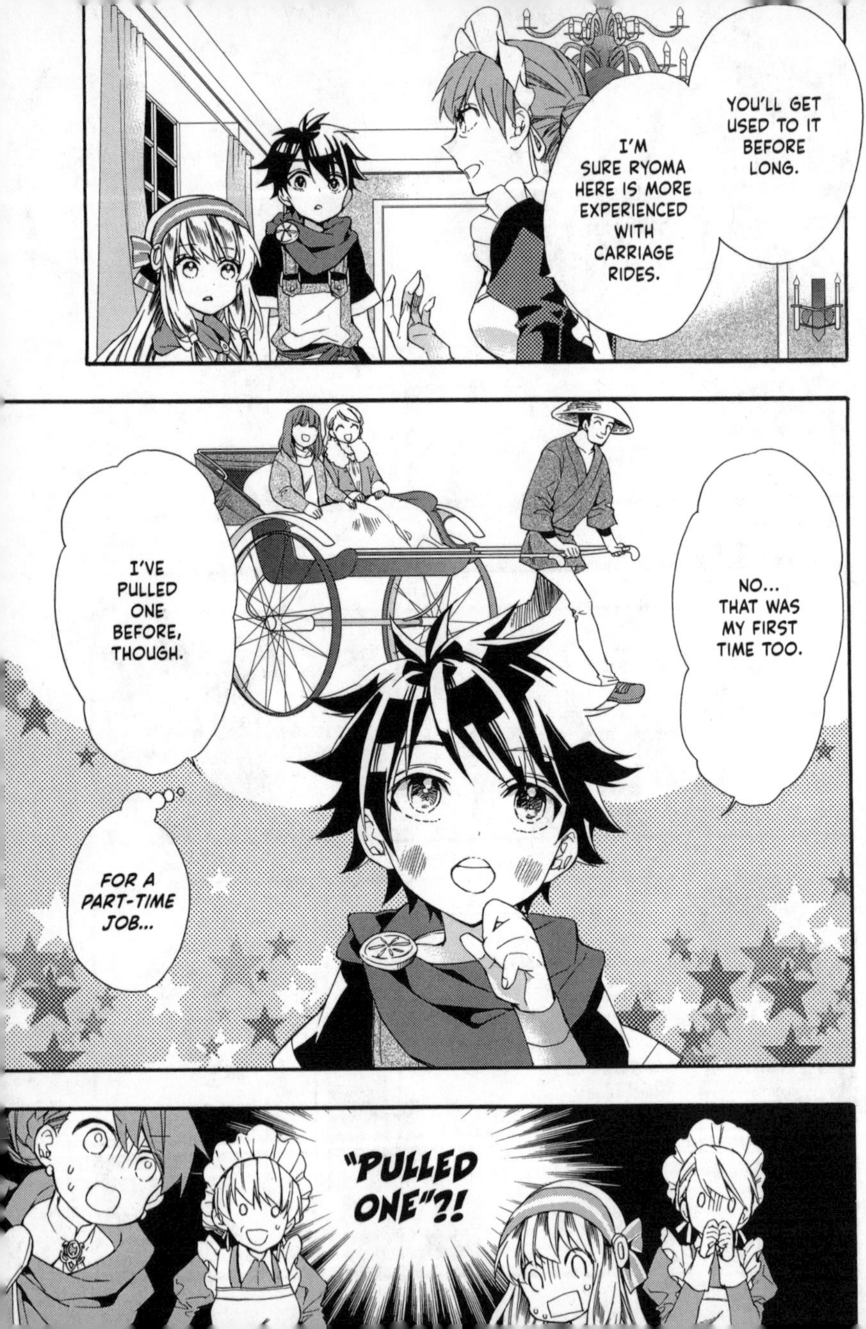
YOU'LL GET USED TO IT BEFORE LONG.
I'M SURE RYOMA HERE IS MORE EXPERIENCED WITH CARRIAGE RIDES.
NO... THAT WAS MY FIRST TIME TOO.
I'VE PULLED ONE BEFORE, THOUGH.
FOR A PART-TIME JOB...
"PULLED ONE"?!

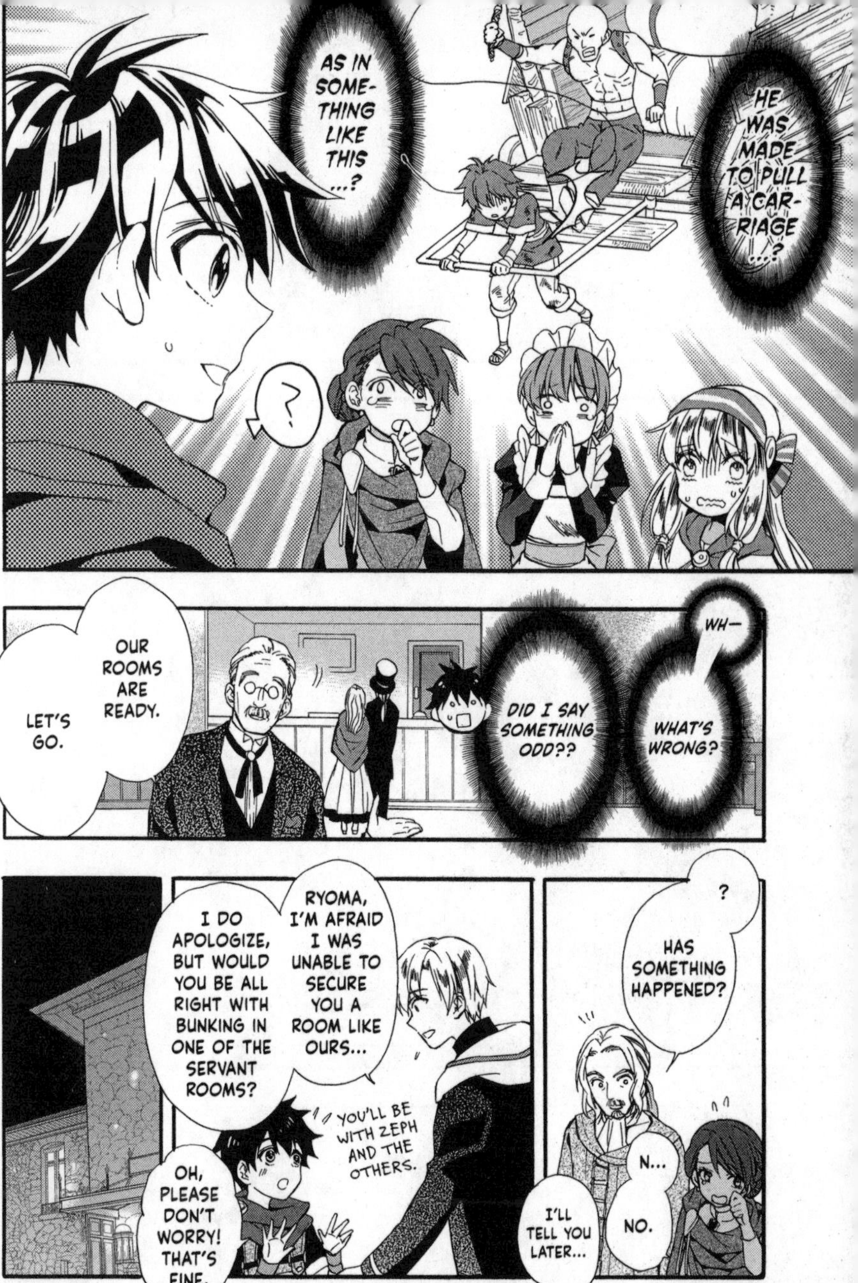
HE WAS MADE TO PULL A CAR-RIAGE ...?
AS IN SOME-THING LIKE THIS ...?
?
WH—
WHAT'S WRONG?
DID I SAY SOMETHING ODD??
OUR ROOMS ARE READY.
LET'S GO.
?
HAS SOMETHING HAPPENED?
N...
NO.
I'LL TELL YOU LATER...
RYOMA, I'M AFRAID I WAS UNABLE TO SECURE YOU A ROOM LIKE OURS...
I DO APOLOGIZE, BUT WOULD YOU BE ALL RIGHT WITH BUNKING IN ONE OF THE SERVANT ROOMS?
YOU'LL BE WITH ZEPH AND THE OTHERS.
OH, PLEASE DON'T WORRY! THAT'S FINE.

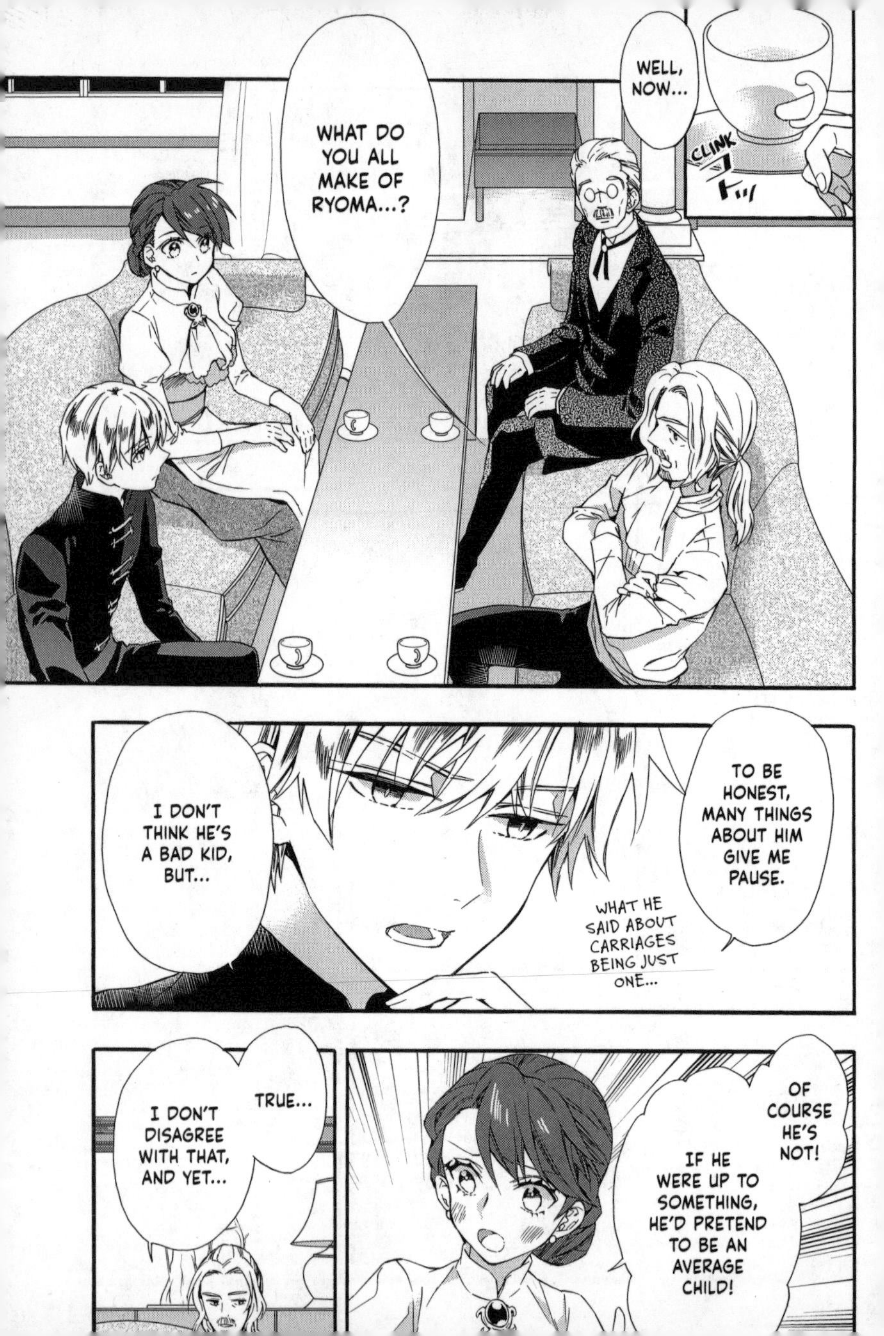
CLINK
WELL, NOW...
WHAT DO YOU ALL MAKE OF RYOMA...?
TO BE HONEST, MANY THINGS ABOUT HIM GIVE ME PAUSE.
WHAT HE SAID ABOUT CARRIAGES BEING JUST ONE...
I DON'T THINK HE'S A BAD KID, BUT...
OF COURSE HE'S NOT!
IF HE WERE UP TO SOMETHING, HE'D PRETEND TO BE AN AVERAGE CHILD!
TRUE...
I DON'T DISAGREE WITH THAT, AND YET...

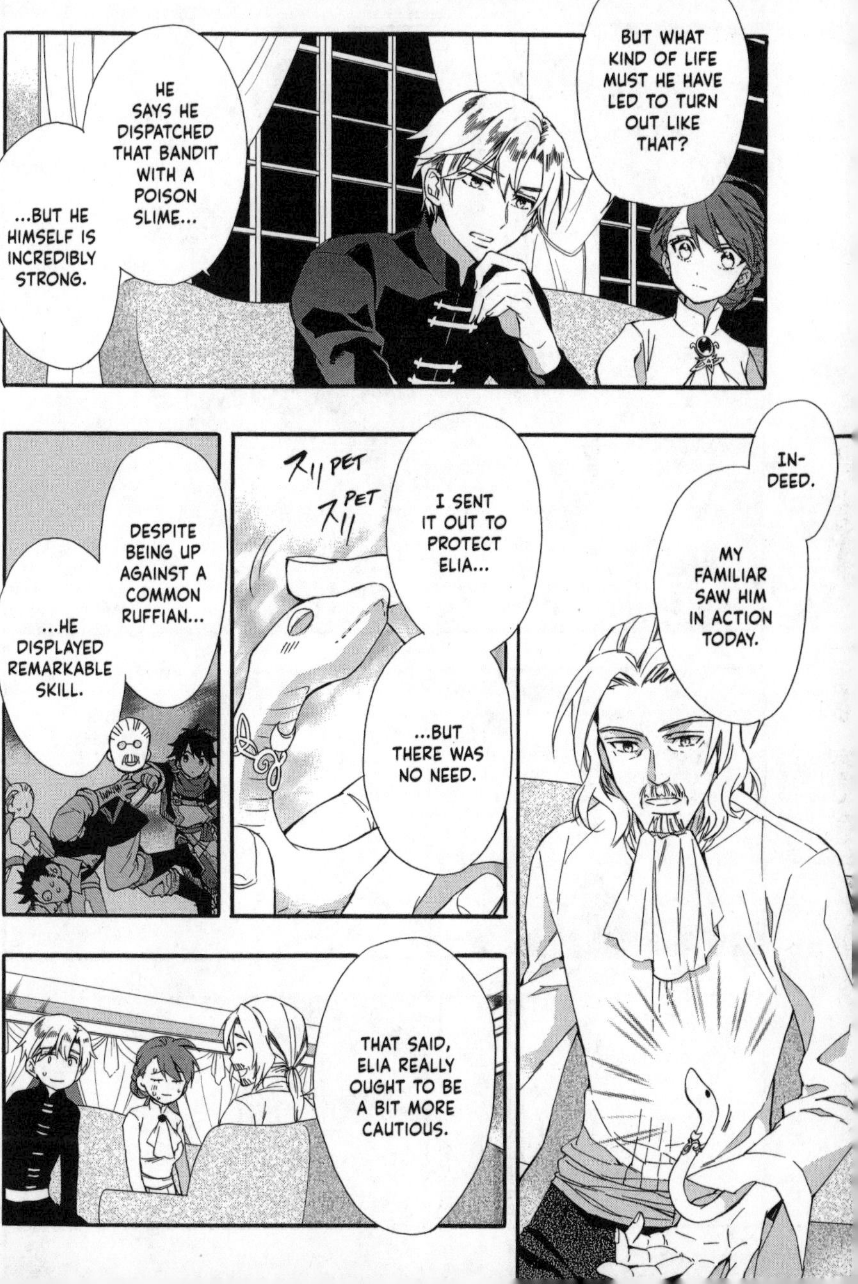
BUT WHAT KIND OF LIFE MUST HE HAVE LED TO TURN OUT LIKE THAT?
HE SAYS HE DISPATCHED THAT BANDIT WITH A POISON SLIME...
...BUT HE HIMSELF IS INCREDIBLY STRONG.
IN-DEED.
MY FAMILIAR SAW HIM IN ACTION TODAY.
スリ PET
スリ PET
I SENT IT OUT TO PROTECT ELIA...
...BUT THERE WAS NO NEED.
DESPITE BEING UP AGAINST A COMMON RUFFIAN...
...HE DISPLAYED REMARKABLE SKILL.
THAT SAID, ELIA REALLY OUGHT TO BE A BIT MORE CAUTIOUS.

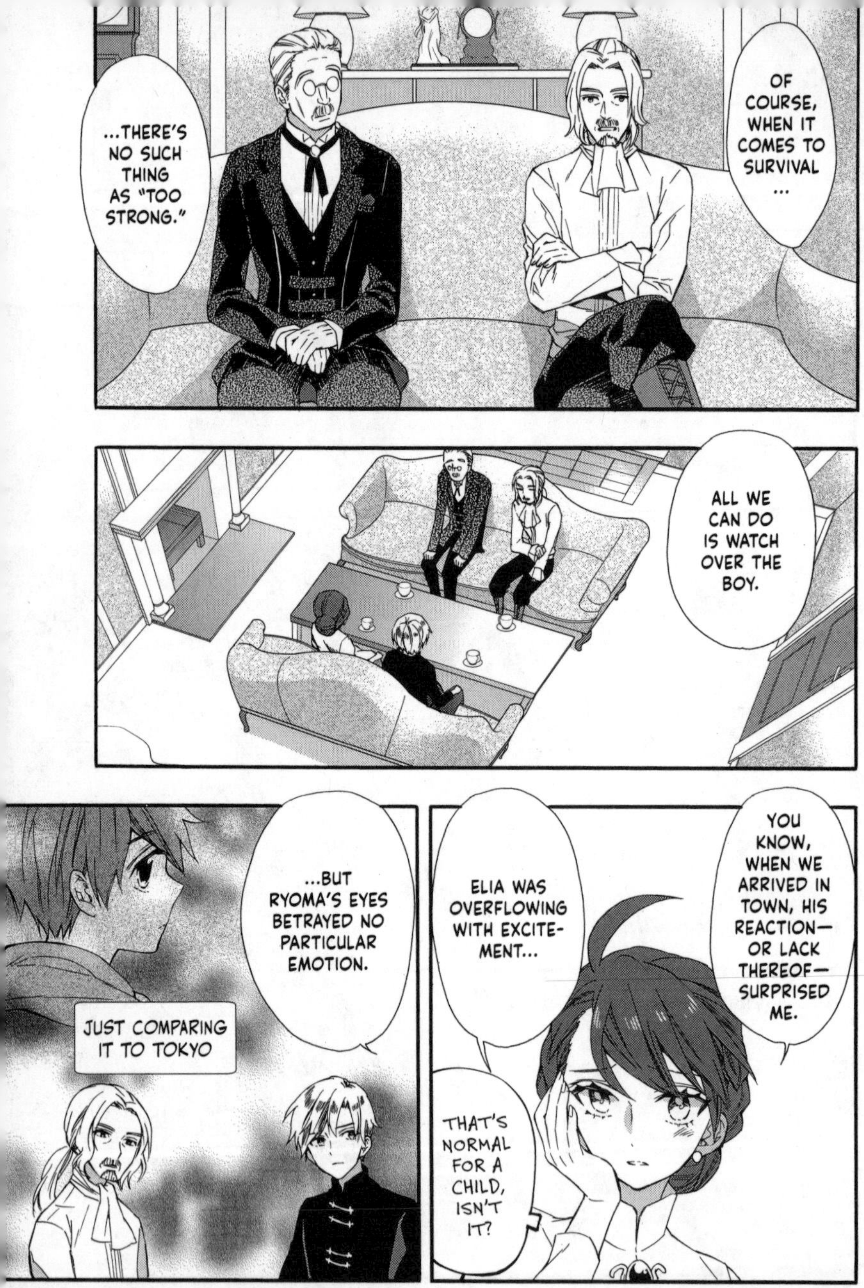
OF COURSE, WHEN IT COMES TO SURVIVAL...
...THERE'S NO SUCH THING AS "TOO STRONG."
ALL WE CAN DO IS WATCH OVER THE BOY.
YOU KNOW, WHEN WE ARRIVED IN TOWN, HIS REACTION—OR LACK THEREOF—SURPRISED ME.
ELIA WAS OVERFLOWING WITH EXCITEMENT...
THAT'S NORMAL FOR A CHILD, ISN'T IT?
...BUT RYOMA'S EYES BETRAYED NO PARTICULAR EMOTION.
JUST COMPARING IT TO TOKYO

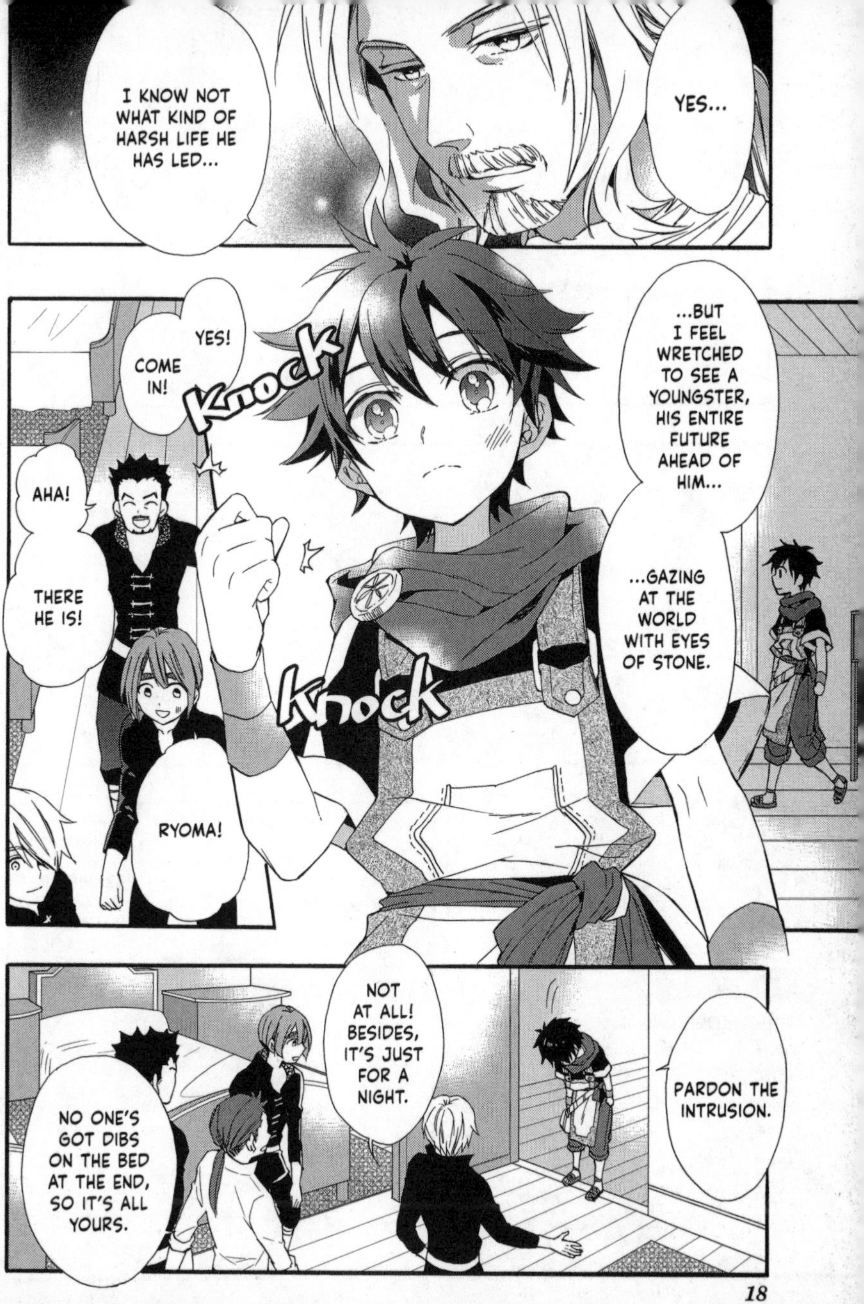
YES...
I KNOW NOT WHAT KIND OF HARSH LIFE HE HAS LED...
...BUT I FEEL WRETCHED TO SEE A YOUNGSTER, HIS ENTIRE FUTURE AHEAD OF HIM...
...GAZING AT THE WORLD WITH EYES OF STONE.
Knock
Knock
YES! COME IN!
AHA!
THERE HE IS!
RYOMA!
PARDON THE INTRUSION.
NOT AT ALL! BESIDES, IT'S JUST FOR A NIGHT.
NO ONE'S GOT DIBS ON THE BED AT THE END, SO IT'S ALL YOURS.

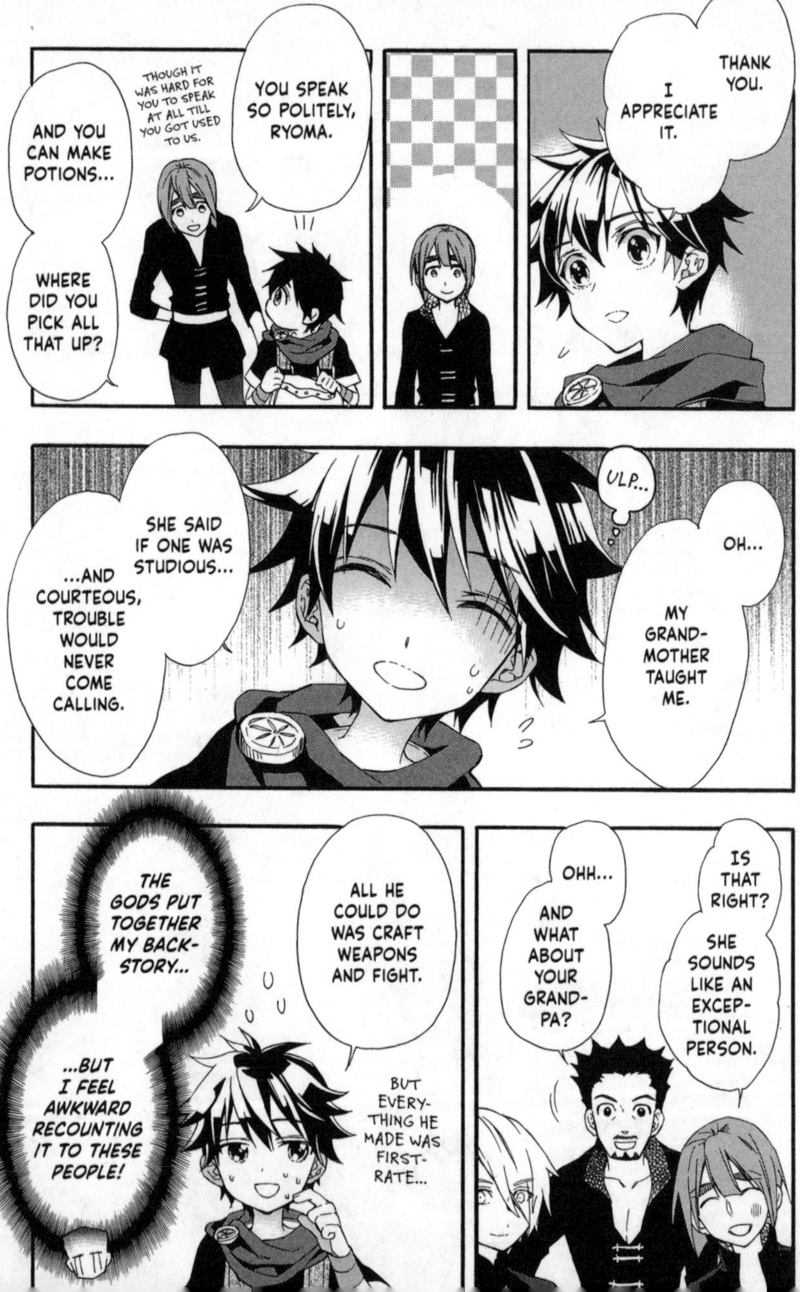
THANK YOU.
I APPRECIATE IT.
YOU SPEAK SO POLITELY, RYOMA.
THOUGH IT WAS HARD FOR YOU TO SPEAK AT ALL TILL YOU GOT USED TO US.
AND YOU CAN MAKE POTIONS...
WHERE DID YOU PICK ALL THAT UP?
ULP...
OH...
MY GRANDMOTHER TAUGHT ME.
SHE SAID IF ONE WAS STUDIOUS...
...AND COURTEOUS, TROUBLE WOULD NEVER COME CALLING.
IS THAT RIGHT?
SHE SOUNDS LIKE AN EXCEPTIONAL PERSON.
OHH...
AND WHAT ABOUT YOUR GRANDPA?
ALL HE COULD DO WAS CRAFT WEAPONS AND FIGHT.
BUT EVERYTHING HE MADE WAS FIRST-RATE...
THE GODS PUT TOGETHER MY BACKSTORY...
...BUT I FEEL AWKWARD RECOUNTING IT TO THESE PEOPLE!

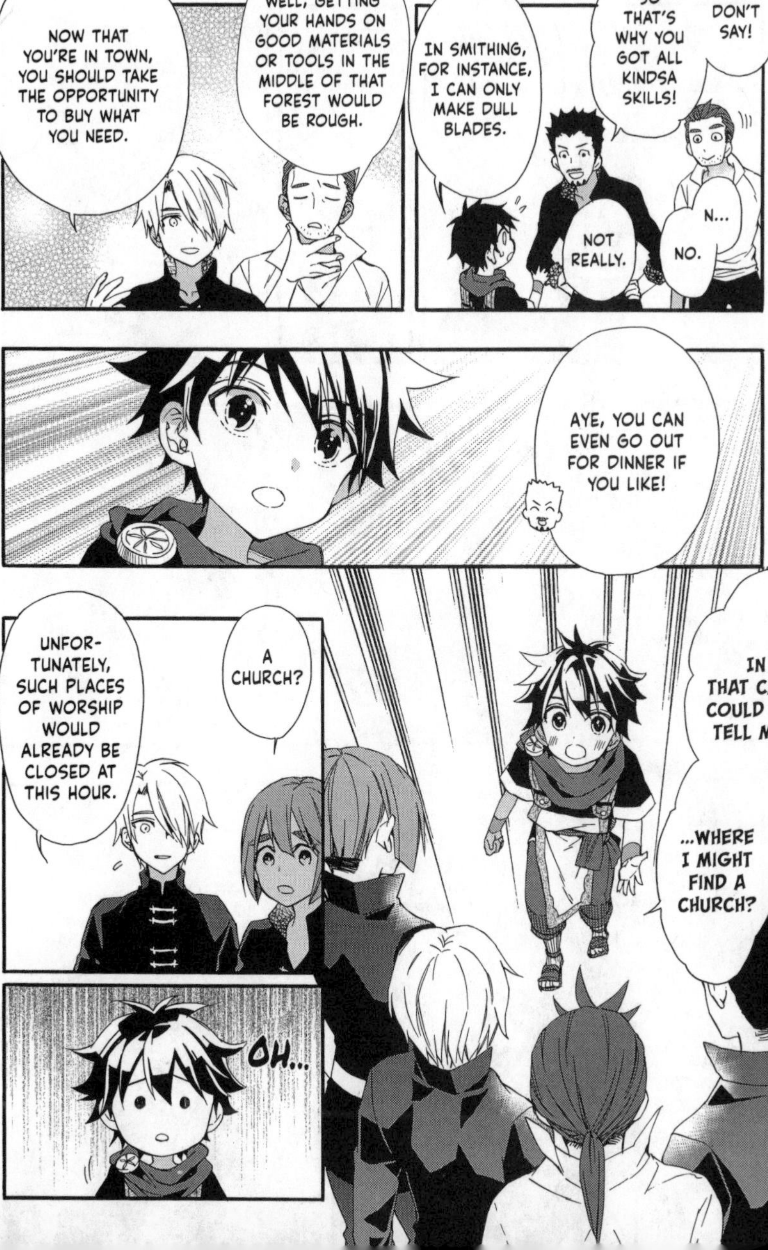
YA DON'T SAY!
SO THAT'S WHY YOU GOT ALL KINDSA SKILLS!
IN SMITHING, FOR INSTANCE, I CAN ONLY MAKE DULL BLADES.
N... NO.
NOT REALLY.
WELL, GETTING YOUR HANDS ON GOOD MATERIALS OR TOOLS IN THE MIDDLE OF THAT FOREST WOULD BE ROUGH.
NOW THAT YOU'RE IN TOWN, YOU SHOULD TAKE THE OPPORTUNITY TO BUY WHAT YOU NEED.
AYE, YOU CAN EVEN GO OUT FOR DINNER IF YOU LIKE!
IN THAT CASE, COULD YOU TELL ME...
...WHERE I MIGHT FIND A CHURCH?
A CHURCH?
UNFOR-TUNATELY, SUCH PLACES OF WORSHIP WOULD ALREADY BE CLOSED AT THIS HOUR.
OH...

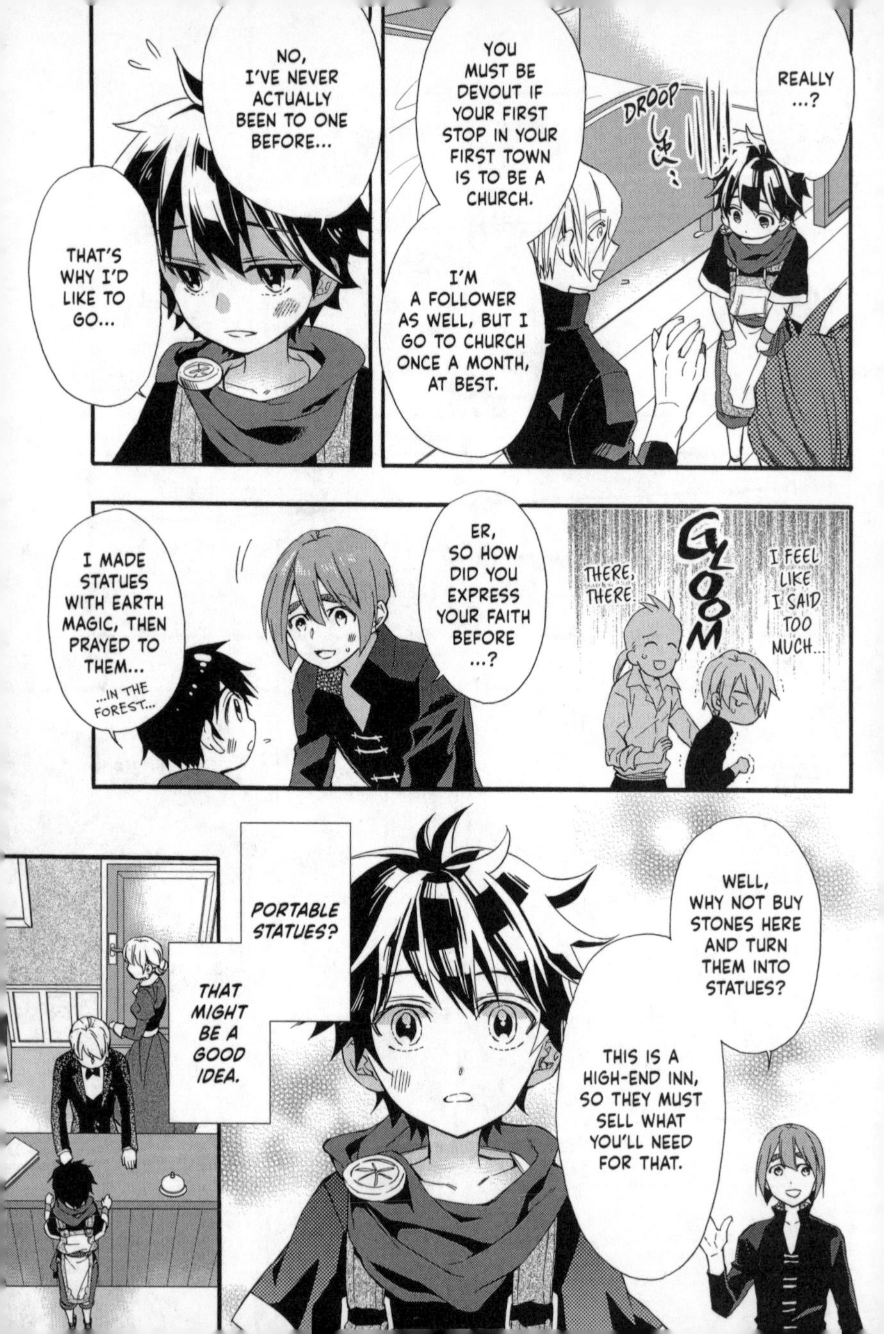
REALLY ...?
DROOP
YOU MUST BE DEVOUT IF YOUR FIRST STOP IN YOUR FIRST TOWN IS TO BE A CHURCH.
I'M A FOLLOWER AS WELL, BUT I GO TO CHURCH ONCE A MONTH, AT BEST.
NO, I'VE NEVER ACTUALLY BEEN TO ONE BEFORE...
THAT'S WHY I'D LIKE TO GO...
I FEEL LIKE I SAID TOO MUCH...
GLOOM
THERE, THERE.
ER, SO HOW DID YOU EXPRESS YOUR FAITH BEFORE ...?
I MADE STATUES WITH EARTH MAGIC, THEN PRAYED TO THEM...
...IN THE FOREST...
WELL, WHY NOT BUY STONES HERE AND TURN THEM INTO STATUES?
THIS IS A HIGH-END INN, SO THEY MUST SELL WHAT YOU'LL NEED FOR THAT.
PORTABLE STATUES?
THAT MIGHT BE A GOOD IDEA.

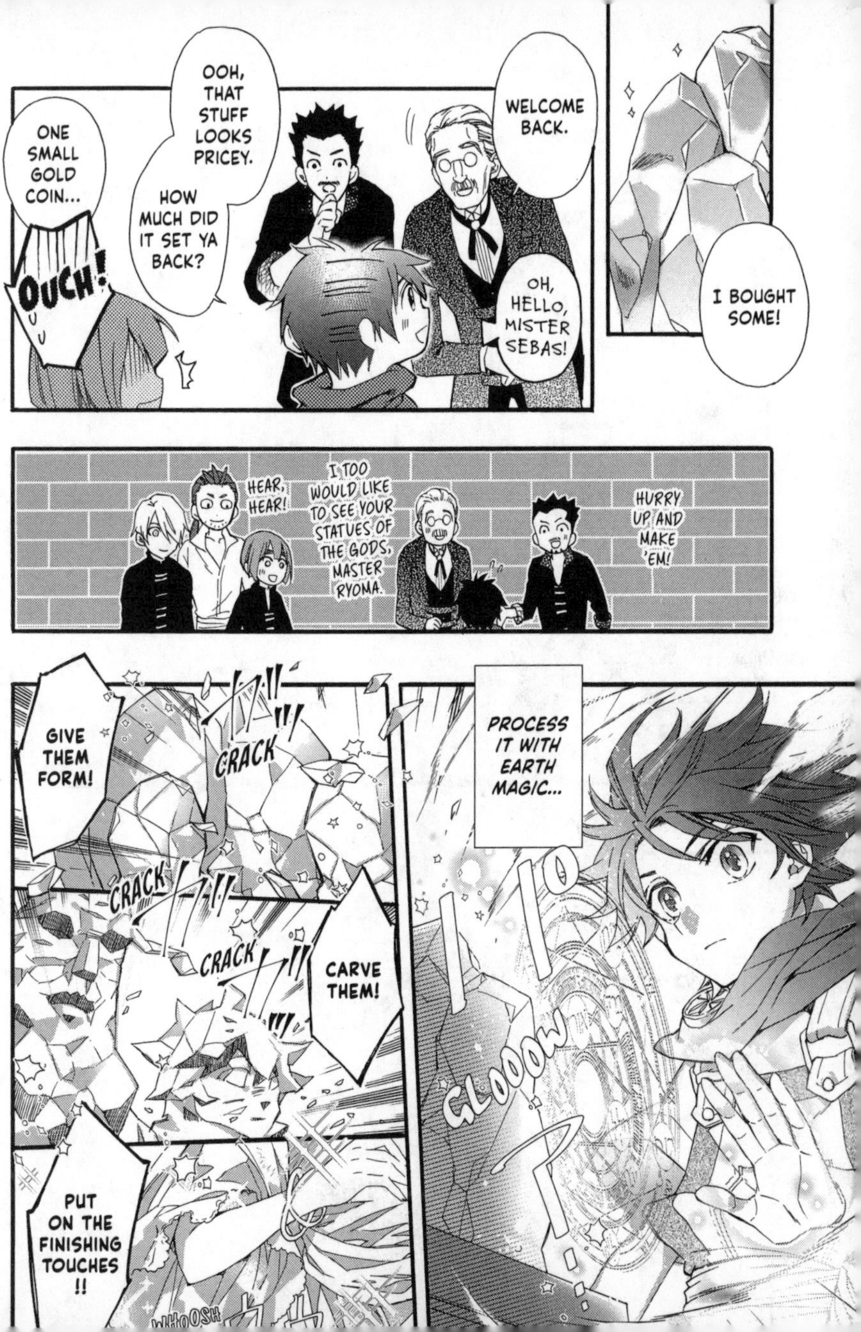

I BOUGHT SOME!
WELCOME BACK.
OH, HELLO, MISTER SEBAS!
OOH, THAT STUFF LOOKS PRICEY.
HOW MUCH DID IT SET YA BACK?
ONE SMALL GOLD COIN...
OUCH!
HURRY UP AND MAKE 'EM!
I TOO WOULD LIKE TO SEE YOUR STATUES OF THE GODS, MASTER RYOMA.
HEAR, HEAR!
PROCESS IT WITH EARTH MAGIC...
GLOOOW
GIVE THEM FORM!
CRACK
CRACK
CRACK
CARVE THEM!
PUT ON THE FINISHING TOUCHES !!
WHOOSH

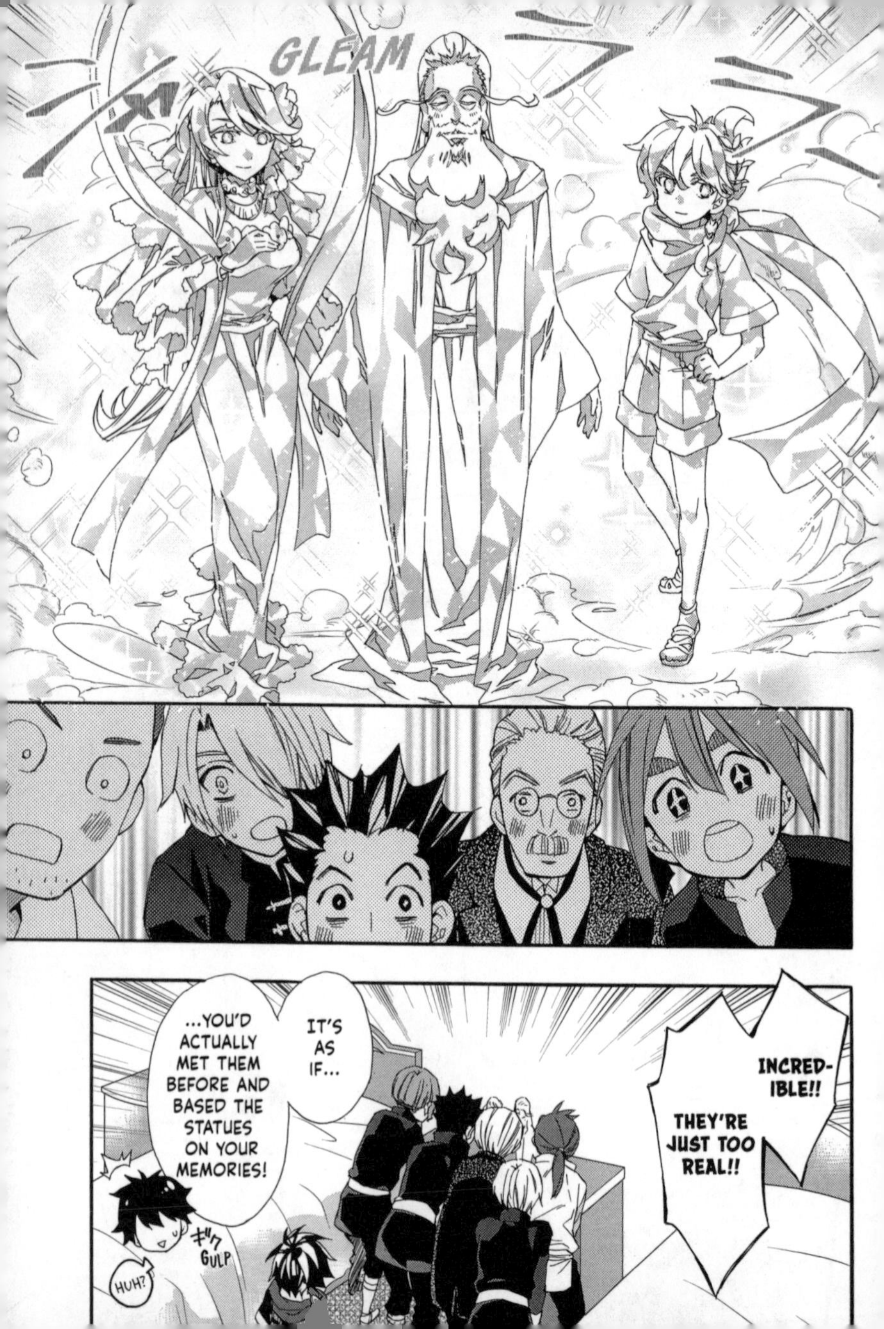
GLEAM
INCRED-IBLE!!
THEY'RE JUST TOO REAL!!
IT'S AS IF...
...YOU'D ACTUALLY MET THEM BEFORE AND BASED THE STATUES ON YOUR MEMORIES!
ギク
GULP
HUH?

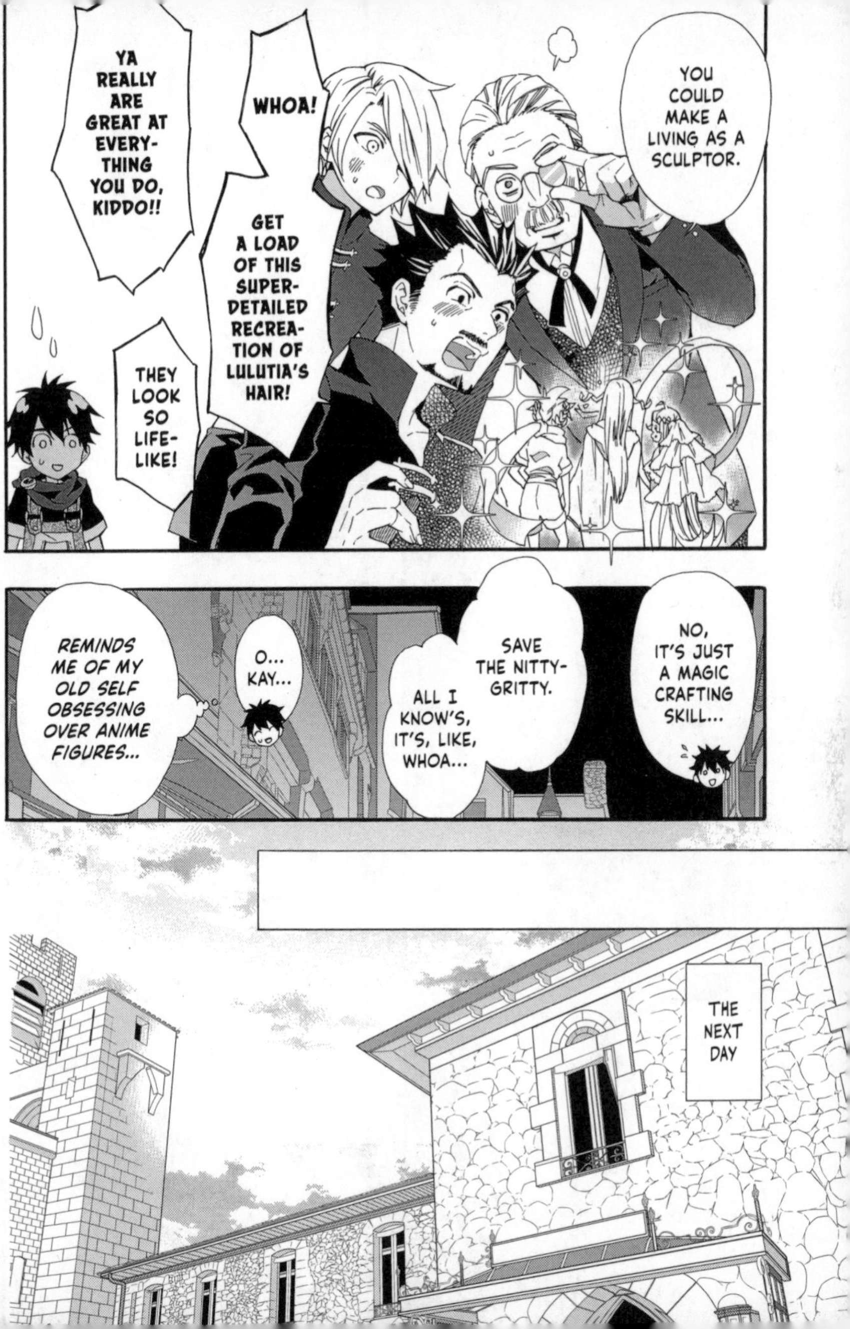
YOU COULD MAKE A LIVING AS A SCULPTOR.
WHOA!
YA REALLY ARE GREAT AT EVERY-THING YOU DO, KIDDO!!
GET A LOAD OF THIS SUPER-DETAILED RECREA-TION OF LULUTIA'S HAIR!
THEY LOOK SO LIFE-LIKE!
NO, IT'S JUST A MAGIC CRAFTING SKILL...
SAVE THE NITTY-GRITTY.
ALL I KNOW'S, IT'S, LIKE, WHOA...
O... KAY...
REMINDS ME OF MY OLD SELF OBSESSING OVER ANIME FIGURES...
THE NEXT DAY

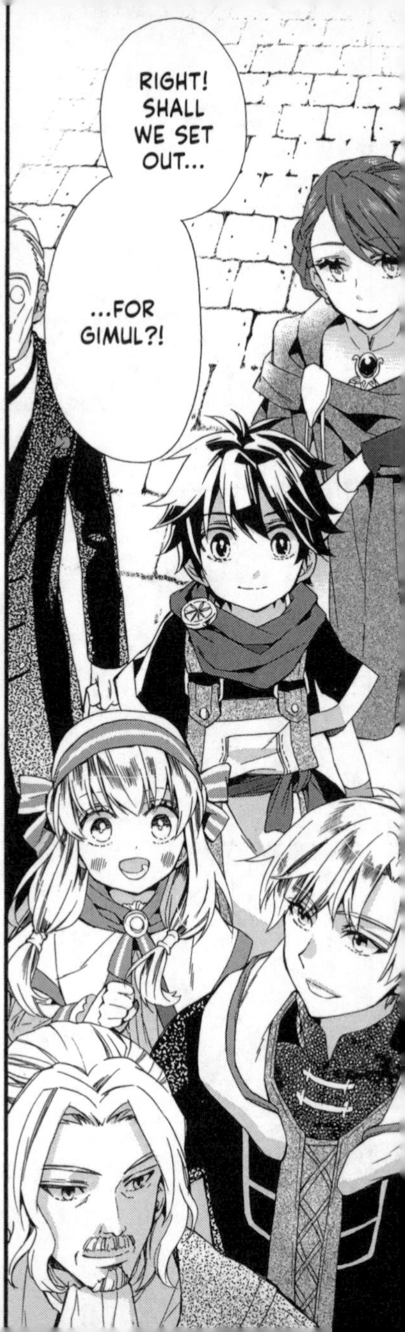
RIGHT! SHALL WE SET OUT...
...FOR GIMUL?!

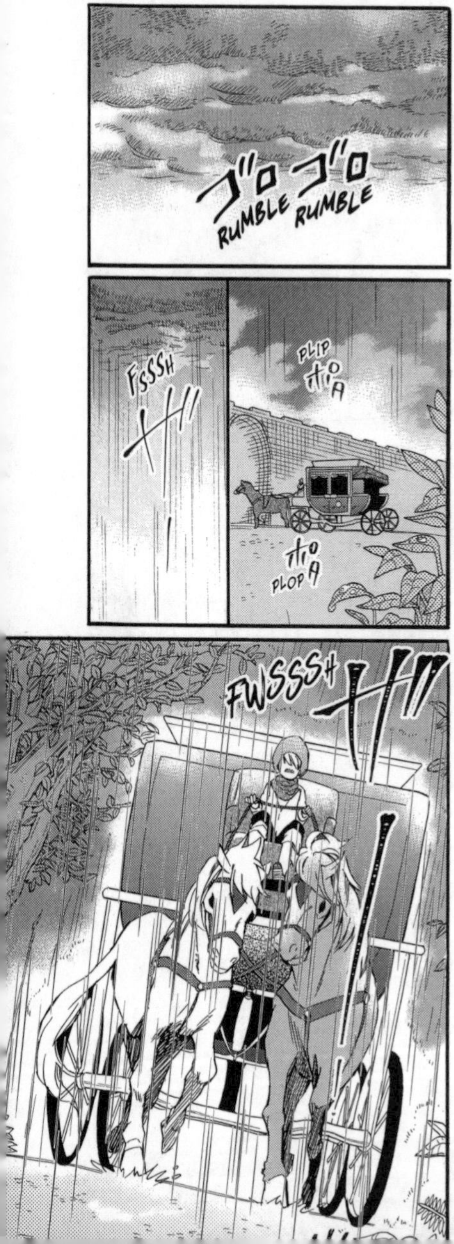
ゴロゴロ
RUMBLE RUMBLE
PLIP
PLOP
FSSSH
FWSSSH

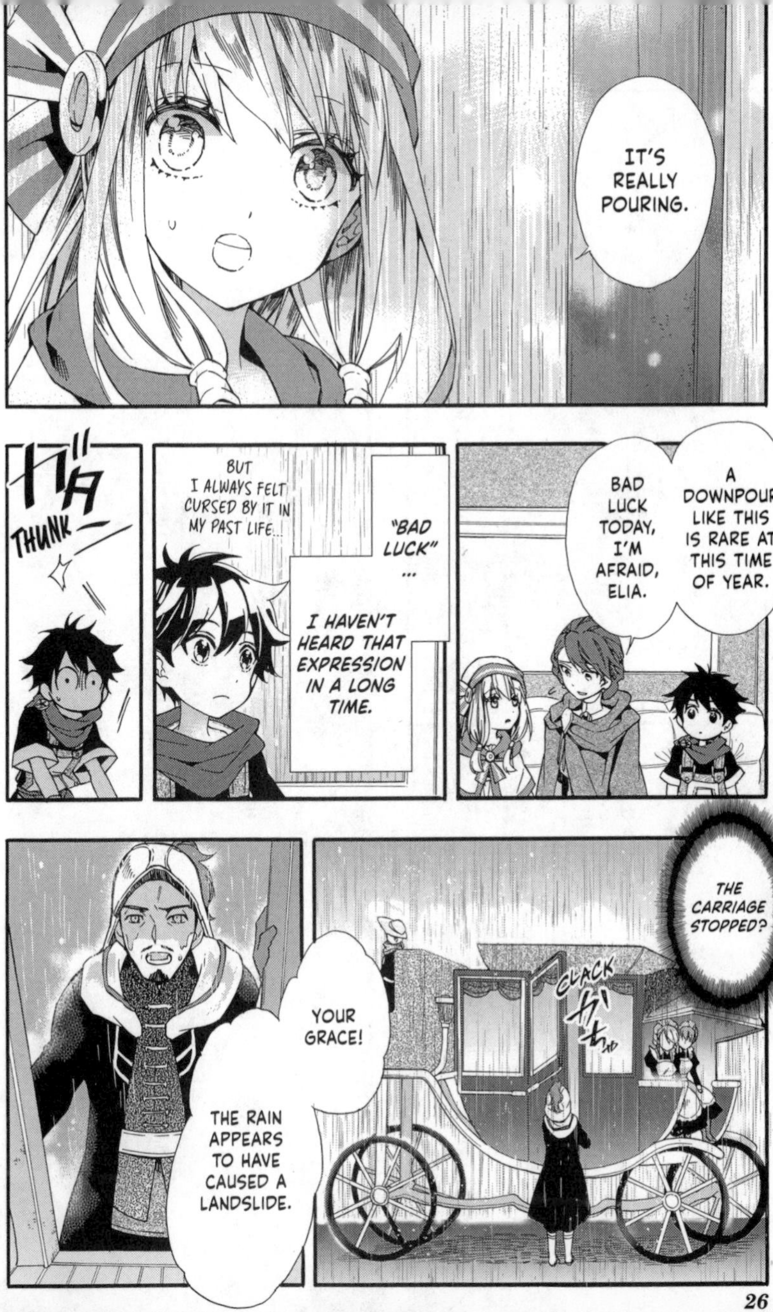
IT'S REALLY POURING.
A DOWNPOUR LIKE THIS IS RARE AT THIS TIME OF YEAR.
BAD LUCK TODAY, I'M AFRAID, ELIA.
"BAD LUCK"...
I HAVEN'T HEARD THAT EXPRESSION IN A LONG TIME.
BUT I ALWAYS FELT CURSED BY IT IN MY PAST LIFE...
THUNK
THE CARRIAGE STOPPED?
CLACK
YOUR GRACE!
THE RAIN APPEARS TO HAVE CAUSED A LANDSLIDE.

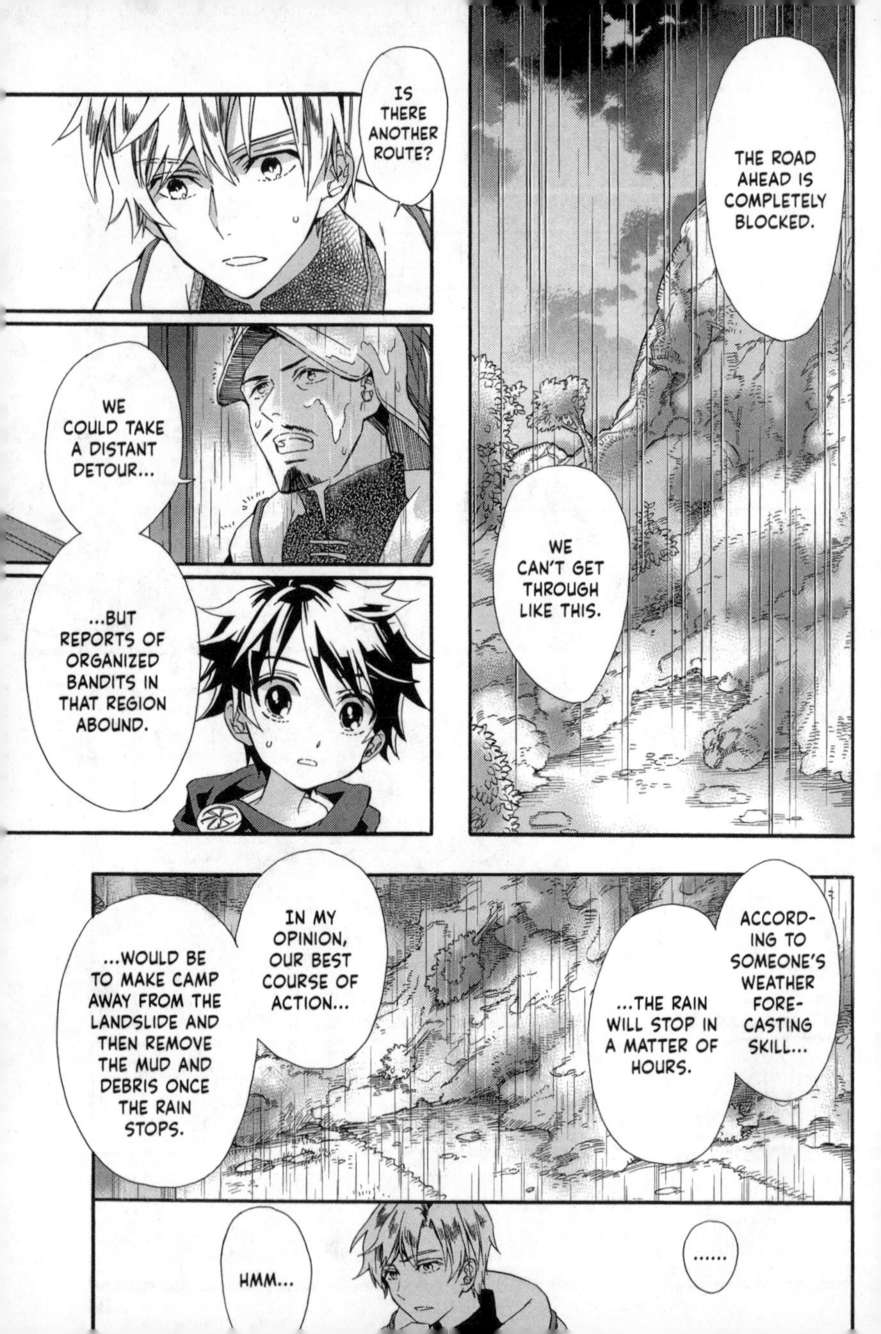
THE ROAD AHEAD IS COMPLETELY BLOCKED.
WE CAN'T GET THROUGH LIKE THIS.
IS THERE ANOTHER ROUTE?
WE COULD TAKE A DISTANT DETOUR...
...BUT REPORTS OF ORGANIZED BANDITS IN THAT REGION ABOUND.
ACCORD-ING TO SOMEONE'S WEATHER FORE-CASTING SKILL...
...THE RAIN WILL STOP IN A MATTER OF HOURS.
IN MY OPINION, OUR BEST COURSE OF ACTION...
...WOULD BE TO MAKE CAMP AWAY FROM THE LANDSLIDE AND THEN REMOVE THE MUD AND DEBRIS ONCE THE RAIN STOPS.
......
HMM...

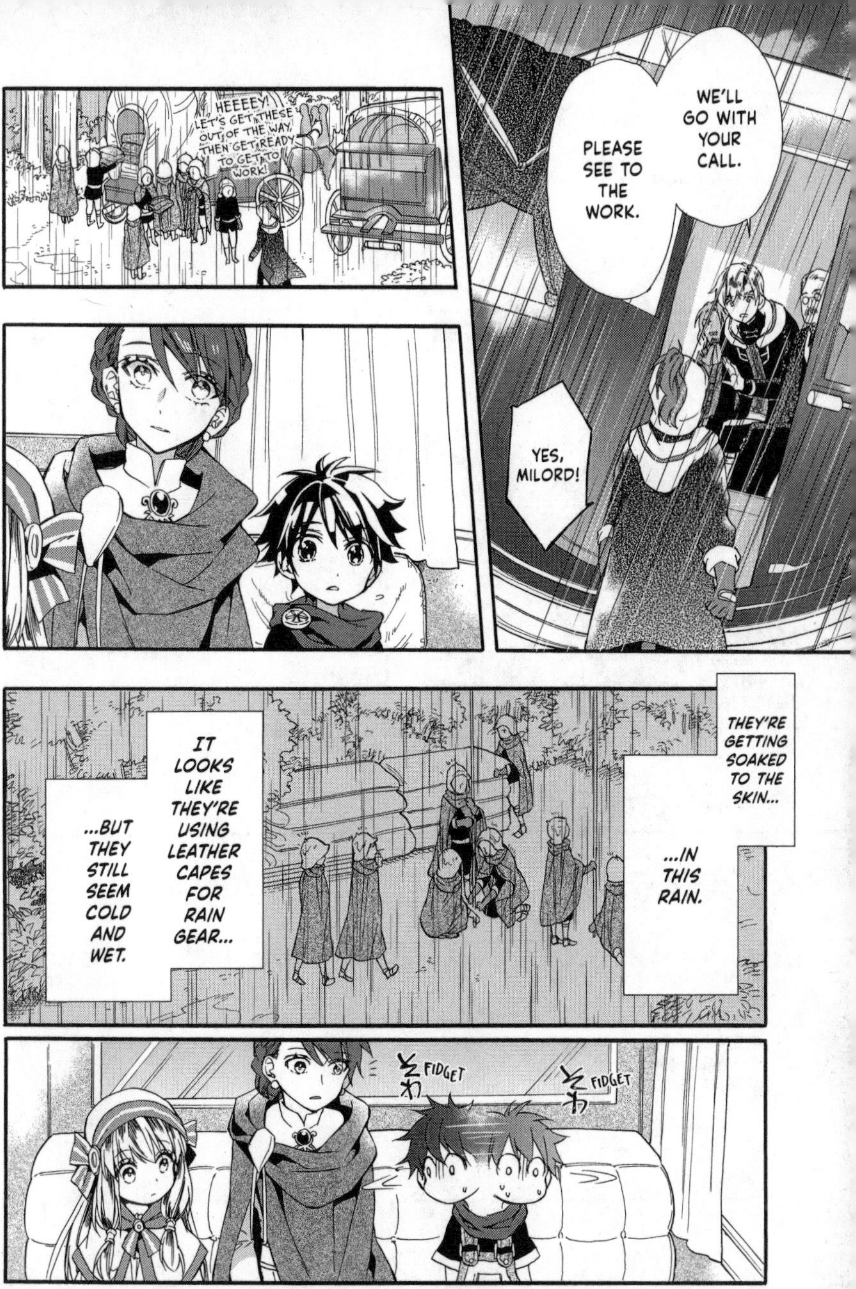
WE'LL GO WITH YOUR CALL.
PLEASE SEE TO THE WORK.
YES, MILORD!
HEEEEY! LET'S GET THESE OUT OF THE WAY, THEN GET READY TO GET TO WORK!
THEY'RE GETTING SOAKED TO THE SKIN...
...IN THIS RAIN.
IT LOOKS LIKE THEY'RE USING LEATHER CAPES FOR RAIN GEAR...
...BUT THEY STILL SEEM COLD AND WET.
そわ FIDGET
そわ FIDGET

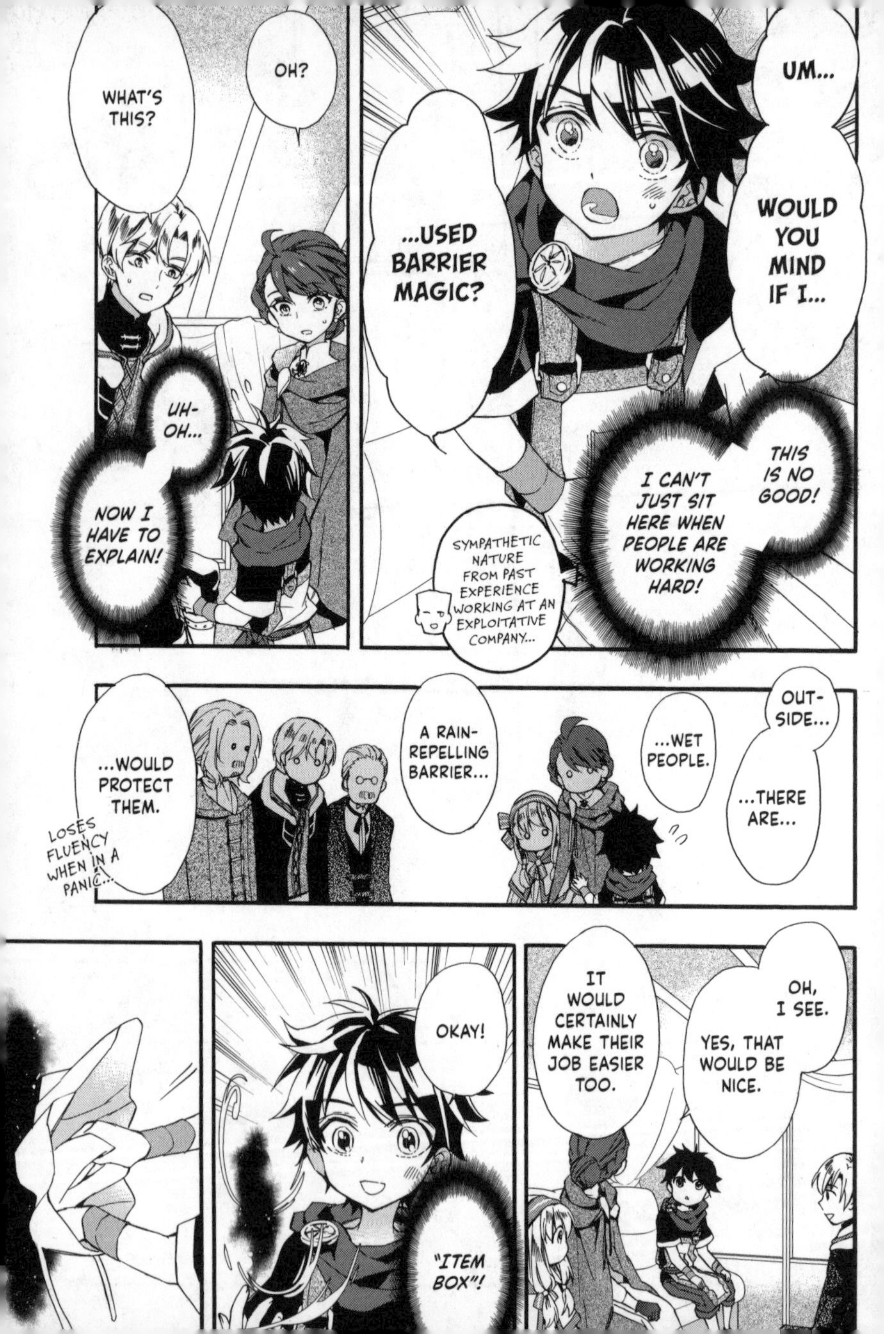
UM...
WOULD YOU MIND IF I...
...USED BARRIER MAGIC?
THIS IS NO GOOD!
I CAN'T JUST SIT HERE WHEN PEOPLE ARE WORKING HARD!
SYMPATHETIC NATURE FROM PAST EXPERIENCE WORKING AT AN EXPLOITATIVE COMPANY...
OH?
WHAT'S THIS?
UH-OH...
NOW I HAVE TO EXPLAIN!
OUT-SIDE...
...THERE ARE...
...WET PEOPLE.
A RAIN-REPELLING BARRIER...
...WOULD PROTECT THEM.
LOSES FLUENCY WHEN IN A PANIC...
OH, I SEE.
YES, THAT WOULD BE NICE.
IT WOULD CERTAINLY MAKE THEIR JOB EASIER TOO.
OKAY!
"ITEM BOX"!

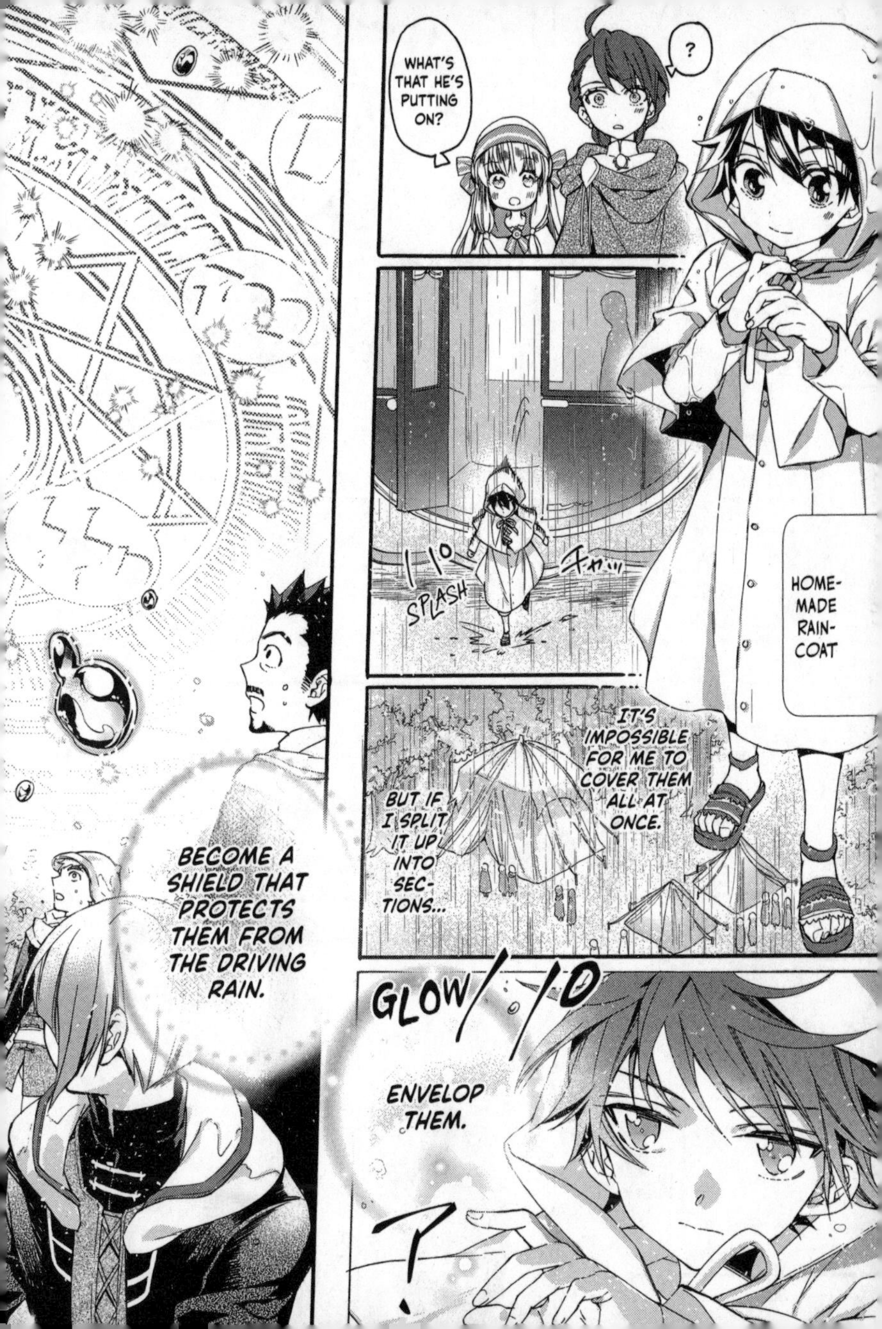

?
WHAT'S THAT HE'S PUTTING ON?
HOME-MADE RAIN-COAT
SPLASH
IT'S IMPOSSIBLE FOR ME TO COVER THEM ALL AT ONCE.
BUT IF I SPLIT IT UP INTO SEC-TIONS...
GLOW
ENVELOP THEM.
BECOME A SHIELD THAT PROTECTS THEM FROM THE DRIVING RAIN.

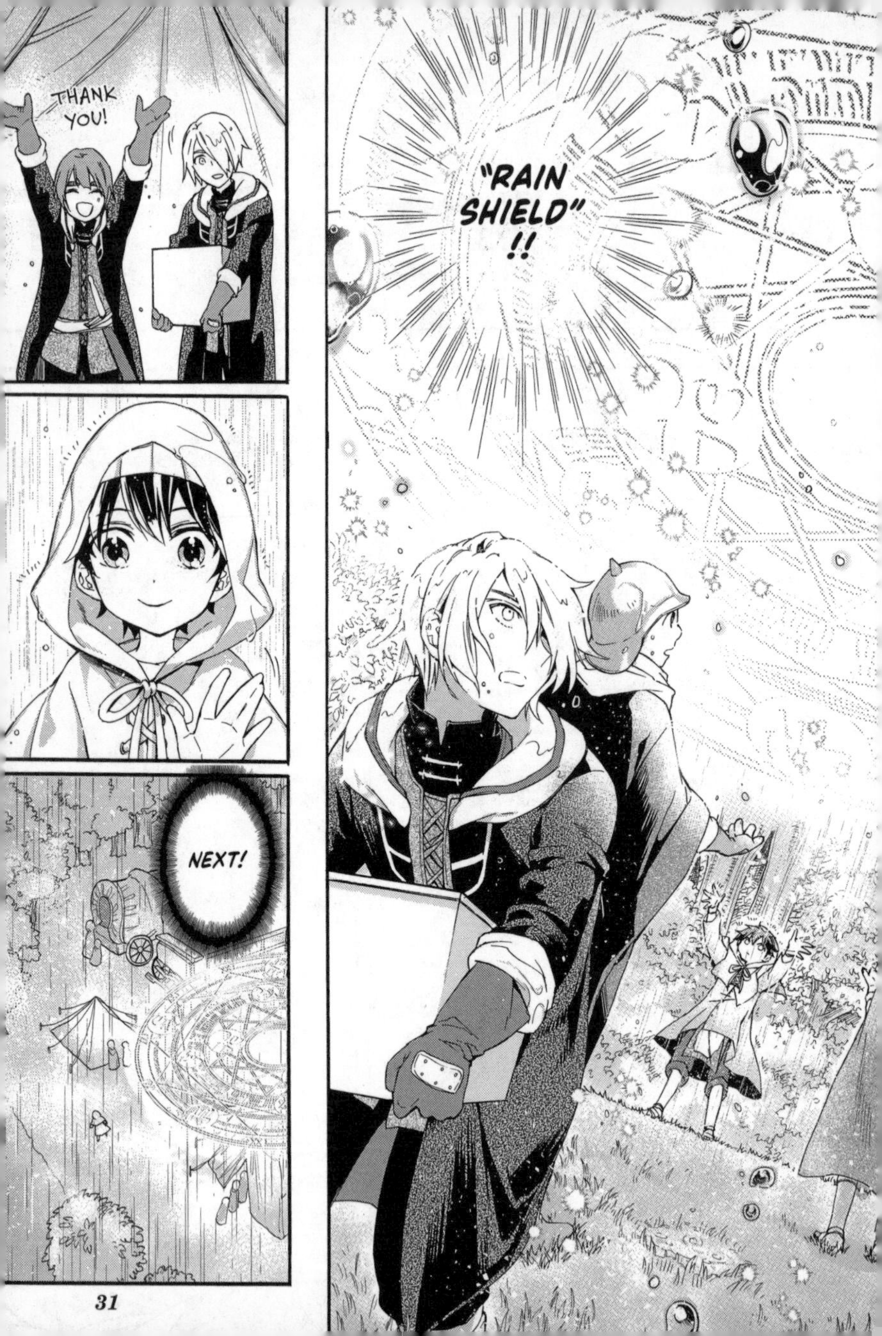
"RAIN SHIELD" !!
THANK YOU!
NEXT!

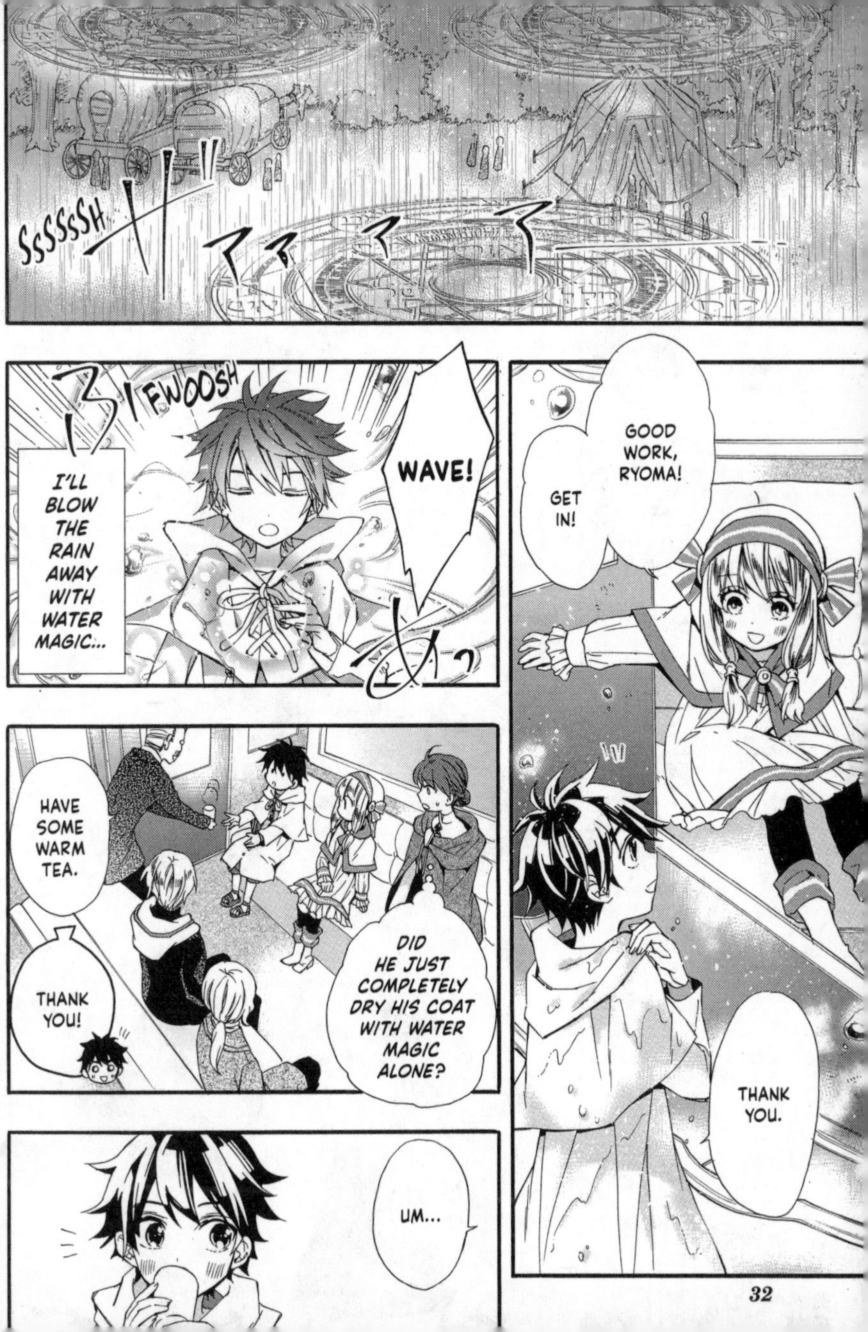
SSSSSSH
GOOD WORK, RYOMA!
GET IN!
THANK YOU.
WAVE!
FWOOSH
I'LL BLOW THE RAIN AWAY WITH WATER MAGIC...
HAVE SOME WARM TEA.
THANK YOU!
DID HE JUST COMPLETELY DRY HIS COAT WITH WATER MAGIC ALONE?
UM...

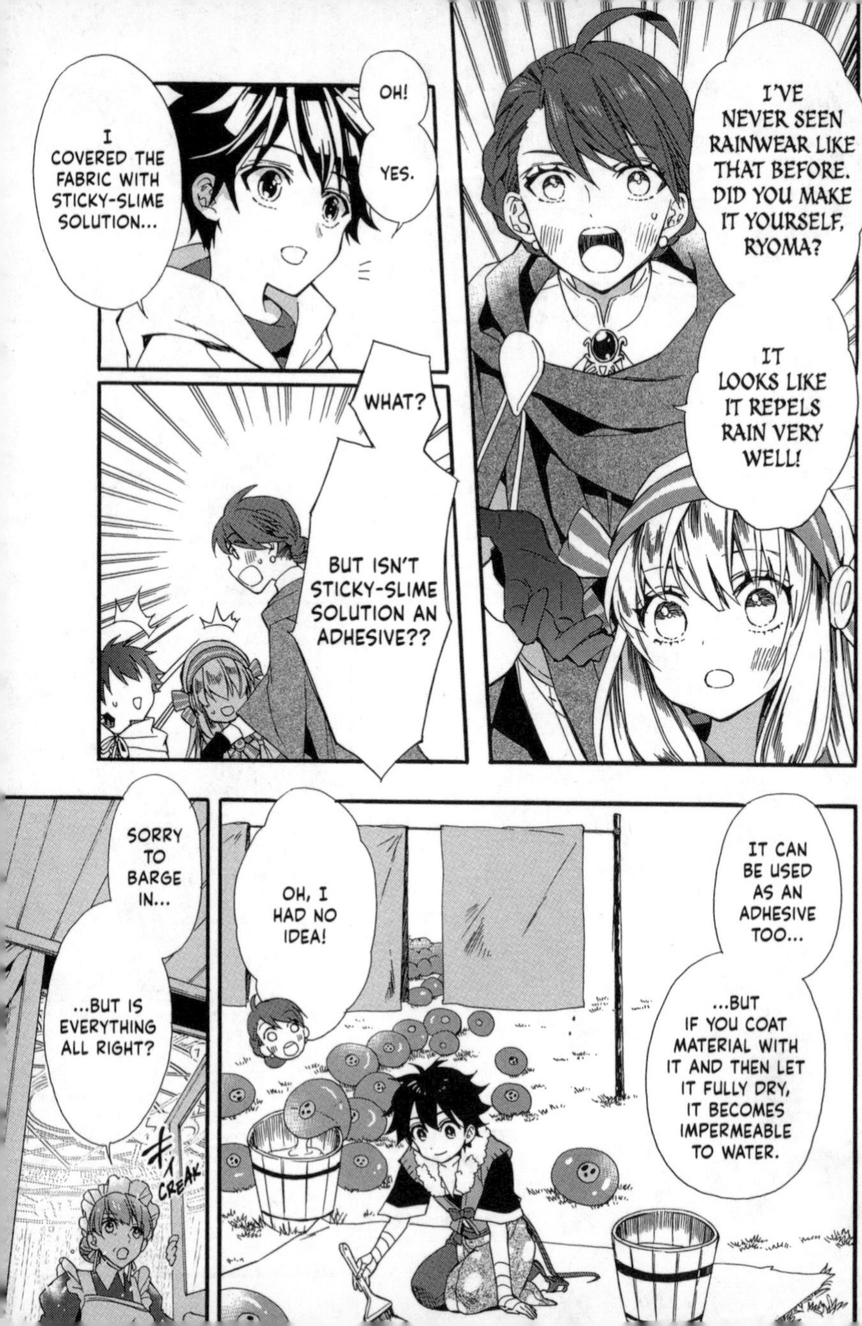
I'VE NEVER SEEN RAINWEAR LIKE THAT BEFORE. DID YOU MAKE IT YOURSELF, RYOMA?
IT LOOKS LIKE IT REPELS RAIN VERY WELL!
OH!
YES.
I COVERED THE FABRIC WITH STICKY-SLIME SOLUTION...
WHAT?
BUT ISN'T STICKY-SLIME SOLUTION AN ADHESIVE??
IT CAN BE USED AS AN ADHESIVE TOO...
...BUT IF YOU COAT MATERIAL WITH IT AND THEN LET IT FULLY DRY, IT BECOMES IMPERMEABLE TO WATER.
OH, I HAD NO IDEA!
SORRY TO BARGE IN...
...BUT IS EVERYTHING ALL RIGHT?
CREAK

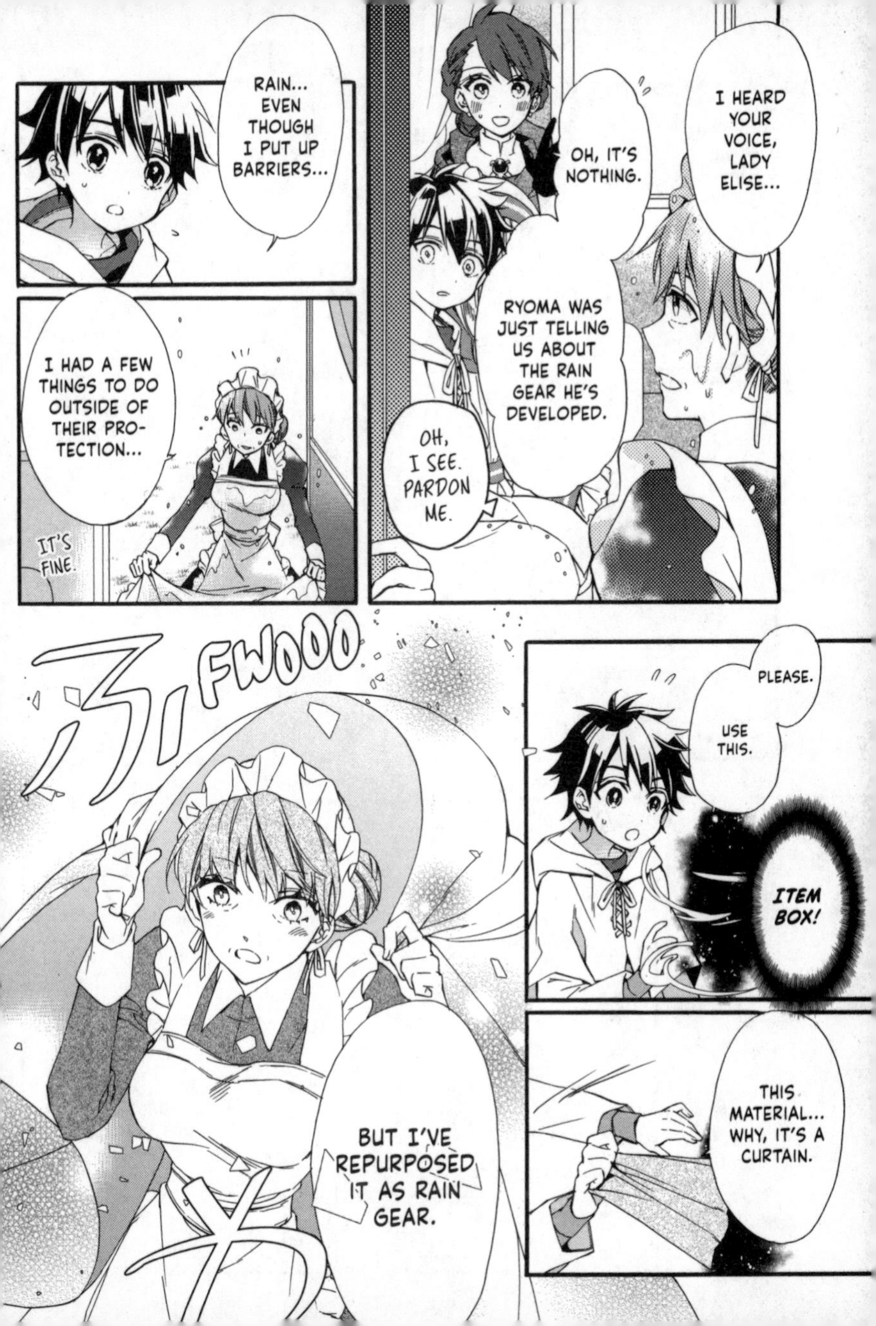
I HEARD YOUR VOICE, LADY ELISE...
OH, IT'S NOTHING.
RYOMA WAS JUST TELLING US ABOUT THE RAIN GEAR HE'S DEVELOPED.
OH, I SEE. PARDON ME.
RAIN... EVEN THOUGH I PUT UP BARRIERS...
I HAD A FEW THINGS TO DO OUTSIDE OF THEIR PRO-TECTION...
IT'S FINE.
PLEASE.
USE THIS.
ITEM BOX!
THIS MATERIAL... WHY, IT'S A CURTAIN.
FWOOO
BUT I'VE REPURPOSED IT AS RAIN GEAR.

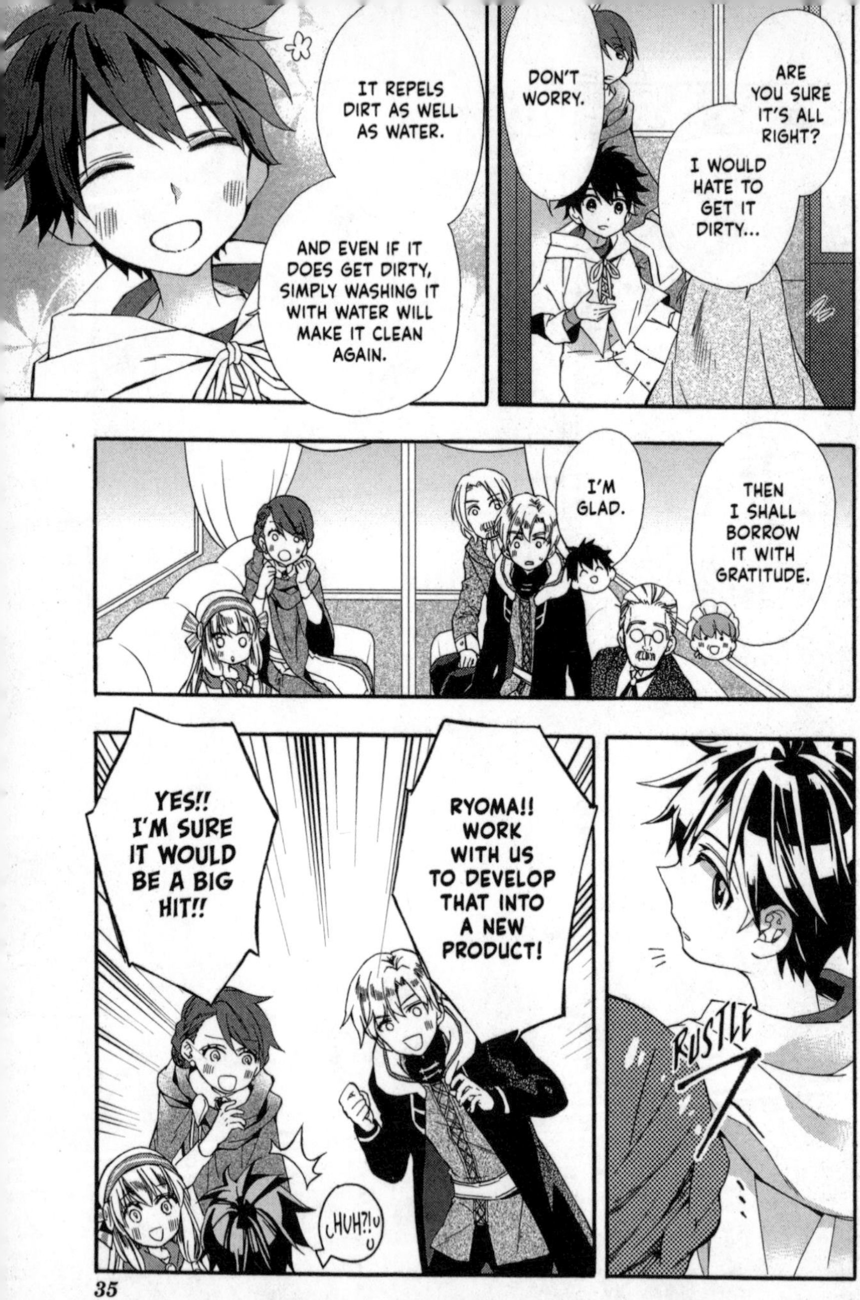
ARE YOU SURE IT'S ALL RIGHT?
I WOULD HATE TO GET IT DIRTY...
DON'T WORRY.
IT REPELS DIRT AS WELL AS WATER.
AND EVEN IF IT DOES GET DIRTY, SIMPLY WASHING IT WITH WATER WILL MAKE IT CLEAN AGAIN.
THEN I SHALL BORROW IT WITH GRATITUDE.
I'M GLAD.
RUSTLE
RYOMA!! WORK WITH US TO DEVELOP THAT INTO A NEW PRODUCT!
YES!! I'M SURE IT WOULD BE A BIG HIT!!
HUH?!

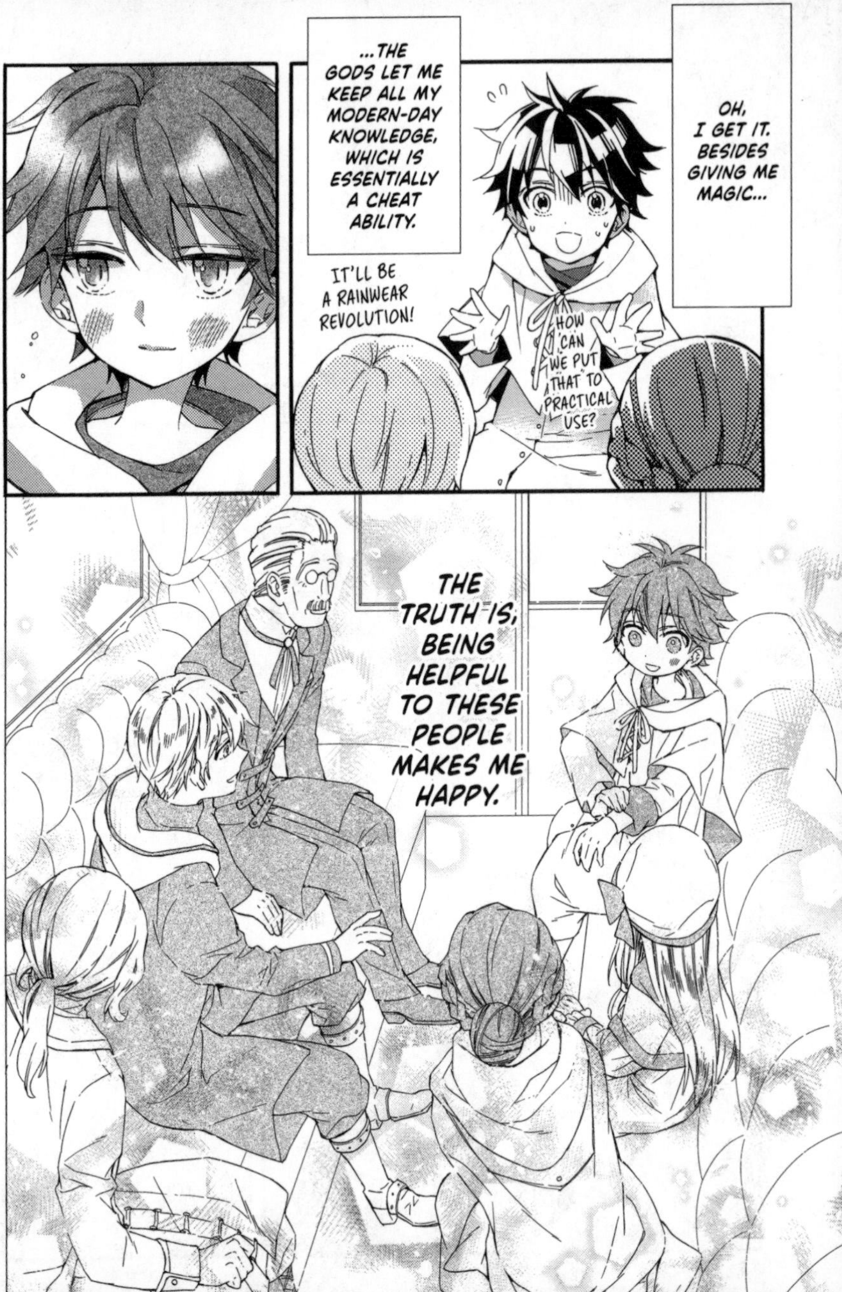
OH, I GET IT. BESIDES GIVING ME MAGIC...
...THE GODS LET ME KEEP ALL MY MODERN-DAY KNOWLEDGE, WHICH IS ESSENTIALLY A CHEAT ABILITY.
HOW CAN WE PUT THAT TO PRACTICAL USE?
IT'LL BE A RAINWEAR REVOLUTION!
THE TRUTH IS, BEING HELPFUL TO THESE PEOPLE MAKES ME HAPPY.

Chapter 6: Public Works

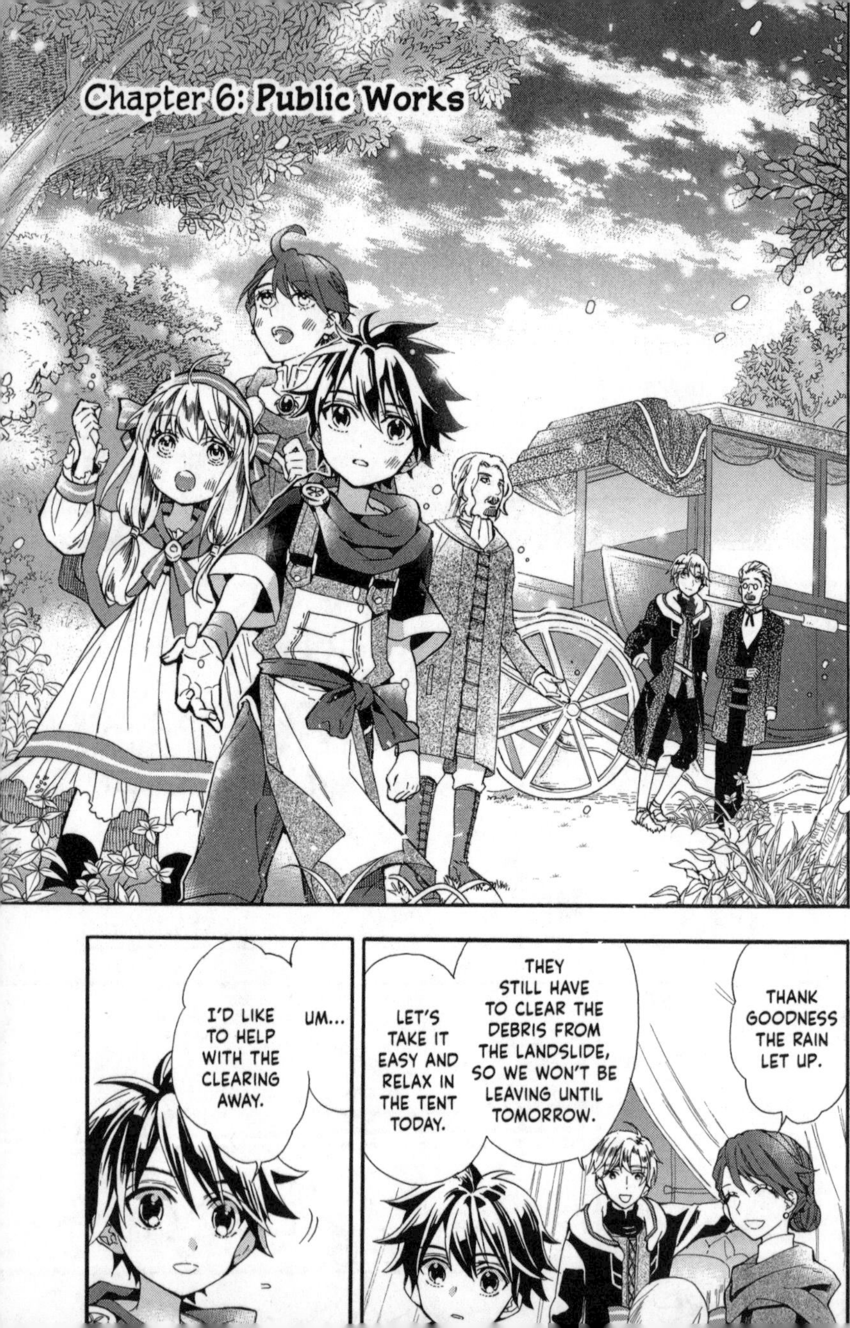
THANK GOODNESS THE RAIN LET UP.
THEY STILL HAVE TO CLEAR THE DEBRIS FROM THE LANDSLIDE, SO WE WON'T BE LEAVING UNTIL TOMORROW.
LET'S TAKE IT EASY AND RELAX IN THE TENT TODAY.
UM...
I'D LIKE TO HELP WITH THE CLEARING AWAY.

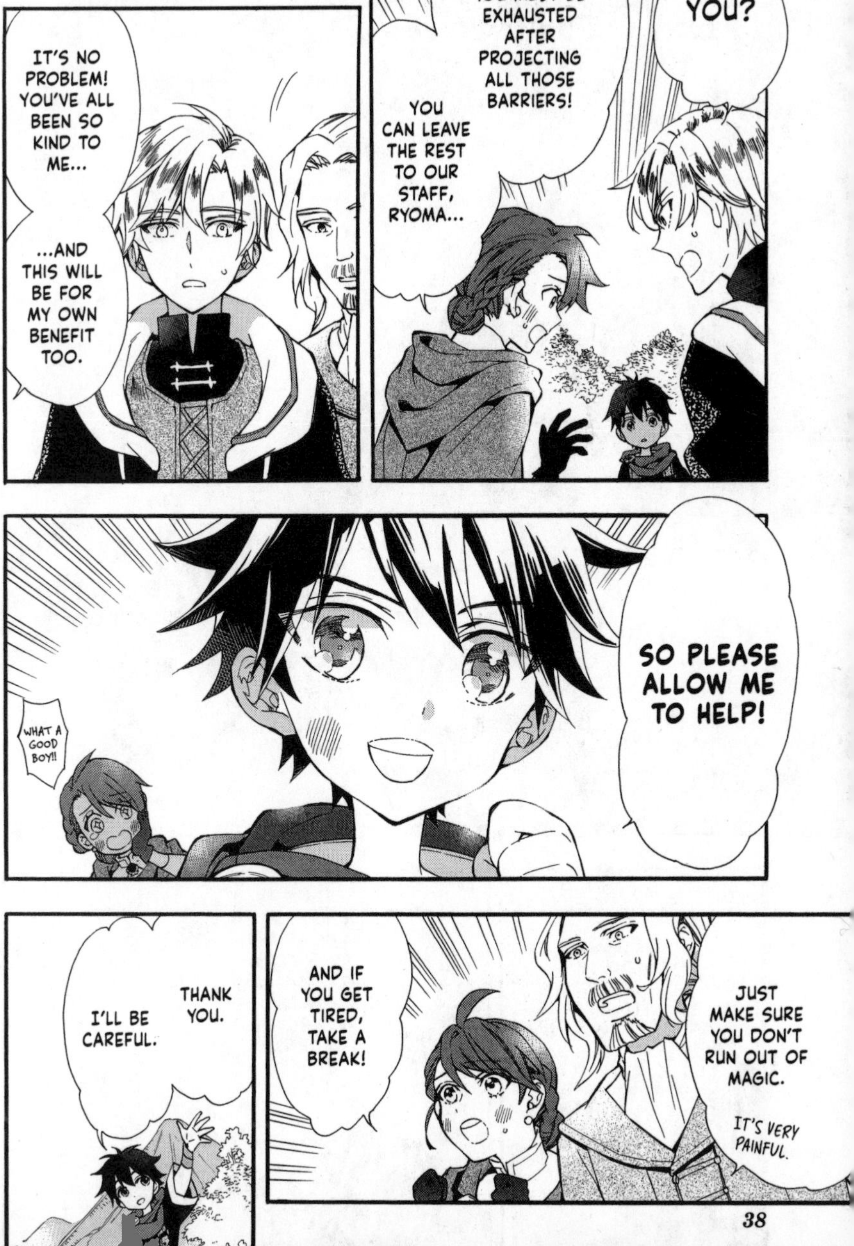
YOU?
BUT... YOU MUST BE EXHAUSTED AFTER PROJECTING ALL THOSE BARRIERS!
YOU CAN LEAVE THE REST TO OUR STAFF, RYOMA...
IT'S NO PROBLEM! YOU'VE ALL BEEN SO KIND TO ME...
...AND THIS WILL BE FOR MY OWN BENEFIT TOO.
SO PLEASE ALLOW ME TO HELP!
WHAT A GOOD BOY!!
JUST MAKE SURE YOU DON'T RUN OUT OF MAGIC.
IT'S VERY PAINFUL.
AND IF YOU GET TIRED, TAKE A BREAK!
THANK YOU.
I'LL BE CAREFUL.

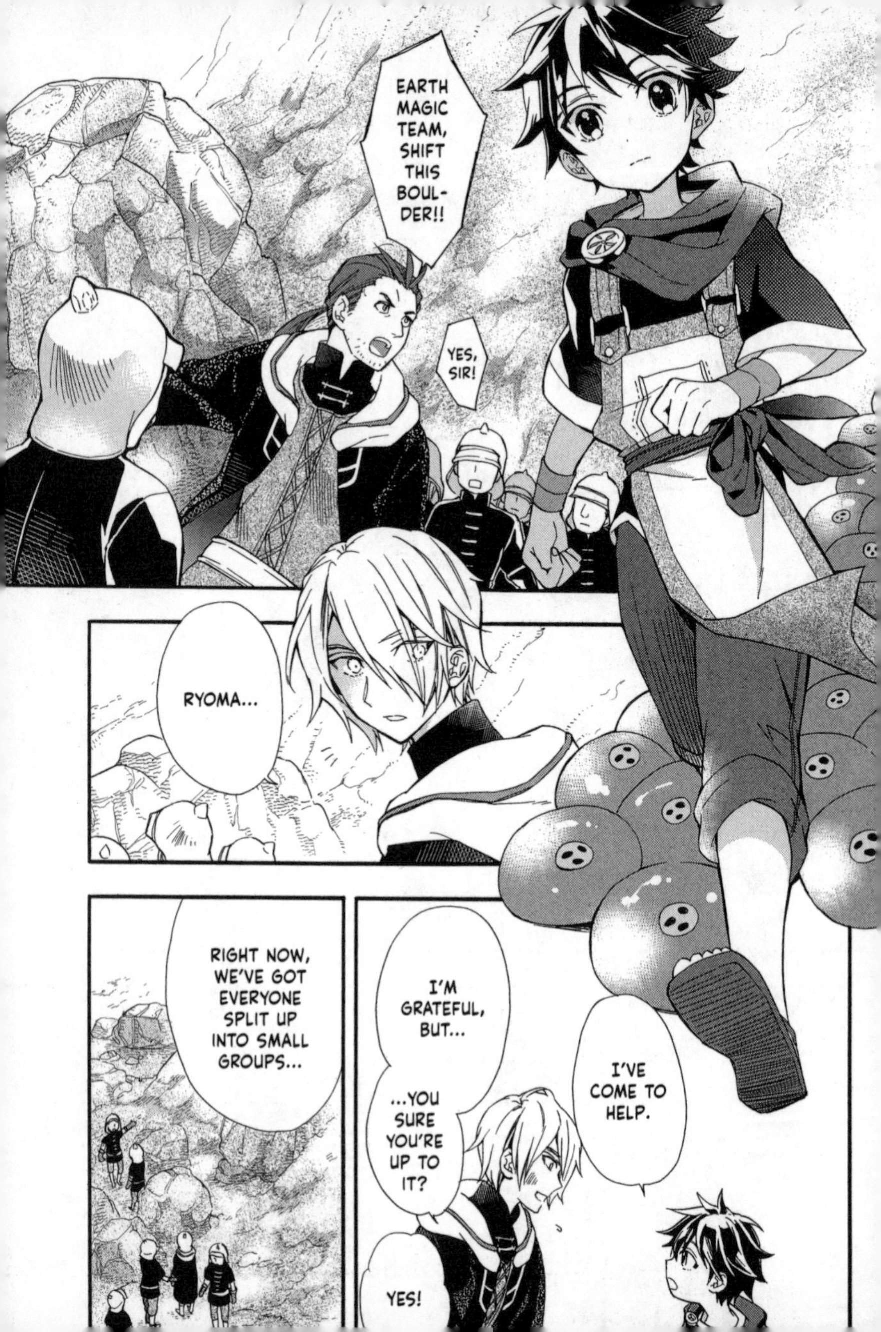
EARTH MAGIC TEAM, SHIFT THIS BOUL-DER!!
YES, SIR!
RYOMA...
I'VE COME TO HELP.
I'M GRATEFUL, BUT...
...YOU SURE YOU'RE UP TO IT?
YES!
RIGHT NOW, WE'VE GOT EVERYONE SPLIT UP INTO SMALL GROUPS...

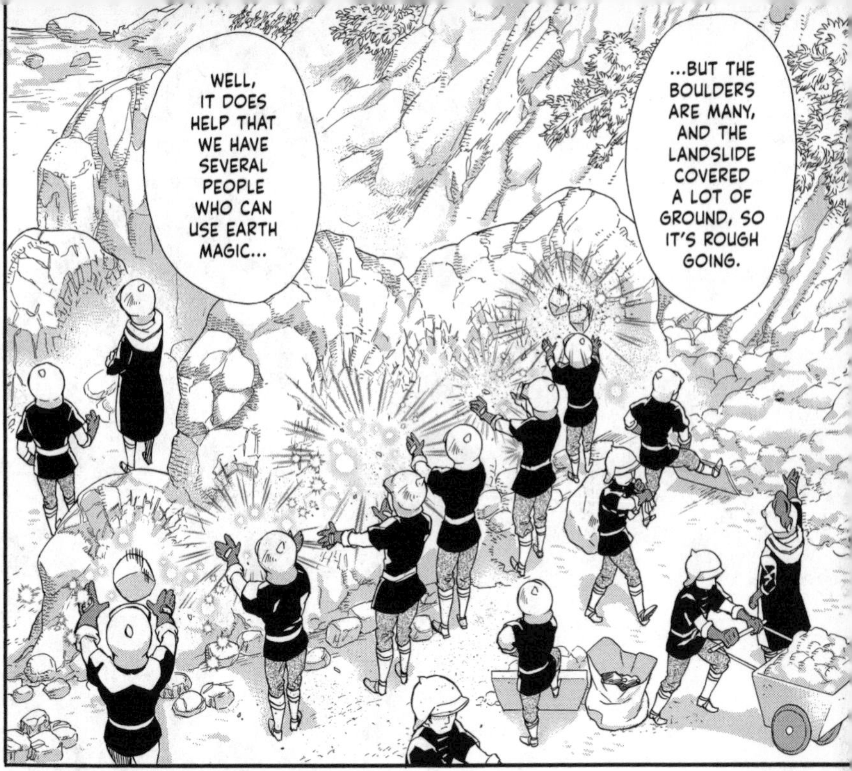
...BUT THE BOULDERS ARE MANY, AND THE LANDSLIDE COVERED A LOT OF GROUND, SO IT'S ROUGH GOING.
WELL, IT DOES HELP THAT WE HAVE SEVERAL PEOPLE WHO CAN USE EARTH MAGIC...
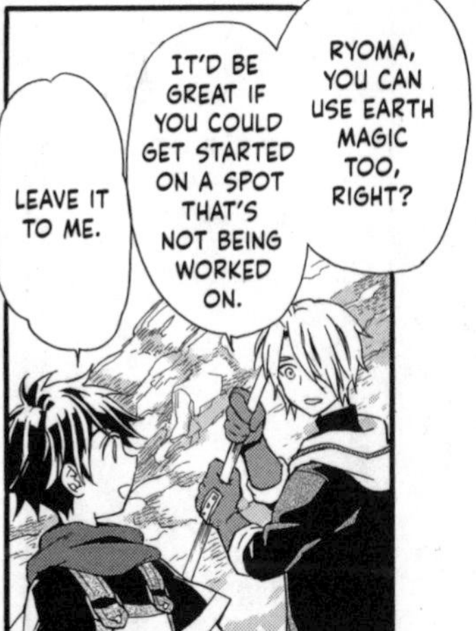
RYOMA, YOU CAN USE EARTH MAGIC TOO, RIGHT?
IT'D BE GREAT IF YOU COULD GET STARTED ON A SPOT THAT'S NOT BEING WORKED ON.
LEAVE IT TO ME.
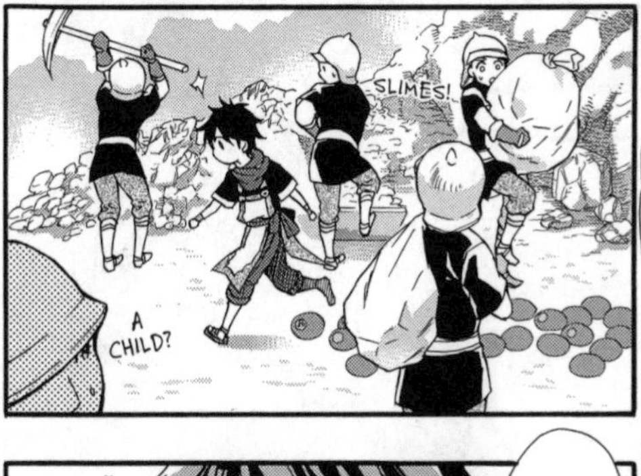
SLIMES!
A CHILD?
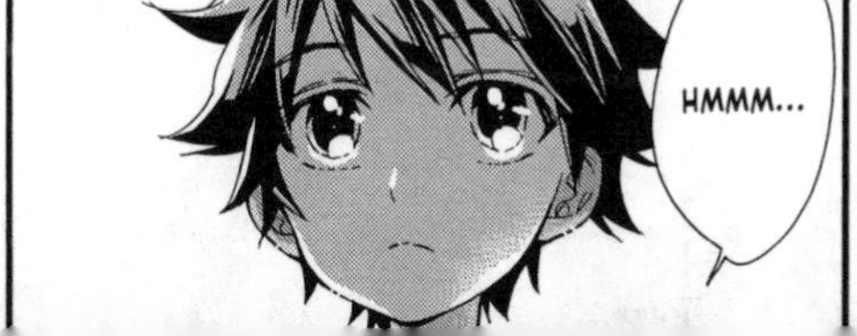
HMMM...

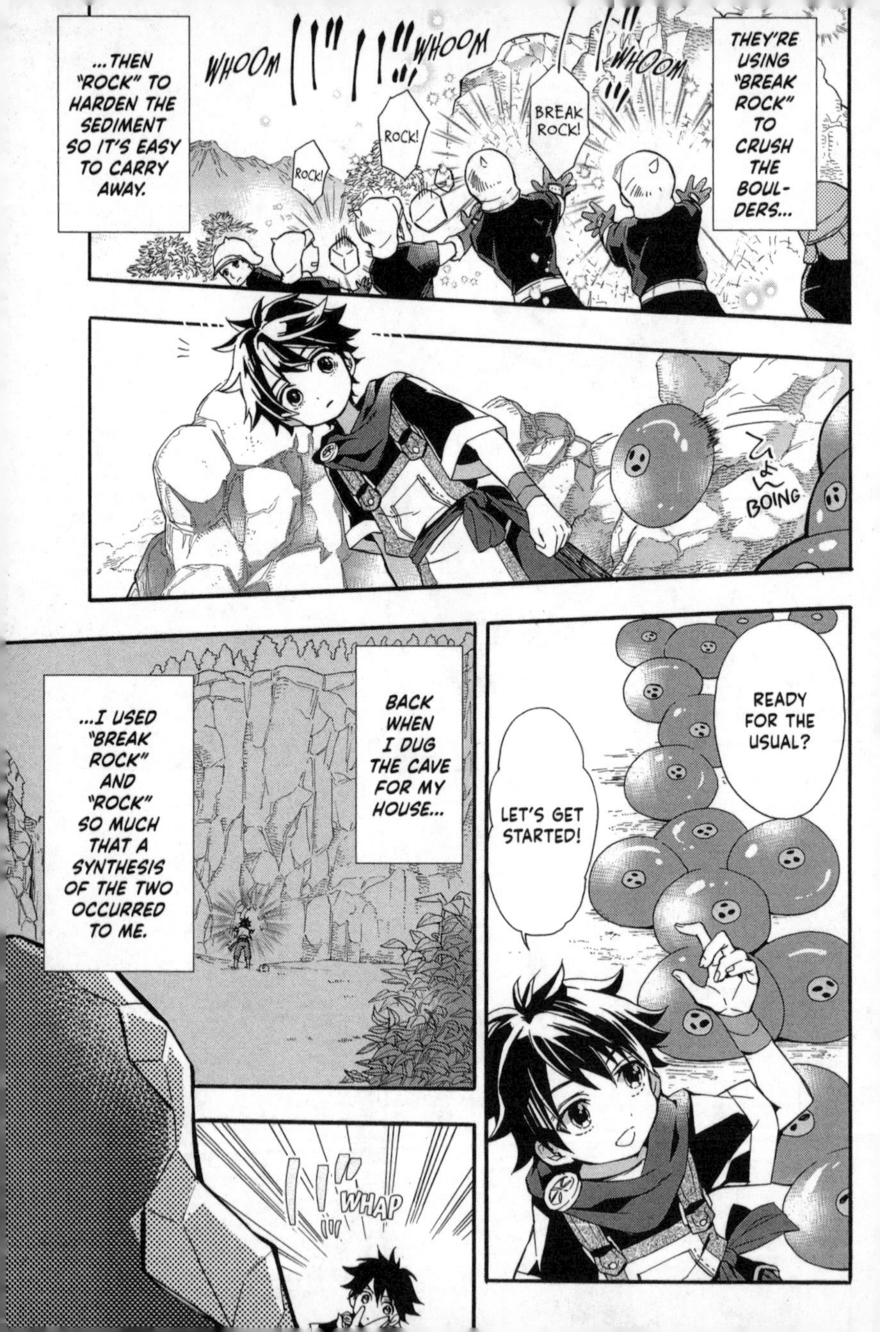
THEY'RE USING "BREAK ROCK" TO CRUSH THE BOULDERS...
WHOOM
BREAK ROCK!
WHOOM
ROCK!
ROCK!
WHOOM
...THEN "ROCK" TO HARDEN THE SEDIMENT SO IT'S EASY TO CARRY AWAY.
BOING
READY FOR THE USUAL?
LET'S GET STARTED!
BACK WHEN I DUG THE CAVE FOR MY HOUSE...
...I USED "BREAK ROCK" AND "ROCK" SO MUCH THAT A SYNTHESIS OF THE TWO OCCURRED TO ME.
WHAP

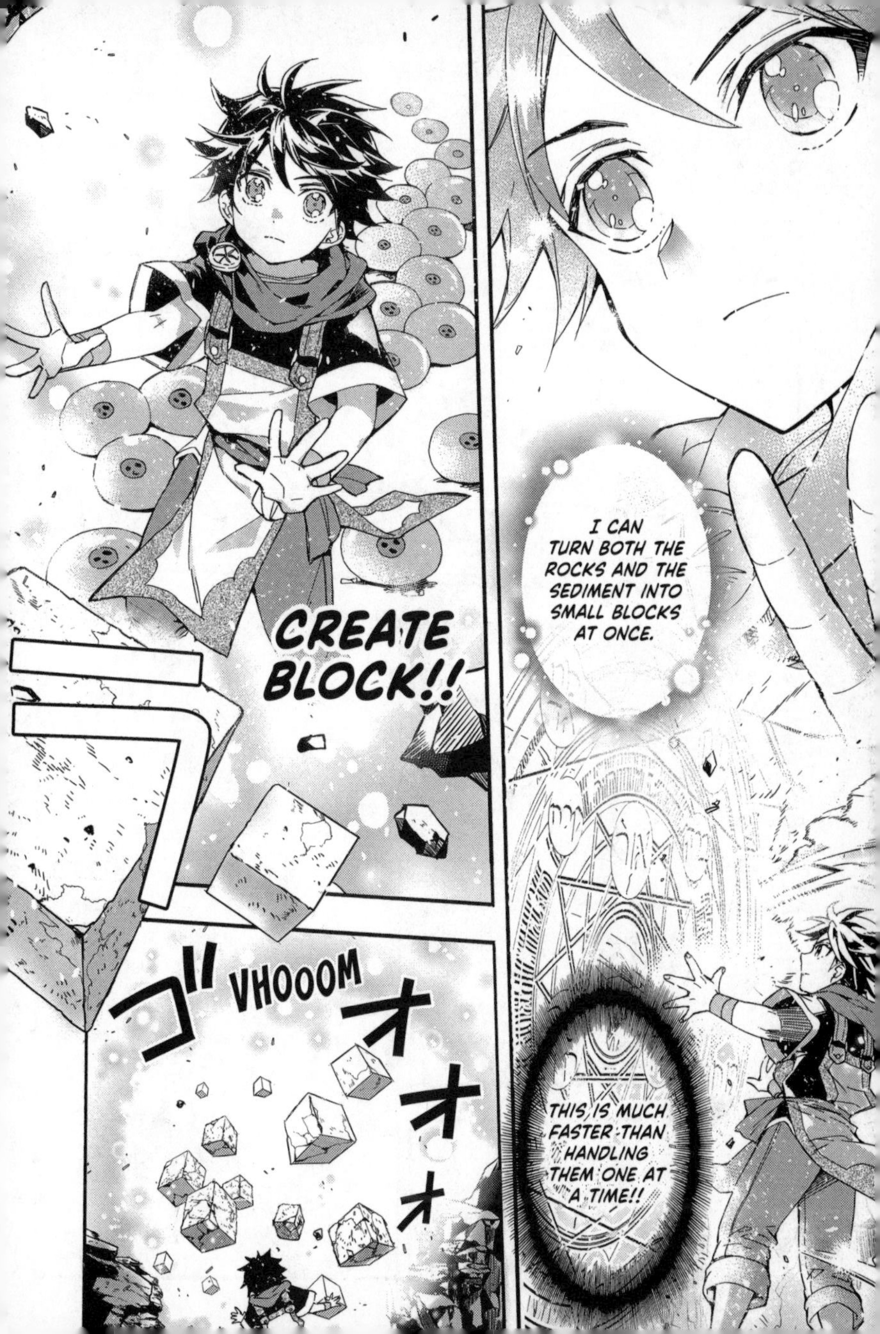
I CAN TURN BOTH THE ROCKS AND THE SEDIMENT INTO SMALL BLOCKS AT ONCE.
THIS IS MUCH FASTER THAN HANDLING THEM ONE AT A TIME!!
CREATE BLOCK!!
VHOOOM

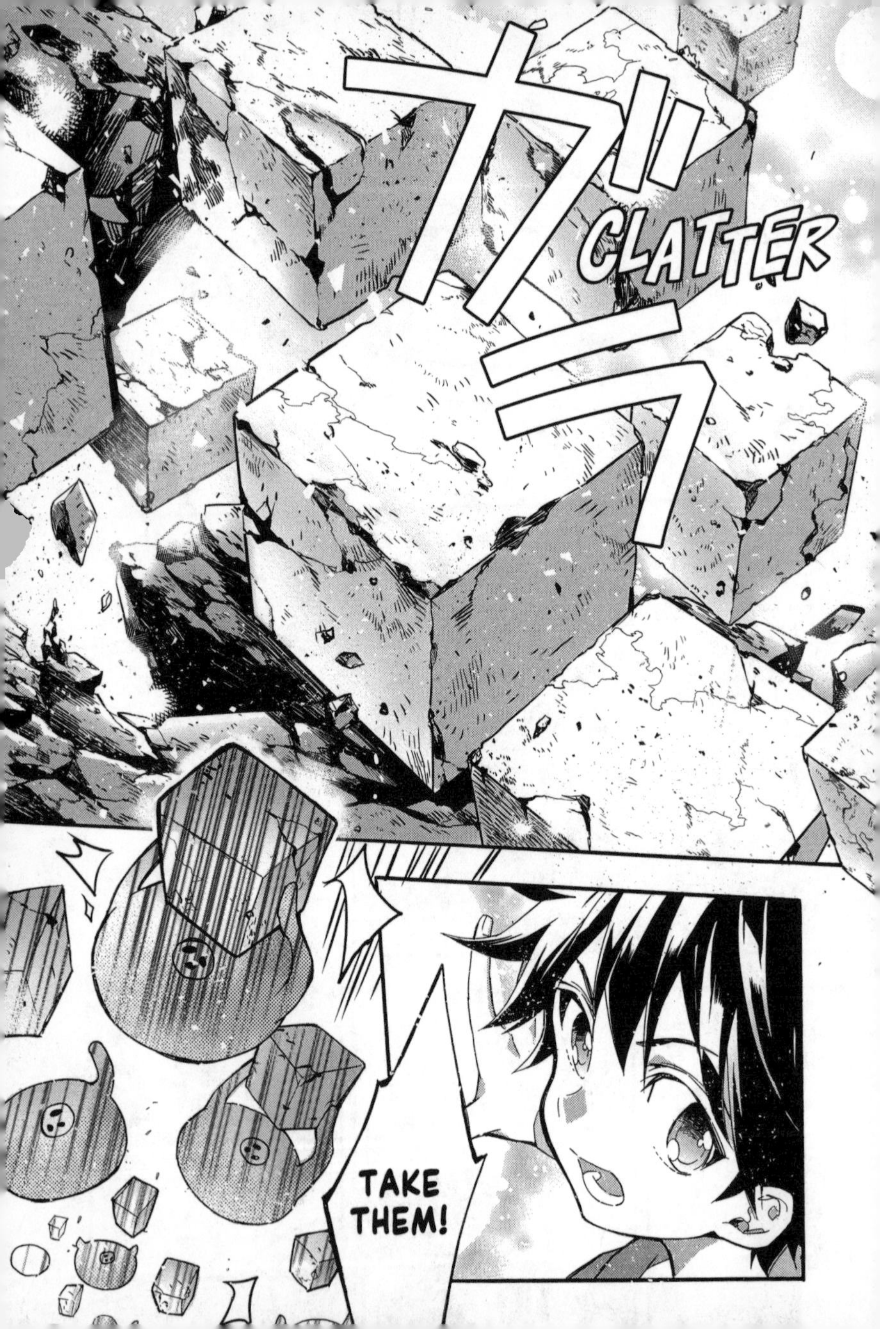
ガラ
CLATTER
TAKE THEM!

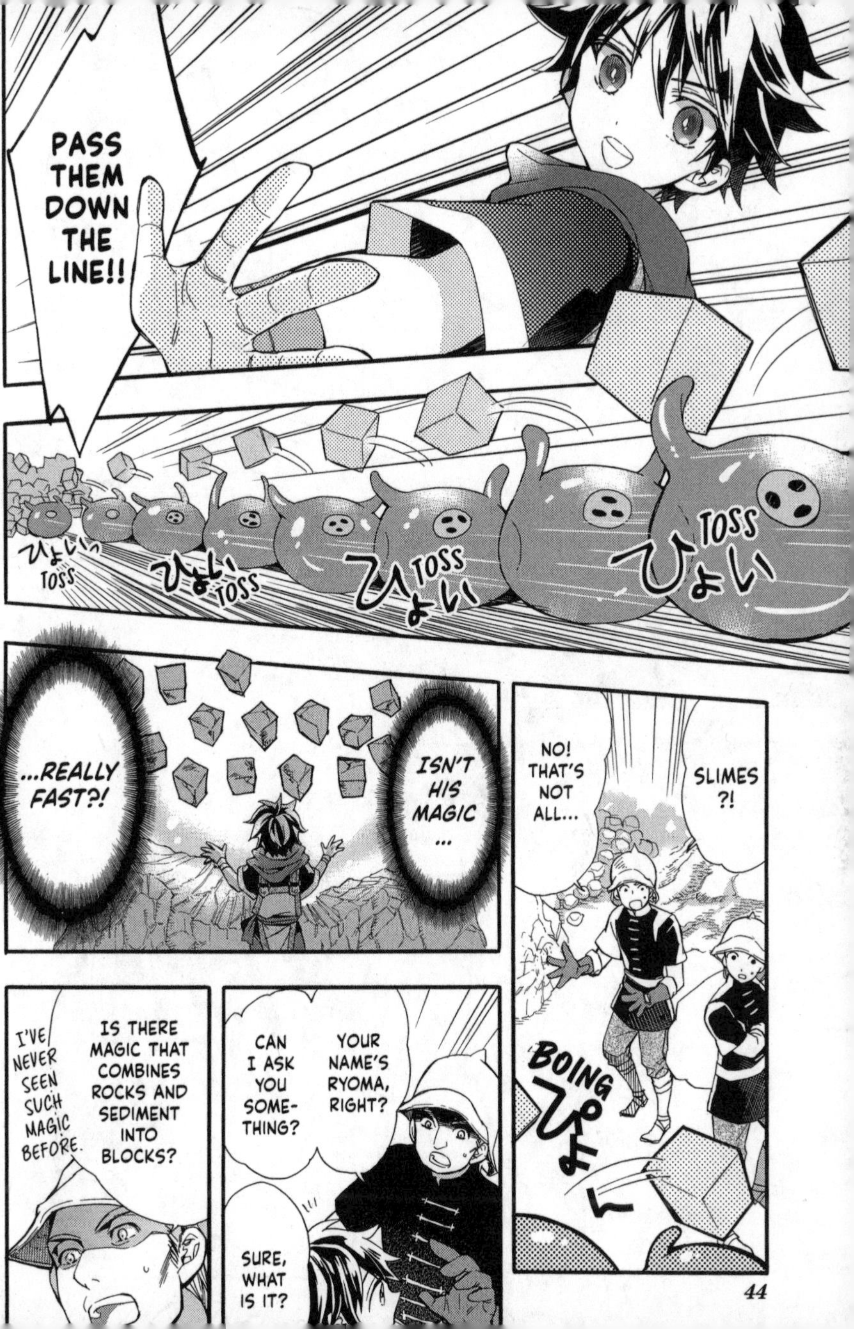
PASS THEM DOWN THE LINE!!
ひょい TOSS
ひょい TOSS
ひょい TOSS
ひょいっ TOSS
SLIMES ?!
NO! THAT'S NOT ALL...
BOING ぴょ
ISN'T HIS MAGIC ...
...REALLY FAST?!
YOUR NAME'S RYOMA, RIGHT?
CAN I ASK YOU SOME-THING?
SURE, WHAT IS IT?
IS THERE MAGIC THAT COMBINES ROCKS AND SEDIMENT INTO BLOCKS?
I'VE NEVER SEEN SUCH MAGIC BEFORE.

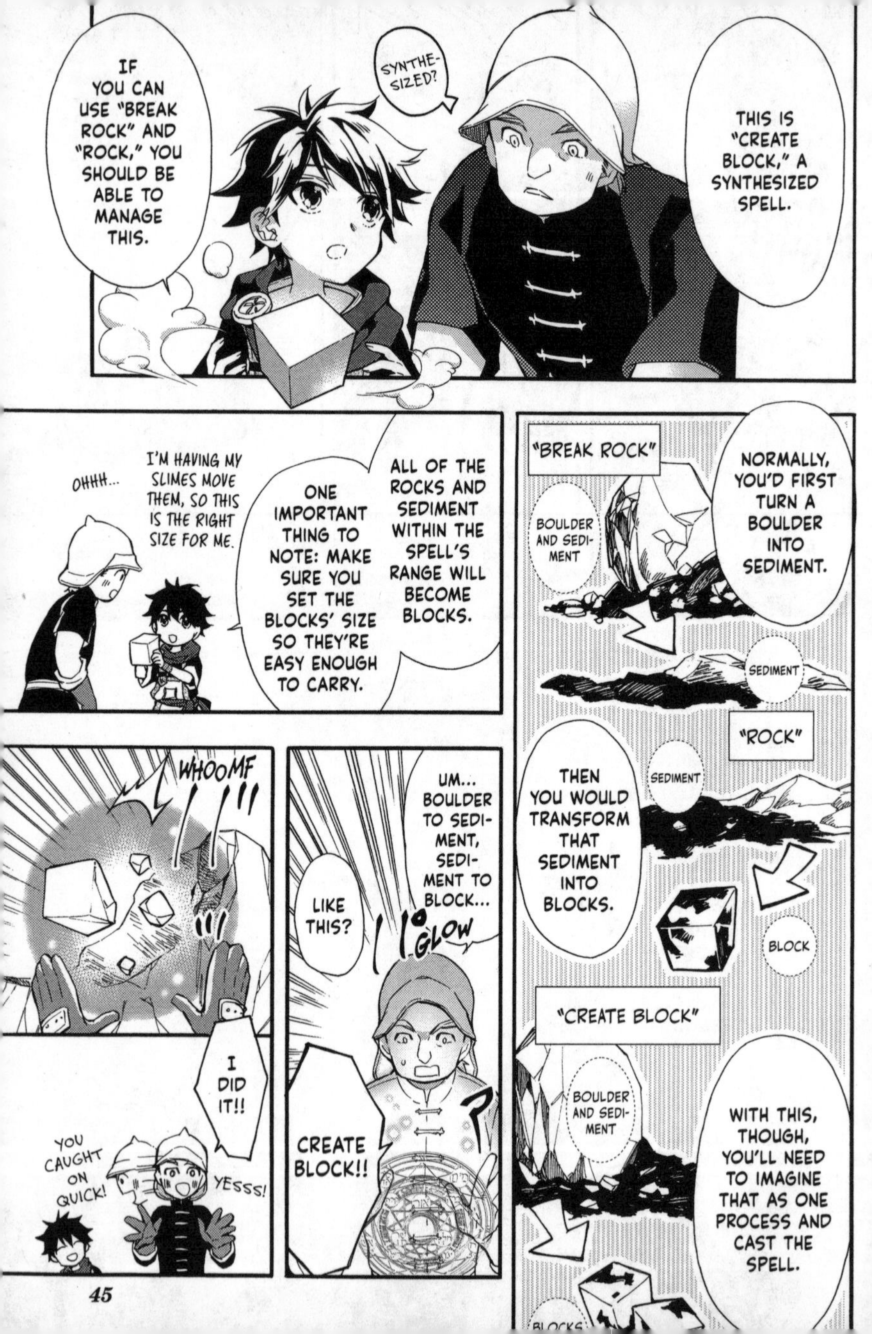
THIS IS "CREATE BLOCK," A SYNTHESIZED SPELL.
SYNTHE-SIZED?
IF YOU CAN USE "BREAK ROCK" AND "ROCK," YOU SHOULD BE ABLE TO MANAGE THIS.
"BREAK ROCK"
NORMALLY, YOU'D FIRST TURN A BOULDER INTO SEDIMENT.
BOULDER AND SEDI-MENT
SEDIMENT
"ROCK"
THEN YOU WOULD TRANSFORM THAT SEDIMENT INTO BLOCKS.
SEDIMENT
BLOCK
"CREATE BLOCK"
WITH THIS, THOUGH, YOU'LL NEED TO IMAGINE THAT AS ONE PROCESS AND CAST THE SPELL.
BOULDER AND SEDI-MENT
BLOCKS
ALL OF THE ROCKS AND SEDIMENT WITHIN THE SPELL'S RANGE WILL BECOME BLOCKS.
ONE IMPORTANT THING TO NOTE: MAKE SURE YOU SET THE BLOCKS' SIZE SO THEY'RE EASY ENOUGH TO CARRY.
I'M HAVING MY SLIMES MOVE THEM, SO THIS IS THE RIGHT SIZE FOR ME.
OHHH...
UM... BOULDER TO SEDI-MENT, SEDI-MENT TO BLOCK...
LIKE THIS?
GLOW
CREATE BLOCK!!
WHOOMF
I DID IT!!
YESSS!
YOU CAUGHT ON QUICK!

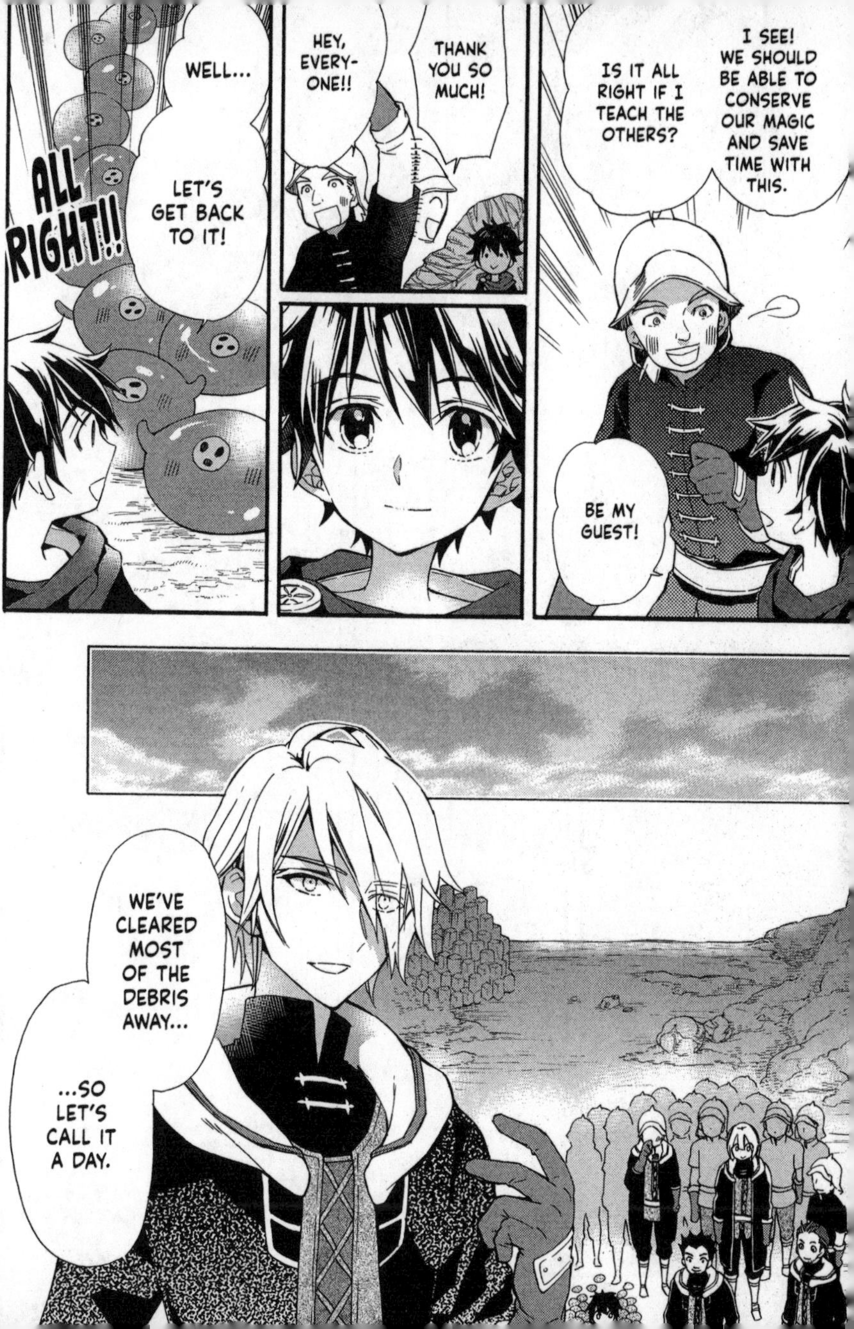
I SEE! WE SHOULD BE ABLE TO CONSERVE OUR MAGIC AND SAVE TIME WITH THIS.
IS IT ALL RIGHT IF I TEACH THE OTHERS?
BE MY GUEST!
THANK YOU SO MUCH!
HEY, EVERYONE!!
WELL...
LET'S GET BACK TO IT!
ALL RIGHT!!
WE'VE CLEARED MOST OF THE DEBRIS AWAY...
...SO LET'S CALL IT A DAY.

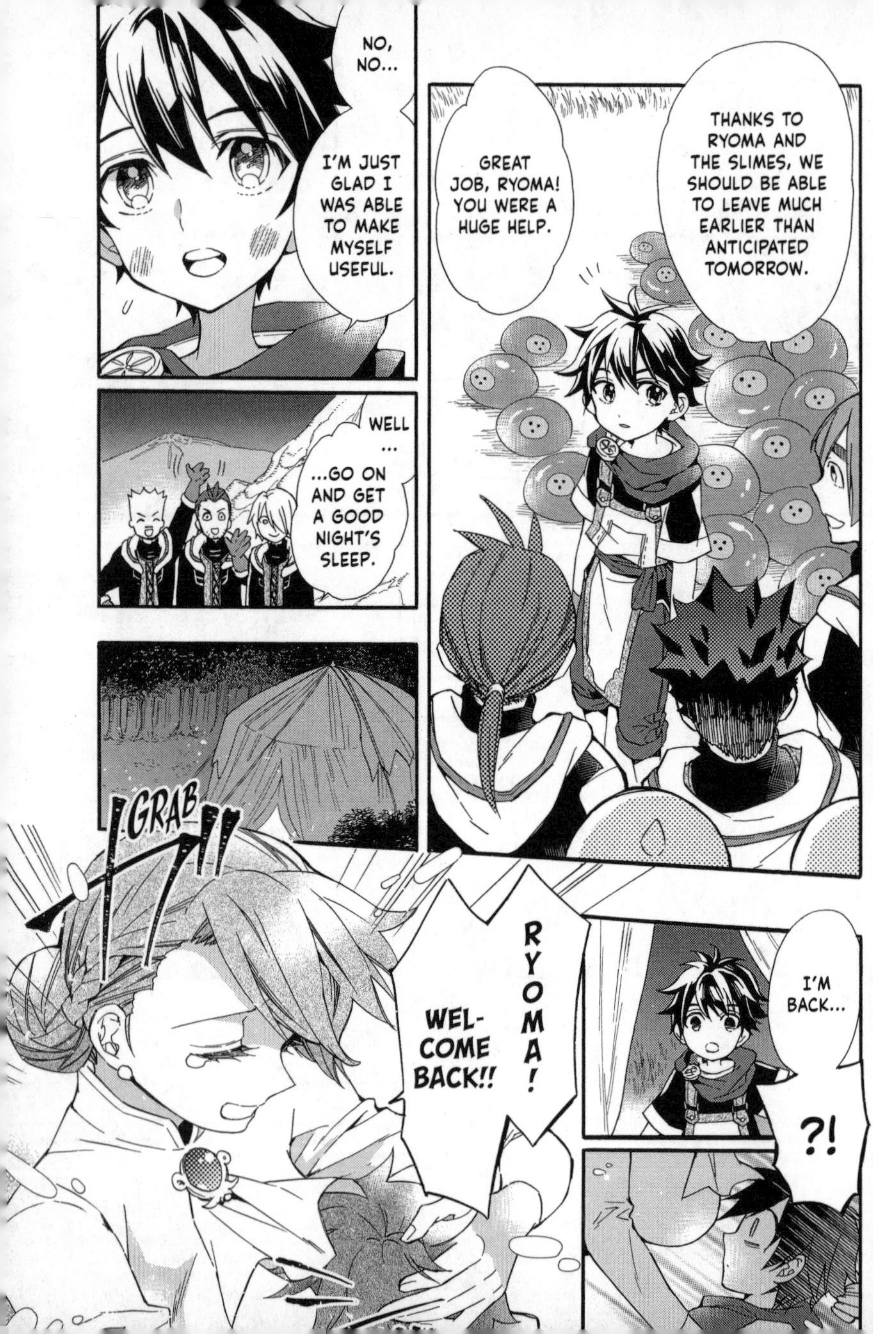
THANKS TO RYOMA AND THE SLIMES, WE SHOULD BE ABLE TO LEAVE MUCH EARLIER THAN ANTICIPATED TOMORROW.
GREAT JOB, RYOMA! YOU WERE A HUGE HELP.
NO, NO...
I'M JUST GLAD I WAS ABLE TO MAKE MYSELF USEFUL.
WELL ...
...GO ON AND GET A GOOD NIGHT'S SLEEP.
I'M BACK...
?!
RYOMA!
WEL-COME BACK!!
GRAB

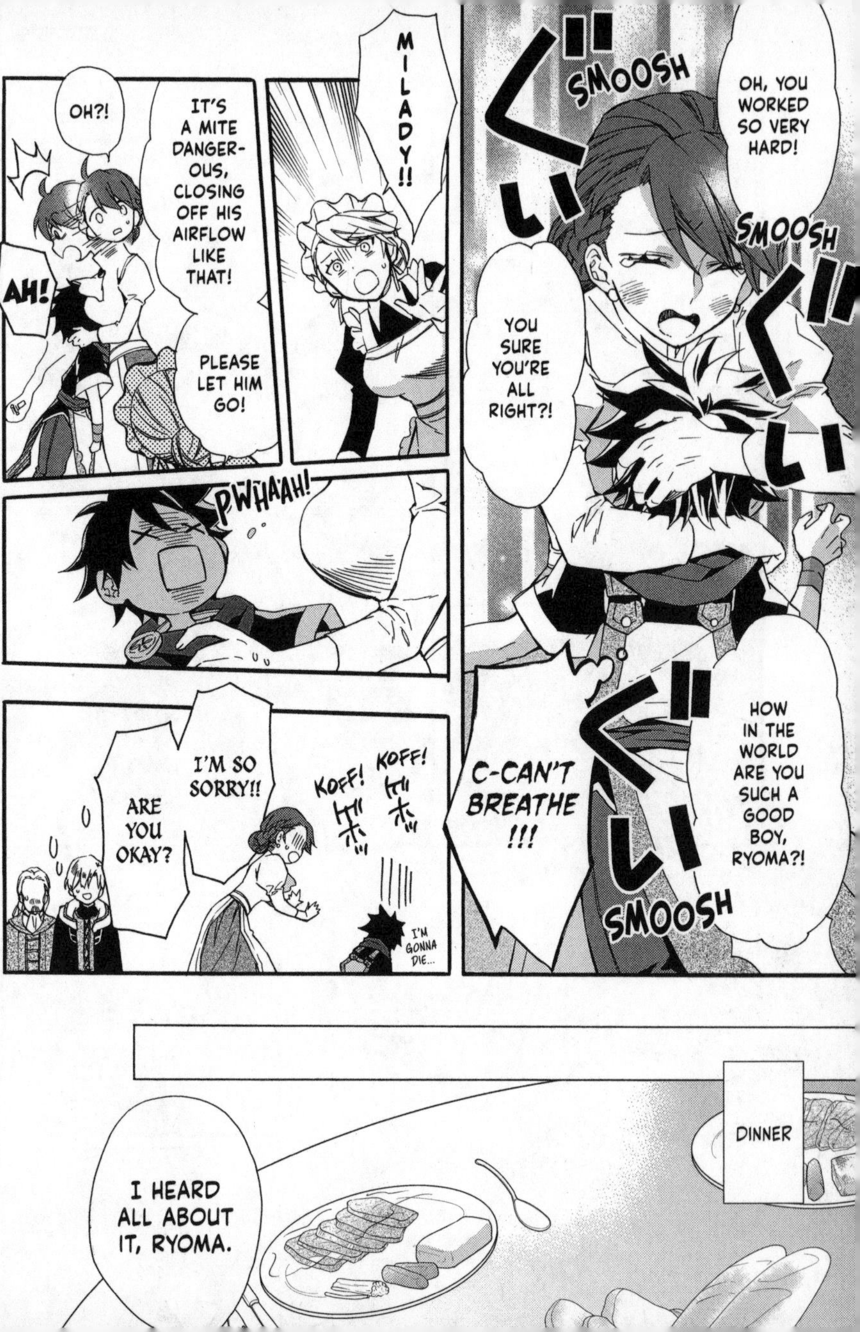

SMOOSH
OH, YOU WORKED SO VERY HARD!
SMOOSH
YOU SURE YOU'RE ALL RIGHT?!
HOW IN THE WORLD ARE YOU SUCH A GOOD BOY, RYOMA?!
C-CAN'T BREATHE!!!
SMOOSH
MILADY!!
IT'S A MITE DANGER-OUS, CLOSING OFF HIS AIRFLOW LIKE THAT!
PLEASE LET HIM GO!
OH?!
AH!
PWHAAH!
KOFF! KOFF!
I'M SO SORRY!!
ARE YOU OKAY?
I'M GONNA DIE...
DINNER
I HEARD ALL ABOUT IT, RYOMA.

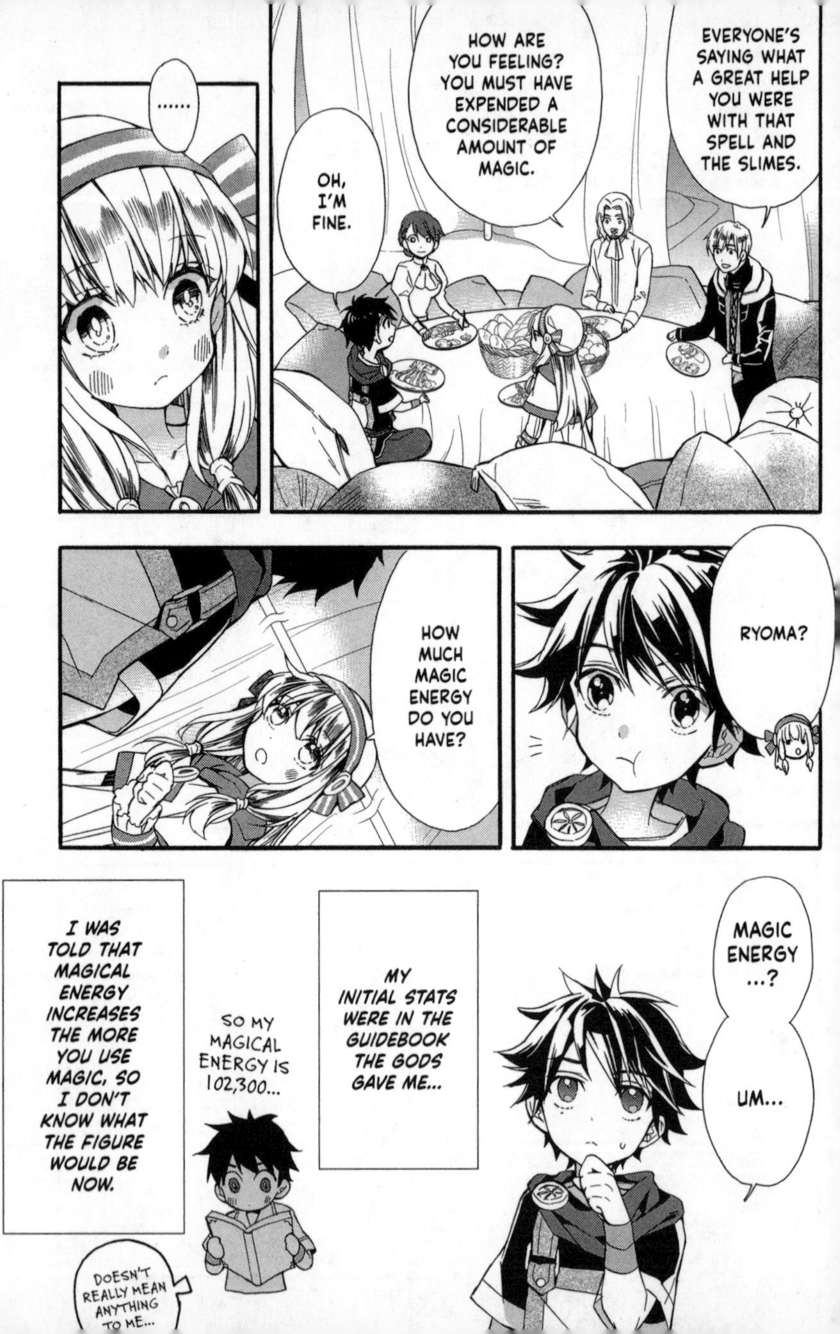
EVERYONE'S SAYING WHAT A GREAT HELP YOU WERE WITH THAT SPELL AND THE SLIMES.
HOW ARE YOU FEELING? YOU MUST HAVE EXPENDED A CONSIDERABLE AMOUNT OF MAGIC.
OH, I'M FINE.
......
RYOMA?
HOW MUCH MAGIC ENERGY DO YOU HAVE?
MAGIC ENERGY ...?
UM...
MY INITIAL STATS WERE IN THE GUIDEBOOK THE GODS GAVE ME...
SO MY MAGICAL ENERGY IS 102,300...
I WAS TOLD THAT MAGICAL ENERGY INCREASES THE MORE YOU USE MAGIC, SO I DON'T KNOW WHAT THE FIGURE WOULD BE NOW.
DOESN'T REALLY MEAN ANYTHING TO ME...

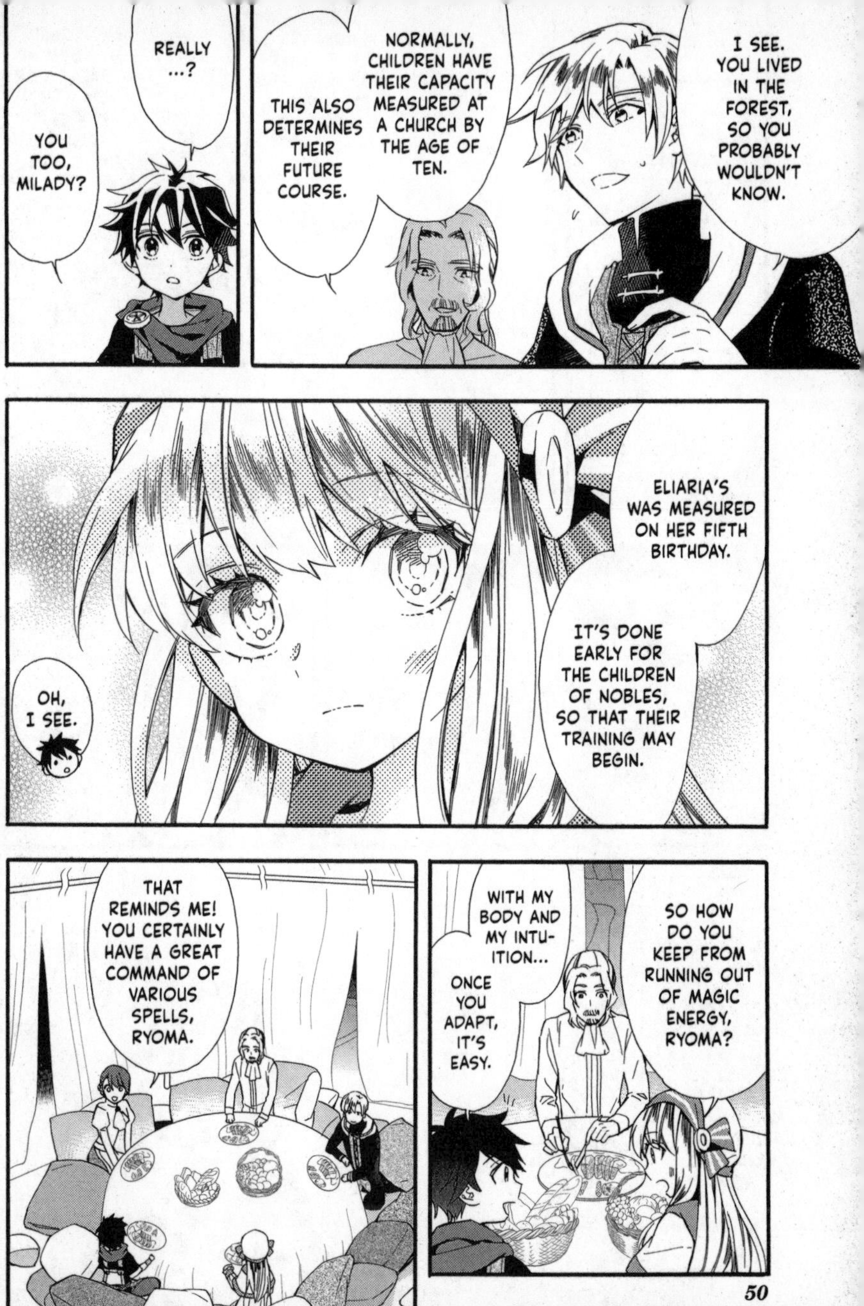
I SEE. YOU LIVED IN THE FOREST, SO YOU PROBABLY WOULDN'T KNOW.
NORMALLY, CHILDREN HAVE THEIR CAPACITY MEASURED AT A CHURCH BY THE AGE OF TEN.
THIS ALSO DETERMINES THEIR FUTURE COURSE.
REALLY ...?
YOU TOO, MILADY?
ELIARIA'S WAS MEASURED ON HER FIFTH BIRTHDAY.
IT'S DONE EARLY FOR THE CHILDREN OF NOBLES, SO THAT THEIR TRAINING MAY BEGIN.
OH, I SEE.
SO HOW DO YOU KEEP FROM RUNNING OUT OF MAGIC ENERGY, RYOMA?
WITH MY BODY AND MY INTU-ITION...
ONCE YOU ADAPT, IT'S EASY.
THAT REMINDS ME! YOU CERTAINLY HAVE A GREAT COMMAND OF VARIOUS SPELLS, RYOMA.

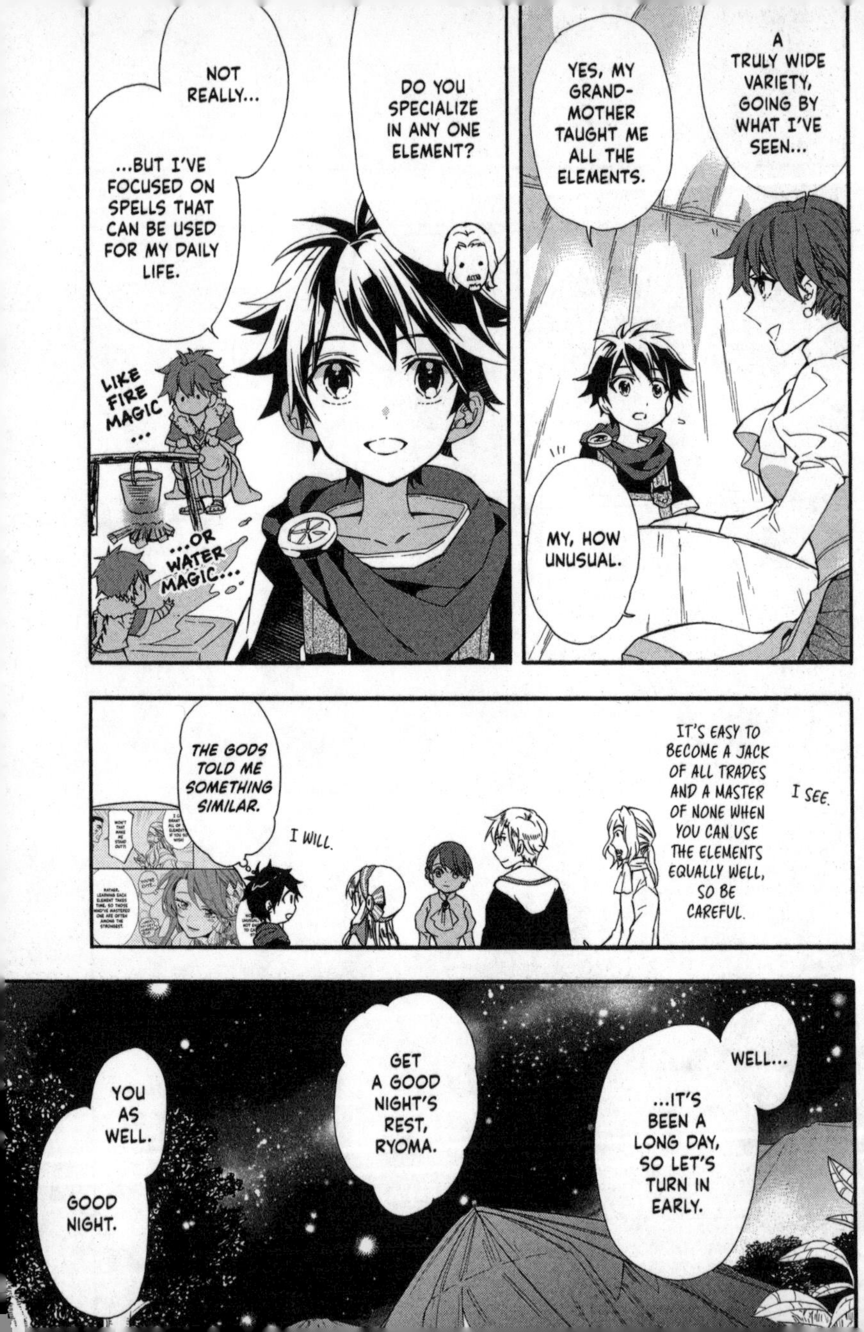
A TRULY WIDE VARIETY, GOING BY WHAT I'VE SEEN...
YES, MY GRANDMOTHER TAUGHT ME ALL THE ELEMENTS.
MY, HOW UNUSUAL.
DO YOU SPECIALIZE IN ANY ONE ELEMENT?
NOT REALLY...
...BUT I'VE FOCUSED ON SPELLS THAT CAN BE USED FOR MY DAILY LIFE.
LIKE FIRE MAGIC...
...OR WATER MAGIC...
I SEE.
IT'S EASY TO BECOME A JACK OF ALL TRADES AND A MASTER OF NONE WHEN YOU CAN USE THE ELEMENTS EQUALLY WELL, SO BE CAREFUL.
I WILL.
THE GODS TOLD ME SOMETHING SIMILAR.
WELL...
...IT'S BEEN A LONG DAY, SO LET'S TURN IN EARLY.
GET A GOOD NIGHT'S REST, RYOMA.
YOU AS WELL.
GOOD NIGHT.

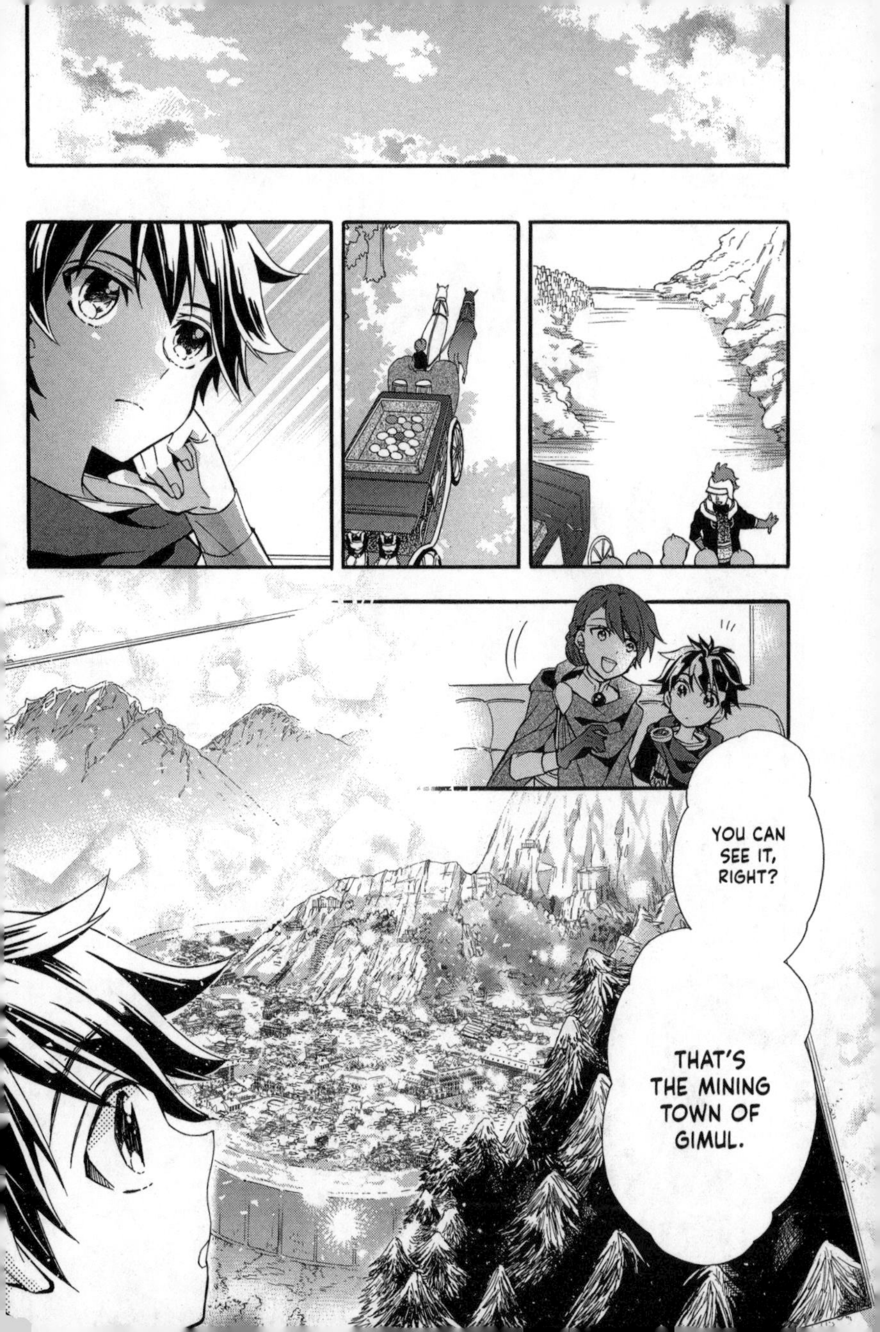
YOU CAN SEE IT, RIGHT?
THAT'S THE MINING TOWN OF GIMUL.

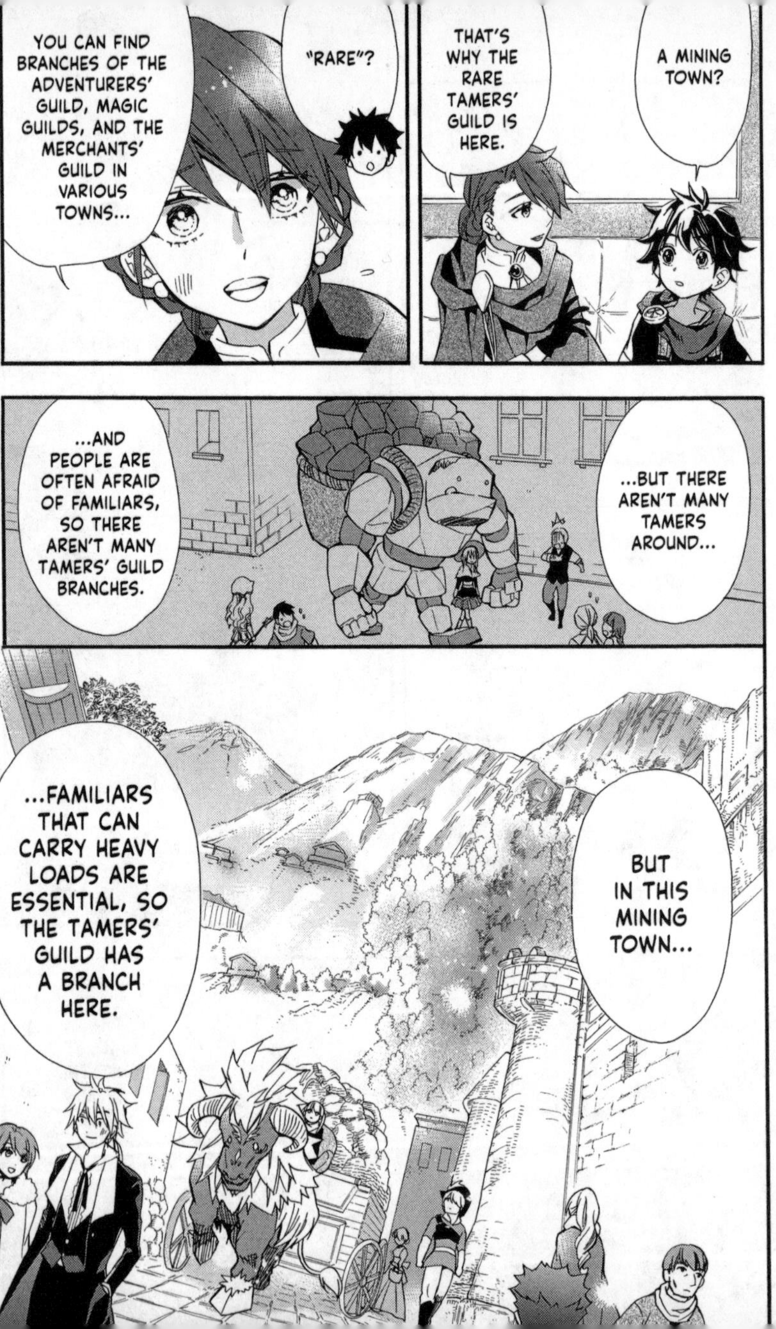
A MINING TOWN?
THAT'S WHY THE RARE TAMERS' GUILD IS HERE.
"RARE"?
YOU CAN FIND BRANCHES OF THE ADVENTURERS' GUILD, MAGIC GUILDS, AND THE MERCHANTS' GUILD IN VARIOUS TOWNS...
...BUT THERE AREN'T MANY TAMERS AROUND...
...AND PEOPLE ARE OFTEN AFRAID OF FAMILIARS, SO THERE AREN'T MANY TAMERS' GUILD BRANCHES.
BUT IN THIS MINING TOWN...
...FAMILIARS THAT CAN CARRY HEAVY LOADS ARE ESSENTIAL, SO THE TAMERS' GUILD HAS A BRANCH HERE.

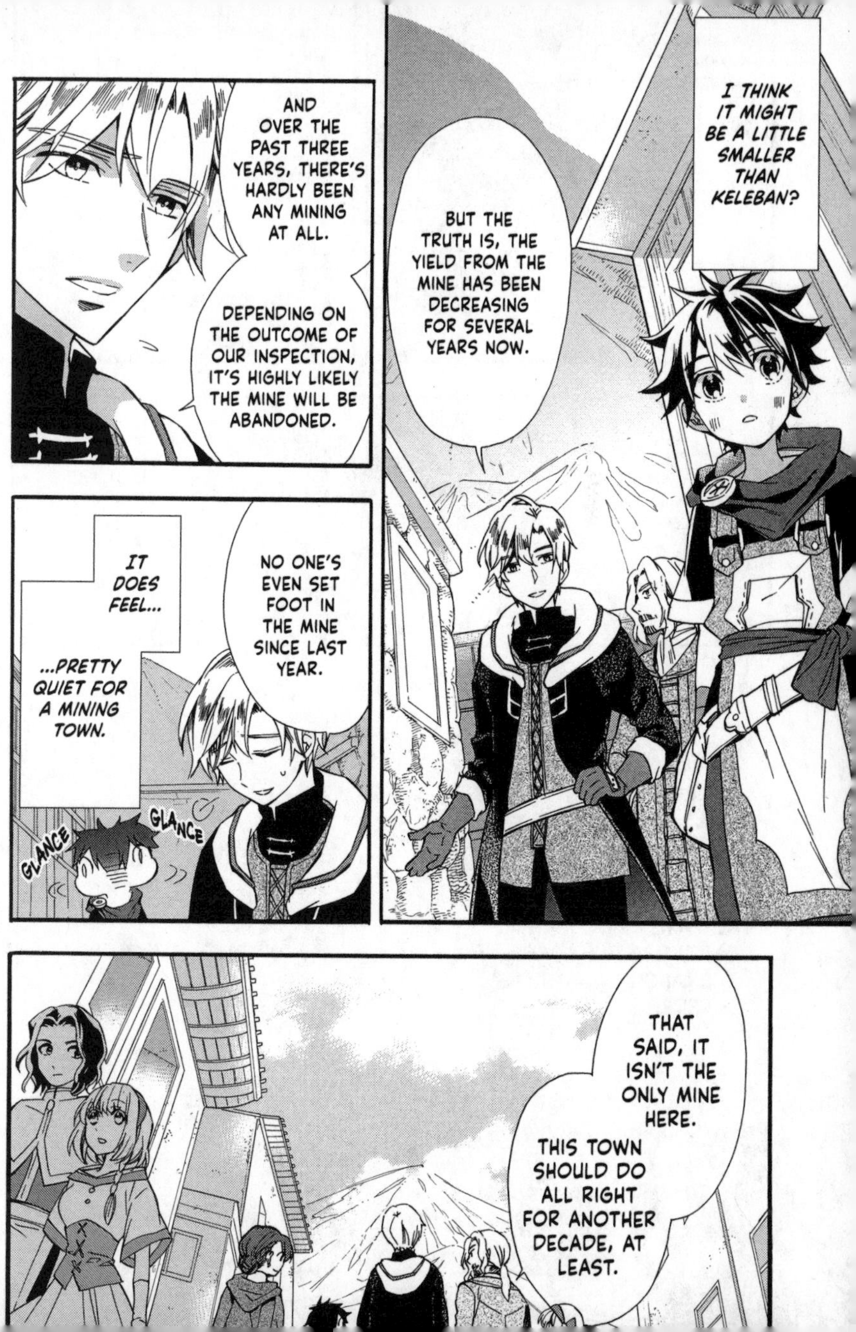
I THINK IT MIGHT BE A LITTLE SMALLER THAN KELEBAN?
BUT THE TRUTH IS, THE YIELD FROM THE MINE HAS BEEN DECREASING FOR SEVERAL YEARS NOW.
AND OVER THE PAST THREE YEARS, THERE'S HARDLY BEEN ANY MINING AT ALL.
DEPENDING ON THE OUTCOME OF OUR INSPECTION, IT'S HIGHLY LIKELY THE MINE WILL BE ABANDONED.
NO ONE'S EVEN SET FOOT IN THE MINE SINCE LAST YEAR.
IT DOES FEEL...
...PRETTY QUIET FOR A MINING TOWN.
GLANCE
GLANCE
THAT SAID, IT ISN'T THE ONLY MINE HERE.
THIS TOWN SHOULD DO ALL RIGHT FOR ANOTHER DECADE, AT LEAST.

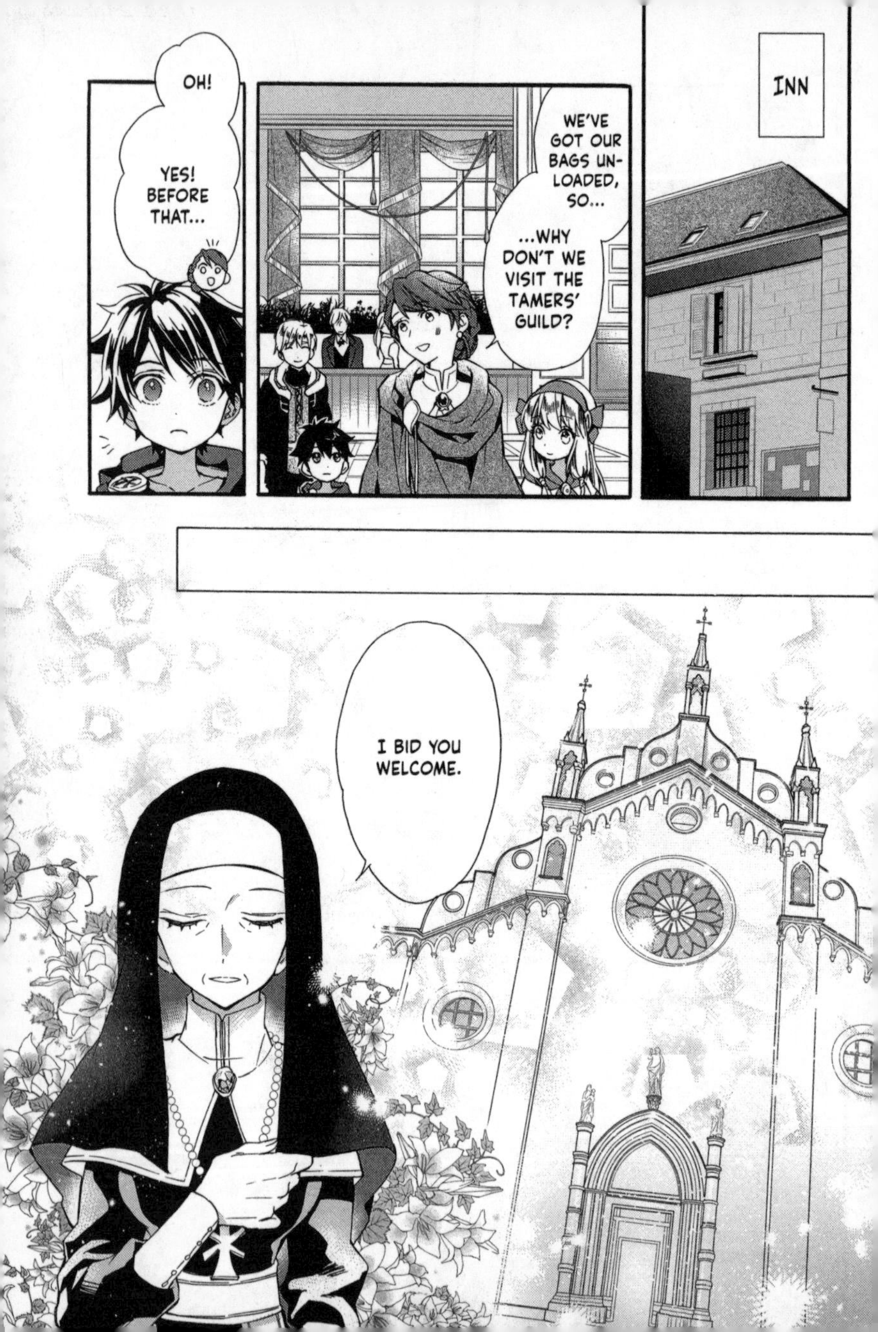
INN
WE'VE GOT OUR BAGS UN-LOADED, SO...
...WHY DON'T WE VISIT THE TAMERS' GUILD?
OH!
YES! BEFORE THAT...
I BID YOU WELCOME.

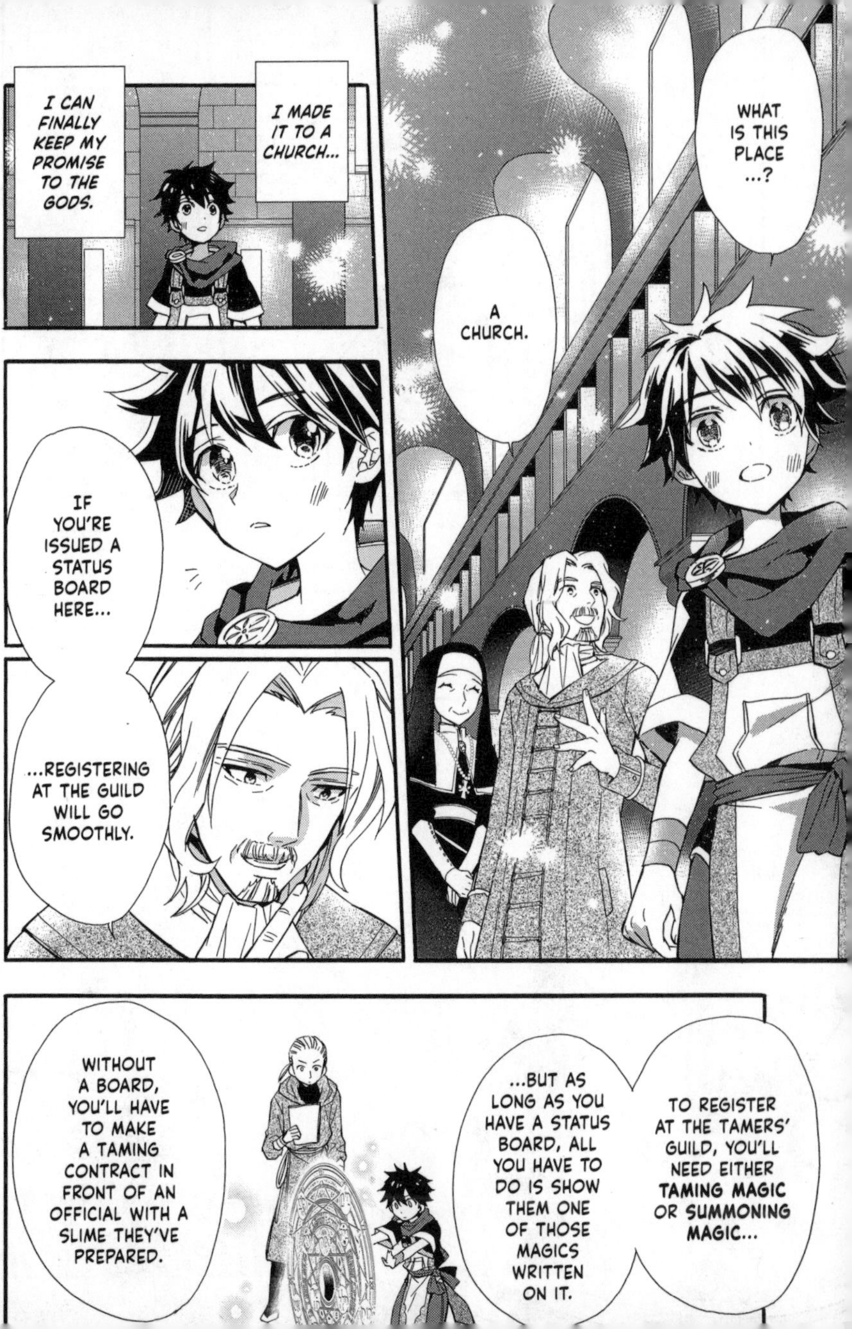
WHAT IS THIS PLACE ...?
A CHURCH.
I MADE IT TO A CHURCH...
I CAN FINALLY KEEP MY PROMISE TO THE GODS.
IF YOU'RE ISSUED A STATUS BOARD HERE...
...REGISTERING AT THE GUILD WILL GO SMOOTHLY.
TO REGISTER AT THE TAMERS' GUILD, YOU'LL NEED EITHER TAMING MAGIC OR SUMMONING MAGIC...
...BUT AS LONG AS YOU HAVE A STATUS BOARD, ALL YOU HAVE TO DO IS SHOW THEM ONE OF THOSE MAGICS WRITTEN ON IT.
WITHOUT A BOARD, YOU'LL HAVE TO MAKE A TAMING CONTRACT IN FRONT OF AN OFFICIAL WITH A SLIME THEY'VE PREPARED.

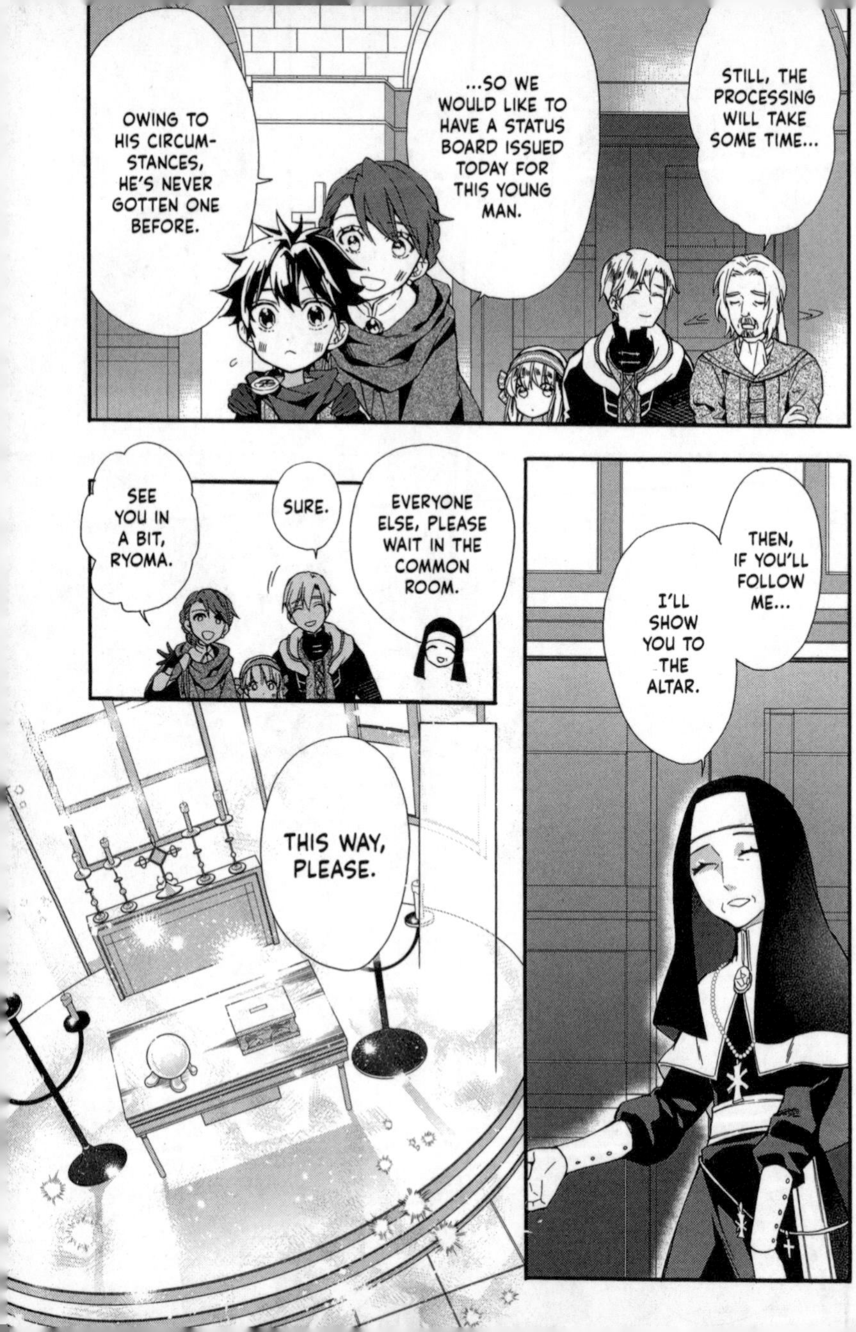
STILL, THE PROCESSING WILL TAKE SOME TIME...
...SO WE WOULD LIKE TO HAVE A STATUS BOARD ISSUED TODAY FOR THIS YOUNG MAN.
OWING TO HIS CIRCUM-STANCES, HE'S NEVER GOTTEN ONE BEFORE.
THEN, IF YOU'LL FOLLOW ME...
I'LL SHOW YOU TO THE ALTAR.
EVERYONE ELSE, PLEASE WAIT IN THE COMMON ROOM.
SURE.
SEE YOU IN A BIT, RYOMA.
THIS WAY, PLEASE.

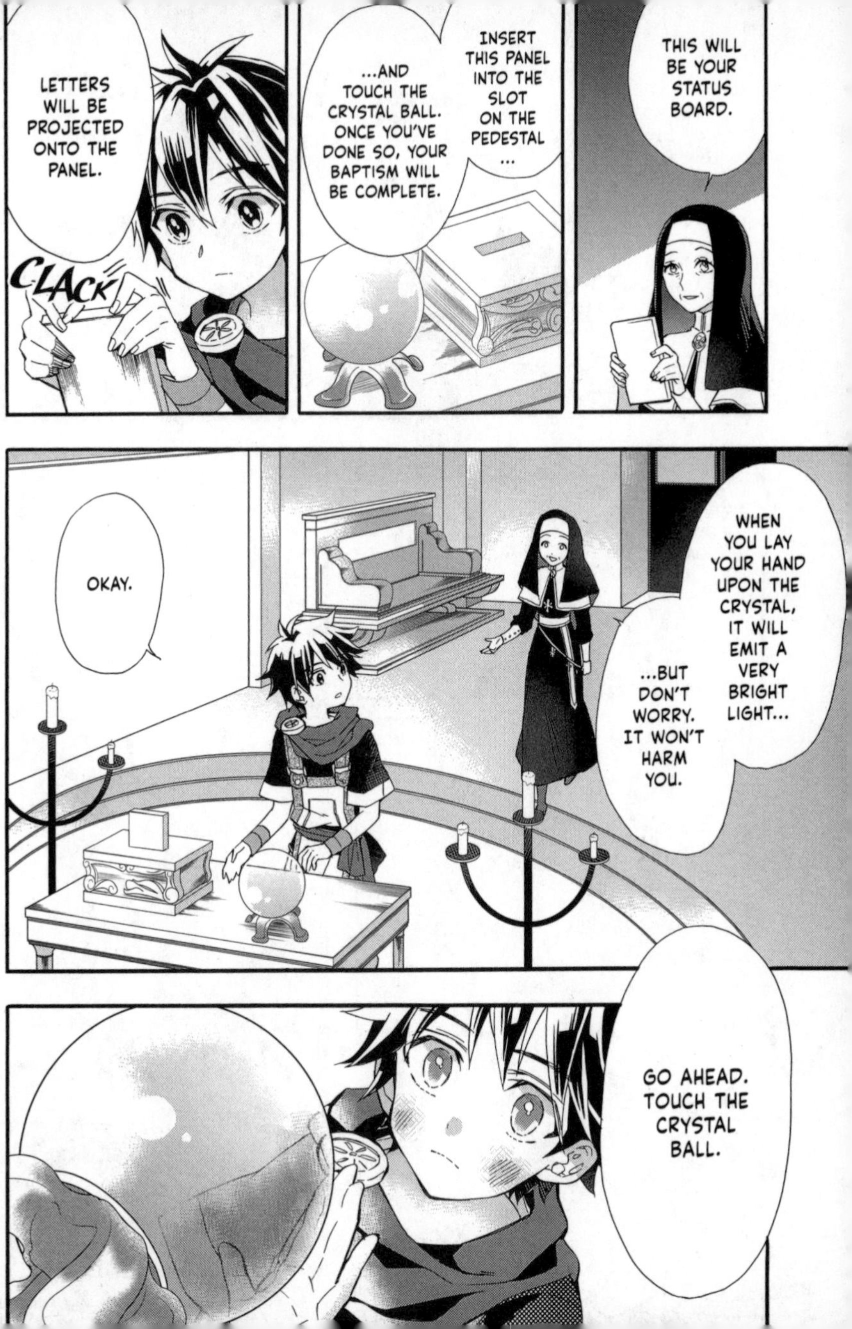
THIS WILL BE YOUR STATUS BOARD.
INSERT THIS PANEL INTO THE SLOT ON THE PEDESTAL ...
...AND TOUCH THE CRYSTAL BALL. ONCE YOU'VE DONE SO, YOUR BAPTISM WILL BE COMPLETE.
LETTERS WILL BE PROJECTED ONTO THE PANEL.
CLACK
WHEN YOU LAY YOUR HAND UPON THE CRYSTAL, IT WILL EMIT A VERY BRIGHT LIGHT...
...BUT DON'T WORRY. IT WON'T HARM YOU.
OKAY.
GO AHEAD. TOUCH THE CRYSTAL BALL.

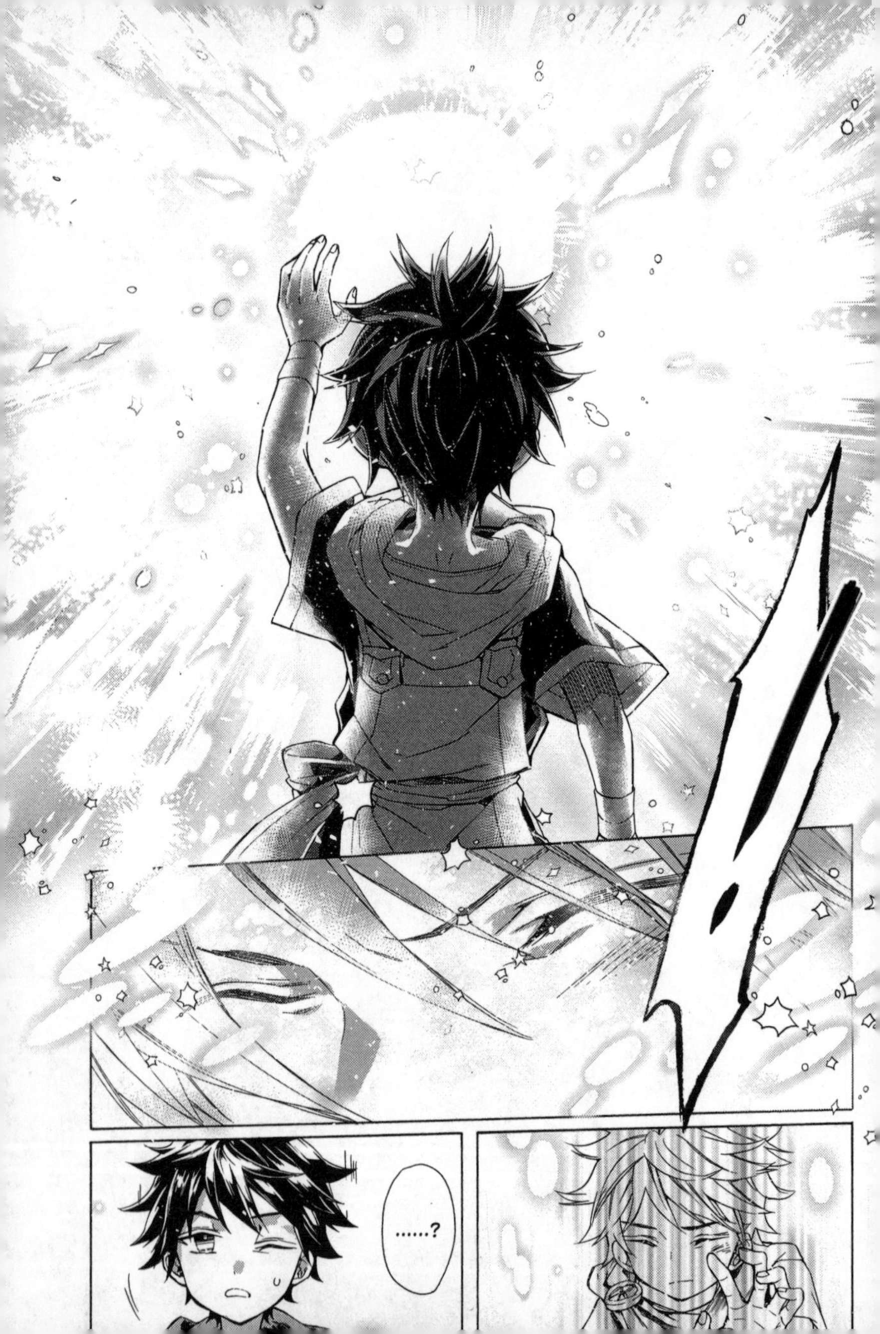
......?

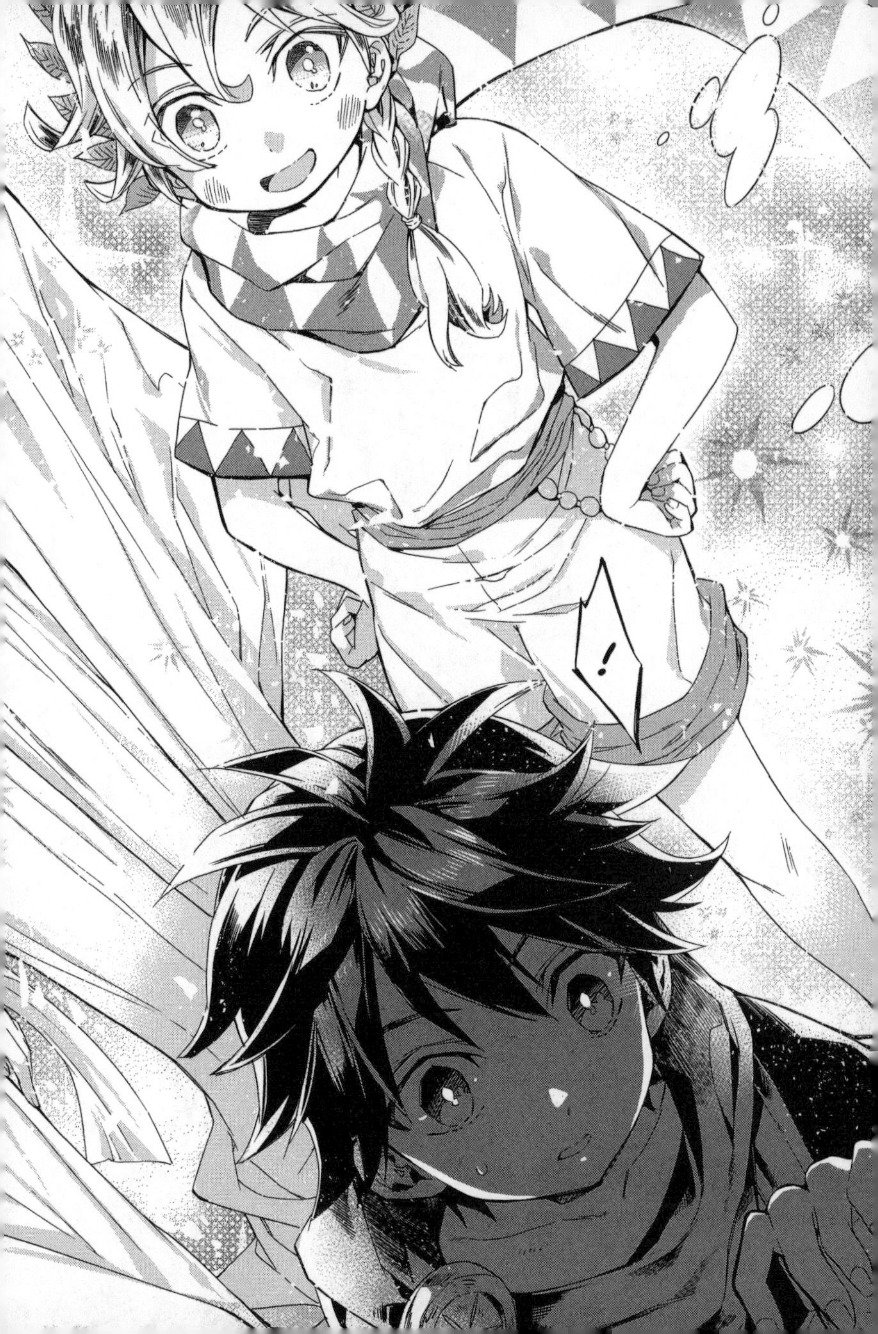
!

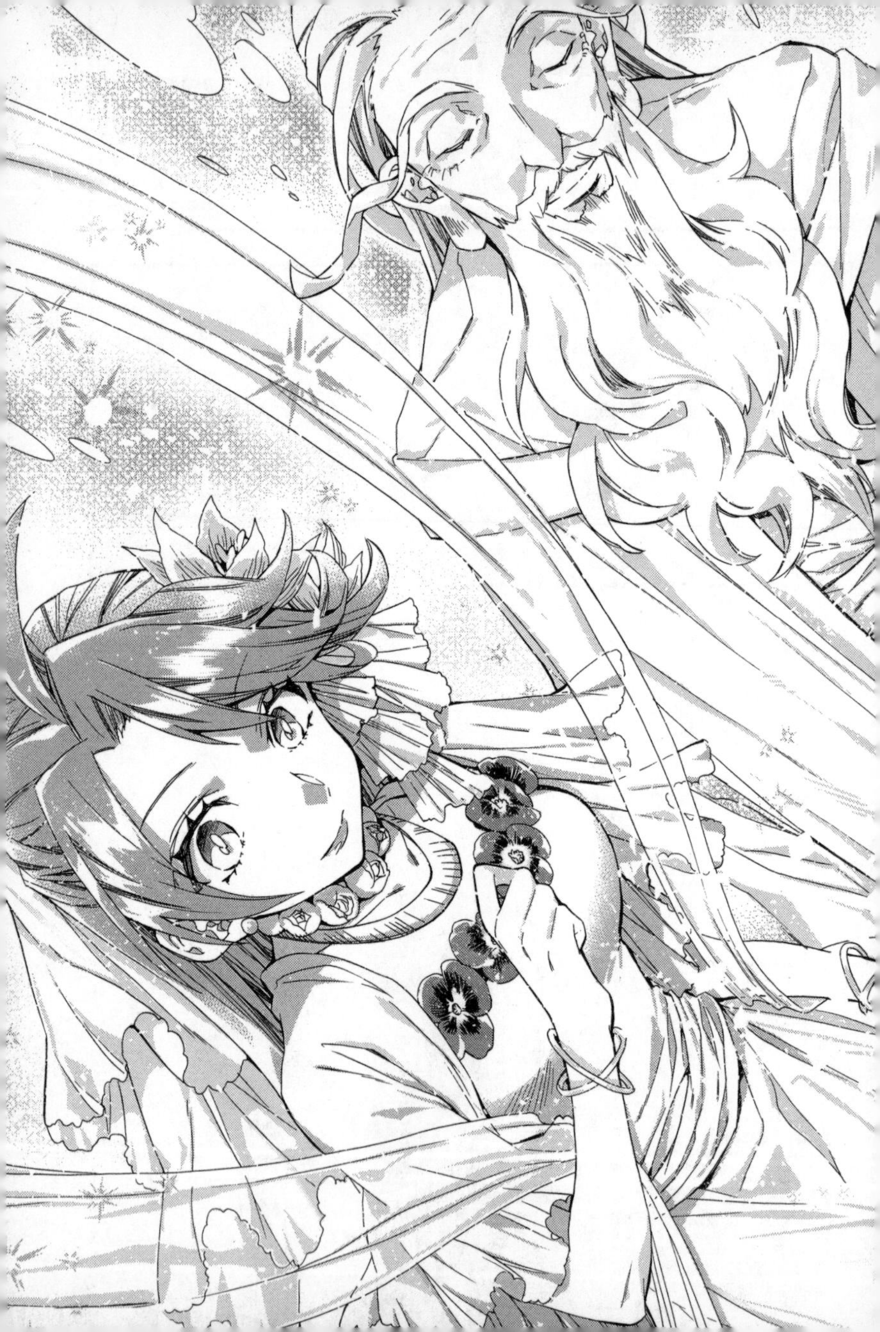

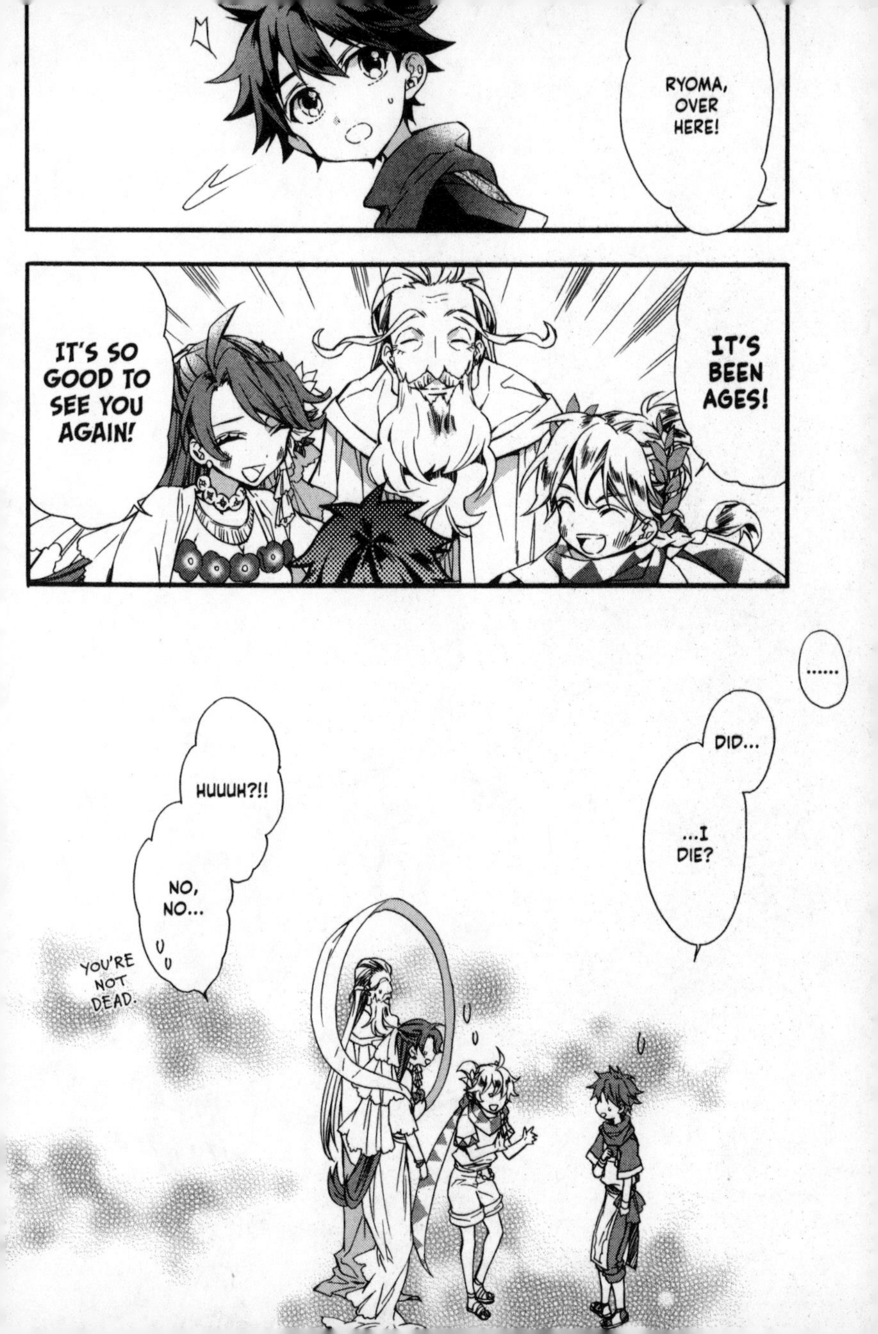
RYOMA, OVER HERE!
IT'S BEEN AGES!
IT'S SO GOOD TO SEE YOU AGAIN!
......
DID...
...I DIE?
HUUUH?!!
NO, NO...
YOU'RE NOT DEAD.

Chapter 7: In Gimul

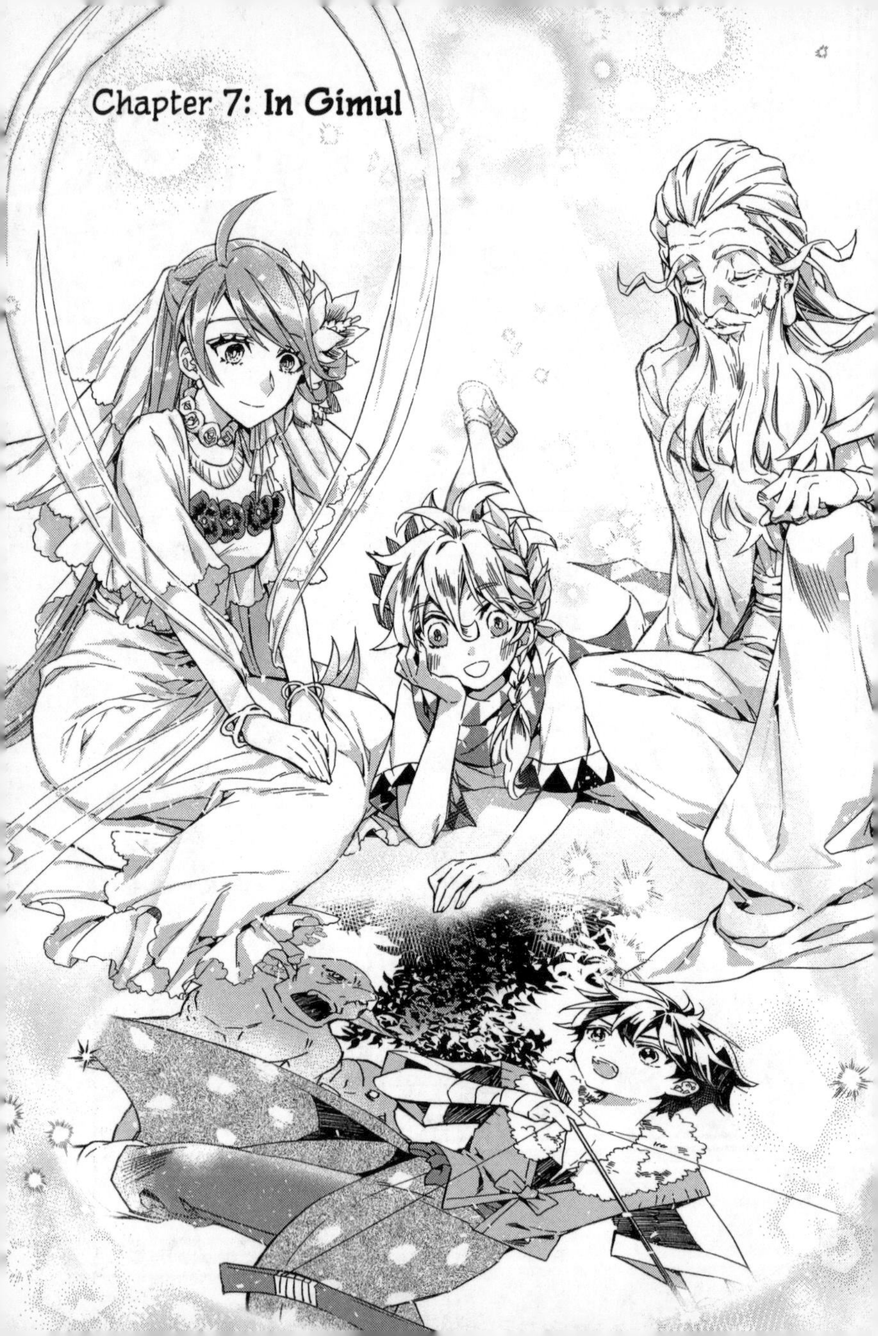

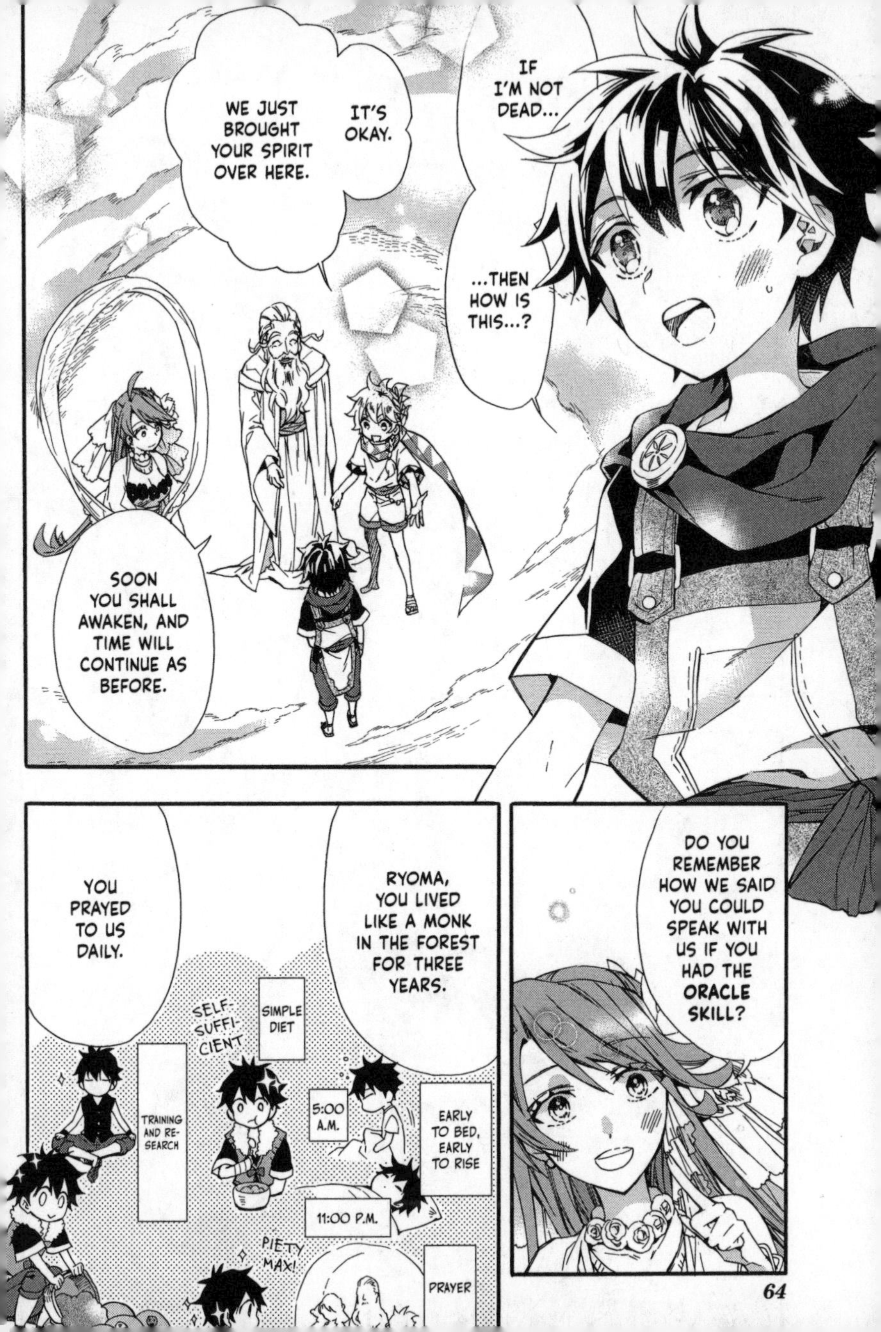
IF I'M NOT DEAD...
...THEN HOW IS THIS...?
IT'S OKAY.
WE JUST BROUGHT YOUR SPIRIT OVER HERE.
SOON YOU SHALL AWAKEN, AND TIME WILL CONTINUE AS BEFORE.
DO YOU REMEMBER HOW WE SAID YOU COULD SPEAK WITH US IF YOU HAD THE ORACLE SKILL?
RYOMA, YOU LIVED LIKE A MONK IN THE FOREST FOR THREE YEARS.
YOU PRAYED TO US DAILY.
SIMPLE DIET
SELF-SUFFICIENT
EARLY TO BED, EARLY TO RISE
5:00 A.M.
11:00 P.M.
TRAINING AND RESEARCH
PIETY MAX!
PRAYER

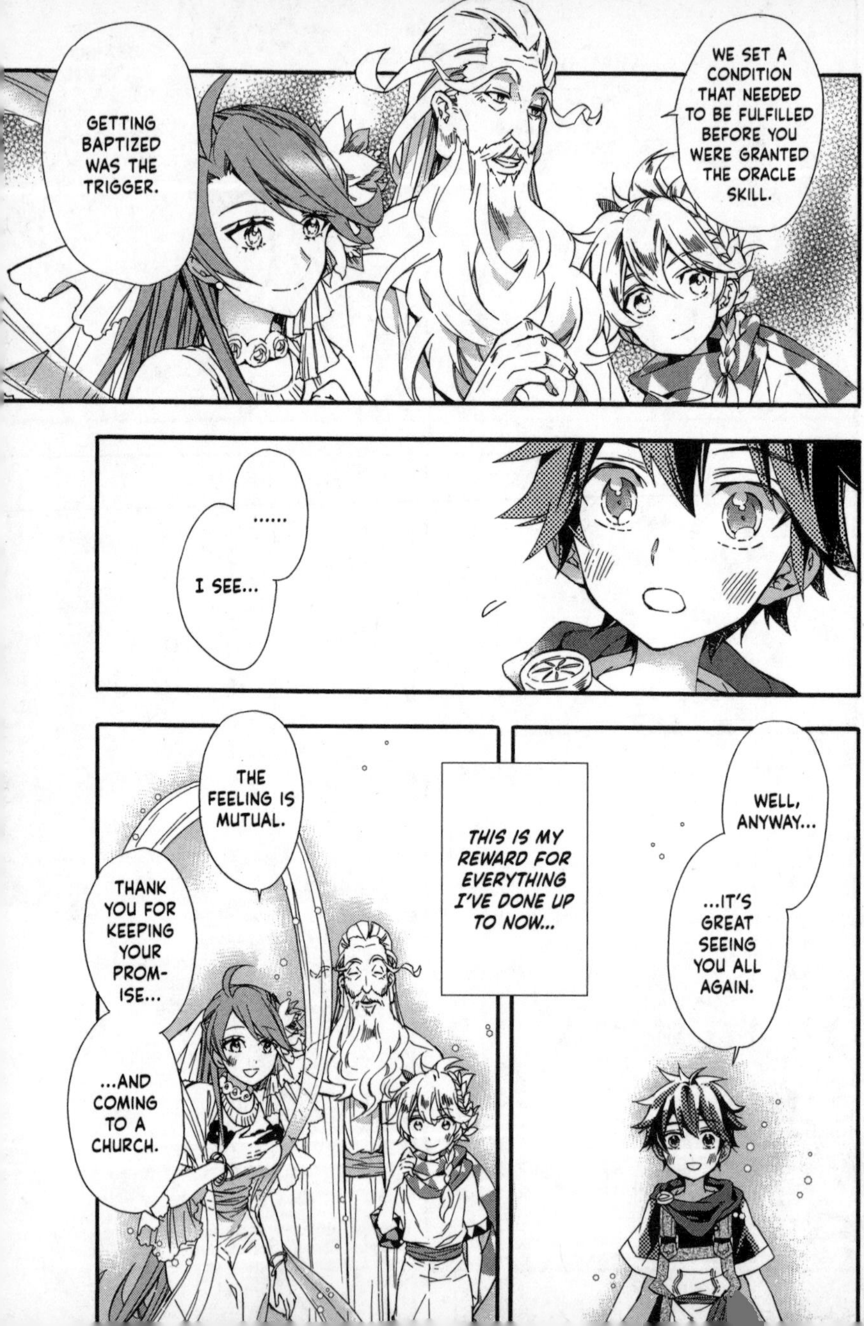
WE SET A CONDITION THAT NEEDED TO BE FULFILLED BEFORE YOU WERE GRANTED THE ORACLE SKILL.
GETTING BAPTIZED WAS THE TRIGGER.
...... I SEE...
WELL, ANYWAY...
...IT'S GREAT SEEING YOU ALL AGAIN.
THIS IS MY REWARD FOR EVERYTHING I'VE DONE UP TO NOW...
THE FEELING IS MUTUAL.
THANK YOU FOR KEEPING YOUR PROM-ISE...
...AND COMING TO A CHURCH.

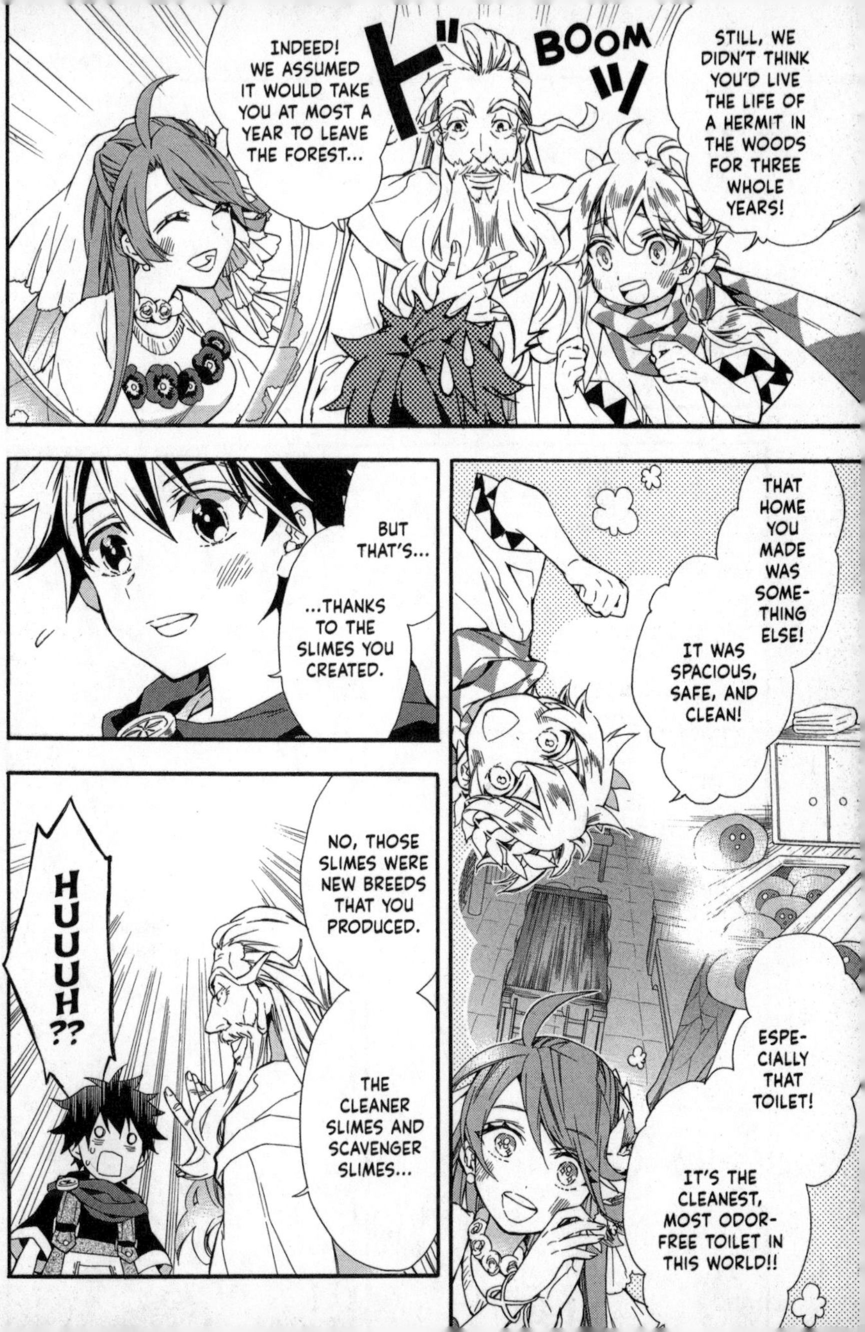
STILL, WE DIDN'T THINK YOU'D LIVE THE LIFE OF A HERMIT IN THE WOODS FOR THREE WHOLE YEARS!
BOOM
ド
INDEED! WE ASSUMED IT WOULD TAKE YOU AT MOST A YEAR TO LEAVE THE FOREST...
THAT HOME YOU MADE WAS SOME-THING ELSE!
IT WAS SPACIOUS, SAFE, AND CLEAN!
ESPE-CIALLY THAT TOILET!
IT'S THE CLEANEST, MOST ODOR-FREE TOILET IN THIS WORLD!!
BUT THAT'S...
...THANKS TO THE SLIMES YOU CREATED.
NO, THOSE SLIMES WERE NEW BREEDS THAT YOU PRODUCED.
THE CLEANER SLIMES AND SCAVENGER SLIMES...
HUUUH??

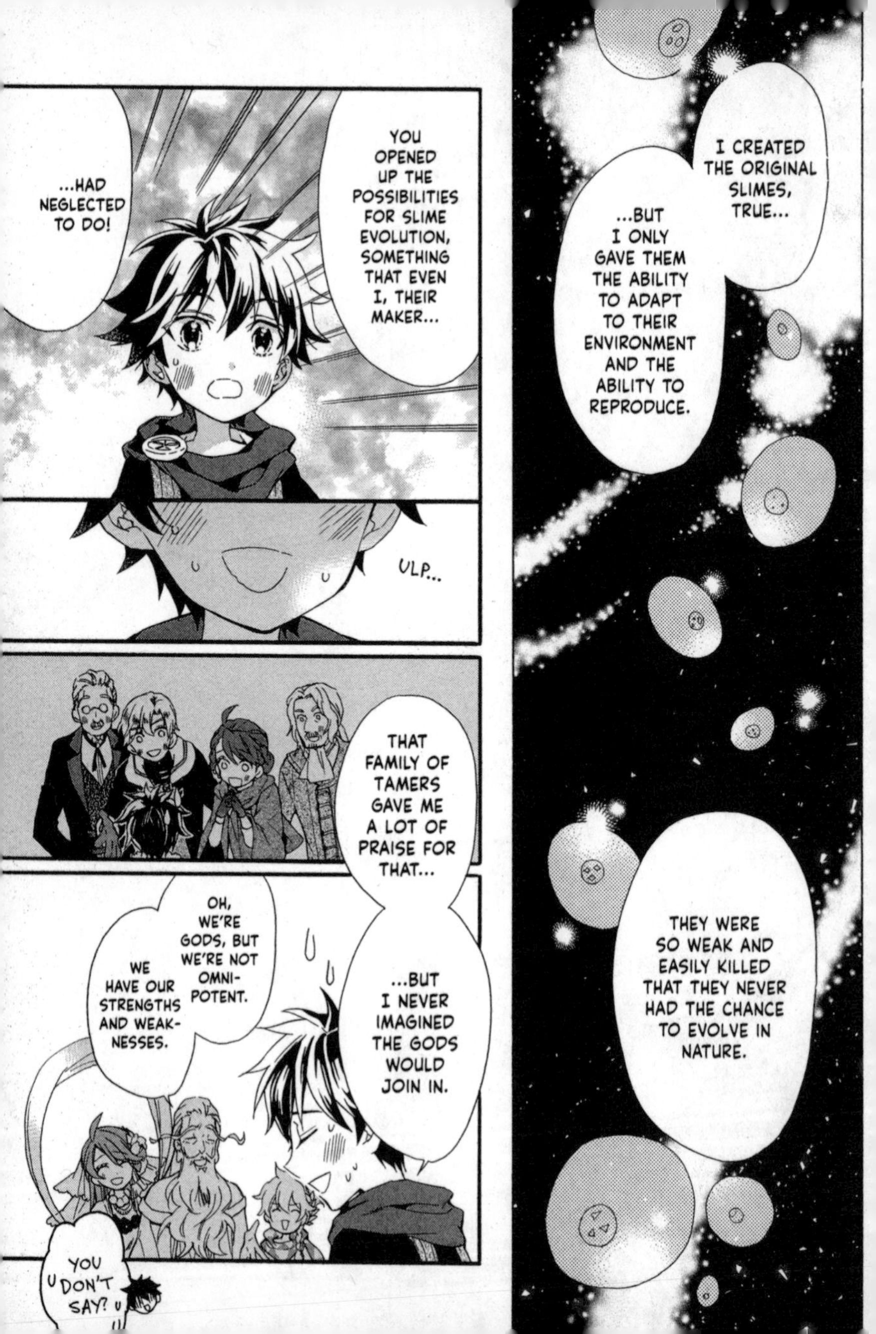
I CREATED THE ORIGINAL SLIMES, TRUE...
...BUT I ONLY GAVE THEM THE ABILITY TO ADAPT TO THEIR ENVIRONMENT AND THE ABILITY TO REPRODUCE.
THEY WERE SO WEAK AND EASILY KILLED THAT THEY NEVER HAD THE CHANCE TO EVOLVE IN NATURE.
YOU OPENED UP THE POSSIBILITIES FOR SLIME EVOLUTION, SOMETHING THAT EVEN I, THEIR MAKER...
...HAD NEGLECTED TO DO!
ULP...
THAT FAMILY OF TAMERS GAVE ME A LOT OF PRAISE FOR THAT...
...BUT I NEVER IMAGINED THE GODS WOULD JOIN IN.
OH, WE'RE GODS, BUT WE'RE NOT OMNI-POTENT.
WE HAVE OUR STRENGTHS AND WEAK-NESSES.
YOU DON'T SAY?

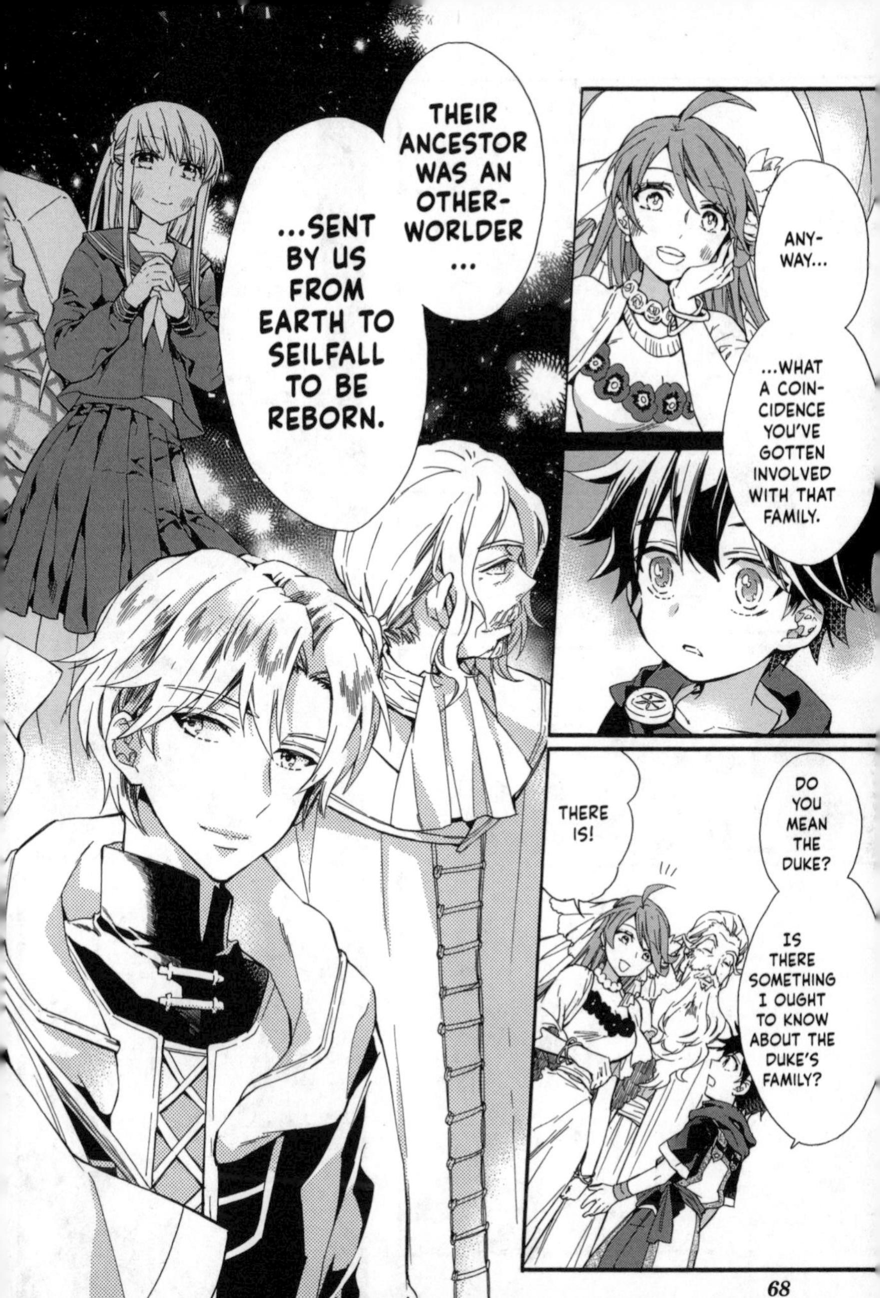
ANY-WAY...
...WHAT A COIN-CIDENCE YOU'VE GOTTEN INVOLVED WITH THAT FAMILY.
DO YOU MEAN THE DUKE?
IS THERE SOMETHING I OUGHT TO KNOW ABOUT THE DUKE'S FAMILY?
THERE IS!
THEIR ANCESTOR WAS AN OTHER-WORLDER...
...SENT BY US FROM EARTH TO SEILFALL TO BE REBORN.

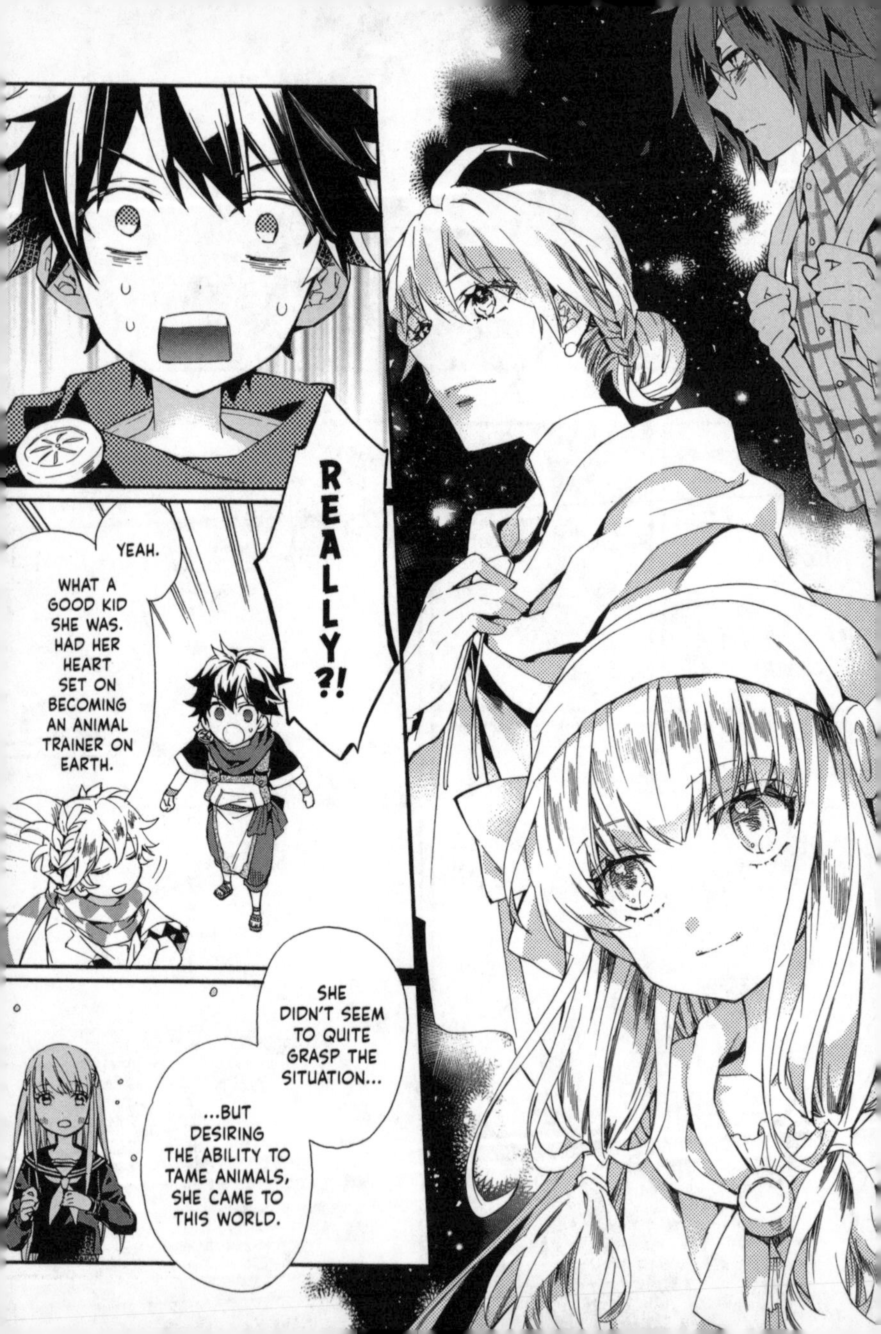
REALLY?!
YEAH.
WHAT A GOOD KID SHE WAS. HAD HER HEART SET ON BECOMING AN ANIMAL TRAINER ON EARTH.
SHE DIDN'T SEEM TO QUITE GRASP THE SITUATION...
...BUT DESIRING THE ABILITY TO TAME ANIMALS, SHE CAME TO THIS WORLD.

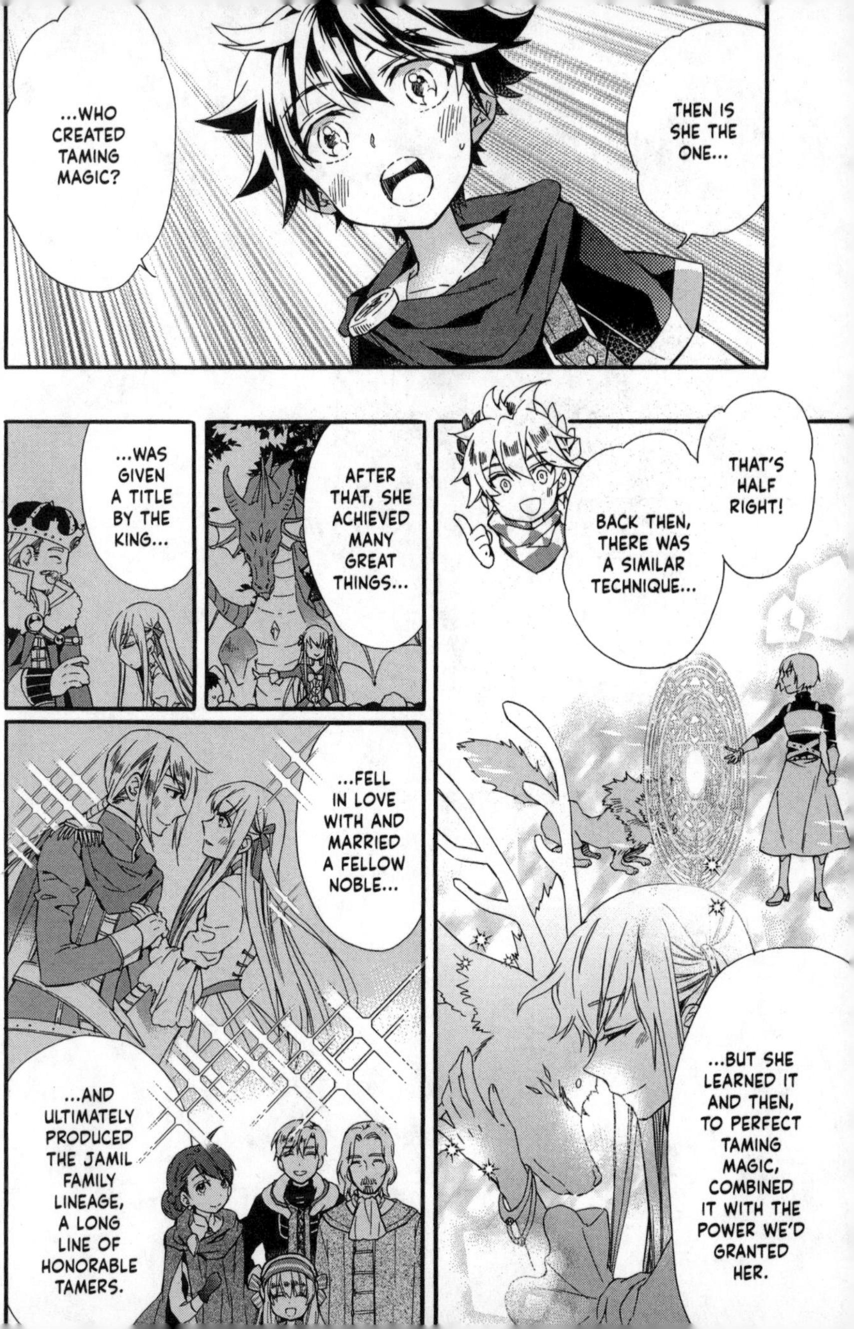
THEN IS SHE THE ONE...
...WHO CREATED TAMING MAGIC?
THAT'S HALF RIGHT!
BACK THEN, THERE WAS A SIMILAR TECHNIQUE...
...BUT SHE LEARNED IT AND THEN, TO PERFECT TAMING MAGIC, COMBINED IT WITH THE POWER WE'D GRANTED HER.
AFTER THAT, SHE ACHIEVED MANY GREAT THINGS...
...WAS GIVEN A TITLE BY THE KING...
...FELL IN LOVE WITH AND MARRIED A FELLOW NOBLE...
...AND ULTIMATELY PRODUCED THE JAMIL FAMILY LINEAGE, A LONG LINE OF HONORABLE TAMERS.

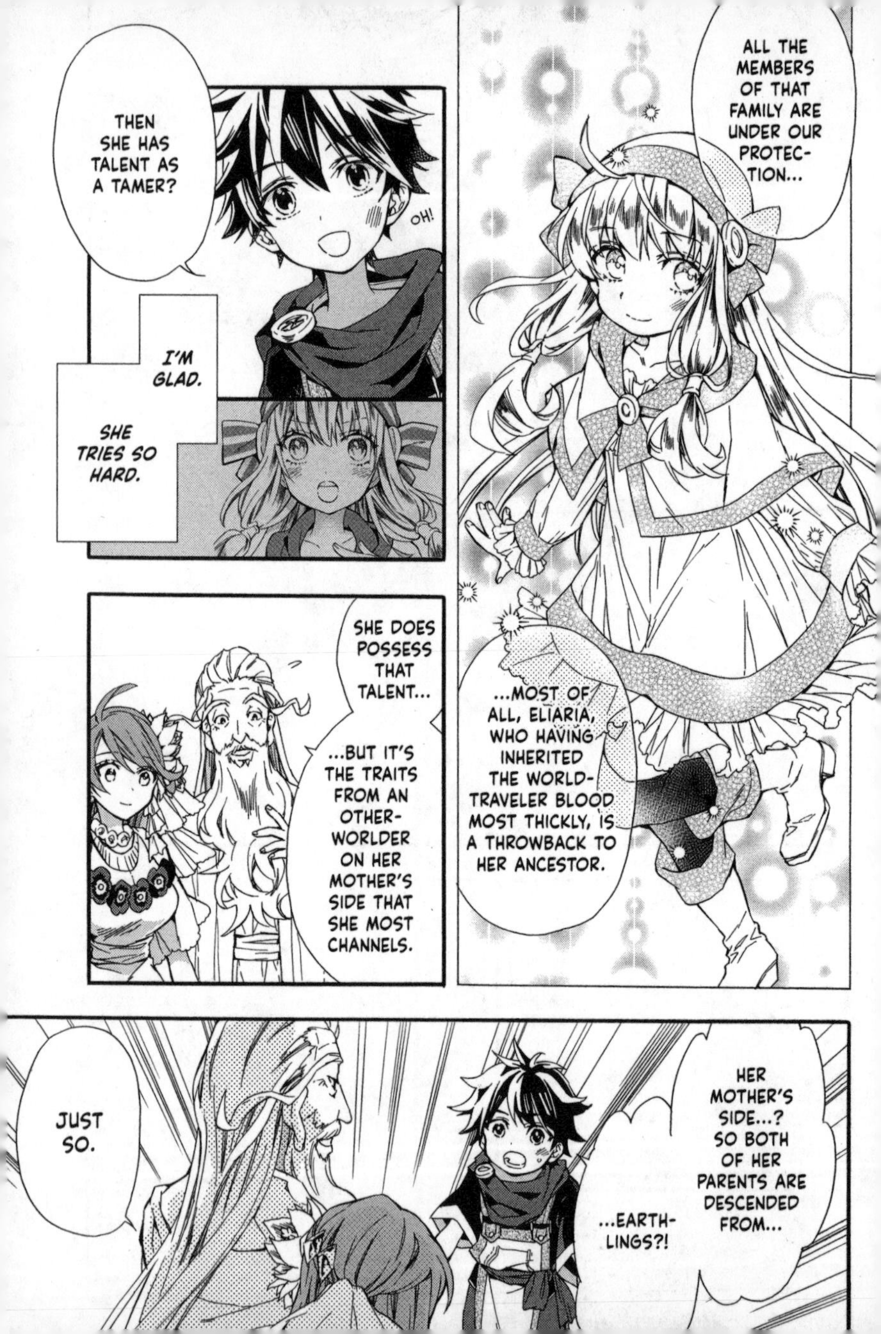
ALL THE MEMBERS OF THAT FAMILY ARE UNDER OUR PROTECTION...
...MOST OF ALL, ELIARIA, WHO HAVING INHERITED THE WORLD-TRAVELER BLOOD MOST THICKLY, IS A THROWBACK TO HER ANCESTOR.
THEN SHE HAS TALENT AS A TAMER?
OH!
I'M GLAD.
SHE TRIES SO HARD.
SHE DOES POSSESS THAT TALENT...
...BUT IT'S THE TRAITS FROM AN OTHER-WORLDER ON HER MOTHER'S SIDE THAT SHE MOST CHANNELS.
HER MOTHER'S SIDE...? SO BOTH OF HER PARENTS ARE DESCENDED FROM...
...EARTH-LINGS?!
JUST SO.

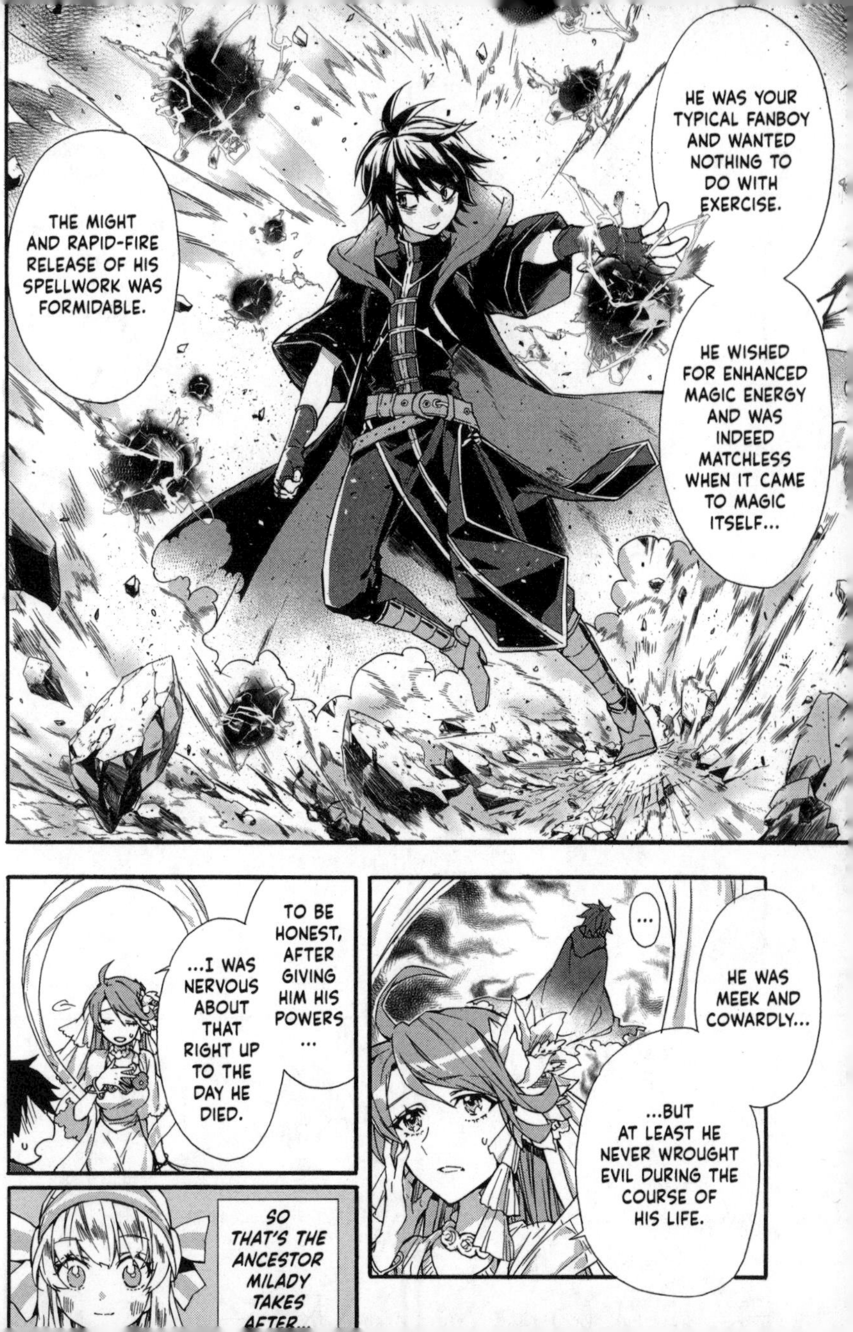
HE WAS YOUR TYPICAL FANBOY AND WANTED NOTHING TO DO WITH EXERCISE.
HE WISHED FOR ENHANCED MAGIC ENERGY AND WAS INDEED MATCHLESS WHEN IT CAME TO MAGIC ITSELF...
THE MIGHT AND RAPID-FIRE RELEASE OF HIS SPELLWORK WAS FORMIDABLE.
...
HE WAS MEEK AND COWARDLY...
...BUT AT LEAST HE NEVER WROUGHT EVIL DURING THE COURSE OF HIS LIFE.
TO BE HONEST, AFTER GIVING HIM HIS POWERS...
...I WAS NERVOUS ABOUT THAT RIGHT UP TO THE DAY HE DIED.
SO THAT'S THE ANCESTOR MILADY TAKES AFTER...

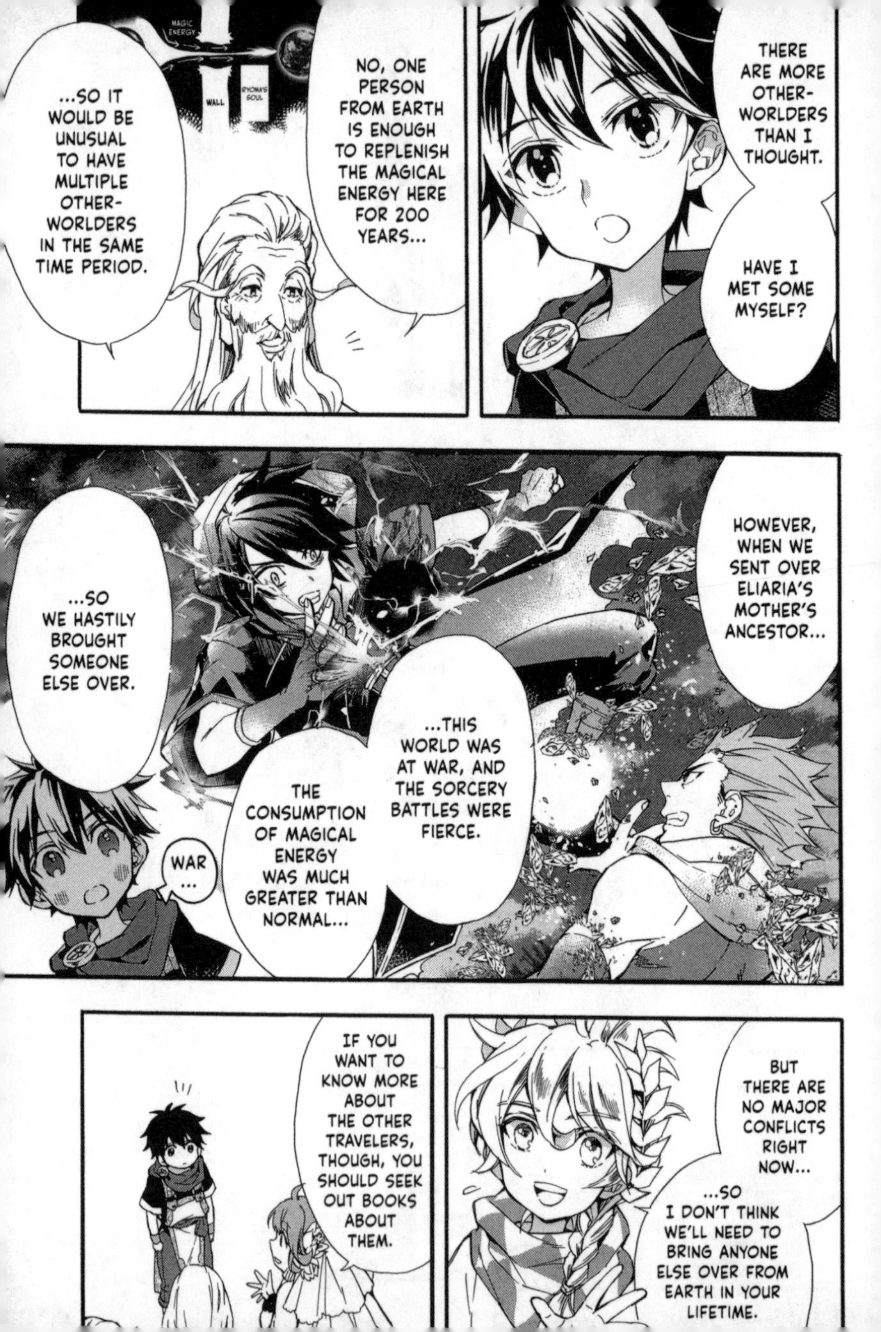
THERE ARE MORE OTHER-WORLDERS THAN I THOUGHT.
HAVE I MET SOME MYSELF?
MAGIC ENERGY
RYOMA'S SOUL
WALL
NO, ONE PERSON FROM EARTH IS ENOUGH TO REPLENISH THE MAGICAL ENERGY HERE FOR 200 YEARS...
...SO IT WOULD BE UNUSUAL TO HAVE MULTIPLE OTHER-WORLDERS IN THE SAME TIME PERIOD.
HOWEVER, WHEN WE SENT OVER ELIARIA'S MOTHER'S ANCESTOR...
...THIS WORLD WAS AT WAR, AND THE SORCERY BATTLES WERE FIERCE.
THE CONSUMPTION OF MAGICAL ENERGY WAS MUCH GREATER THAN NORMAL...
...SO WE HASTILY BROUGHT SOMEONE ELSE OVER.
WAR...
BUT THERE ARE NO MAJOR CONFLICTS RIGHT NOW...
...SO I DON'T THINK WE'LL NEED TO BRING ANYONE ELSE OVER FROM EARTH IN YOUR LIFETIME.
IF YOU WANT TO KNOW MORE ABOUT THE OTHER TRAVELERS, THOUGH, YOU SHOULD SEEK OUT BOOKS ABOUT THEM.

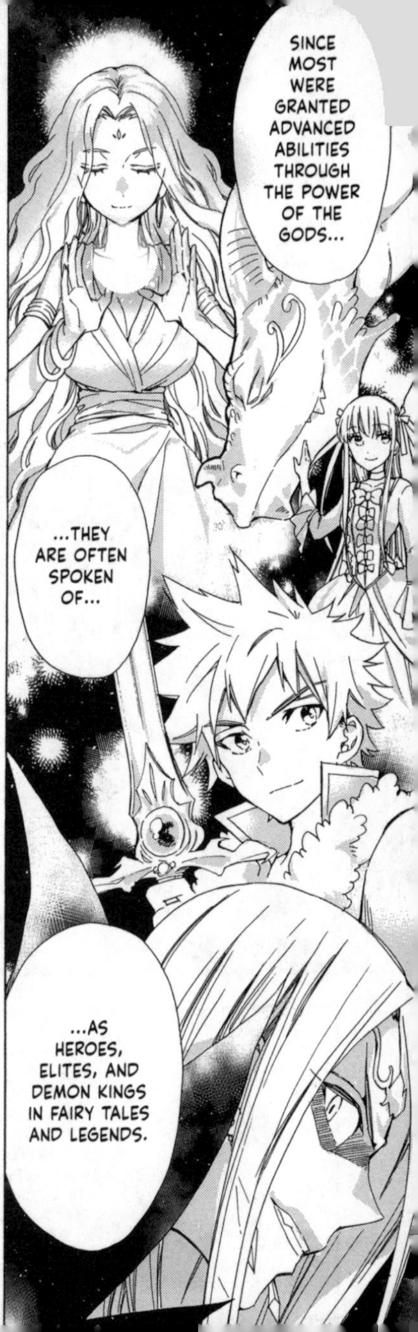
SINCE MOST WERE GRANTED ADVANCED ABILITIES THROUGH THE POWER OF THE GODS...
...THEY ARE OFTEN SPOKEN OF...
...AS HEROES, ELITES, AND DEMON KINGS IN FAIRY TALES AND LEGENDS.

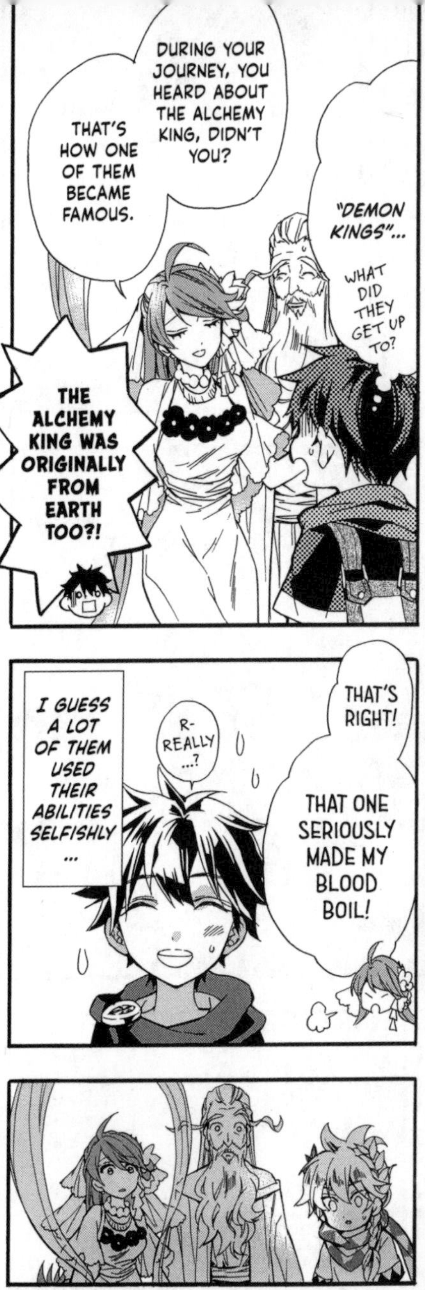
"DEMON KINGS"...
WHAT DID THEY GET UP TO?
DURING YOUR JOURNEY, YOU HEARD ABOUT THE ALCHEMY KING, DIDN'T YOU?
THAT'S HOW ONE OF THEM BECAME FAMOUS.
THE ALCHEMY KING WAS ORIGINALLY FROM EARTH TOO?!
THAT'S RIGHT!
THAT ONE SERIOUSLY MADE MY BLOOD BOIL!
R-REALLY ...?
I GUESS A LOT OF THEM USED THEIR ABILITIES SELFISHLY ...

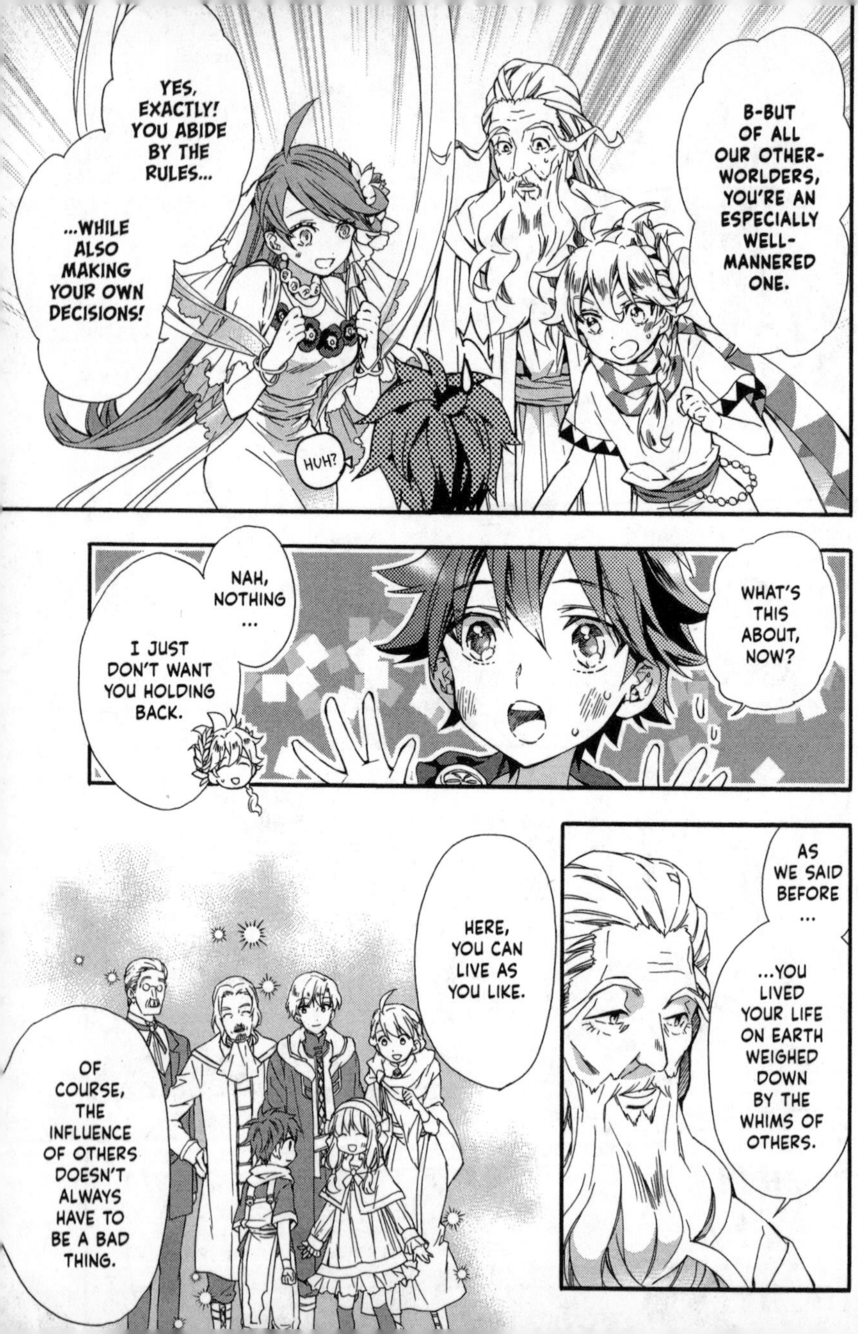
B-BUT OF ALL OUR OTHER-WORLDERS, YOU'RE AN ESPECIALLY WELL-MANNERED ONE.
YES, EXACTLY! YOU ABIDE BY THE RULES...
...WHILE ALSO MAKING YOUR OWN DECISIONS!
HUH?
WHAT'S THIS ABOUT, NOW?
NAH, NOTHING...
I JUST DON'T WANT YOU HOLDING BACK.
AS WE SAID BEFORE...
...YOU LIVED YOUR LIFE ON EARTH WEIGHED DOWN BY THE WHIMS OF OTHERS.
HERE, YOU CAN LIVE AS YOU LIKE.
OF COURSE, THE INFLUENCE OF OTHERS DOESN'T ALWAYS HAVE TO BE A BAD THING.

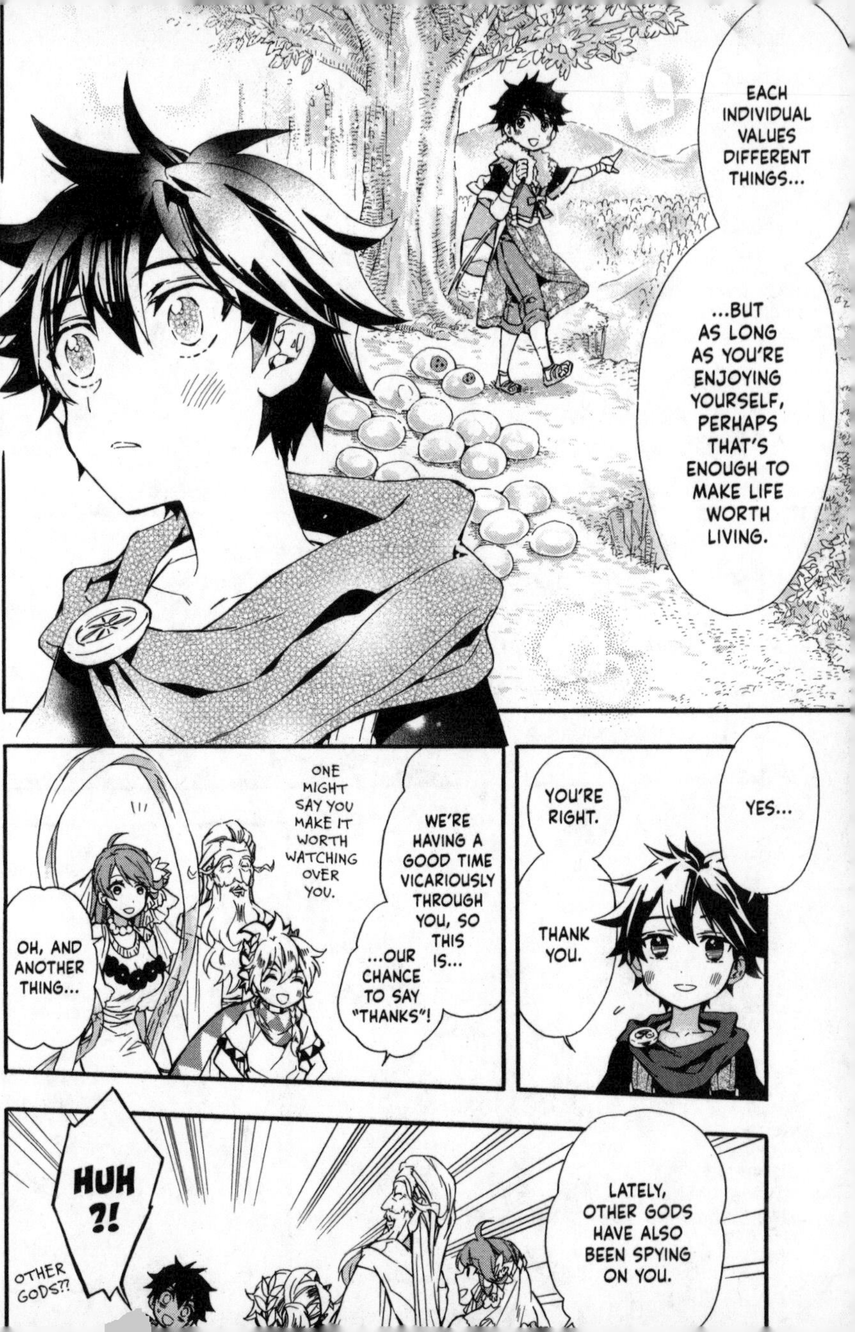
EACH INDIVIDUAL VALUES DIFFERENT THINGS...
...BUT AS LONG AS YOU'RE ENJOYING YOURSELF, PERHAPS THAT'S ENOUGH TO MAKE LIFE WORTH LIVING.
YES...
YOU'RE RIGHT.
THANK YOU.
WE'RE HAVING A GOOD TIME VICARIOUSLY THROUGH YOU, SO THIS IS...
ONE MIGHT SAY YOU MAKE IT WORTH WATCHING OVER YOU.
...OUR CHANCE TO SAY "THANKS"!
OH, AND ANOTHER THING...
LATELY, OTHER GODS HAVE ALSO BEEN SPYING ON YOU.
HUH ?!
OTHER GODS??

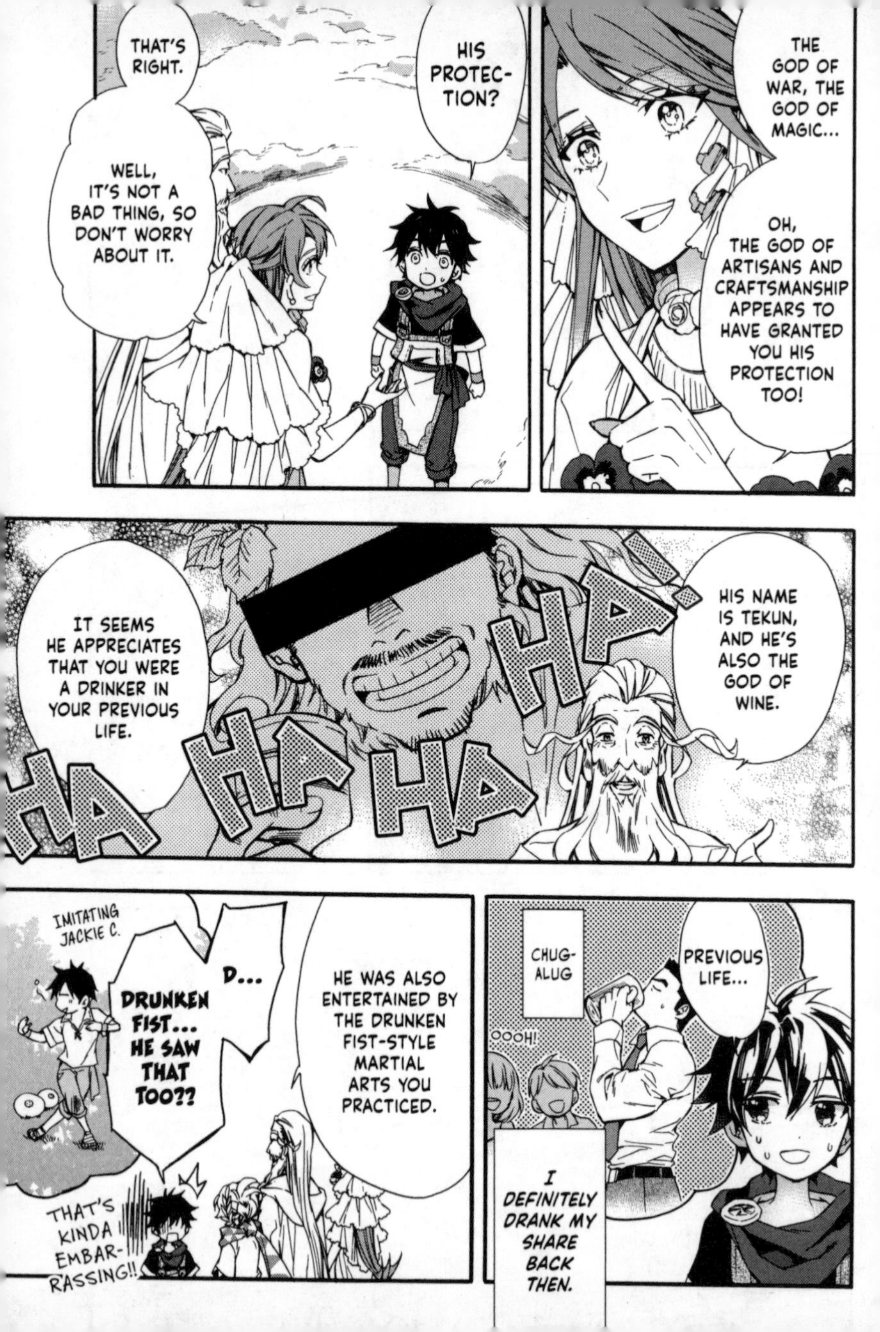
THE GOD OF WAR, THE GOD OF MAGIC...
OH, THE GOD OF ARTISANS AND CRAFTSMANSHIP APPEARS TO HAVE GRANTED YOU HIS PROTECTION TOO!
HIS PROTECTION?
THAT'S RIGHT.
WELL, IT'S NOT A BAD THING, SO DON'T WORRY ABOUT IT.
HIS NAME IS TEKUN, AND HE'S ALSO THE GOD OF WINE.
HA HA HA HA!
IT SEEMS HE APPRECIATES THAT YOU WERE A DRINKER IN YOUR PREVIOUS LIFE.
PREVIOUS LIFE...
CHUG-ALUG
OOOH!
I DEFINITELY DRANK MY SHARE BACK THEN.
HE WAS ALSO ENTERTAINED BY THE DRUNKEN FIST-STYLE MARTIAL ARTS YOU PRACTICED.
D...
DRUNKEN FIST... HE SAW THAT TOO??
IMITATING JACKIE C.
THAT'S KINDA EMBARRASSING!!

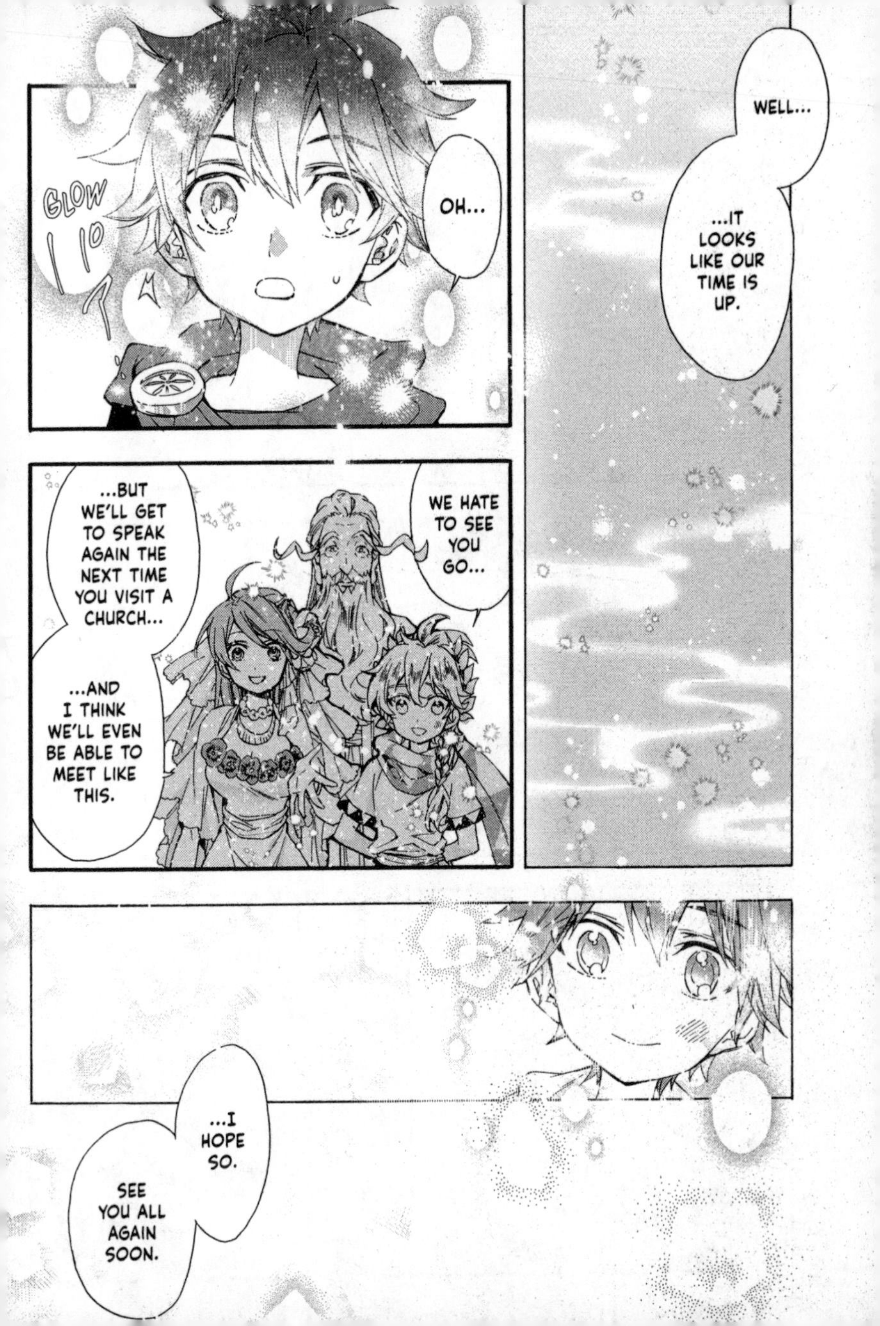
WELL...
...IT LOOKS LIKE OUR TIME IS UP.
GLOW
OH...
WE HATE TO SEE YOU GO...
...BUT WE'LL GET TO SPEAK AGAIN THE NEXT TIME YOU VISIT A CHURCH...
...AND I THINK WE'LL EVEN BE ABLE TO MEET LIKE THIS.
...I HOPE SO.
SEE YOU ALL AGAIN SOON.

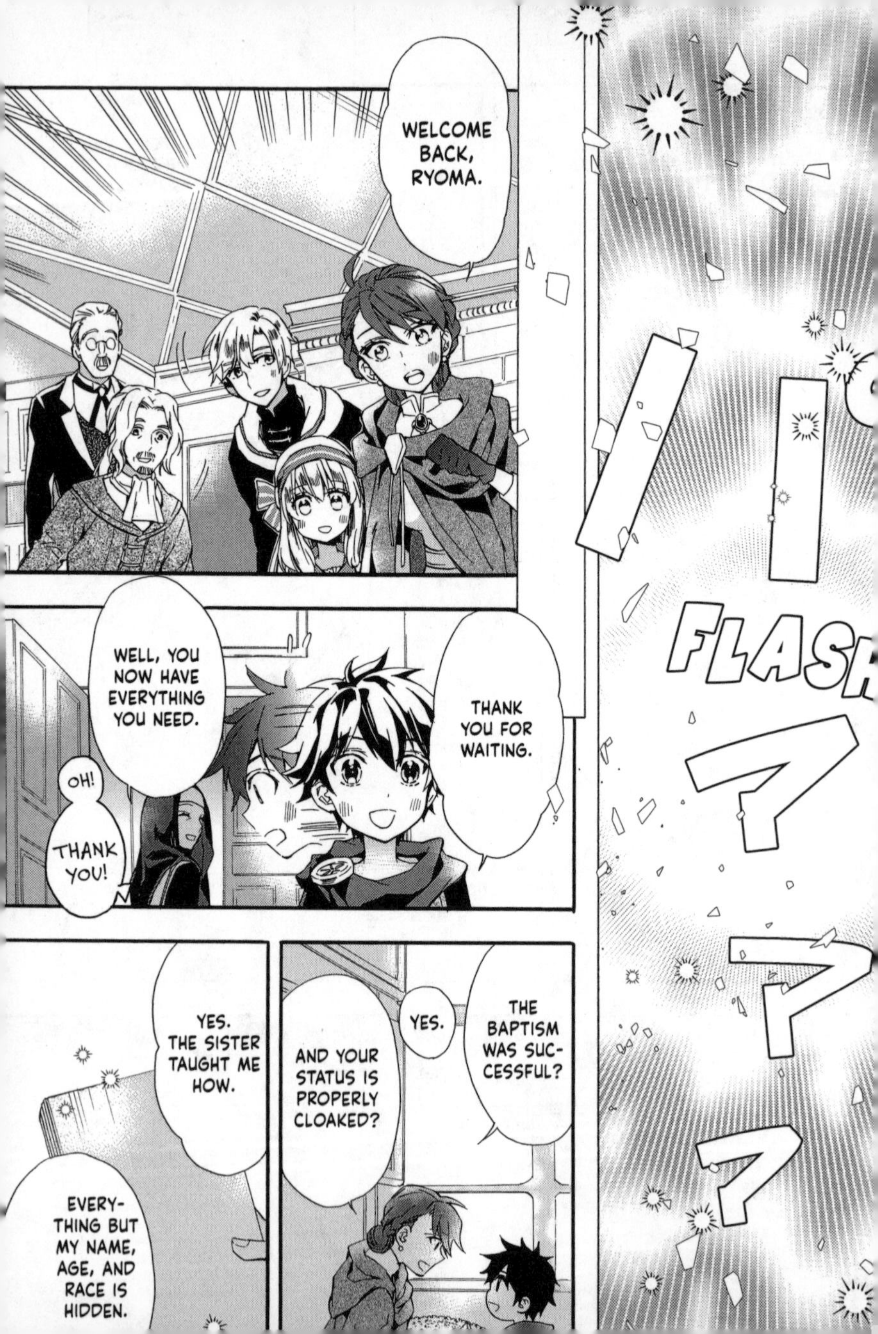
FLASH
WELCOME BACK, RYOMA.
THANK YOU FOR WAITING.
WELL, YOU NOW HAVE EVERYTHING YOU NEED.
OH!
THANK YOU!
THE BAPTISM WAS SUC-CESSFUL?
YES.
AND YOUR STATUS IS PROPERLY CLOAKED?
YES. THE SISTER TAUGHT ME HOW.
EVERY-THING BUT MY NAME, AGE, AND RACE IS HIDDEN.

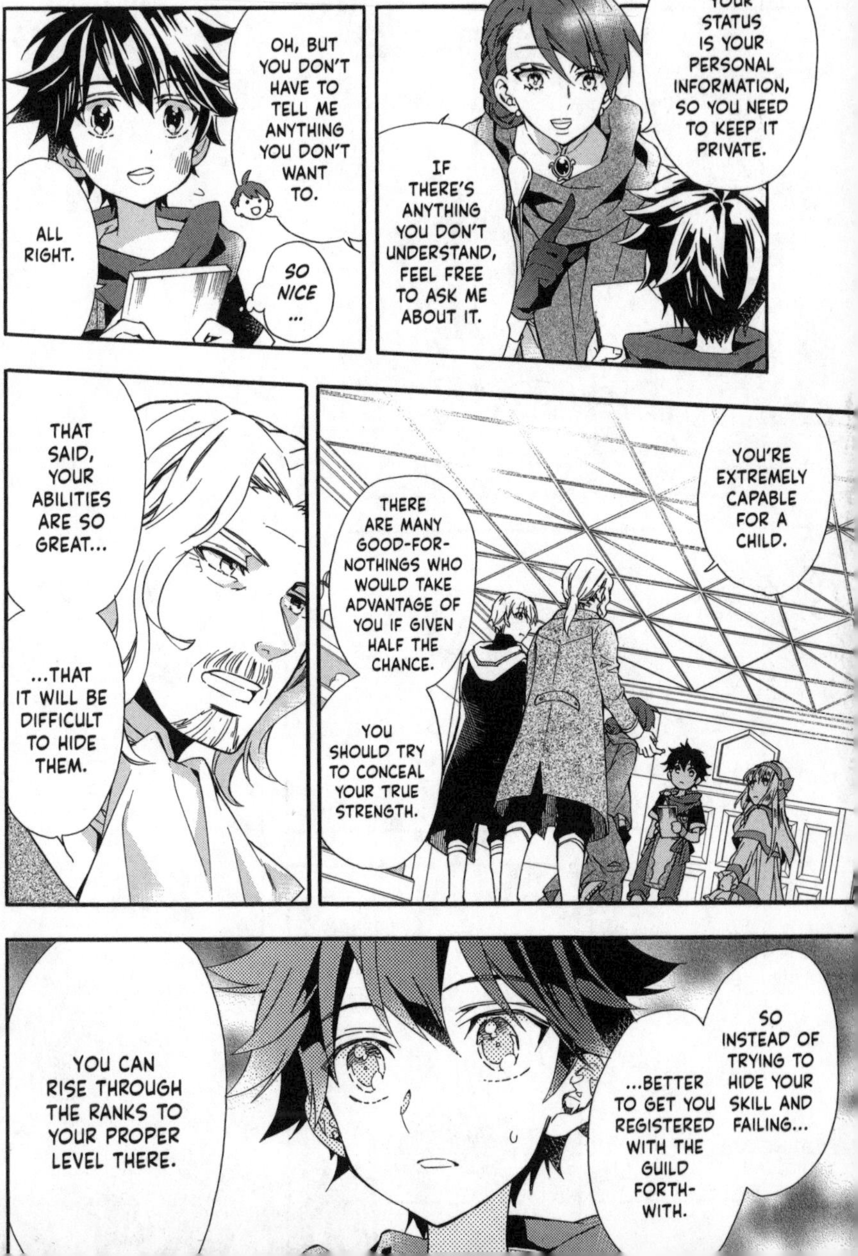
GOOD. YOUR STATUS IS YOUR PERSONAL INFORMATION, SO YOU NEED TO KEEP IT PRIVATE.
IF THERE'S ANYTHING YOU DON'T UNDERSTAND, FEEL FREE TO ASK ME ABOUT IT.
OH, BUT YOU DON'T HAVE TO TELL ME ANYTHING YOU DON'T WANT TO.
SO NICE ...
ALL RIGHT.
YOU'RE EXTREMELY CAPABLE FOR A CHILD.
THERE ARE MANY GOOD-FOR-NOTHINGS WHO WOULD TAKE ADVANTAGE OF YOU IF GIVEN HALF THE CHANCE.
YOU SHOULD TRY TO CONCEAL YOUR TRUE STRENGTH.
THAT SAID, YOUR ABILITIES ARE SO GREAT...
...THAT IT WILL BE DIFFICULT TO HIDE THEM.
SO INSTEAD OF TRYING TO HIDE YOUR SKILL AND FAILING...
...BETTER TO GET YOU REGISTERED WITH THE GUILD FORTH-WITH.
YOU CAN RISE THROUGH THE RANKS TO YOUR PROPER LEVEL THERE.

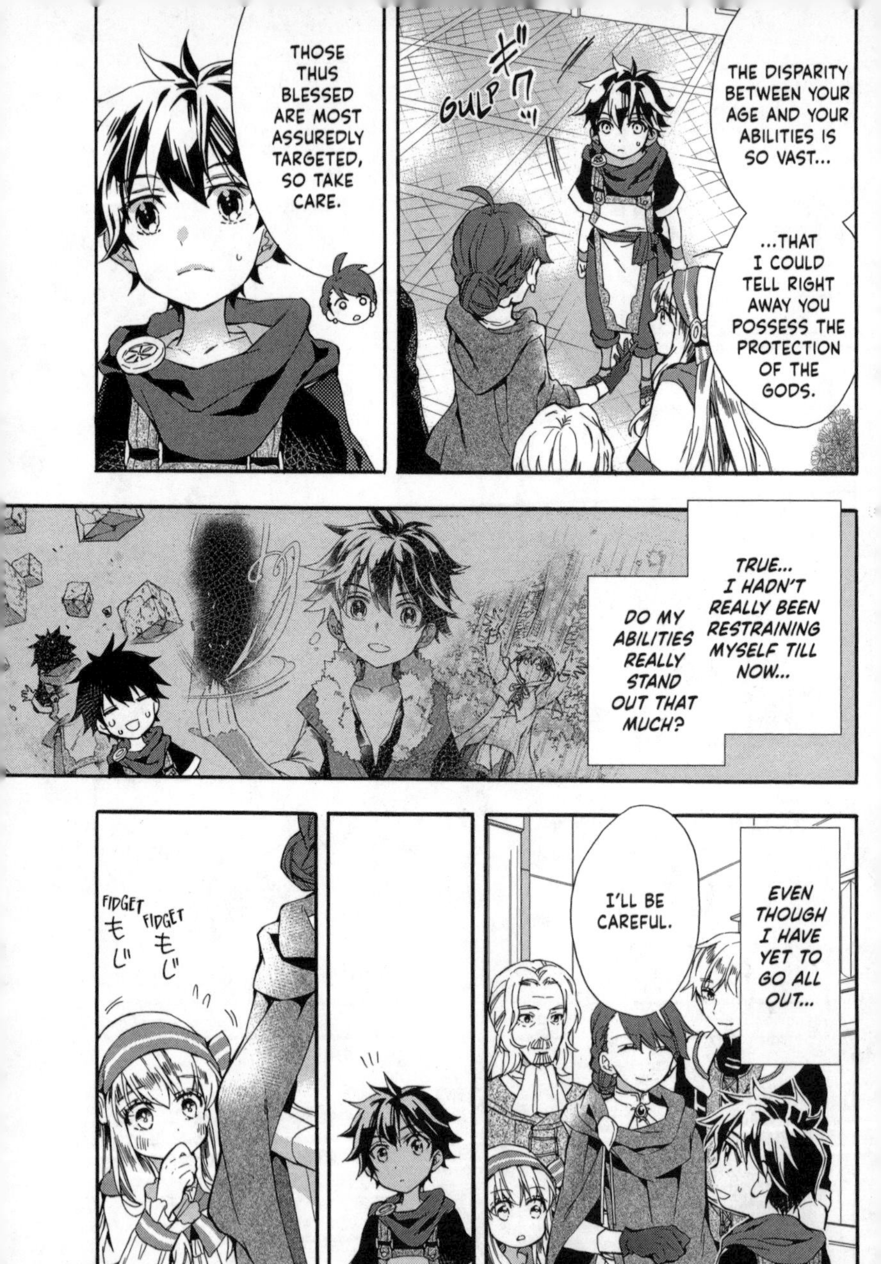
THE DISPARITY BETWEEN YOUR AGE AND YOUR ABILITIES IS SO VAST...
...THAT I COULD TELL RIGHT AWAY YOU POSSESS THE PROTECTION OF THE GODS.
GULP ギクッ
THOSE THUS BLESSED ARE MOST ASSUREDLY TARGETED, SO TAKE CARE.
TRUE... I HADN'T REALLY BEEN RESTRAINING MYSELF TILL NOW...
DO MY ABILITIES REALLY STAND OUT THAT MUCH?
EVEN THOUGH I HAVE YET TO GO ALL OUT...
I'LL BE CAREFUL.
FIDGET もじ
FIDGET もじ

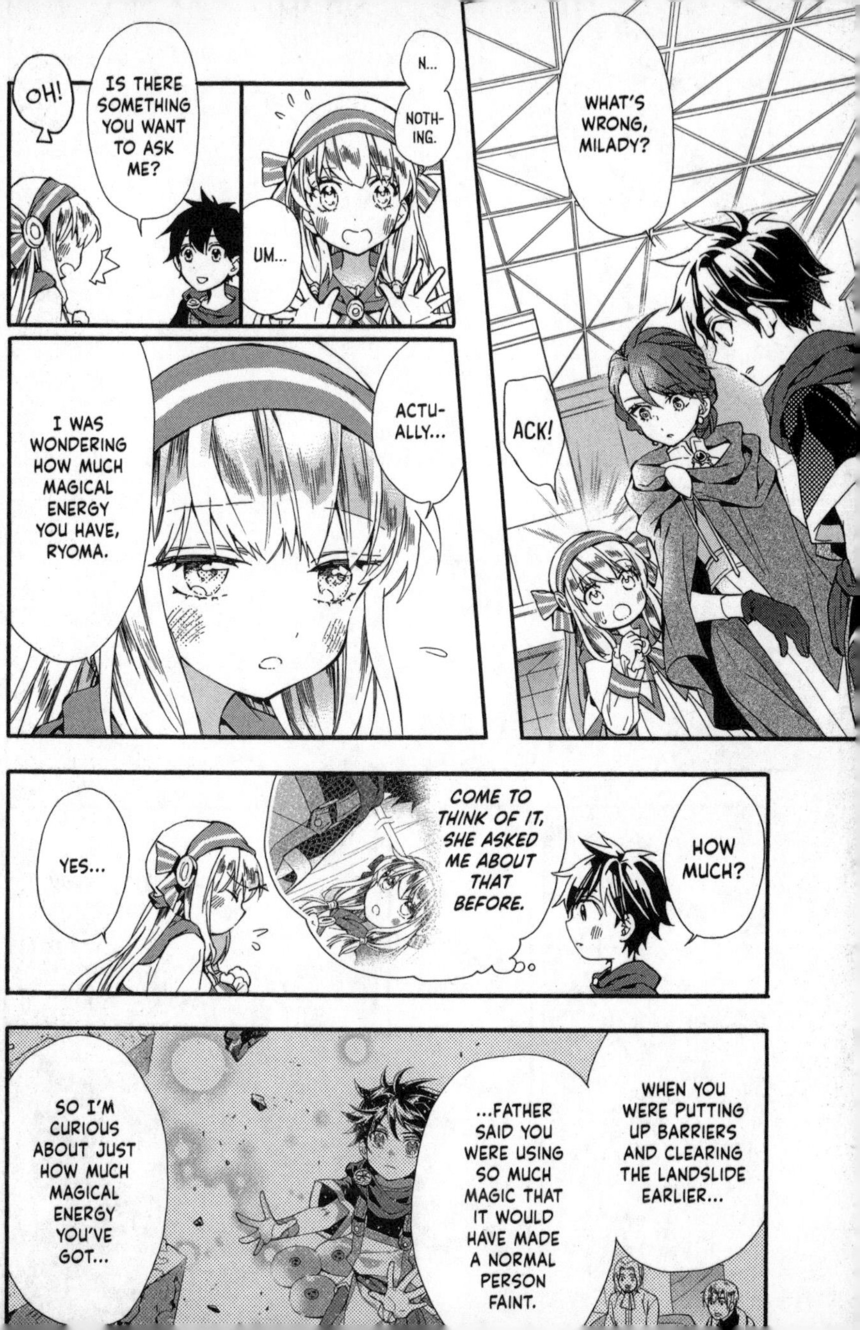

WHAT'S WRONG, MILADY?
ACK!
N... NOTHING.
UM...
IS THERE SOMETHING YOU WANT TO ASK ME?
OH!
ACTUALLY...
I WAS WONDERING HOW MUCH MAGICAL ENERGY YOU HAVE, RYOMA.
HOW MUCH?
COME TO THINK OF IT, SHE ASKED ME ABOUT THAT BEFORE.
YES...
WHEN YOU WERE PUTTING UP BARRIERS AND CLEARING THE LANDSLIDE EARLIER...
...FATHER SAID YOU WERE USING SO MUCH MAGIC THAT IT WOULD HAVE MADE A NORMAL PERSON FAINT.
SO I'M CURIOUS ABOUT JUST HOW MUCH MAGICAL ENERGY YOU'VE GOT...

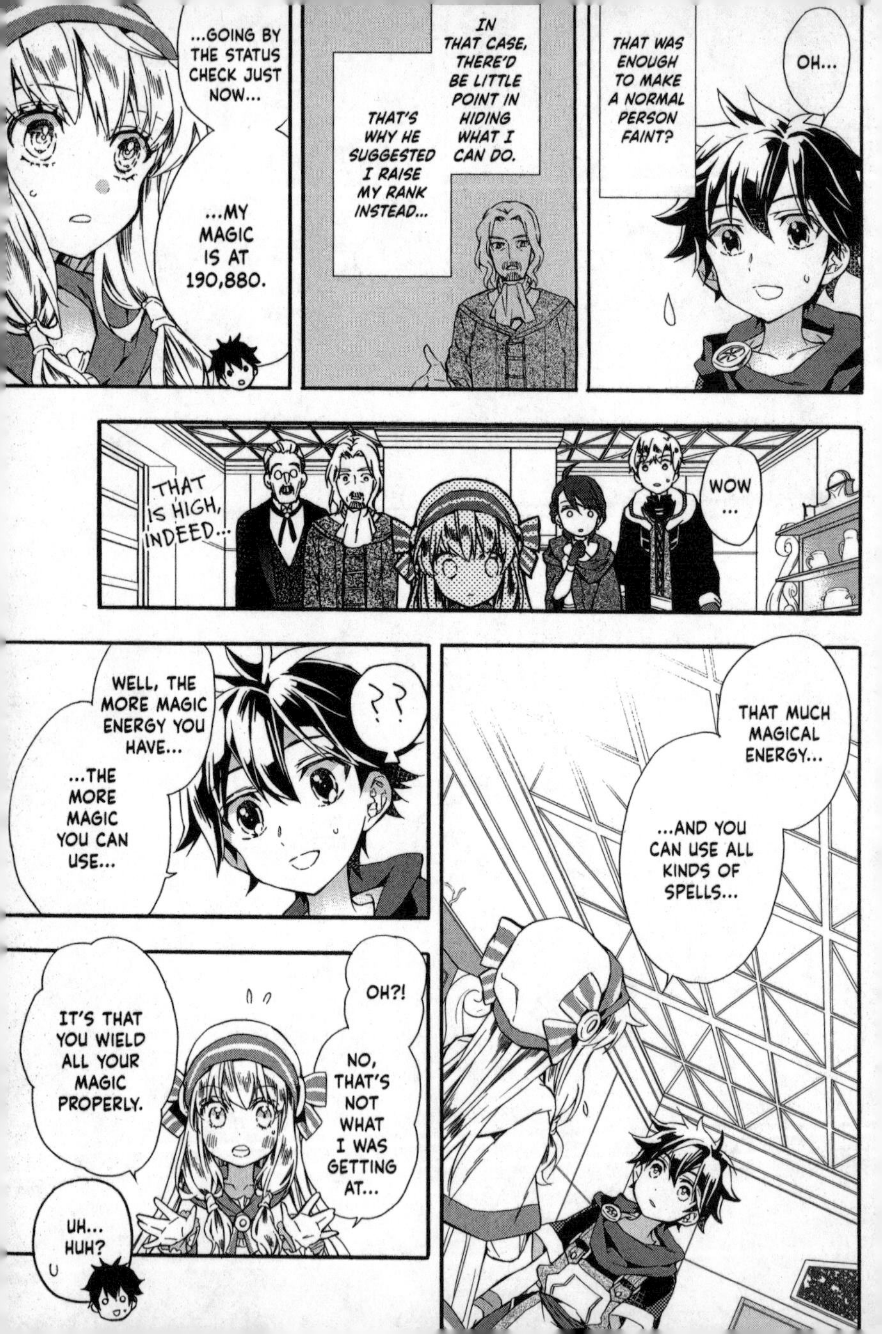
OH...
THAT WAS ENOUGH TO MAKE A NORMAL PERSON FAINT?
IN THAT CASE, THERE'D BE LITTLE POINT IN HIDING WHAT I CAN DO.
THAT'S WHY HE SUGGESTED I RAISE MY RANK INSTEAD...
...GOING BY THE STATUS CHECK JUST NOW...
...MY MAGIC IS AT 190,880.
WOW...
THAT IS HIGH, INDEED...
THAT MUCH MAGICAL ENERGY...
...AND YOU CAN USE ALL KINDS OF SPELLS...
??
WELL, THE MORE MAGIC ENERGY YOU HAVE...
...THE MORE MAGIC YOU CAN USE...
OH?!
NO, THAT'S NOT WHAT I WAS GETTING AT...
IT'S THAT YOU WIELD ALL YOUR MAGIC PROPERLY.
UH... HUH?

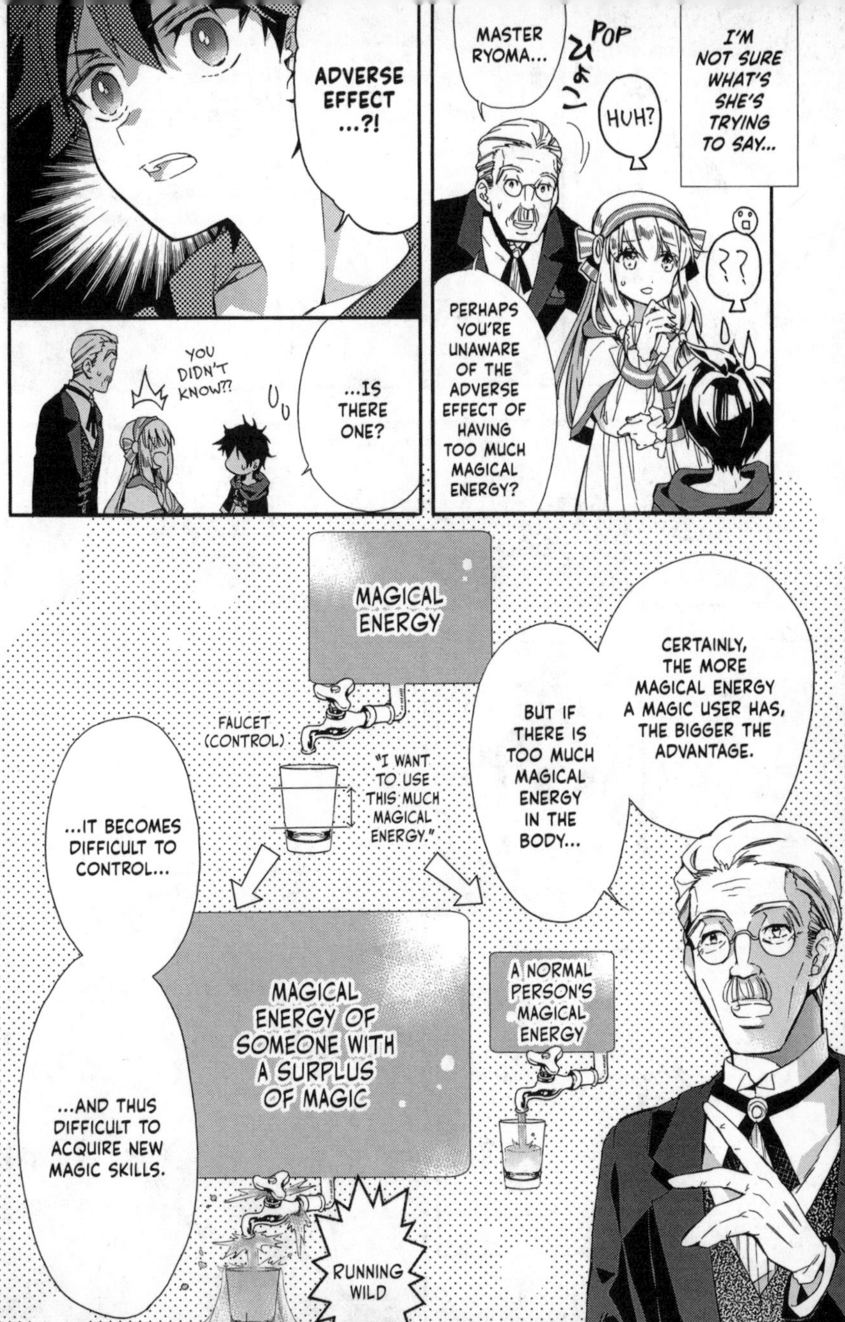
I'M NOT SURE WHAT'S SHE'S TRYING TO SAY...
MASTER RYOMA...
POP
ひょこ
HUH?
??
PERHAPS YOU'RE UNAWARE OF THE ADVERSE EFFECT OF HAVING TOO MUCH MAGICAL ENERGY?
ADVERSE EFFECT ...?!
...IS THERE ONE?
YOU DIDN'T KNOW??
CERTAINLY, THE MORE MAGICAL ENERGY A MAGIC USER HAS, THE BIGGER THE ADVANTAGE.
BUT IF THERE IS TOO MUCH MAGICAL ENERGY IN THE BODY...
MAGICAL ENERGY
FAUCET (CONTROL)
"I WANT TO USE THIS MUCH MAGICAL ENERGY."
...IT BECOMES DIFFICULT TO CONTROL...
A NORMAL PERSON'S MAGICAL ENERGY
MAGICAL ENERGY OF SOMEONE WITH A SURPLUS OF MAGIC
...AND THUS DIFFICULT TO ACQUIRE NEW MAGIC SKILLS.
RUNNING WILD

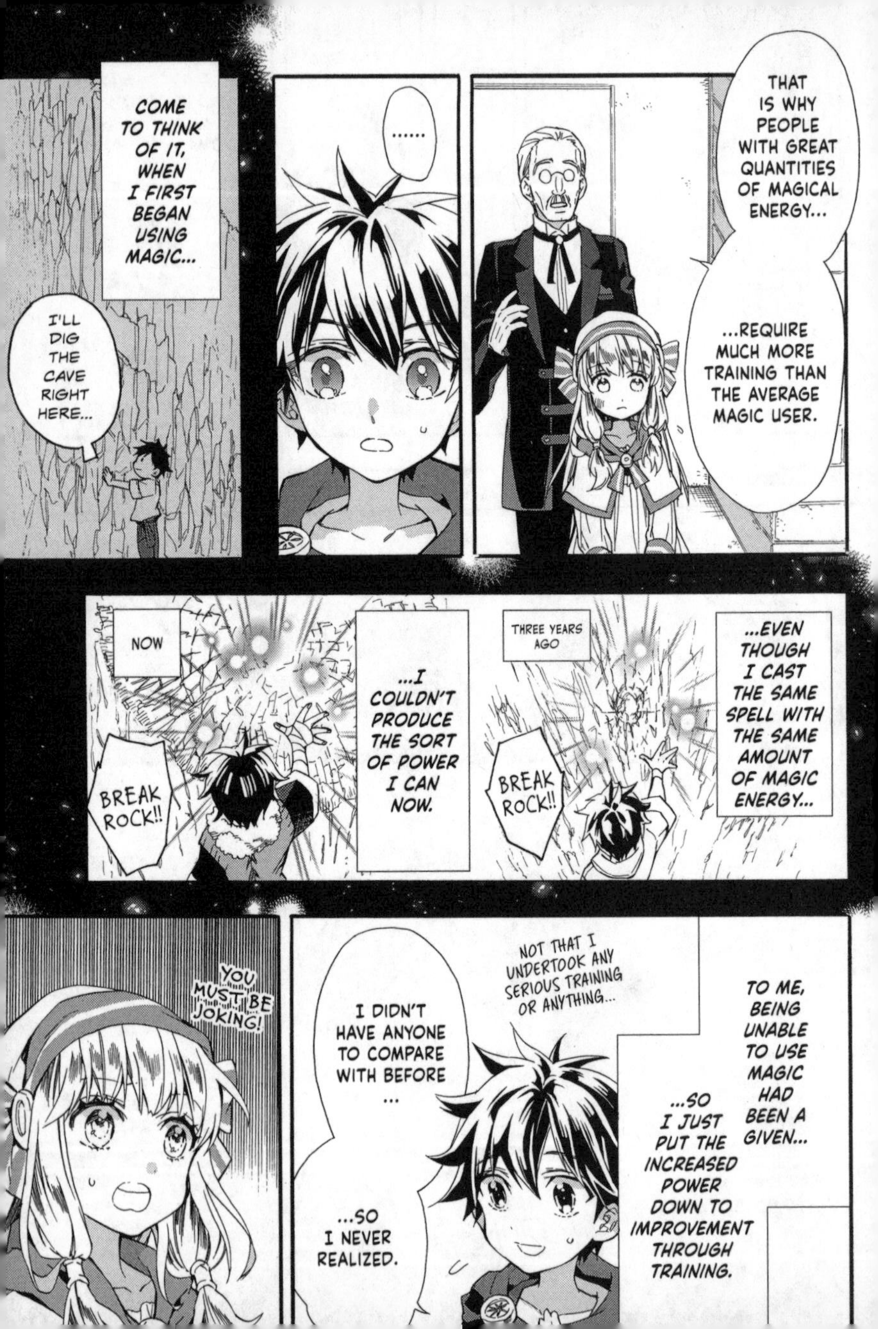
THAT IS WHY PEOPLE WITH GREAT QUANTITIES OF MAGICAL ENERGY...
...REQUIRE MUCH MORE TRAINING THAN THE AVERAGE MAGIC USER.
......
COME TO THINK OF IT, WHEN I FIRST BEGAN USING MAGIC...
I'LL DIG THE CAVE RIGHT HERE...
...EVEN THOUGH I CAST THE SAME SPELL WITH THE SAME AMOUNT OF MAGIC ENERGY...
THREE YEARS AGO
BREAK ROCK!!
...I COULDN'T PRODUCE THE SORT OF POWER I CAN NOW.
NOW
BREAK ROCK!!
TO ME, BEING UNABLE TO USE MAGIC HAD BEEN A GIVEN...
...SO I JUST PUT THE INCREASED POWER DOWN TO IMPROVEMENT THROUGH TRAINING.
NOT THAT I UNDERTOOK ANY SERIOUS TRAINING OR ANYTHING...
I DIDN'T HAVE ANYONE TO COMPARE WITH BEFORE ...
...SO I NEVER REALIZED.
YOU MUST BE JOKING!

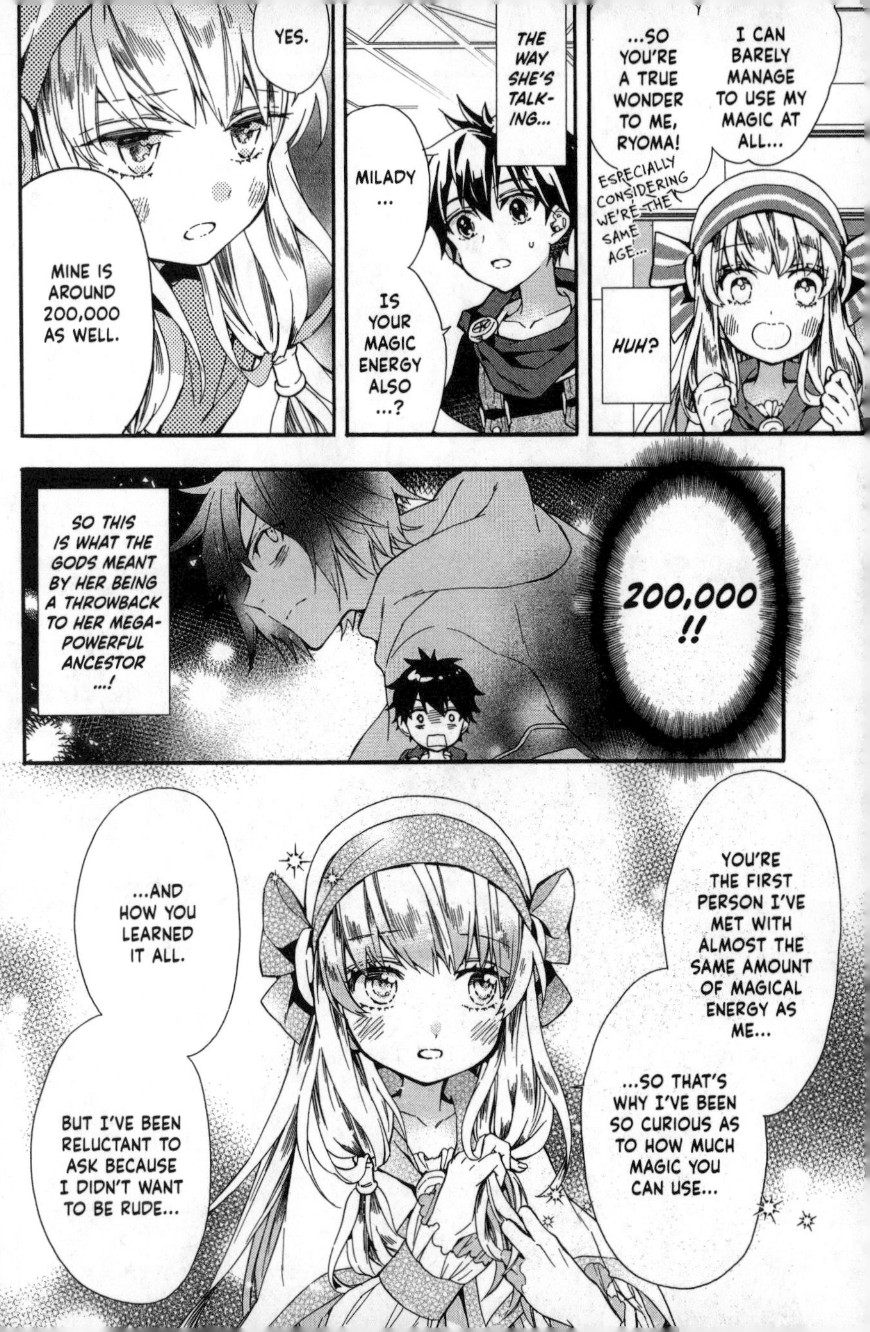
I CAN BARELY MANAGE TO USE MY MAGIC AT ALL...
...SO YOU'RE A TRUE WONDER TO ME, RYOMA!
ESPECIALLY CONSIDERING WE'RE THE SAME AGE...
HUH?
THE WAY SHE'S TALK-ING...
MILADY...
IS YOUR MAGIC ENERGY ALSO...?
YES.
MINE IS AROUND 200,000 AS WELL.
200,000!!
SO THIS IS WHAT THE GODS MEANT BY HER BEING A THROWBACK TO HER MEGA-POWERFUL ANCESTOR...!
YOU'RE THE FIRST PERSON I'VE MET WITH ALMOST THE SAME AMOUNT OF MAGICAL ENERGY AS ME...
...SO THAT'S WHY I'VE BEEN SO CURIOUS AS TO HOW MUCH MAGIC YOU CAN USE...
...AND HOW YOU LEARNED IT ALL.
BUT I'VE BEEN RELUCTANT TO ASK BECAUSE I DIDN'T WANT TO BE RUDE...

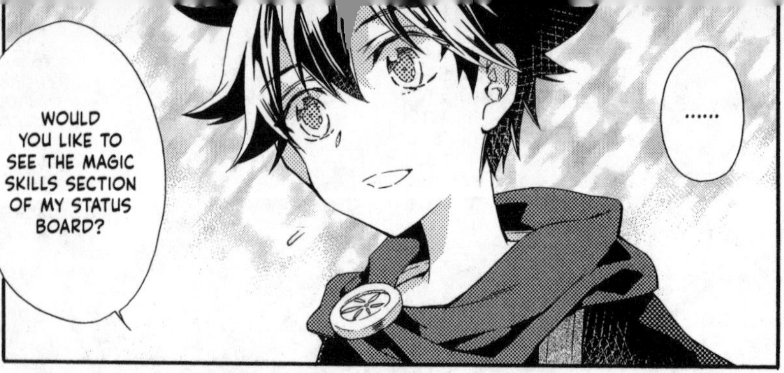
......
WOULD YOU LIKE TO SEE THE MAGIC SKILLS SECTION OF MY STATUS BOARD?

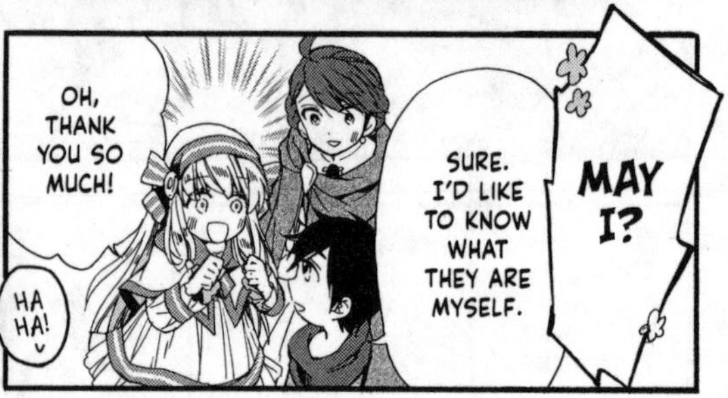
MAY I?
SURE. I'D LIKE TO KNOW WHAT THEY ARE MYSELF.
OH, THANK YOU SO MUCH!
HA HA!

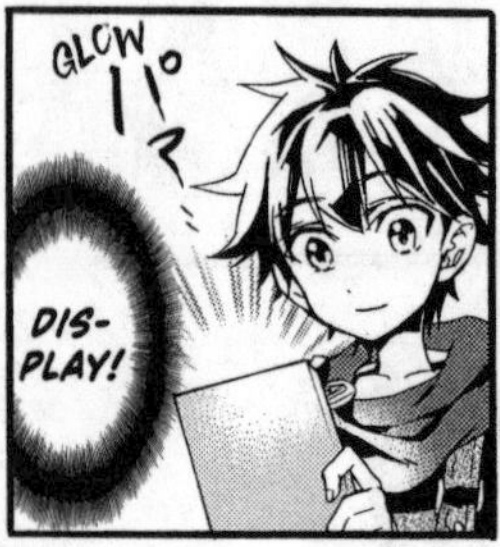
GLOW
DIS-PLAY!

TAMING	2	BARRIER	2	HEALING	1	ALCHEMY	2
FIRE	3	WATER	3	WIND	2	EARTH	4
NEUTRAL	3	LIGHTNING	1	ICE	2	POISON	2
WOOD	3	LIGHT	2	DARK	1	SPACE	3
MAGIC DETECTION	3	MAGIC CONTROL	4	MAGIC RECOVERY	2		

*LEVEL 3 IS COMPETENT. LEVEL 5 IS FIRST-RATE.

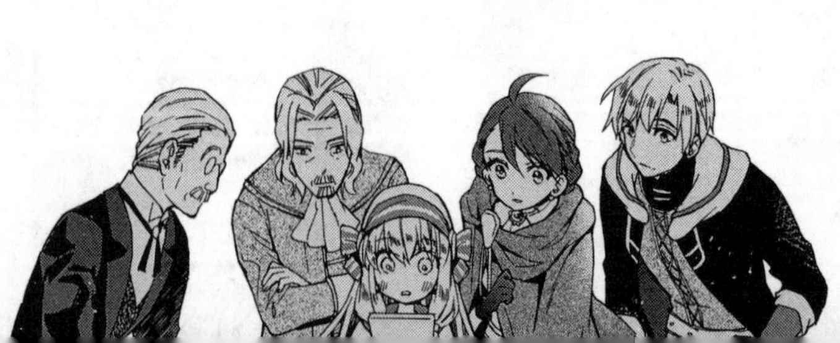

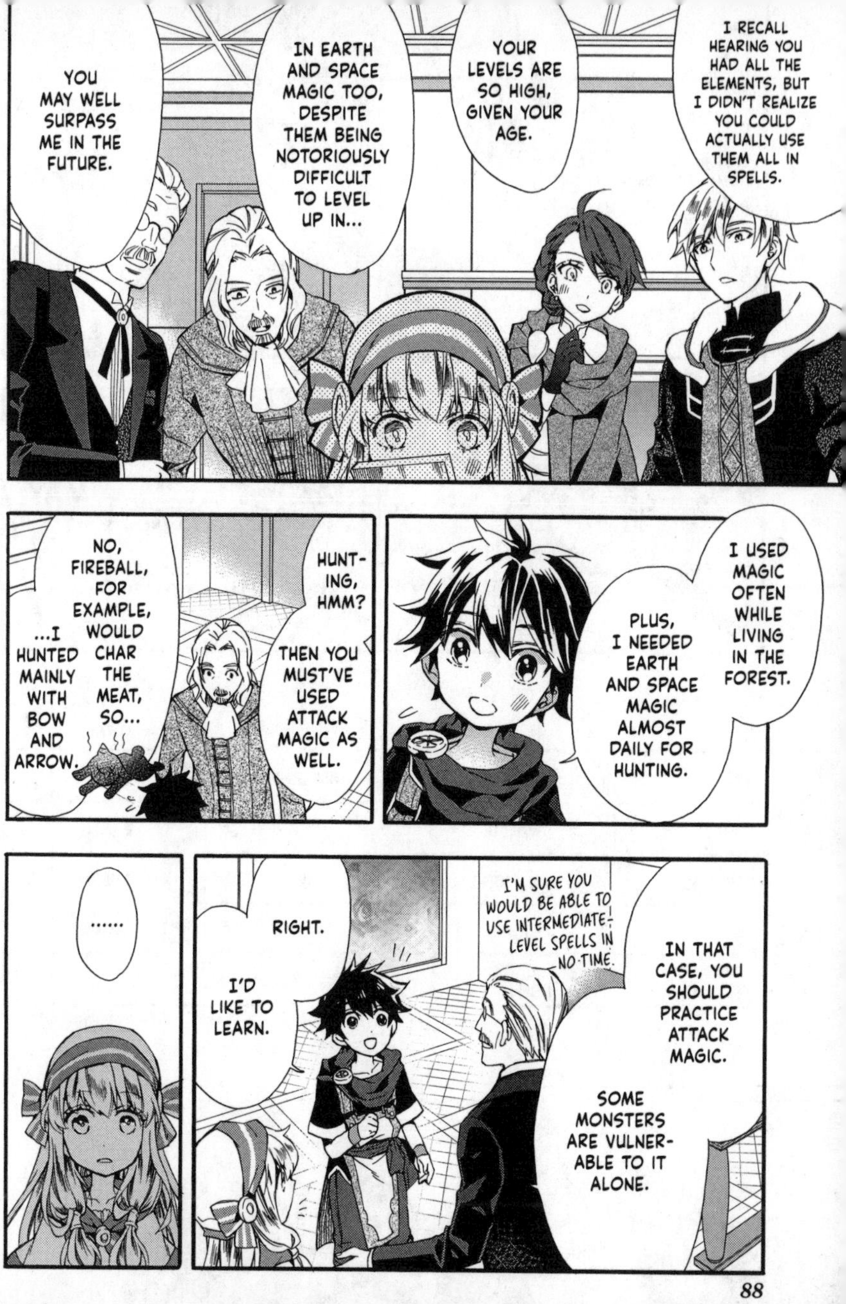
I RECALL HEARING YOU HAD ALL THE ELEMENTS, BUT I DIDN'T REALIZE YOU COULD ACTUALLY USE THEM ALL IN SPELLS.
YOUR LEVELS ARE SO HIGH, GIVEN YOUR AGE.
IN EARTH AND SPACE MAGIC TOO, DESPITE THEM BEING NOTORIOUSLY DIFFICULT TO LEVEL UP IN...
YOU MAY WELL SURPASS ME IN THE FUTURE.
I USED MAGIC OFTEN WHILE LIVING IN THE FOREST.
PLUS, I NEEDED EARTH AND SPACE MAGIC ALMOST DAILY FOR HUNTING.
HUNTING, HMM?
THEN YOU MUST'VE USED ATTACK MAGIC AS WELL.
NO, FIREBALL, FOR EXAMPLE, WOULD CHAR THE MEAT, SO...
...I HUNTED MAINLY WITH BOW AND ARROW.
IN THAT CASE, YOU SHOULD PRACTICE ATTACK MAGIC.
SOME MONSTERS ARE VULNERABLE TO IT ALONE.
I'M SURE YOU WOULD BE ABLE TO USE INTERMEDIATE-LEVEL SPELLS IN NO TIME.
RIGHT.
I'D LIKE TO LEARN.
......

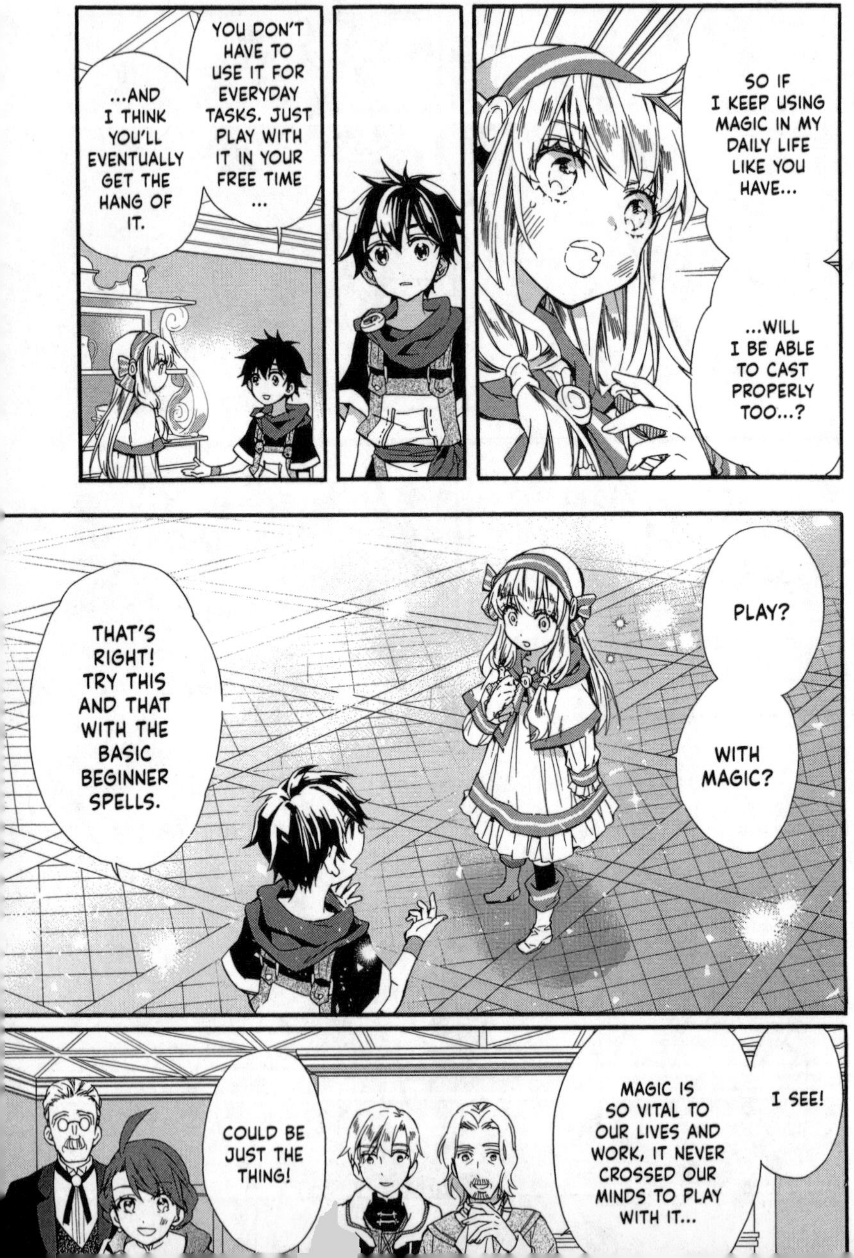
SO IF I KEEP USING MAGIC IN MY DAILY LIFE LIKE YOU HAVE...
...WILL I BE ABLE TO CAST PROPERLY TOO...?
YOU DON'T HAVE TO USE IT FOR EVERYDAY TASKS. JUST PLAY WITH IT IN YOUR FREE TIME ...
...AND I THINK YOU'LL EVENTUALLY GET THE HANG OF IT.
PLAY?
WITH MAGIC?
THAT'S RIGHT! TRY THIS AND THAT WITH THE BASIC BEGINNER SPELLS.
I SEE!
MAGIC IS SO VITAL TO OUR LIVES AND WORK, IT NEVER CROSSED OUR MINDS TO PLAY WITH IT...
COULD BE JUST THE THING!

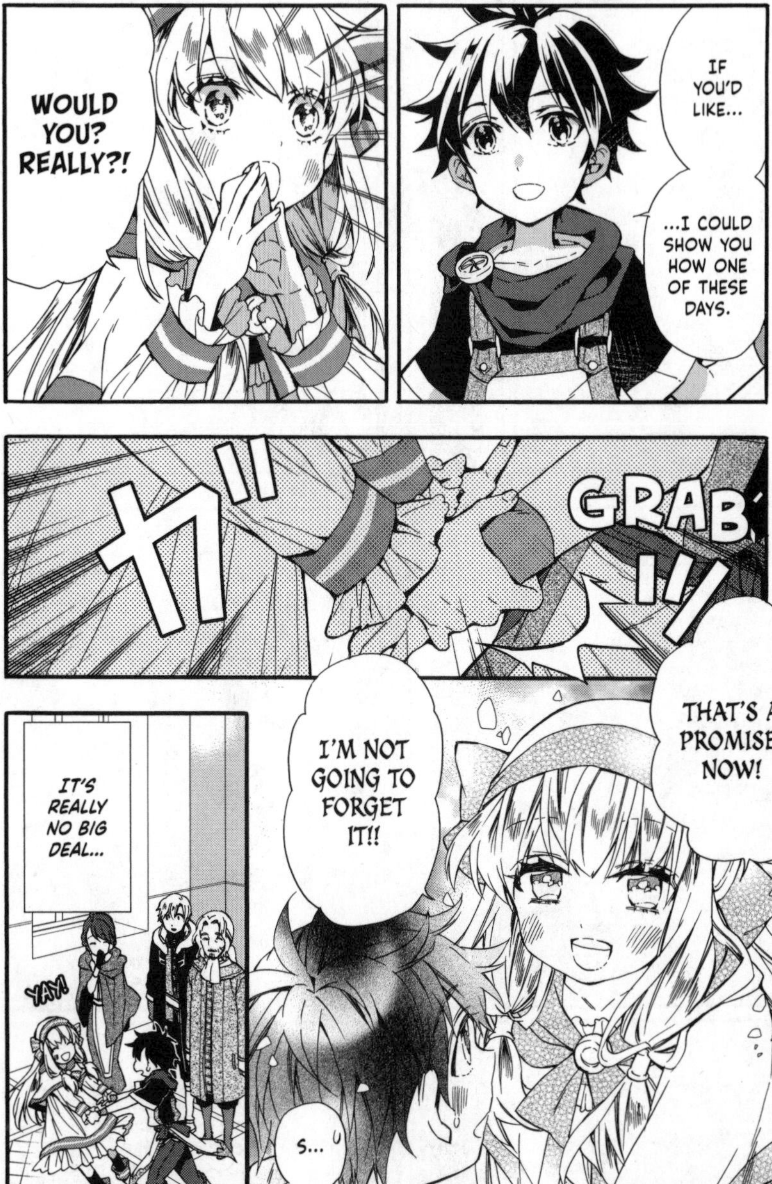
IF YOU'D LIKE...
...I COULD SHOW YOU HOW ONE OF THESE DAYS.
WOULD YOU? REALLY?!
GRAB
ガッ
THAT'S A PROMISE, NOW!
I'M NOT GOING TO FORGET IT!!
S...
SURE...
IT'S REALLY NO BIG DEAL...
YAY!

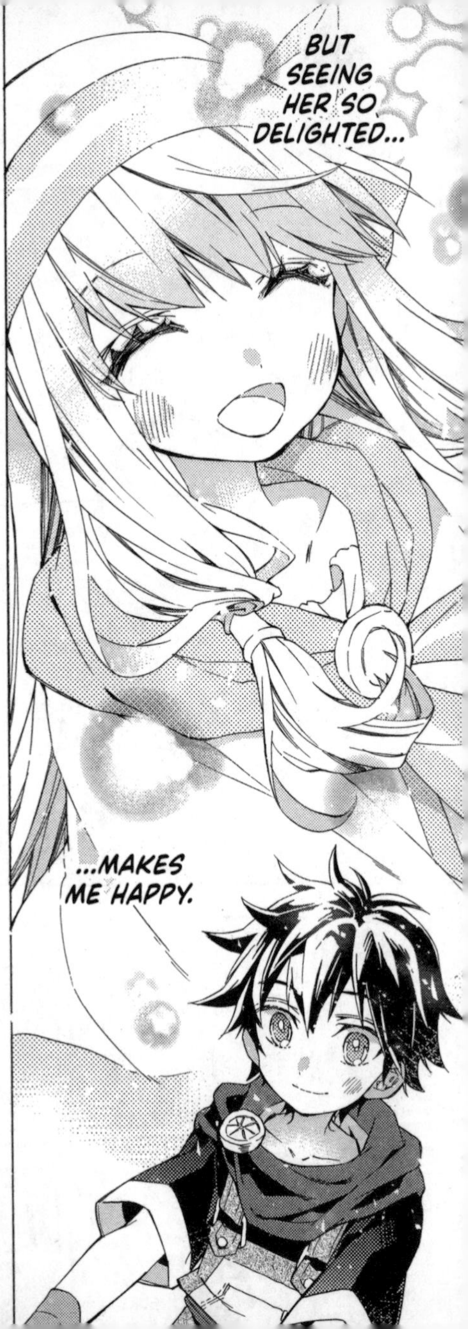
BUT SEEING HER SO DELIGHTED...
...MAKES ME HAPPY.

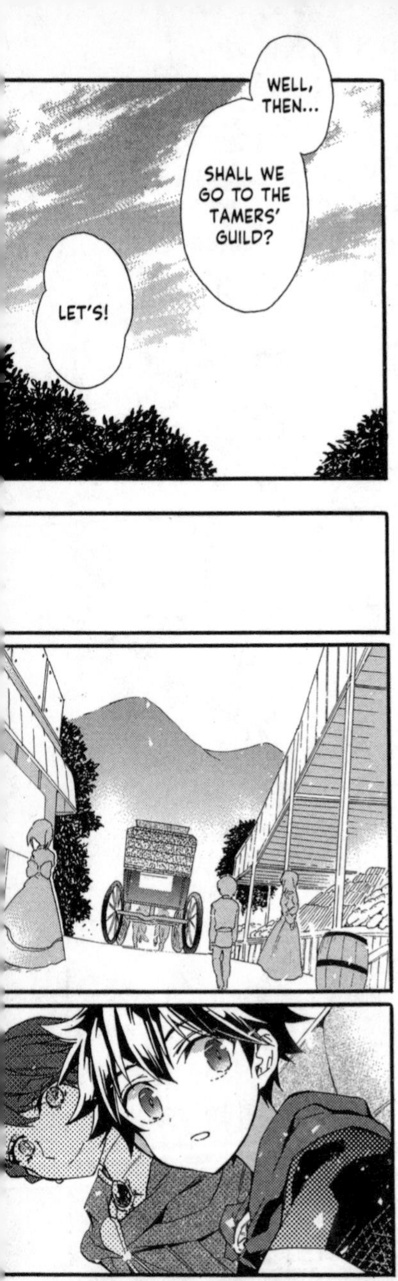
WELL, THEN...
SHALL WE GO TO THE TAMERS' GUILD?
LET'S!

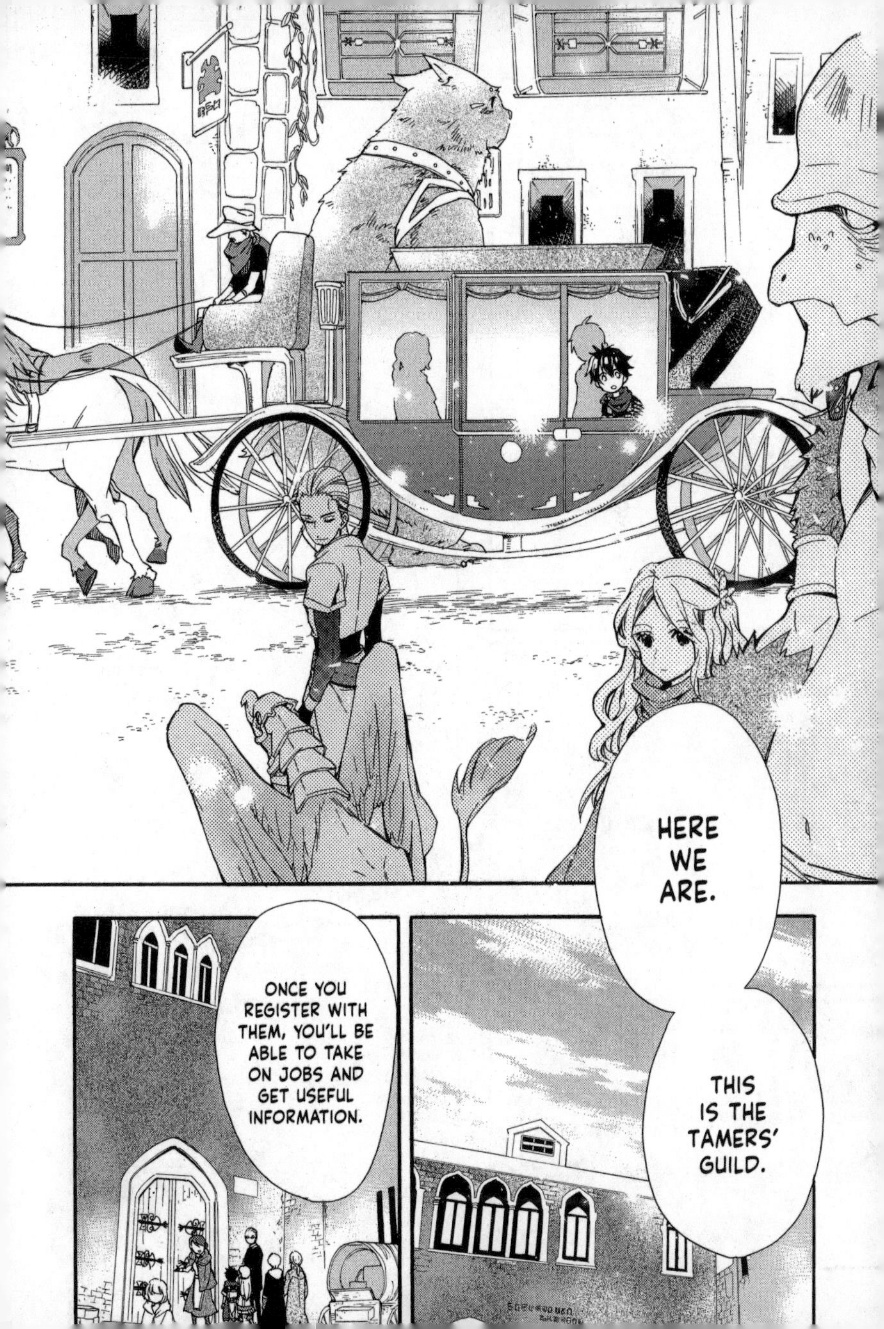
HERE WE ARE.
THIS IS THE TAMERS' GUILD.
ONCE YOU REGISTER WITH THEM, YOU'LL BE ABLE TO TAKE ON JOBS AND GET USEFUL INFORMATION.

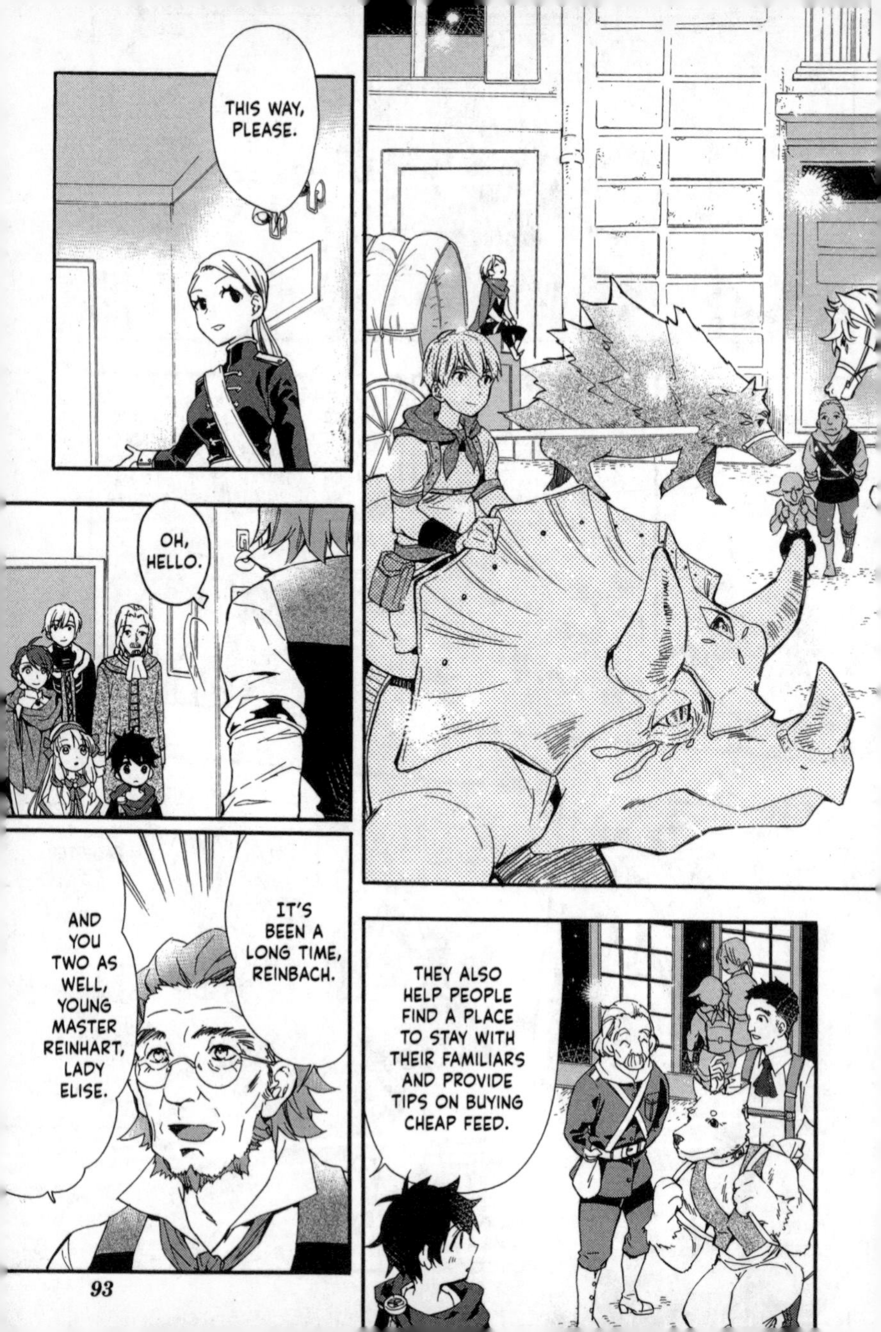
THIS WAY, PLEASE.
OH, HELLO.
THEY ALSO HELP PEOPLE FIND A PLACE TO STAY WITH THEIR FAMILIARS AND PROVIDE TIPS ON BUYING CHEAP FEED.
IT'S BEEN A LONG TIME, REINBACH.
AND YOU TWO AS WELL, YOUNG MASTER REINHART, LADY ELISE.

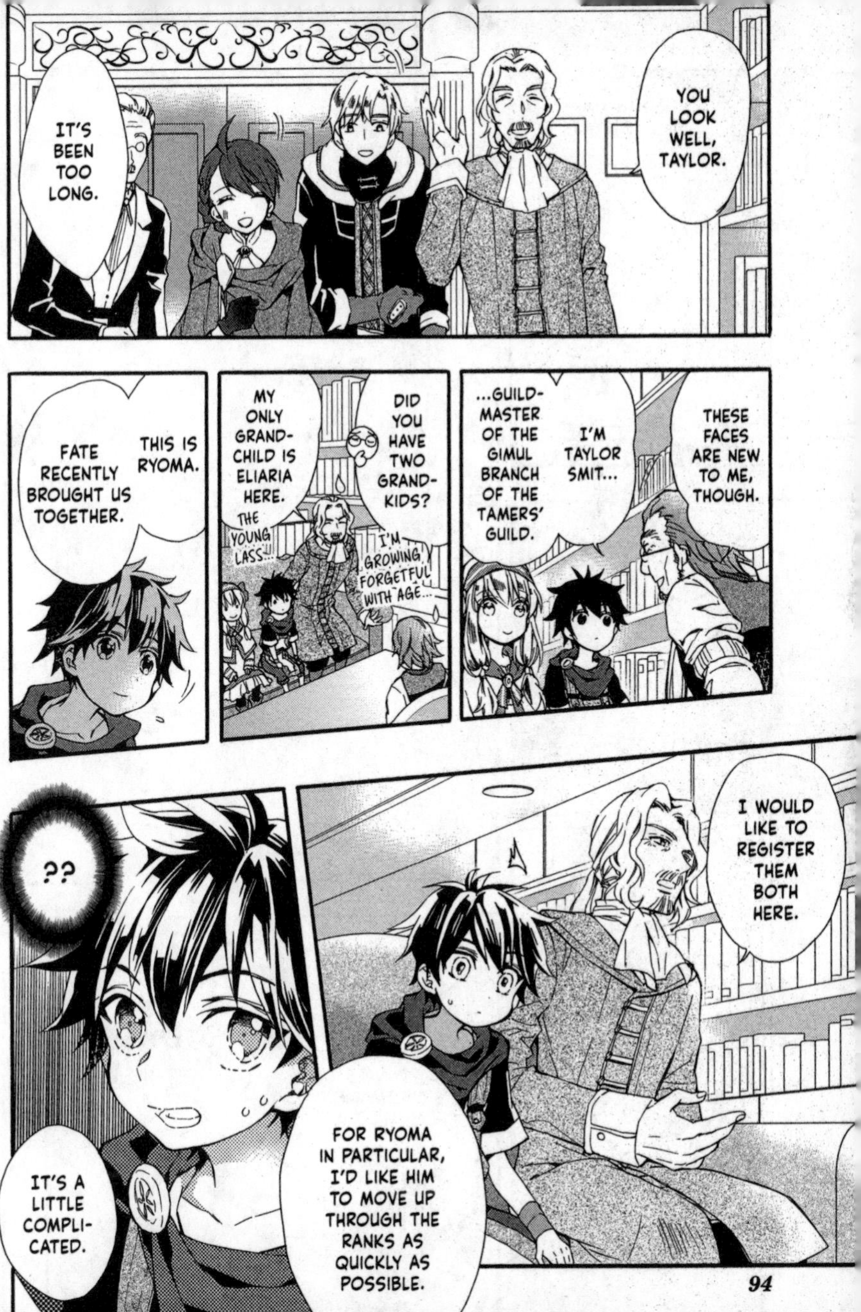
YOU LOOK WELL, TAYLOR.
IT'S BEEN TOO LONG.
THESE FACES ARE NEW TO ME, THOUGH.
I'M TAYLOR SMIT...
...GUILD-MASTER OF THE GIMUL BRANCH OF THE TAMERS' GUILD.
DID YOU HAVE TWO GRAND-KIDS?
MY ONLY GRAND-CHILD IS ELIARIA HERE.
THE YOUNG LASS...
I'M GROWING FORGETFUL WITH AGE...
THIS IS RYOMA.
FATE RECENTLY BROUGHT US TOGETHER.
I WOULD LIKE TO REGISTER THEM BOTH HERE.
FOR RYOMA IN PARTICULAR, I'D LIKE HIM TO MOVE UP THROUGH THE RANKS AS QUICKLY AS POSSIBLE.
??
IT'S A LITTLE COMPLICATED.

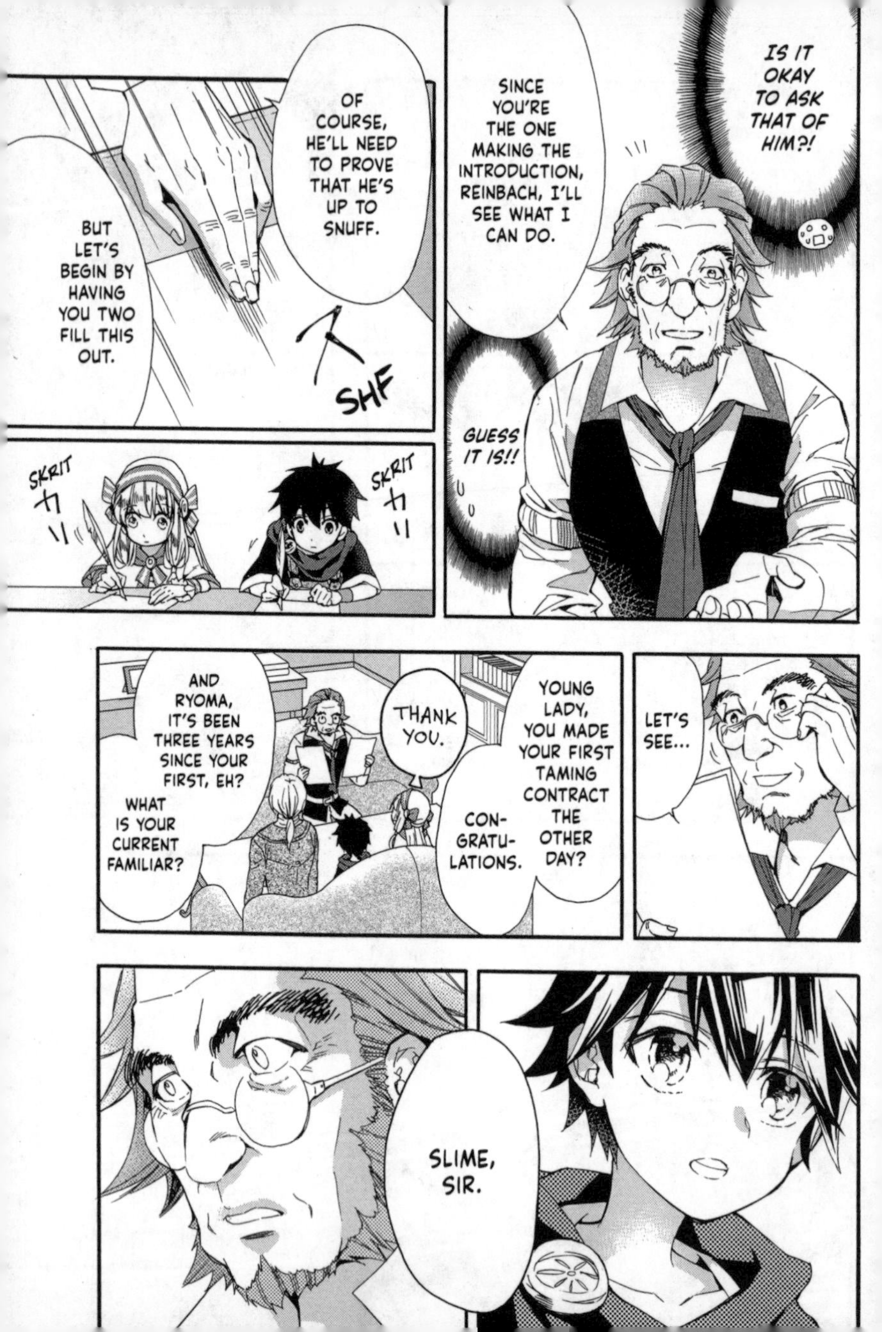
IS IT OKAY TO ASK THAT OF HIM?!
SINCE YOU'RE THE ONE MAKING THE INTRODUCTION, REINBACH, I'LL SEE WHAT I CAN DO.
GUESS IT IS!!
OF COURSE, HE'LL NEED TO PROVE THAT HE'S UP TO SNUFF.
BUT LET'S BEGIN BY HAVING YOU TWO FILL THIS OUT.
SHF
SKRIT
SKRIT
LET'S SEE...
YOUNG LADY, YOU MADE YOUR FIRST TAMING CONTRACT THE OTHER DAY?
CON-GRATU-LATIONS.
THANK YOU.
AND RYOMA, IT'S BEEN THREE YEARS SINCE YOUR FIRST, EH?
WHAT IS YOUR CURRENT FAMILIAR?
SLIME, SIR.

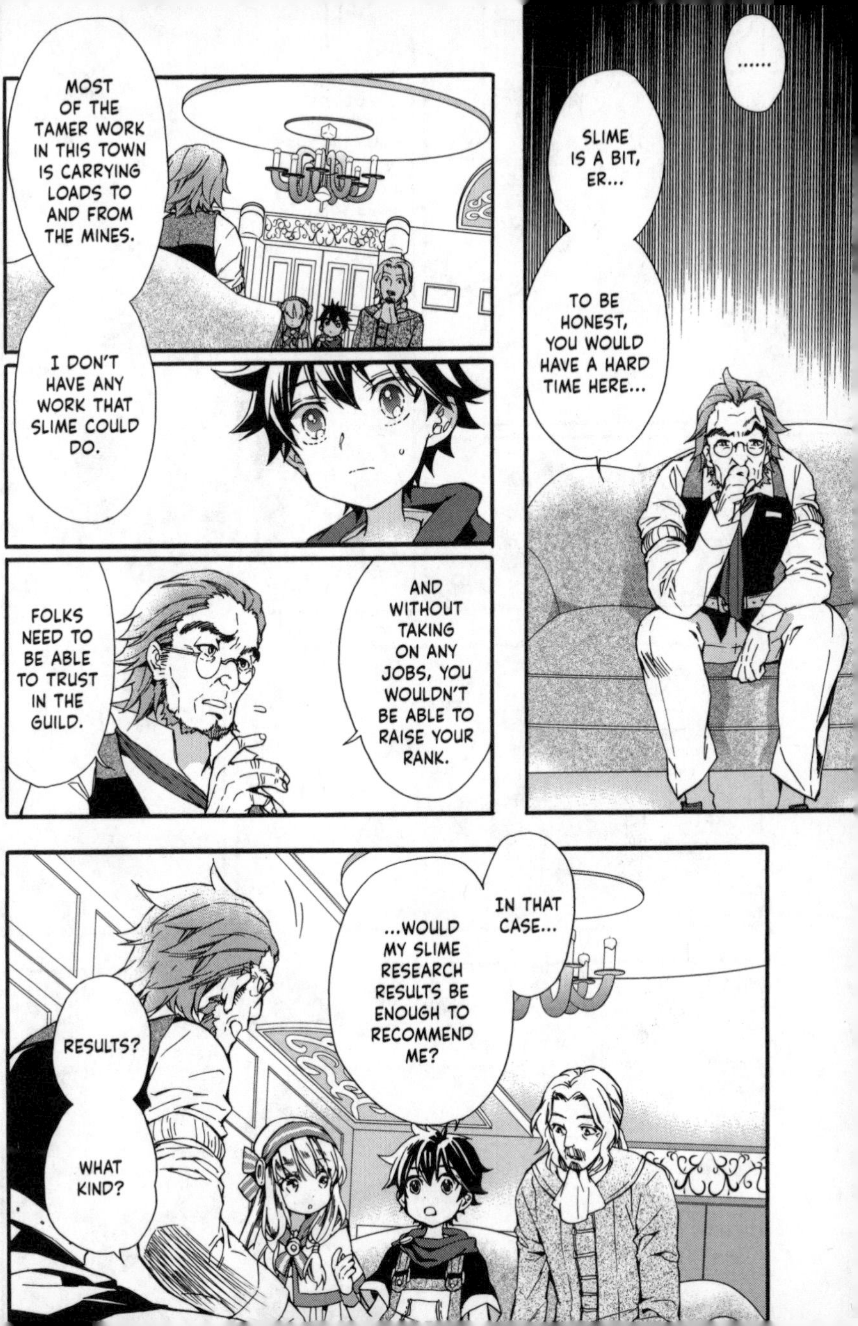

......
SLIME IS A BIT, ER...
TO BE HONEST, YOU WOULD HAVE A HARD TIME HERE...
MOST OF THE TAMER WORK IN THIS TOWN IS CARRYING LOADS TO AND FROM THE MINES.
I DON'T HAVE ANY WORK THAT SLIME COULD DO.
AND WITHOUT TAKING ON ANY JOBS, YOU WOULDN'T BE ABLE TO RAISE YOUR RANK.
FOLKS NEED TO BE ABLE TO TRUST IN THE GUILD.
IN THAT CASE...
...WOULD MY SLIME RESEARCH RESULTS BE ENOUGH TO RECOMMEND ME?
RESULTS?
WHAT KIND?

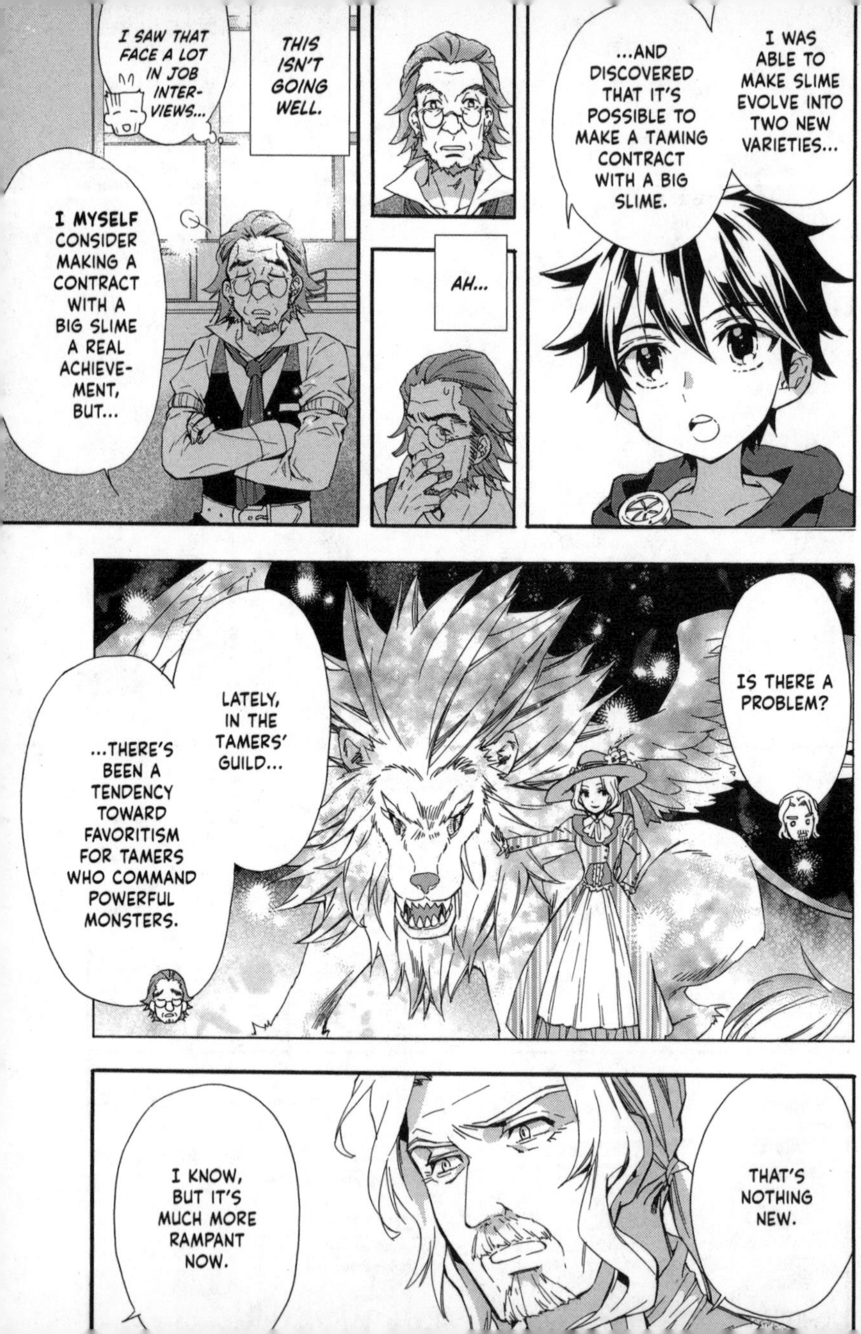
I WAS ABLE TO MAKE SLIME EVOLVE INTO TWO NEW VARIETIES...
...AND DISCOVERED THAT IT'S POSSIBLE TO MAKE A TAMING CONTRACT WITH A BIG SLIME.
AH...
THIS ISN'T GOING WELL.
I SAW THAT FACE A LOT IN JOB INTERVIEWS...
I MYSELF CONSIDER MAKING A CONTRACT WITH A BIG SLIME A REAL ACHIEVEMENT, BUT...
IS THERE A PROBLEM?
LATELY, IN THE TAMERS' GUILD...
...THERE'S BEEN A TENDENCY TOWARD FAVORITISM FOR TAMERS WHO COMMAND POWERFUL MONSTERS.
THAT'S NOTHING NEW.
I KNOW, BUT IT'S MUCH MORE RAMPANT NOW.

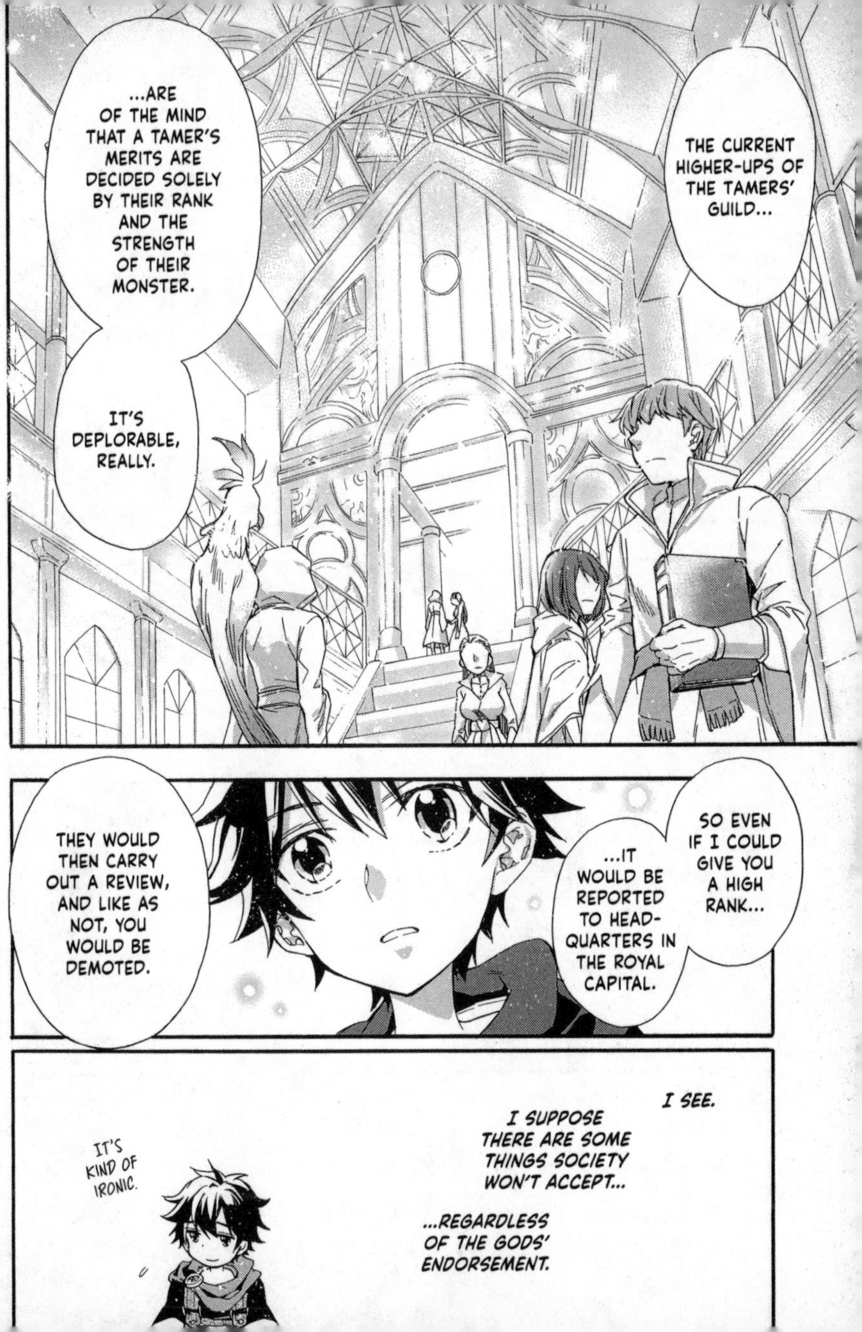
THE CURRENT HIGHER-UPS OF THE TAMERS' GUILD...
...ARE OF THE MIND THAT A TAMER'S MERITS ARE DECIDED SOLELY BY THEIR RANK AND THE STRENGTH OF THEIR MONSTER.
IT'S DEPLORABLE, REALLY.
SO EVEN IF I COULD GIVE YOU A HIGH RANK...
...IT WOULD BE REPORTED TO HEAD-QUARTERS IN THE ROYAL CAPITAL.
THEY WOULD THEN CARRY OUT A REVIEW, AND LIKE AS NOT, YOU WOULD BE DEMOTED.
I SEE.
I SUPPOSE THERE ARE SOME THINGS SOCIETY WON'T ACCEPT...
...REGARDLESS OF THE GODS' ENDORSEMENT.
IT'S KIND OF IRONIC.

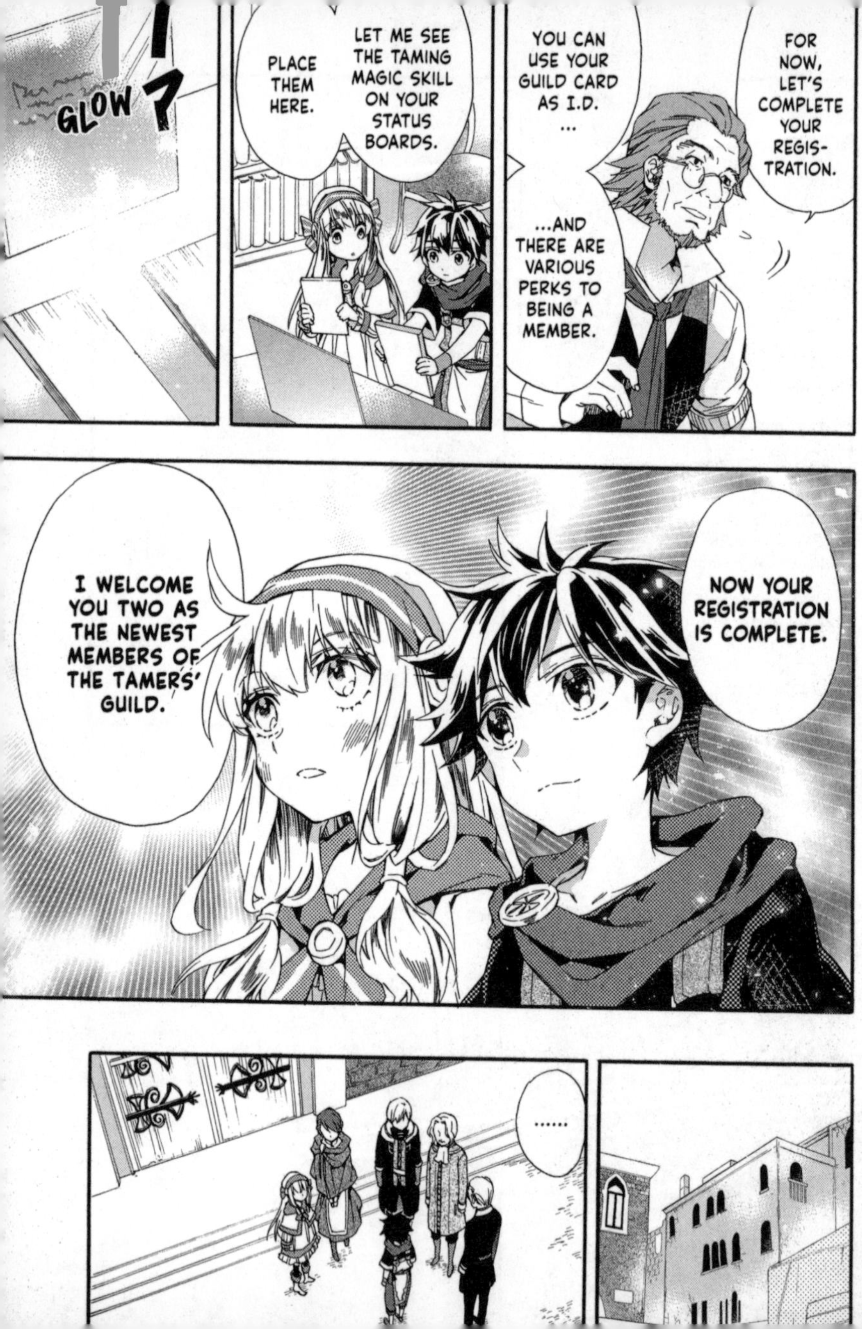
FOR NOW, LET'S COMPLETE YOUR REGISTRATION.
YOU CAN USE YOUR GUILD CARD AS I.D. ...
...AND THERE ARE VARIOUS PERKS TO BEING A MEMBER.
LET ME SEE THE TAMING MAGIC SKILL ON YOUR STATUS BOARDS.
PLACE THEM HERE.
GLOW
NOW YOUR REGISTRATION IS COMPLETE.
I WELCOME YOU TWO AS THE NEWEST MEMBERS OF THE TAMERS' GUILD.
......

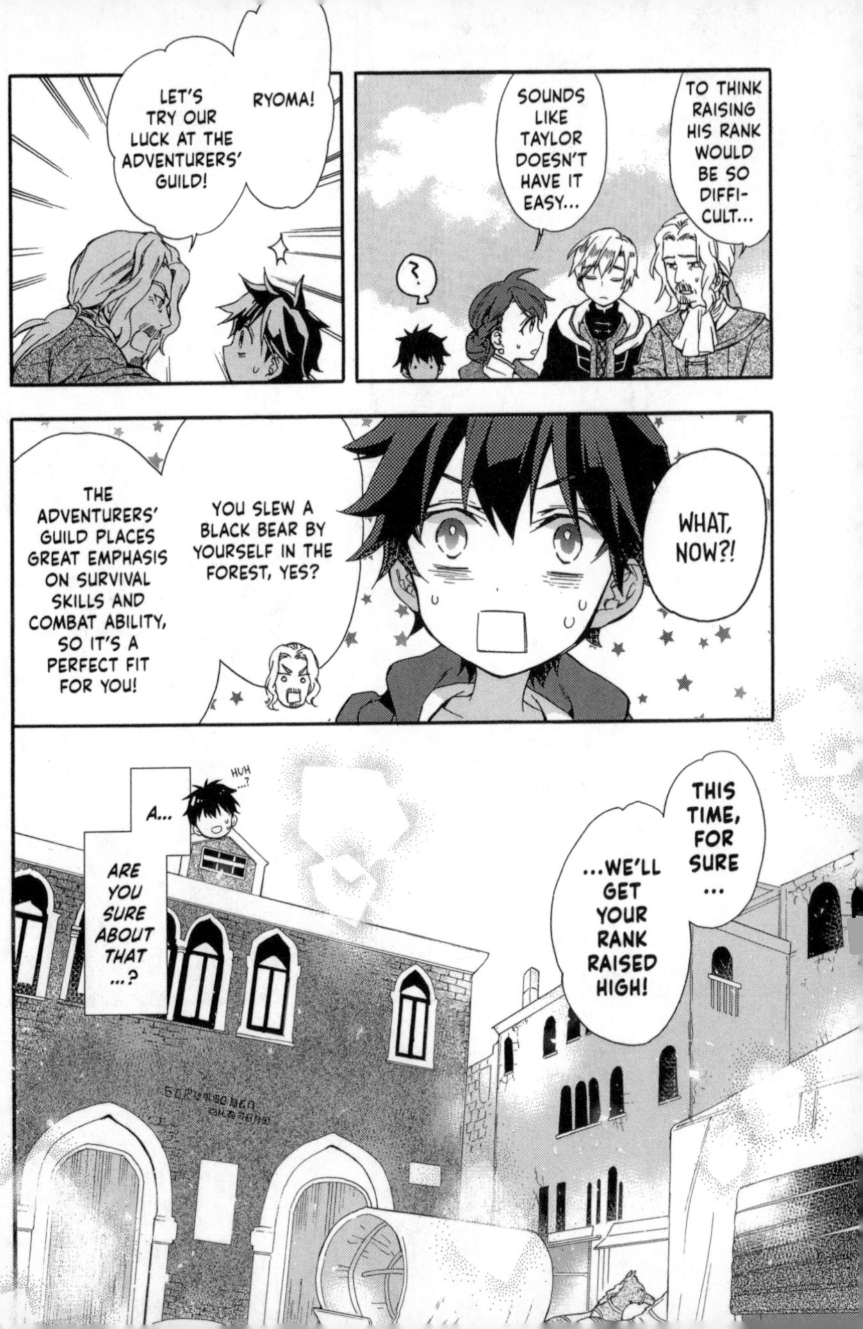
TO THINK RAISING HIS RANK WOULD BE SO DIFFI-CULT...
SOUNDS LIKE TAYLOR DOESN'T HAVE IT EASY...
?
RYOMA!
LET'S TRY OUR LUCK AT THE ADVENTURERS' GUILD!
WHAT, NOW?!
YOU SLEW A BLACK BEAR BY YOURSELF IN THE FOREST, YES?
THE ADVENTURERS' GUILD PLACES GREAT EMPHASIS ON SURVIVAL SKILLS AND COMBAT ABILITY, SO IT'S A PERFECT FIT FOR YOU!
THIS TIME, FOR SURE...
...WE'LL GET YOUR RANK RAISED HIGH!
HUH ...?
A...
ARE YOU SURE ABOUT THAT ...?

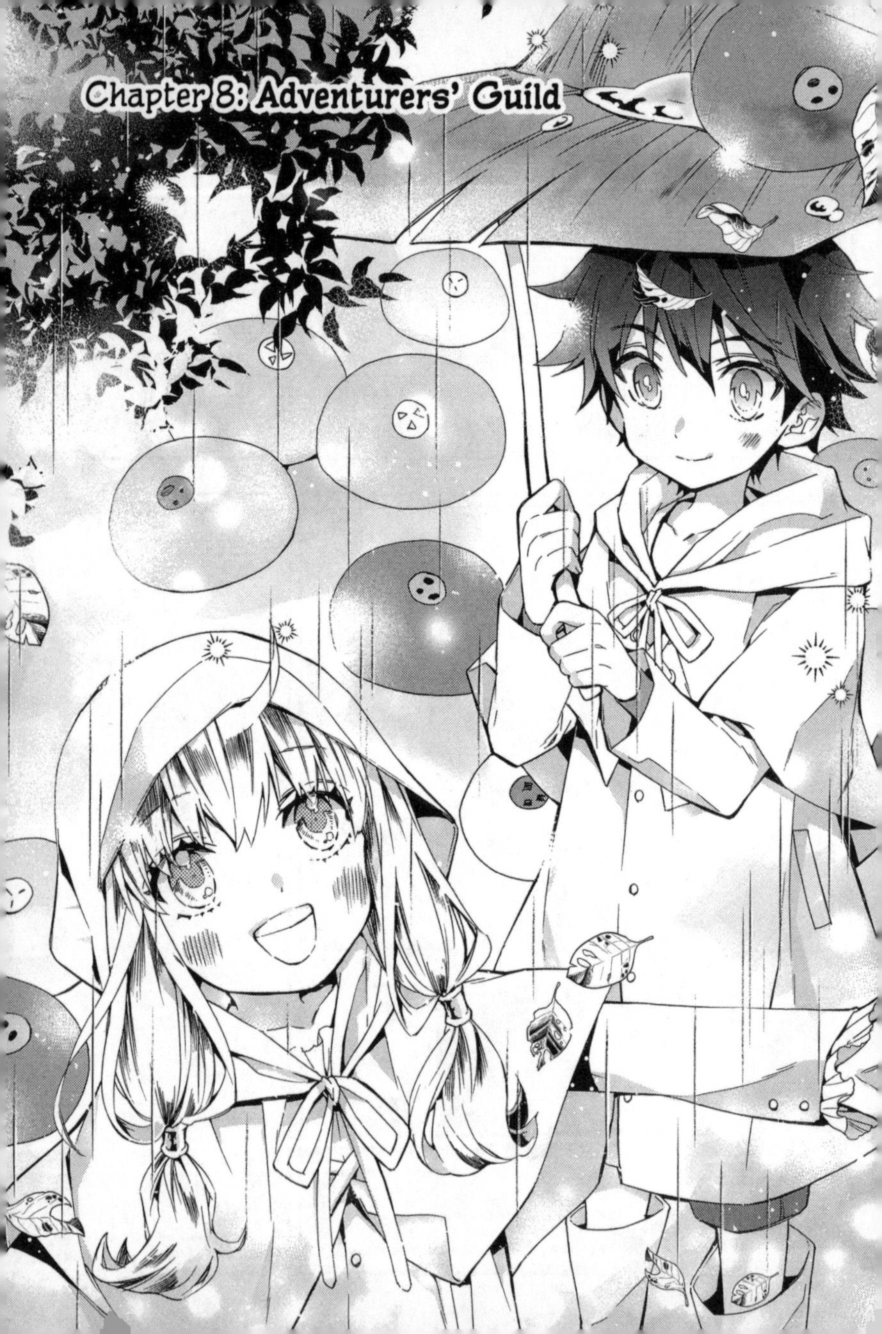
Chapter 8: Adventurers' Guild

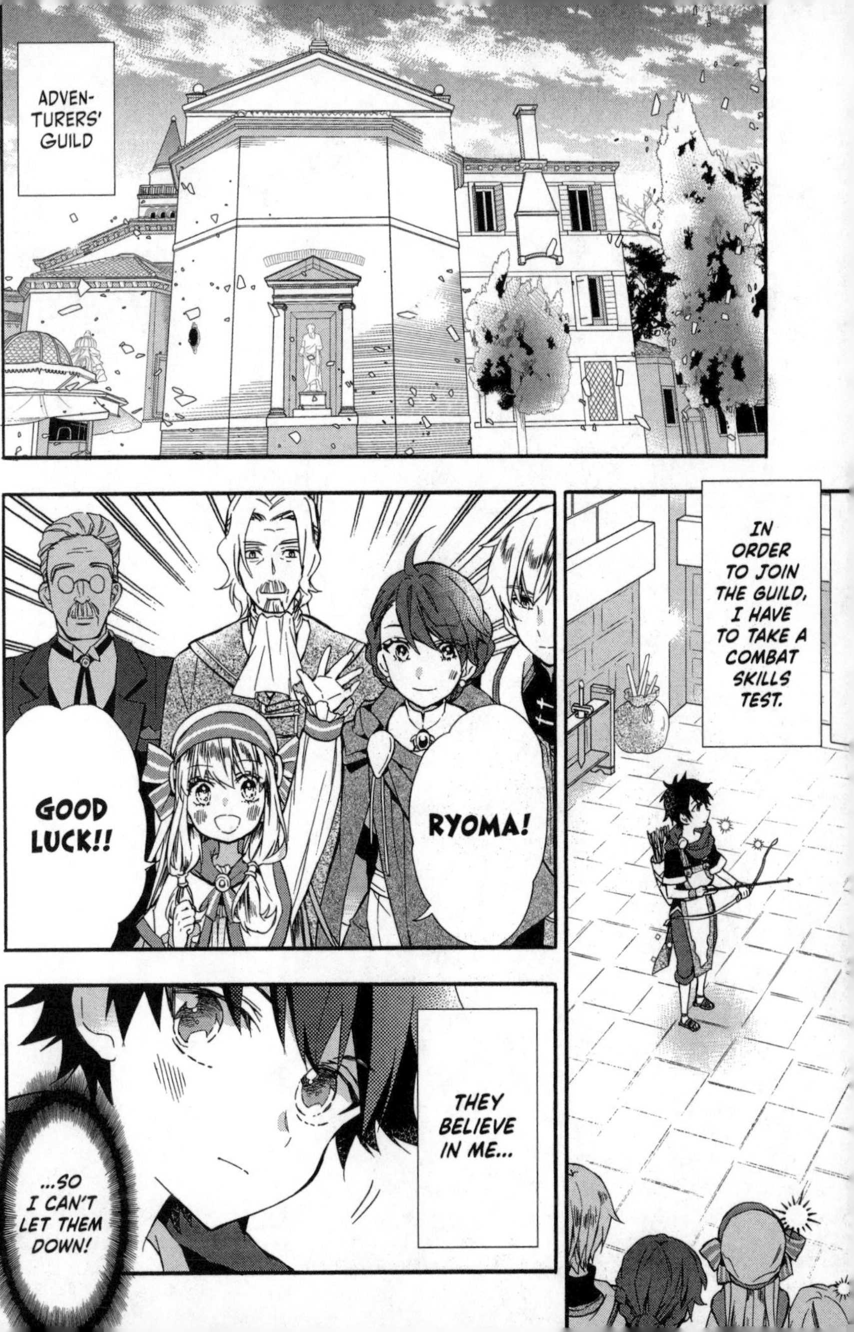
ADVEN-TURERS' GUILD
IN ORDER TO JOIN THE GUILD, I HAVE TO TAKE A COMBAT SKILLS TEST.
RYOMA!
GOOD LUCK!!
THEY BELIEVE IN ME...
...SO I CAN'T LET THEM DOWN!

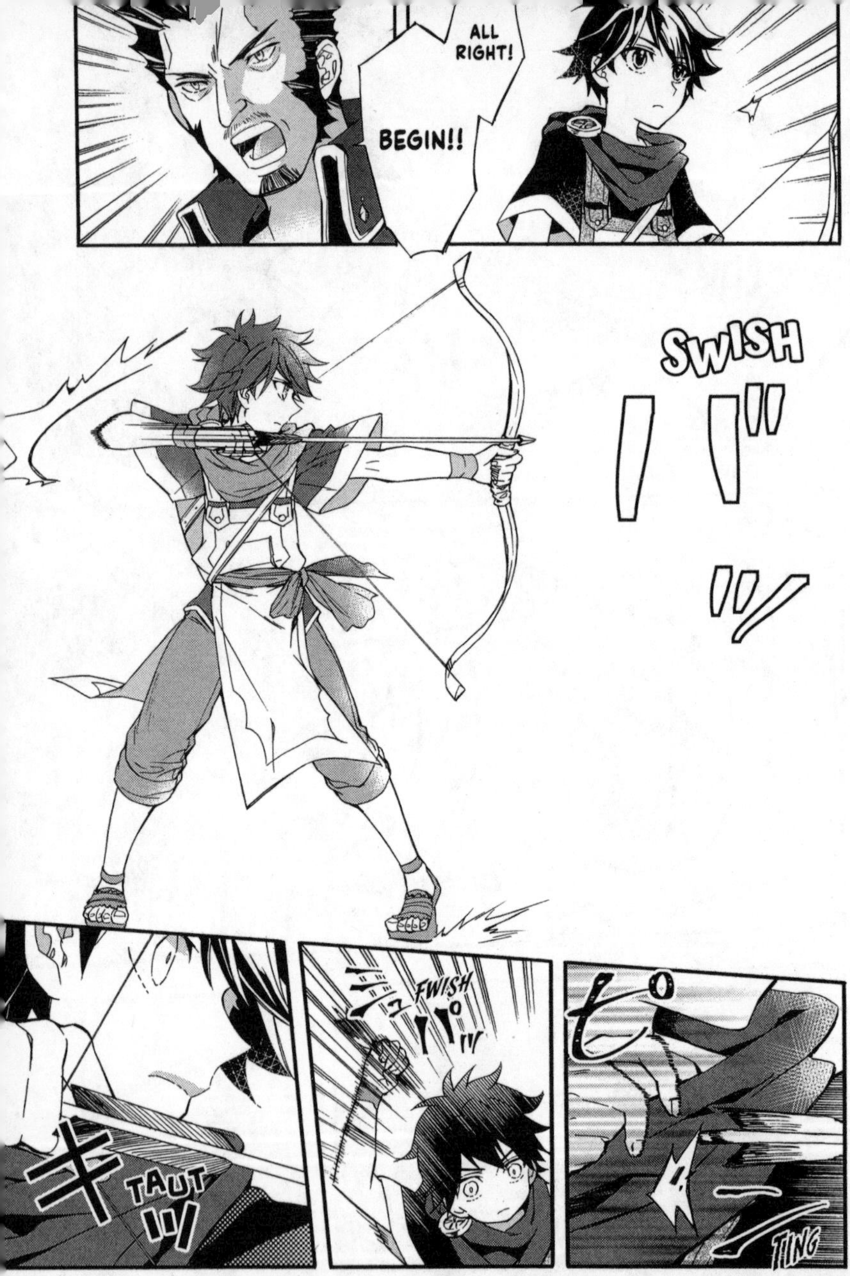
ALL RIGHT!
BEGIN!!
SWISH
TING
FWISH
TAUT

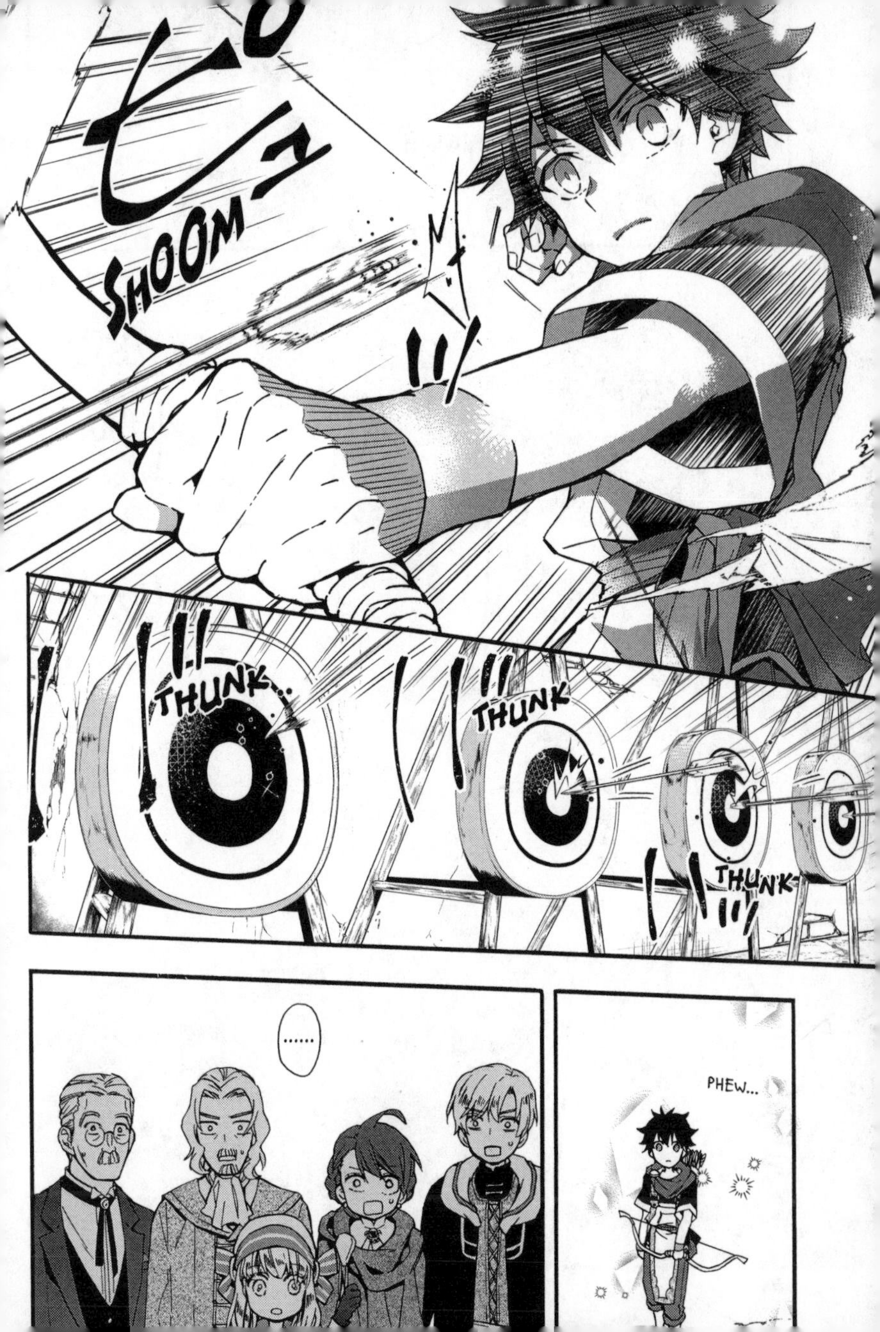
SHOOM
THUNK
THUNK
THUNK...
PHEW...
......

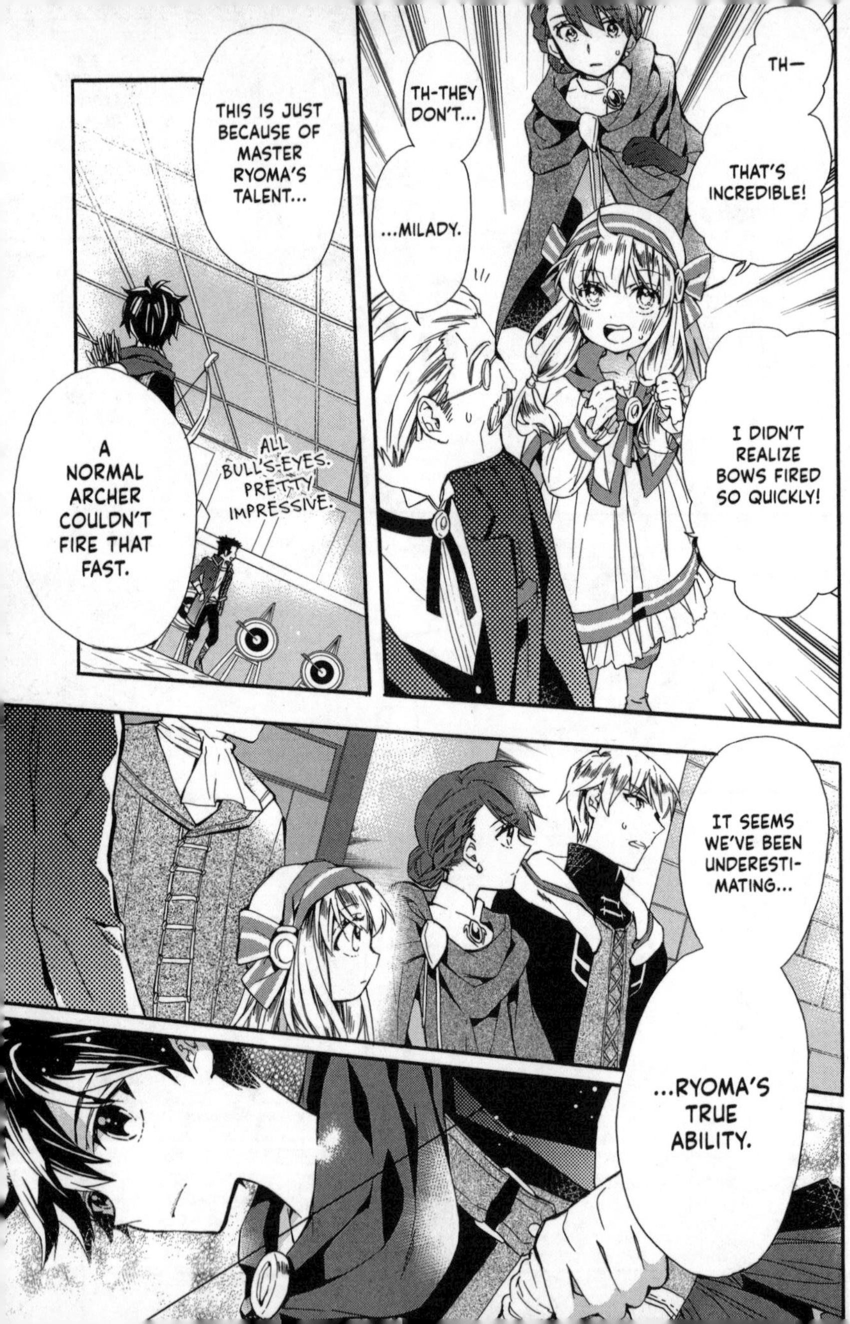
TH—
THAT'S INCREDIBLE!
I DIDN'T REALIZE BOWS FIRED SO QUICKLY!
TH-THEY DON'T...
...MILADY.
THIS IS JUST BECAUSE OF MASTER RYOMA'S TALENT...
ALL BULL'S-EYES. PRETTY IMPRESSIVE.
A NORMAL ARCHER COULDN'T FIRE THAT FAST.
IT SEEMS WE'VE BEEN UNDERESTI-MATING...
...RYOMA'S TRUE ABILITY.

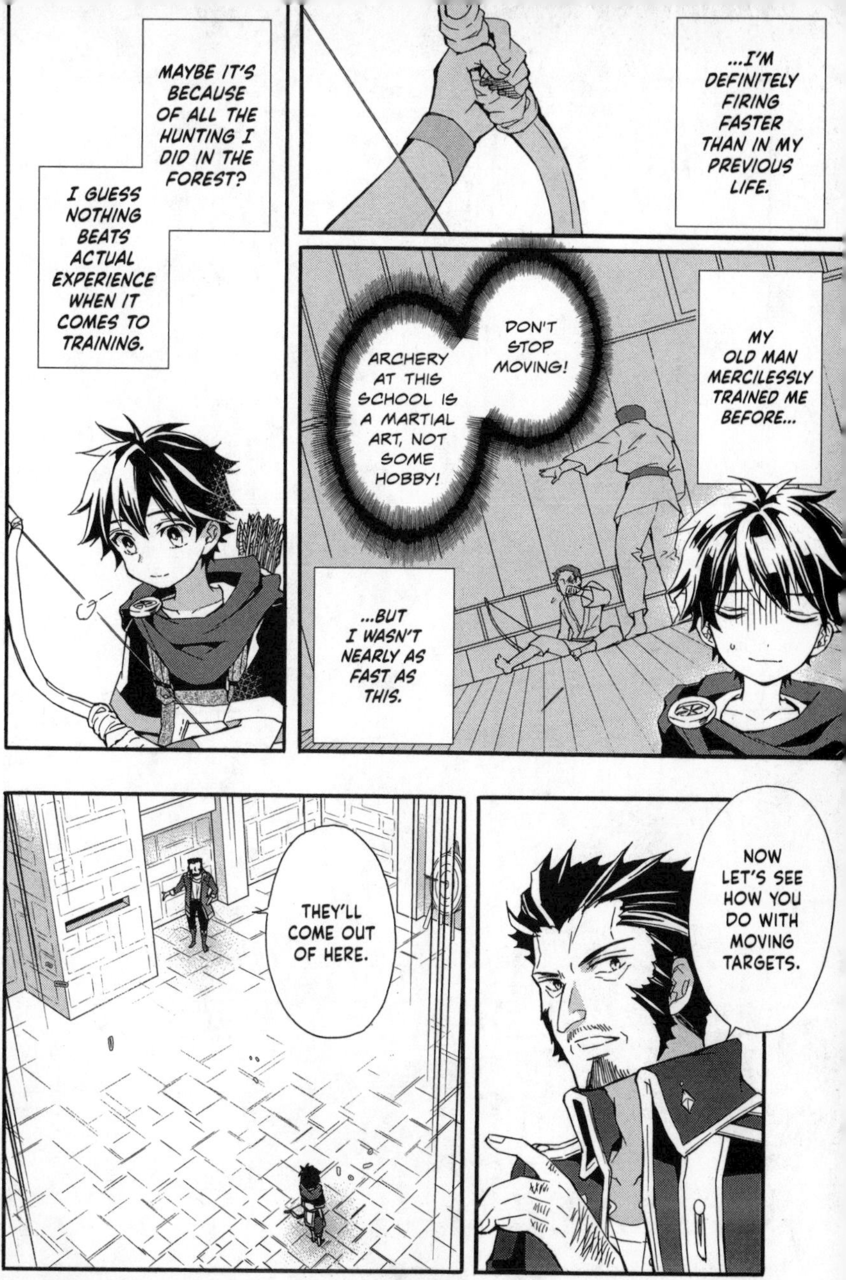
...I'M DEFINITELY FIRING FASTER THAN IN MY PREVIOUS LIFE.
MY OLD MAN MERCILESSLY TRAINED ME BEFORE...
DON'T STOP MOVING!
ARCHERY AT THIS SCHOOL IS A MARTIAL ART, NOT SOME HOBBY!
...BUT I WASN'T NEARLY AS FAST AS THIS.
MAYBE IT'S BECAUSE OF ALL THE HUNTING I DID IN THE FOREST?
I GUESS NOTHING BEATS ACTUAL EXPERIENCE WHEN IT COMES TO TRAINING.
NOW LET'S SEE HOW YOU DO WITH MOVING TARGETS.
THEY'LL COME OUT OF HERE.

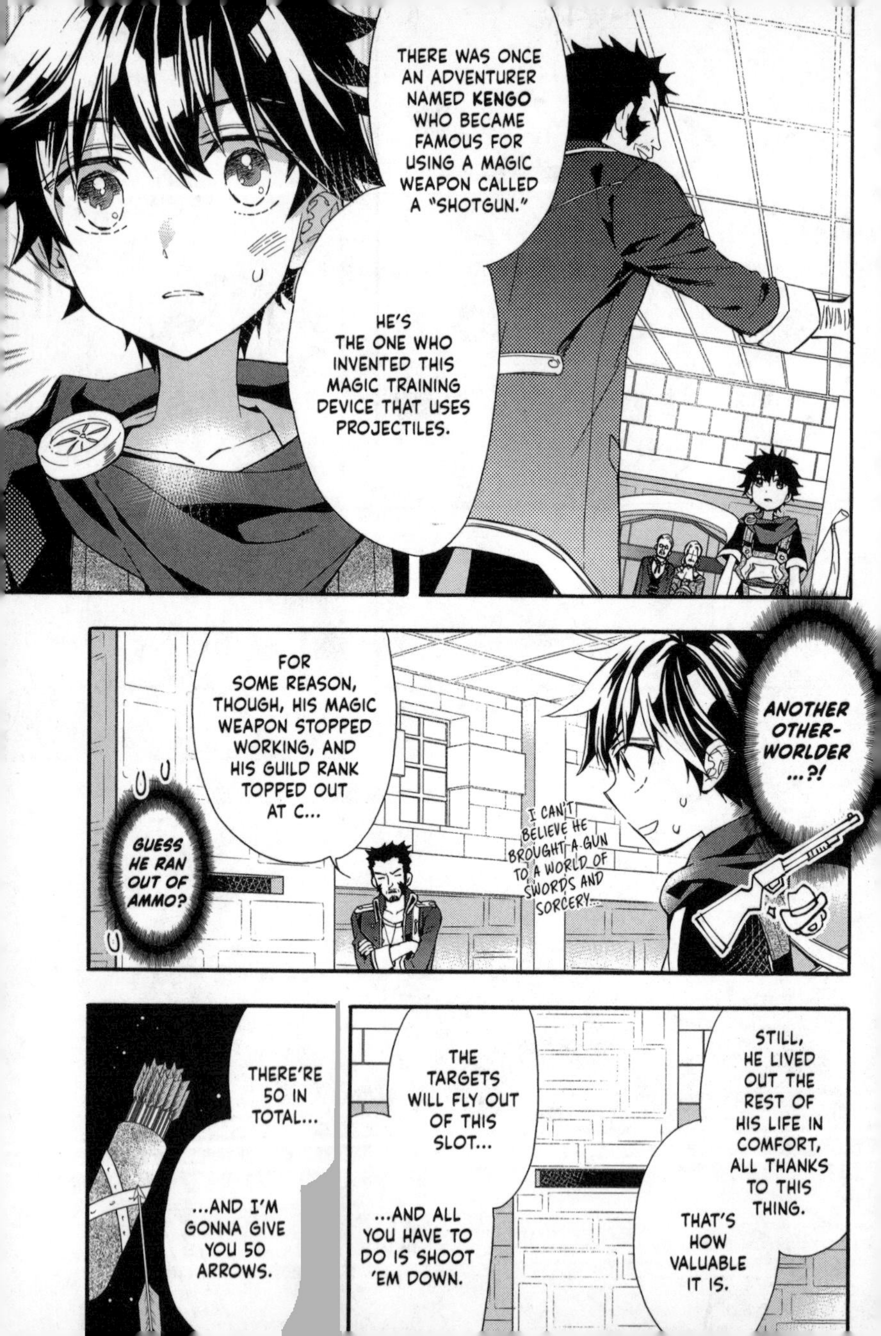
THERE WAS ONCE AN ADVENTURER NAMED KENGO WHO BECAME FAMOUS FOR USING A MAGIC WEAPON CALLED A "SHOTGUN."
HE'S THE ONE WHO INVENTED THIS MAGIC TRAINING DEVICE THAT USES PROJECTILES.
ANOTHER OTHER-WORLDER ...?!
FOR SOME REASON, THOUGH, HIS MAGIC WEAPON STOPPED WORKING, AND HIS GUILD RANK TOPPED OUT AT C...
I CAN'T BELIEVE HE BROUGHT A GUN TO A WORLD OF SWORDS AND SORCERY...
GUESS HE RAN OUT OF AMMO?
STILL, HE LIVED OUT THE REST OF HIS LIFE IN COMFORT, ALL THANKS TO THIS THING.
THAT'S HOW VALUABLE IT IS.
THE TARGETS WILL FLY OUT OF THIS SLOT...
...AND ALL YOU HAVE TO DO IS SHOOT 'EM DOWN.
THERE'RE 50 IN TOTAL...
...AND I'M GONNA GIVE YOU 50 ARROWS.

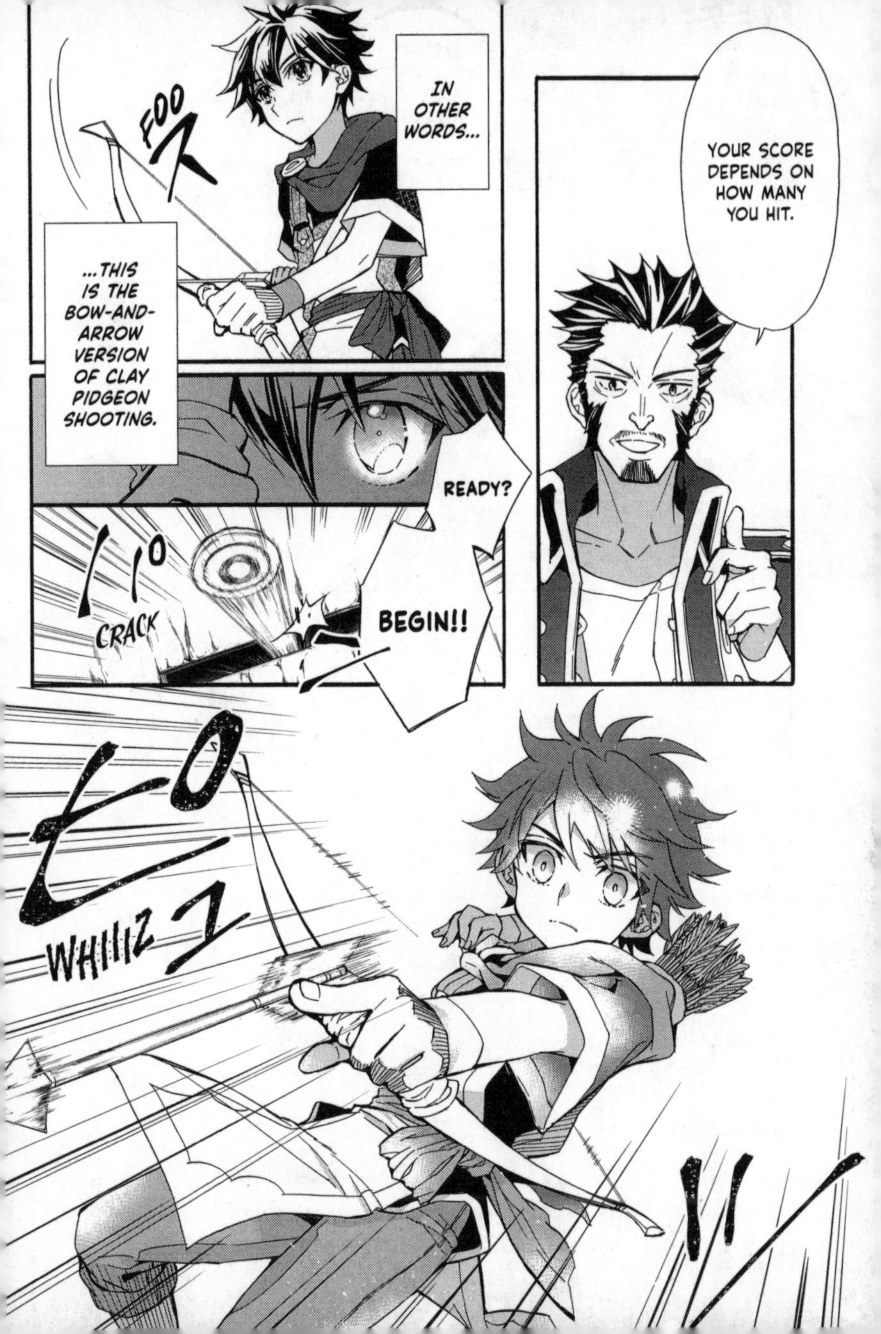
YOUR SCORE DEPENDS ON HOW MANY YOU HIT.
IN OTHER WORDS...
FOO
...THIS IS THE BOW-AND-ARROW VERSION OF CLAY PIDGEON SHOOTING.
READY?
CRACK
BEGIN!!
WHIIIZ

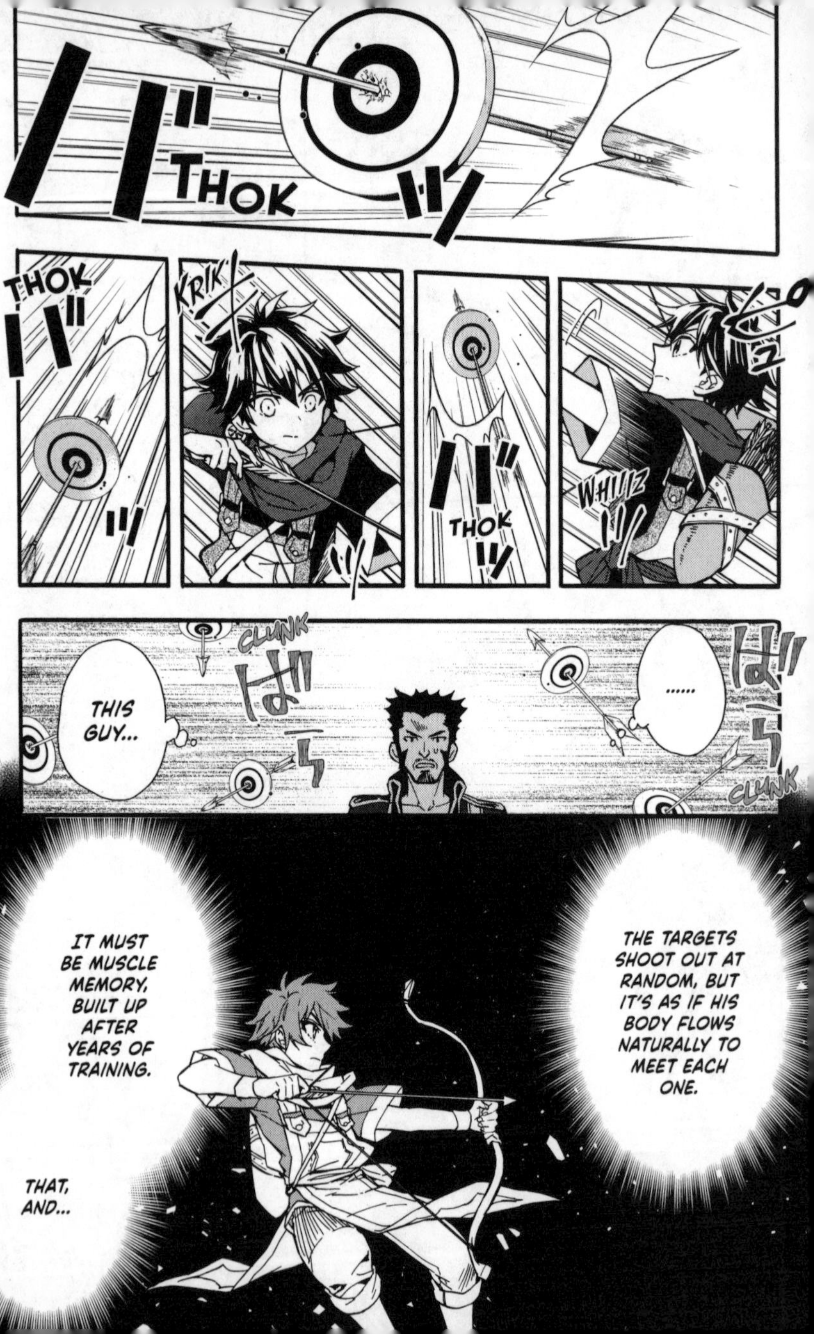
THOK
WHIIIZ
THOK
KRIK!
THOK
......
CLUNK
THIS GUY...
CLUNK
THE TARGETS SHOOT OUT AT RANDOM, BUT IT'S AS IF HIS BODY FLOWS NATURALLY TO MEET EACH ONE.
IT MUST BE MUSCLE MEMORY, BUILT UP AFTER YEARS OF TRAINING.
THAT, AND...

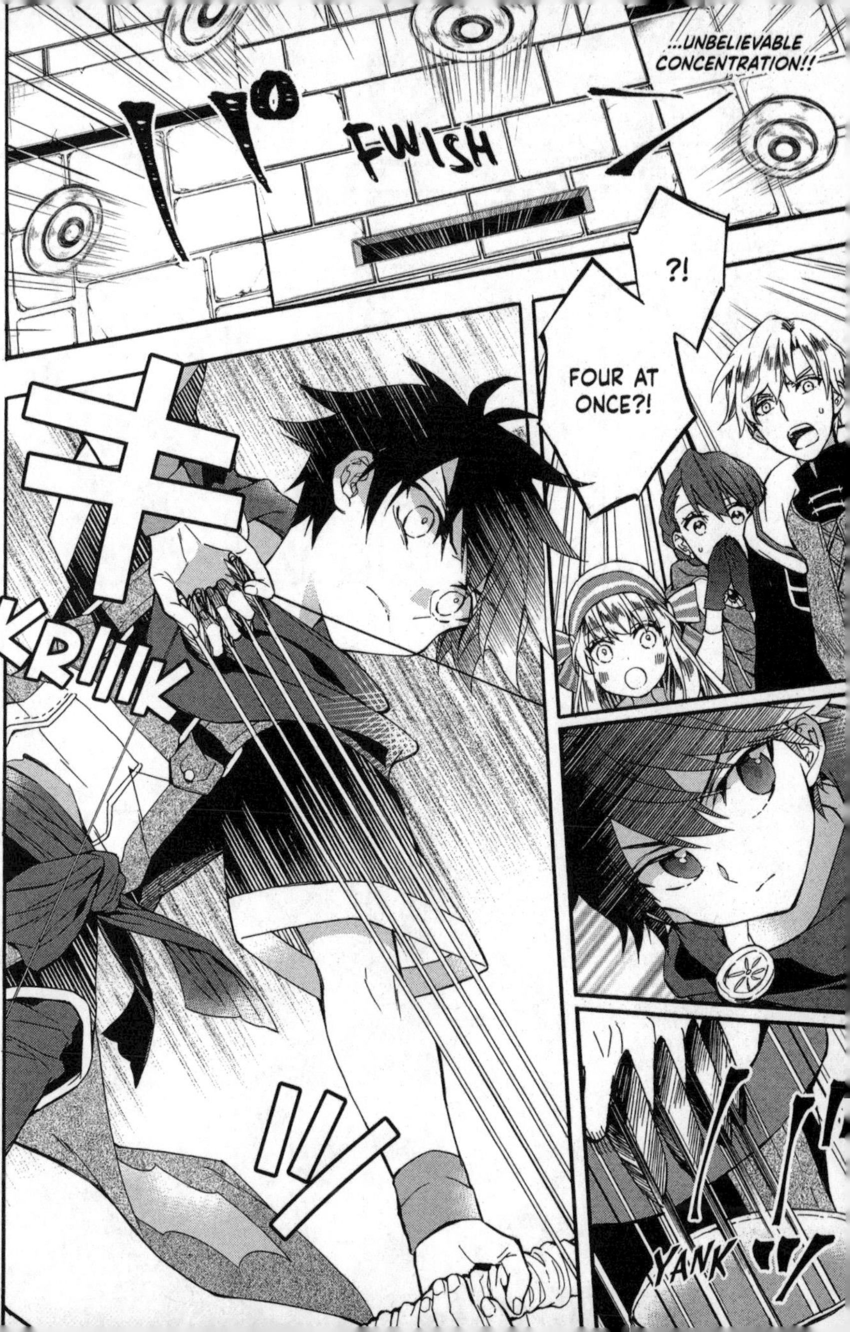
...UNBELIEVABLE CONCENTRATION!!
FWISH
?!
FOUR AT ONCE?!
KRIIIK
YANK

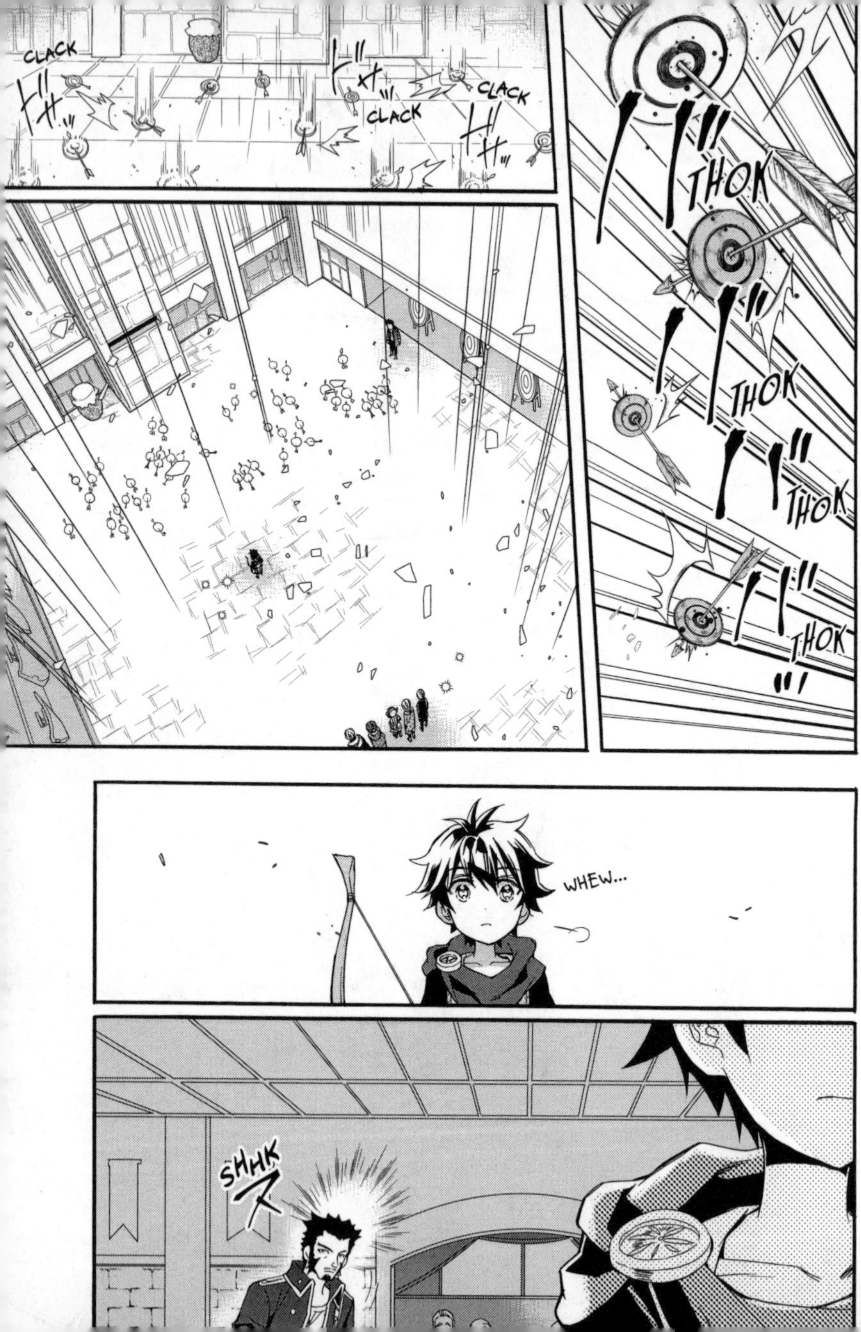
THOK
THOK
THOK
THOK
CLACK
CLACK
CLACK
WHEW...
SHHK

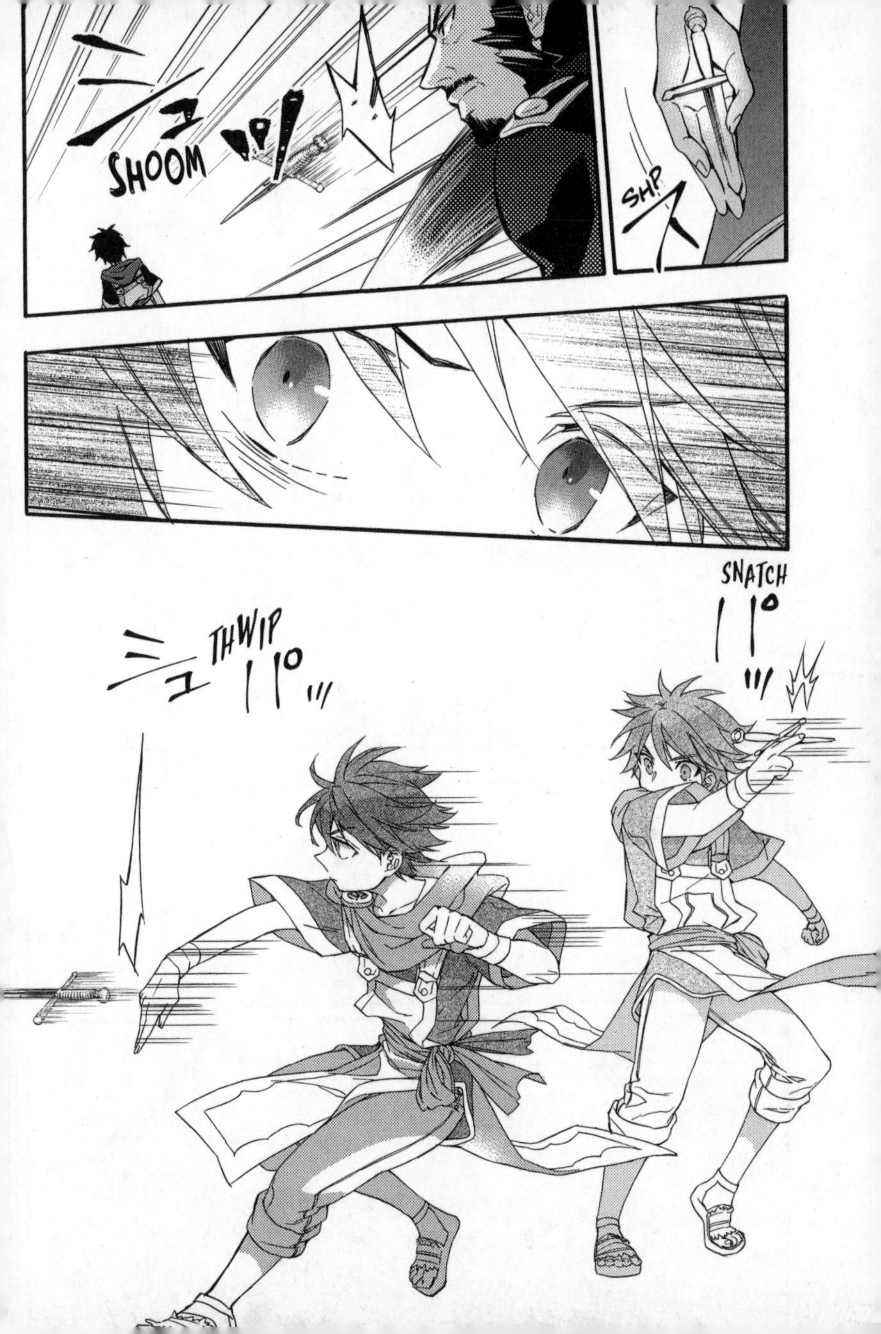
SHP
SHOOM
SNATCH
THWIP

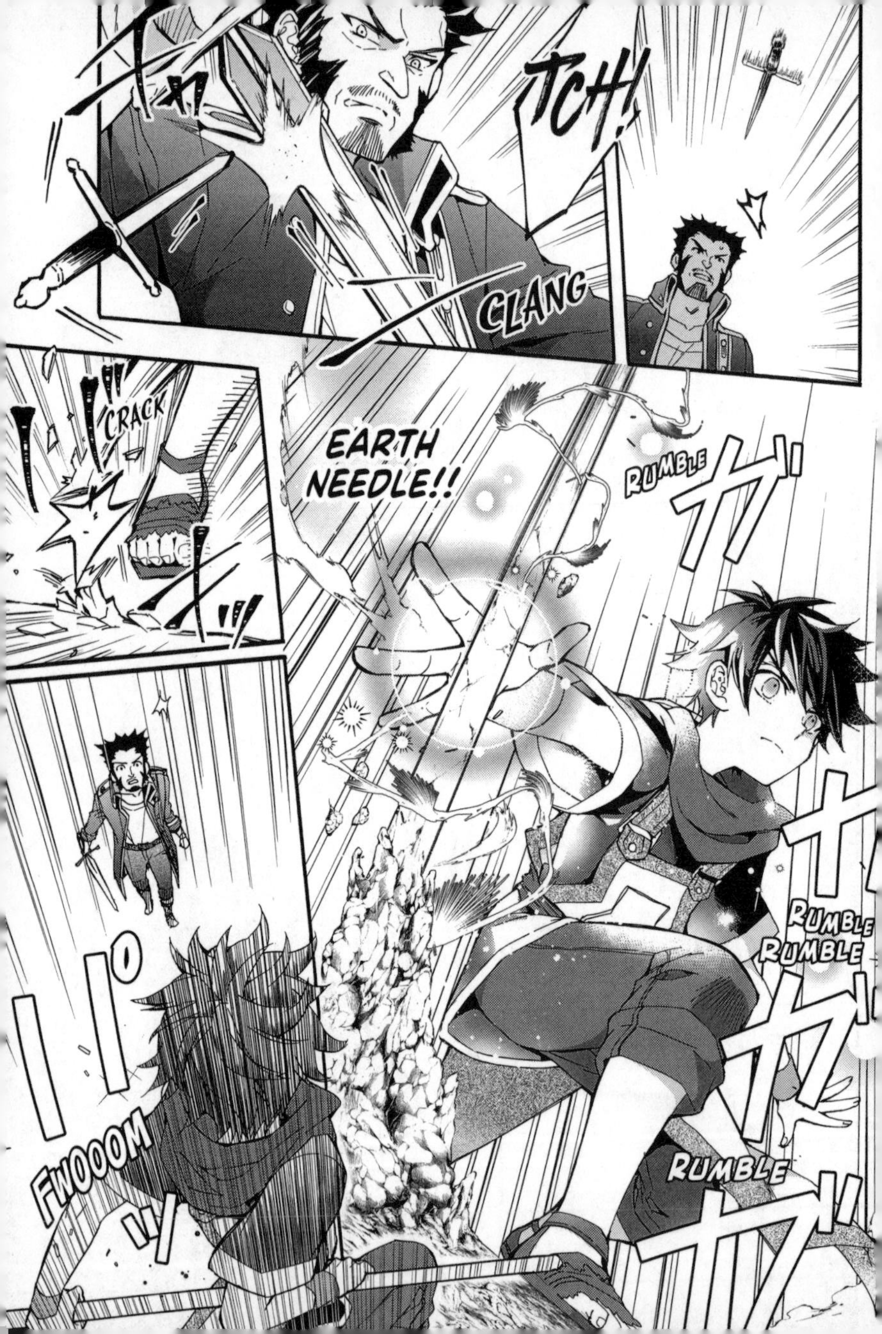
TCH!
CLANG
EARTH NEEDLE!!
RUMBLE
RUMBLE RUMBLE
RUMBLE
CRACK
FWOOOM

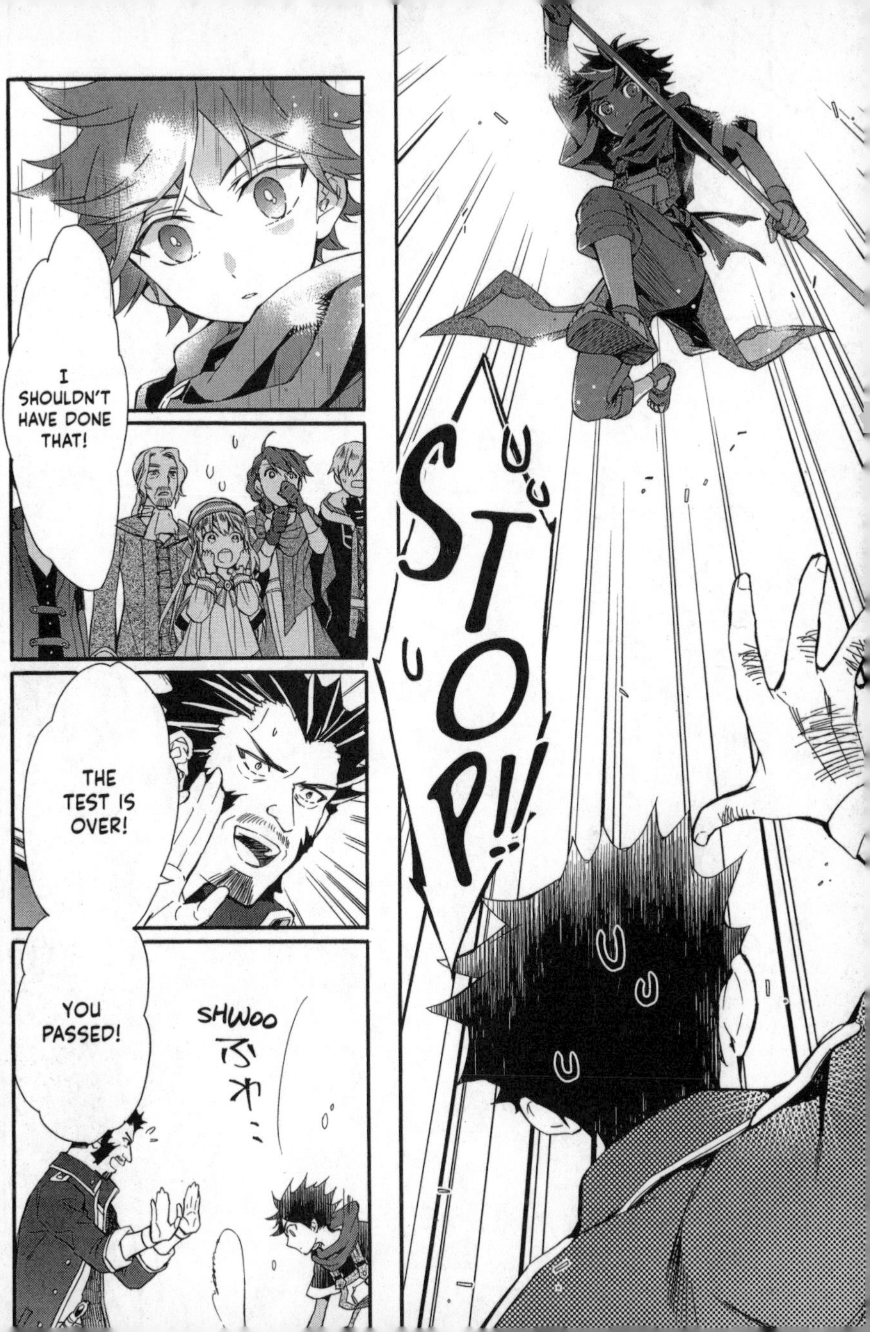
STOP!!
I SHOULDN'T HAVE DONE THAT!
THE TEST IS OVER!
YOU PASSED!
SHWOO

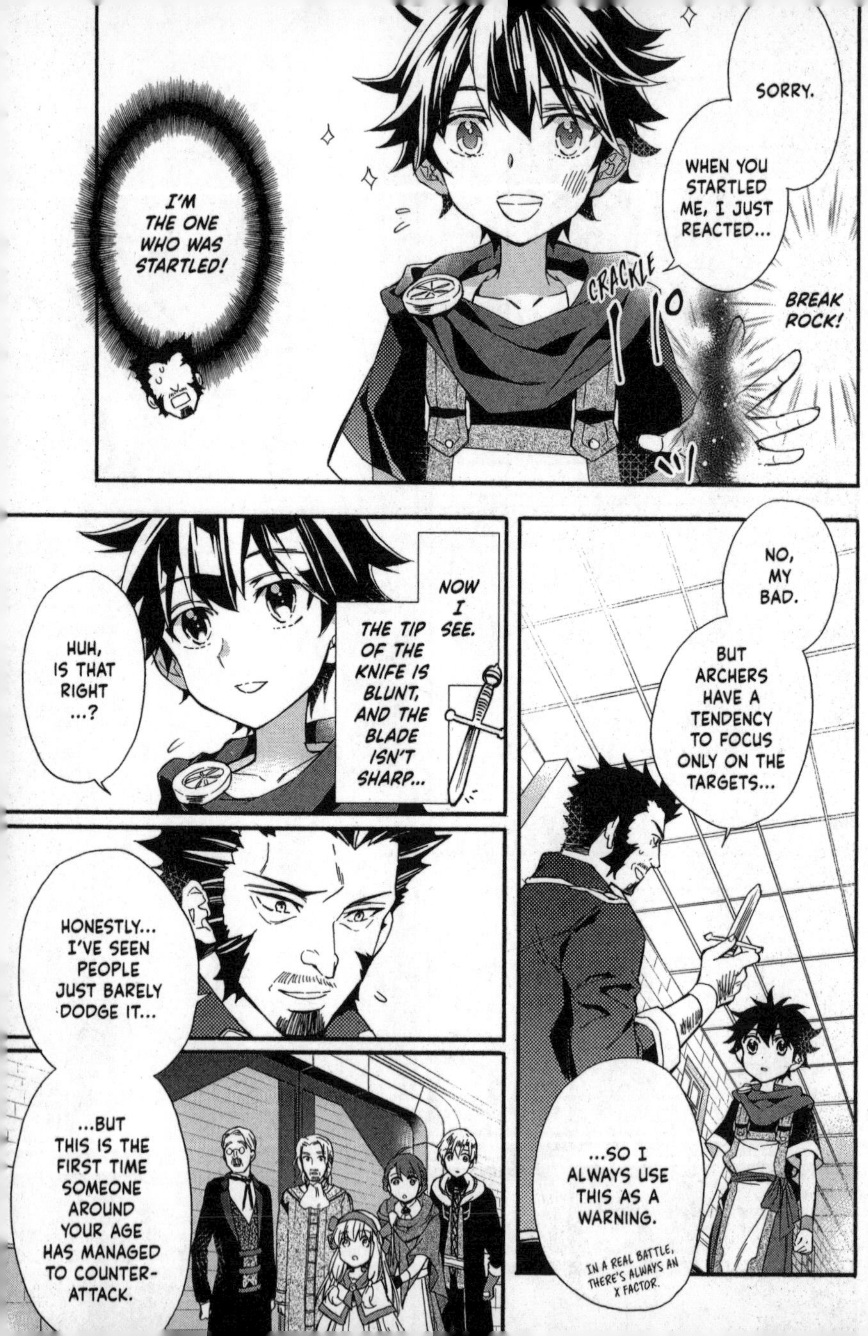
SORRY.
WHEN YOU STARTLED ME, I JUST REACTED...
CRACKLE
BREAK ROCK!
I'M THE ONE WHO WAS STARTLED!
NO, MY BAD.
BUT ARCHERS HAVE A TENDENCY TO FOCUS ONLY ON THE TARGETS...
...SO I ALWAYS USE THIS AS A WARNING.
IN A REAL BATTLE, THERE'S ALWAYS AN X FACTOR.
NOW I SEE.
THE TIP OF THE KNIFE IS BLUNT, AND THE BLADE ISN'T SHARP...
HUH, IS THAT RIGHT ...?
HONESTLY... I'VE SEEN PEOPLE JUST BARELY DODGE IT...
...BUT THIS IS THE FIRST TIME SOMEONE AROUND YOUR AGE HAS MANAGED TO COUNTER-ATTACK.

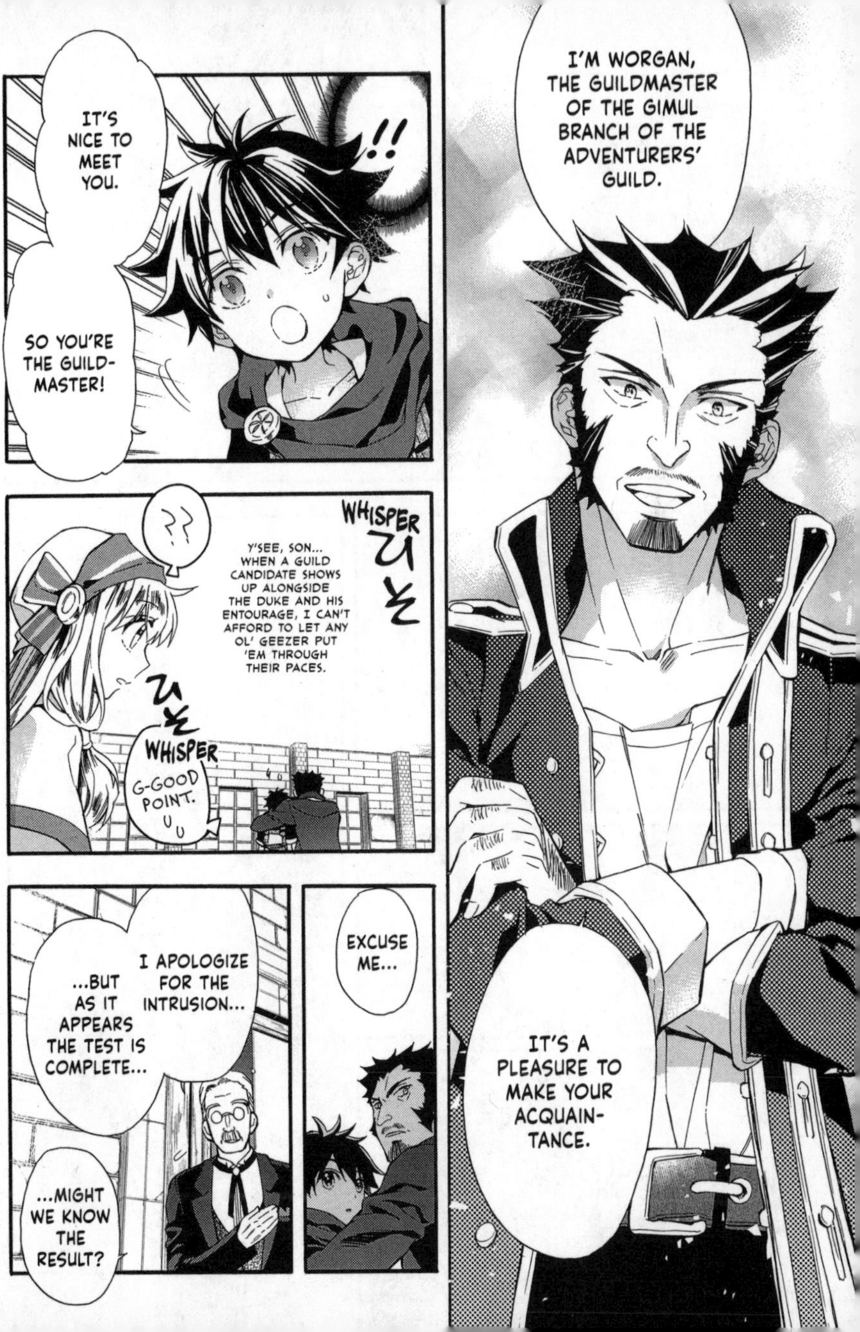
I'M WORGAN, THE GUILDMASTER OF THE GIMUL BRANCH OF THE ADVENTURERS' GUILD.
IT'S A PLEASURE TO MAKE YOUR ACQUAINTANCE.
!!
IT'S NICE TO MEET YOU.
SO YOU'RE THE GUILD-MASTER!
WHISPER ひそ
??
Y'SEE, SON... WHEN A GUILD CANDIDATE SHOWS UP ALONGSIDE THE DUKE AND HIS ENTOURAGE, I CAN'T AFFORD TO LET ANY OL' GEEZER PUT 'EM THROUGH THEIR PACES.
ひそ WHISPER
G-GOOD POINT.
EXCUSE ME...
I APOLOGIZE FOR THE INTRUSION...
...BUT AS IT APPEARS THE TEST IS COMPLETE...
...MIGHT WE KNOW THE RESULT?

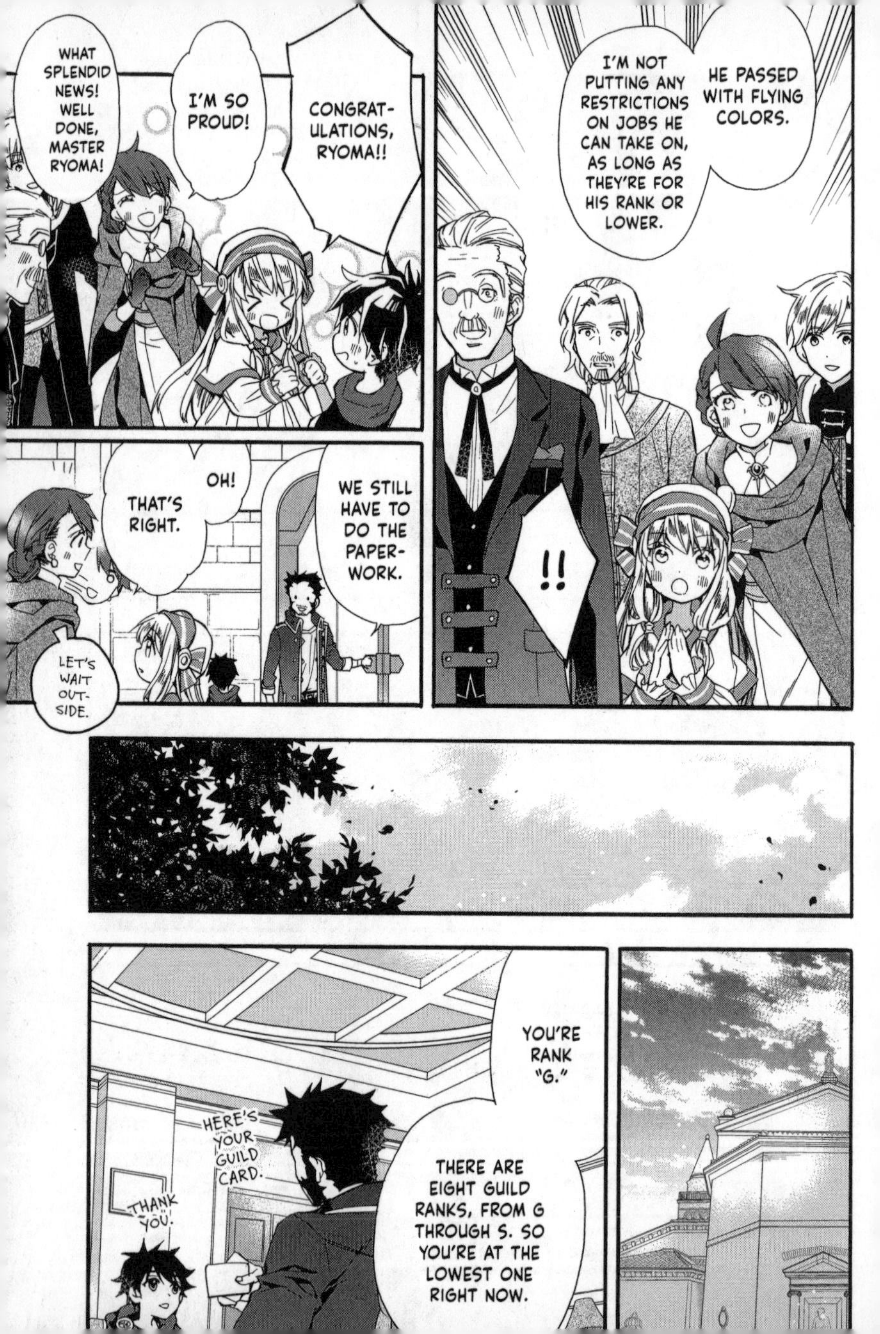
HE PASSED WITH FLYING COLORS.
I'M NOT PUTTING ANY RESTRICTIONS ON JOBS HE CAN TAKE ON, AS LONG AS THEY'RE FOR HIS RANK OR LOWER.
!!
CONGRAT-ULATIONS, RYOMA!!
I'M SO PROUD!
WHAT SPLENDID NEWS! WELL DONE, MASTER RYOMA!
WE STILL HAVE TO DO THE PAPER-WORK.
OH! THAT'S RIGHT.
LET'S WAIT OUT-SIDE.
YOU'RE RANK "G."
HERE'S YOUR GUILD CARD.
THERE ARE EIGHT GUILD RANKS, FROM G THROUGH S. SO YOU'RE AT THE LOWEST ONE RIGHT NOW.
THANK YOU.

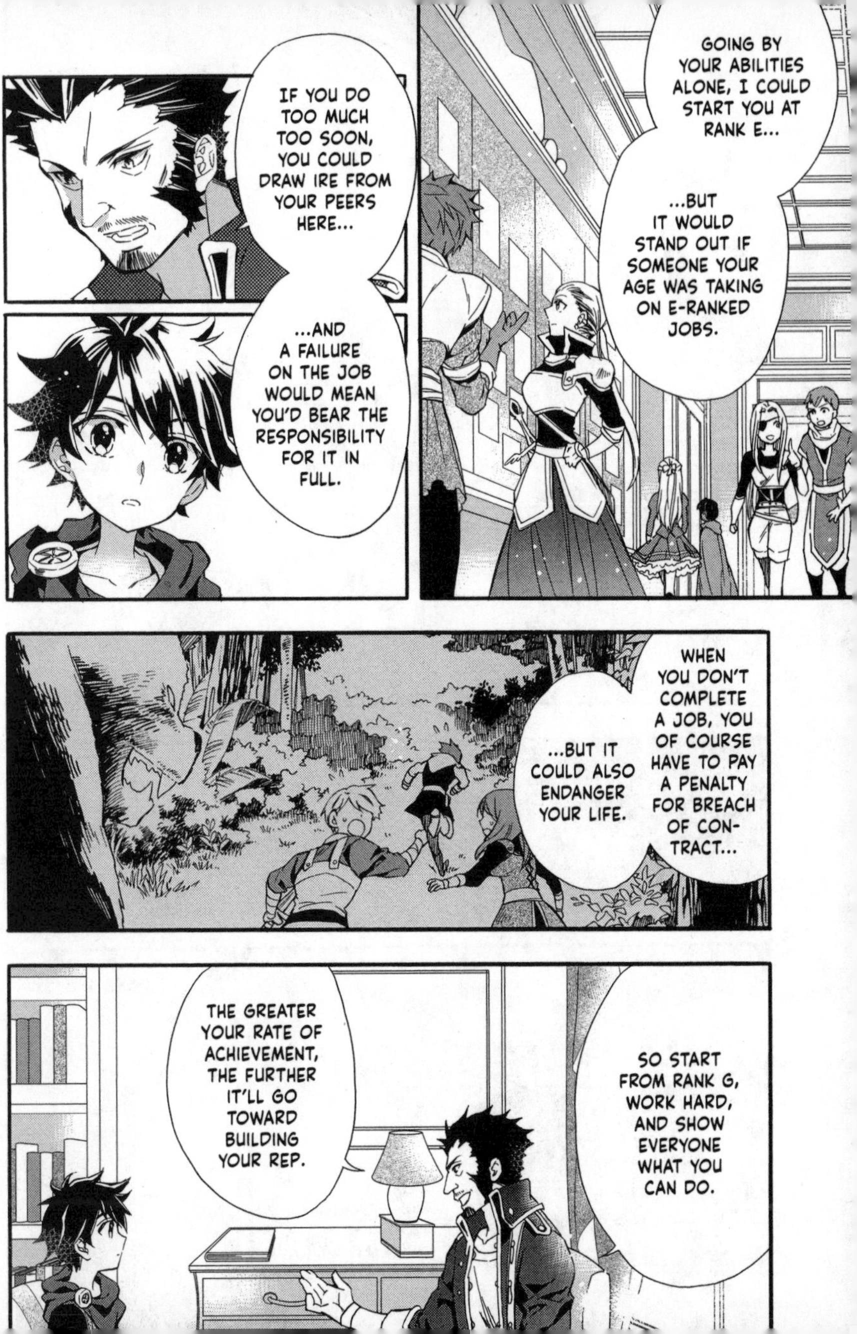
GOING BY YOUR ABILITIES ALONE, I COULD START YOU AT RANK E...
...BUT IT WOULD STAND OUT IF SOMEONE YOUR AGE WAS TAKING ON E-RANKED JOBS.
IF YOU DO TOO MUCH TOO SOON, YOU COULD DRAW IRE FROM YOUR PEERS HERE...
...AND A FAILURE ON THE JOB WOULD MEAN YOU'D BEAR THE RESPONSIBILITY FOR IT IN FULL.
WHEN YOU DON'T COMPLETE A JOB, YOU OF COURSE HAVE TO PAY A PENALTY FOR BREACH OF CONTRACT...
...BUT IT COULD ALSO ENDANGER YOUR LIFE.
SO START FROM RANK G, WORK HARD, AND SHOW EVERYONE WHAT YOU CAN DO.
THE GREATER YOUR RATE OF ACHIEVEMENT, THE FURTHER IT'LL GO TOWARD BUILDING YOUR REP.

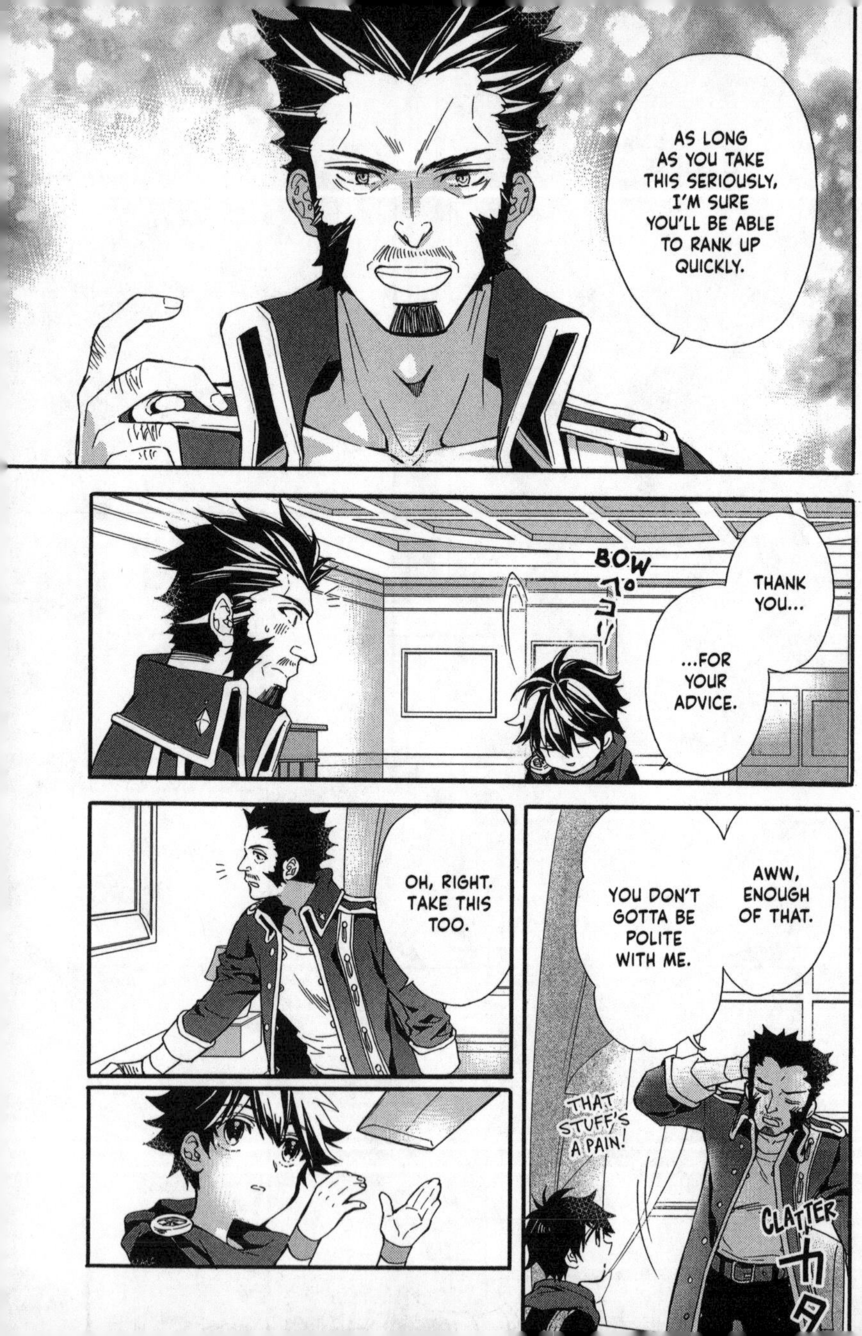
AS LONG AS YOU TAKE THIS SERIOUSLY, I'M SURE YOU'LL BE ABLE TO RANK UP QUICKLY.
THANK YOU...
...FOR YOUR ADVICE.
BOW
AWW, ENOUGH OF THAT.
YOU DON'T GOTTA BE POLITE WITH ME.
THAT STUFF'S A PAIN!
CLATTER
OH, RIGHT. TAKE THIS TOO.

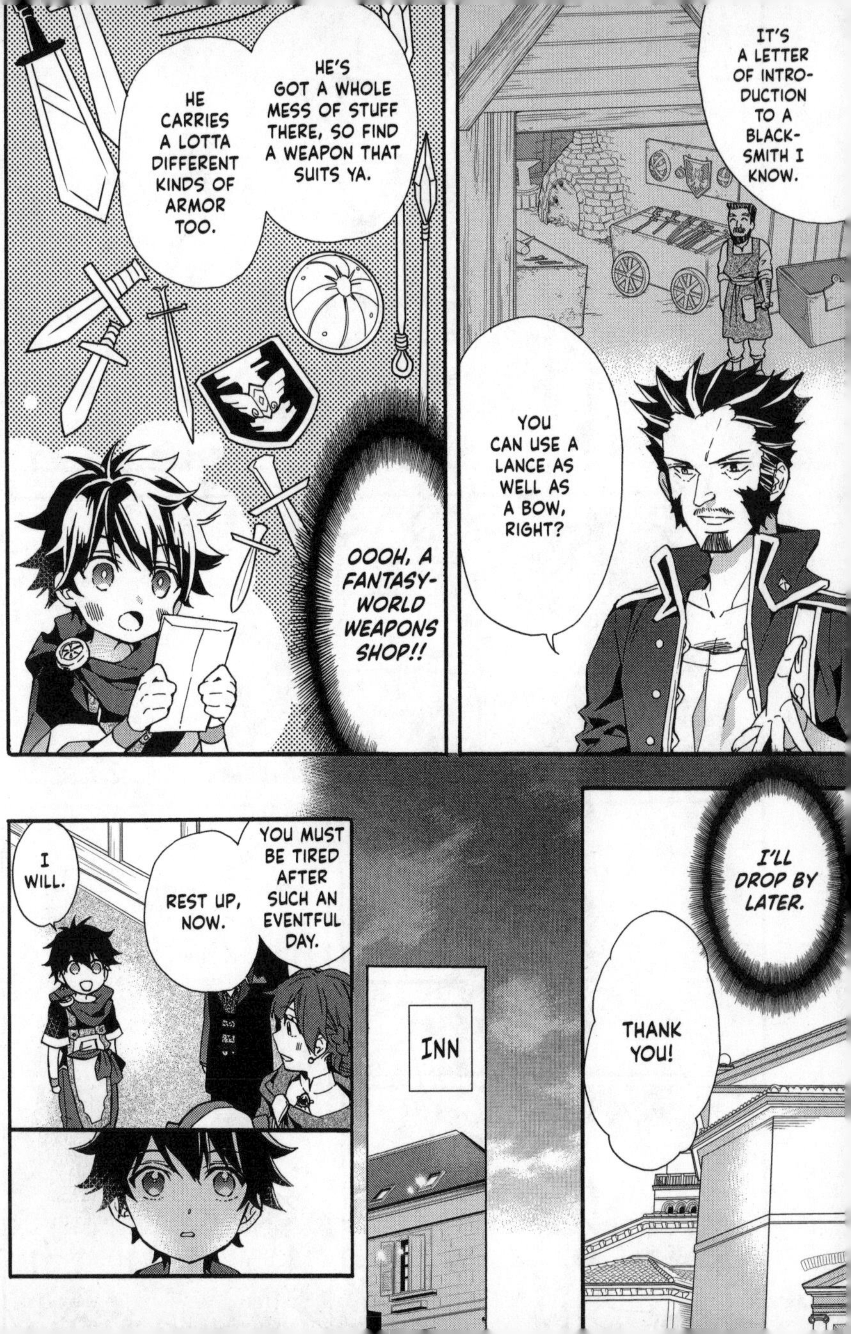
IT'S A LETTER OF INTRO-DUCTION TO A BLACK-SMITH I KNOW.
YOU CAN USE A LANCE AS WELL AS A BOW, RIGHT?
HE'S GOT A WHOLE MESS OF STUFF THERE, SO FIND A WEAPON THAT SUITS YA.
HE CARRIES A LOTTA DIFFERENT KINDS OF ARMOR TOO.
OOOH, A FANTASY-WORLD WEAPONS SHOP!!
I'LL DROP BY LATER.
THANK YOU!
INN
YOU MUST BE TIRED AFTER SUCH AN EVENTFUL DAY.
REST UP, NOW.
I WILL.

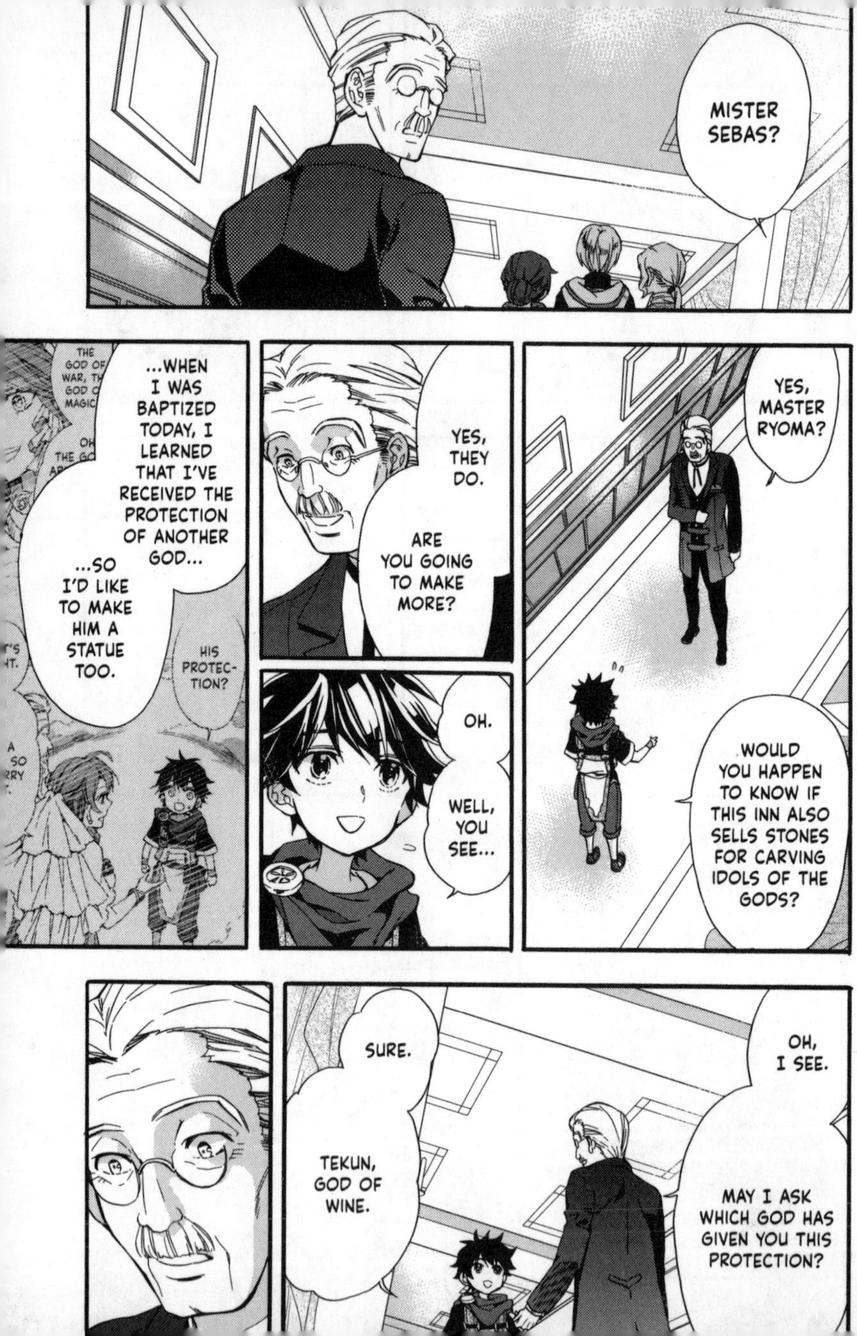
MISTER SEBAS?
YES, MASTER RYOMA?
WOULD YOU HAPPEN TO KNOW IF THIS INN ALSO SELLS STONES FOR CARVING IDOLS OF THE GODS?
YES, THEY DO.
ARE YOU GOING TO MAKE MORE?
OH.
WELL, YOU SEE...
...WHEN I WAS BAPTIZED TODAY, I LEARNED THAT I'VE RECEIVED THE PROTECTION OF ANOTHER GOD...
...SO I'D LIKE TO MAKE HIM A STATUE TOO.
HIS PROTECTION?
OH, I SEE.
MAY I ASK WHICH GOD HAS GIVEN YOU THIS PROTECTION?
SURE.
TEKUN, GOD OF WINE.

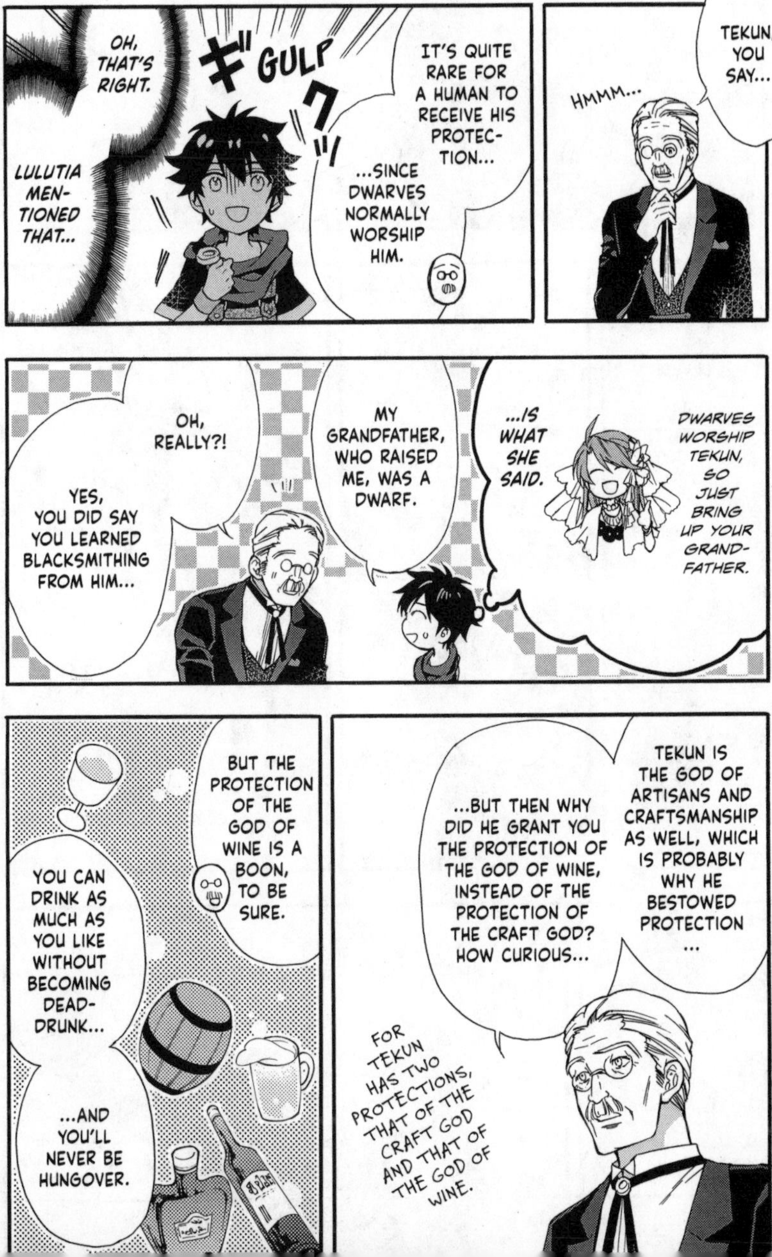
TEKUN, YOU SAY...
HMMM...
IT'S QUITE RARE FOR A HUMAN TO RECEIVE HIS PROTECTION...
...SINCE DWARVES NORMALLY WORSHIP HIM.
ギ GULP ク
OH, THAT'S RIGHT.
LULUTIA MENTIONED THAT...
DWARVES WORSHIP TEKUN, SO JUST BRING UP YOUR GRANDFATHER.
...IS WHAT SHE SAID.
MY GRANDFATHER, WHO RAISED ME, WAS A DWARF.
OH, REALLY?!
YES, YOU DID SAY YOU LEARNED BLACKSMITHING FROM HIM...
TEKUN IS THE GOD OF ARTISANS AND CRAFTSMANSHIP AS WELL, WHICH IS PROBABLY WHY HE BESTOWED PROTECTION ...
...BUT THEN WHY DID HE GRANT YOU THE PROTECTION OF THE GOD OF WINE, INSTEAD OF THE PROTECTION OF THE CRAFT GOD? HOW CURIOUS...
FOR TEKUN HAS TWO PROTECTIONS, THAT OF THE CRAFT GOD AND THAT OF THE GOD OF WINE.
BUT THE PROTECTION OF THE GOD OF WINE IS A BOON, TO BE SURE.
YOU CAN DRINK AS MUCH AS YOU LIKE WITHOUT BECOMING DEAD-DRUNK...
...AND YOU'LL NEVER BE HUNGOVER.

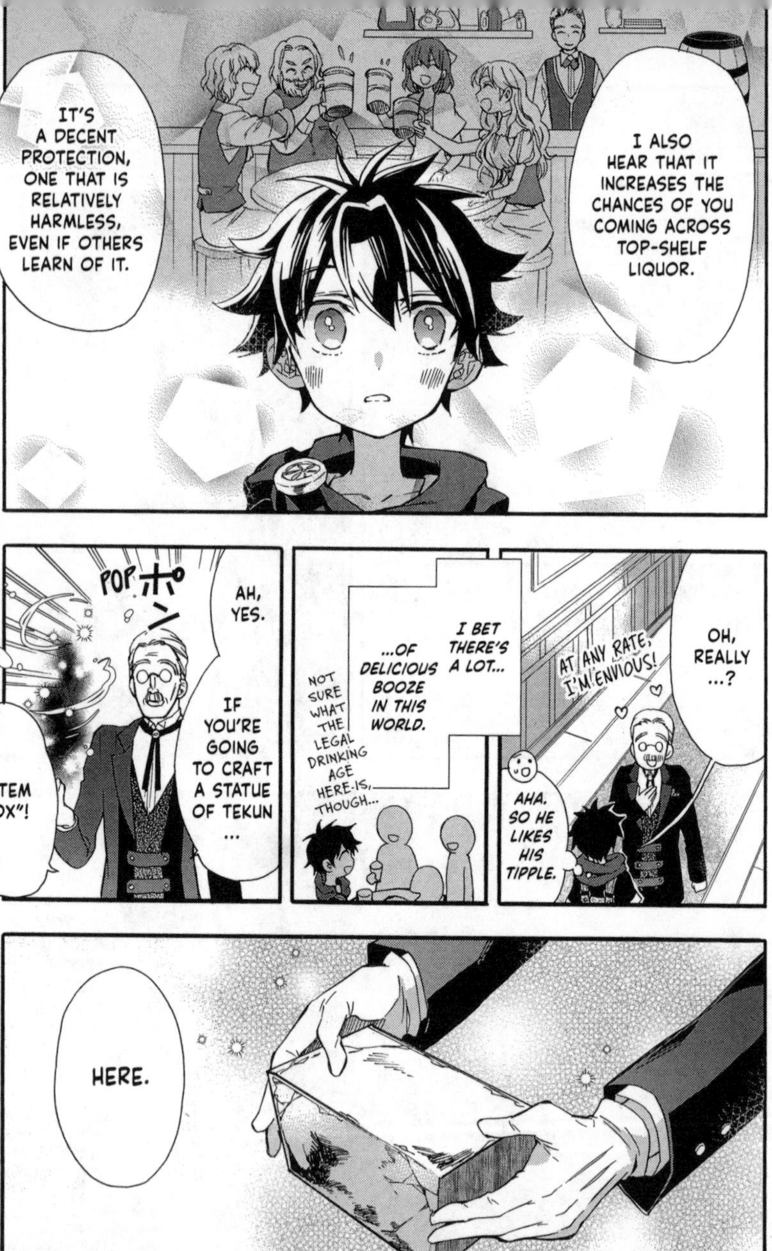
I ALSO HEAR THAT IT INCREASES THE CHANCES OF YOU COMING ACROSS TOP-SHELF LIQUOR.
IT'S A DECENT PROTECTION, ONE THAT IS RELATIVELY HARMLESS, EVEN IF OTHERS LEARN OF IT.
OH, REALLY ...?
AT ANY RATE, I'M ENVIOUS!
AHA. SO HE LIKES HIS TIPPLE.
I BET THERE'S A LOT...
...OF DELICIOUS BOOZE IN THIS WORLD.
NOT SURE WHAT THE LEGAL DRINKING AGE HERE IS, THOUGH...
AH, YES.
IF YOU'RE GOING TO CRAFT A STATUE OF TEKUN ...
POP ポン
"ITEM BOX"!
HERE.

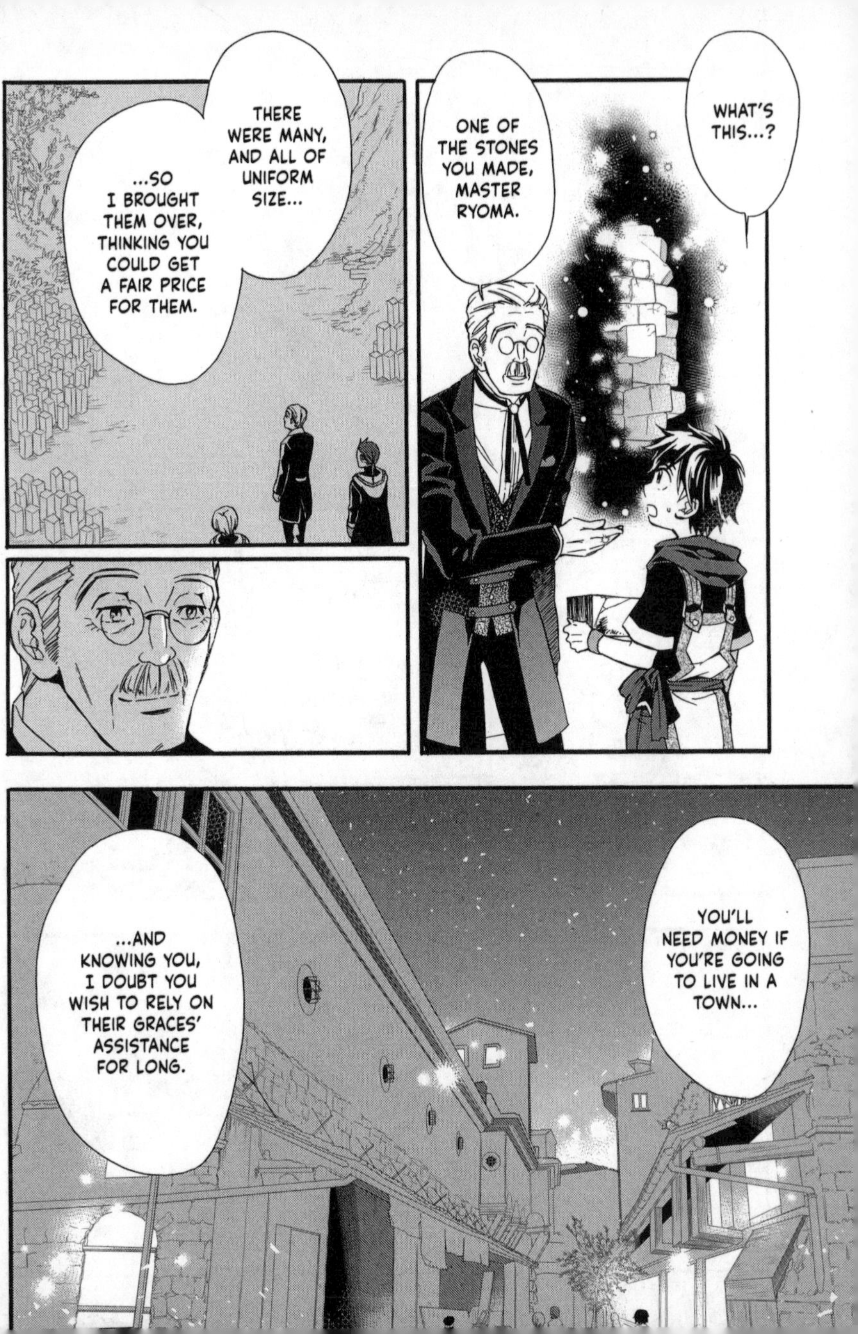
WHAT'S THIS...?
ONE OF THE STONES YOU MADE, MASTER RYOMA.
THERE WERE MANY, AND ALL OF UNIFORM SIZE...
...SO I BROUGHT THEM OVER, THINKING YOU COULD GET A FAIR PRICE FOR THEM.
YOU'LL NEED MONEY IF YOU'RE GOING TO LIVE IN A TOWN...
...AND KNOWING YOU, I DOUBT YOU WISH TO RELY ON THEIR GRACES' ASSISTANCE FOR LONG.

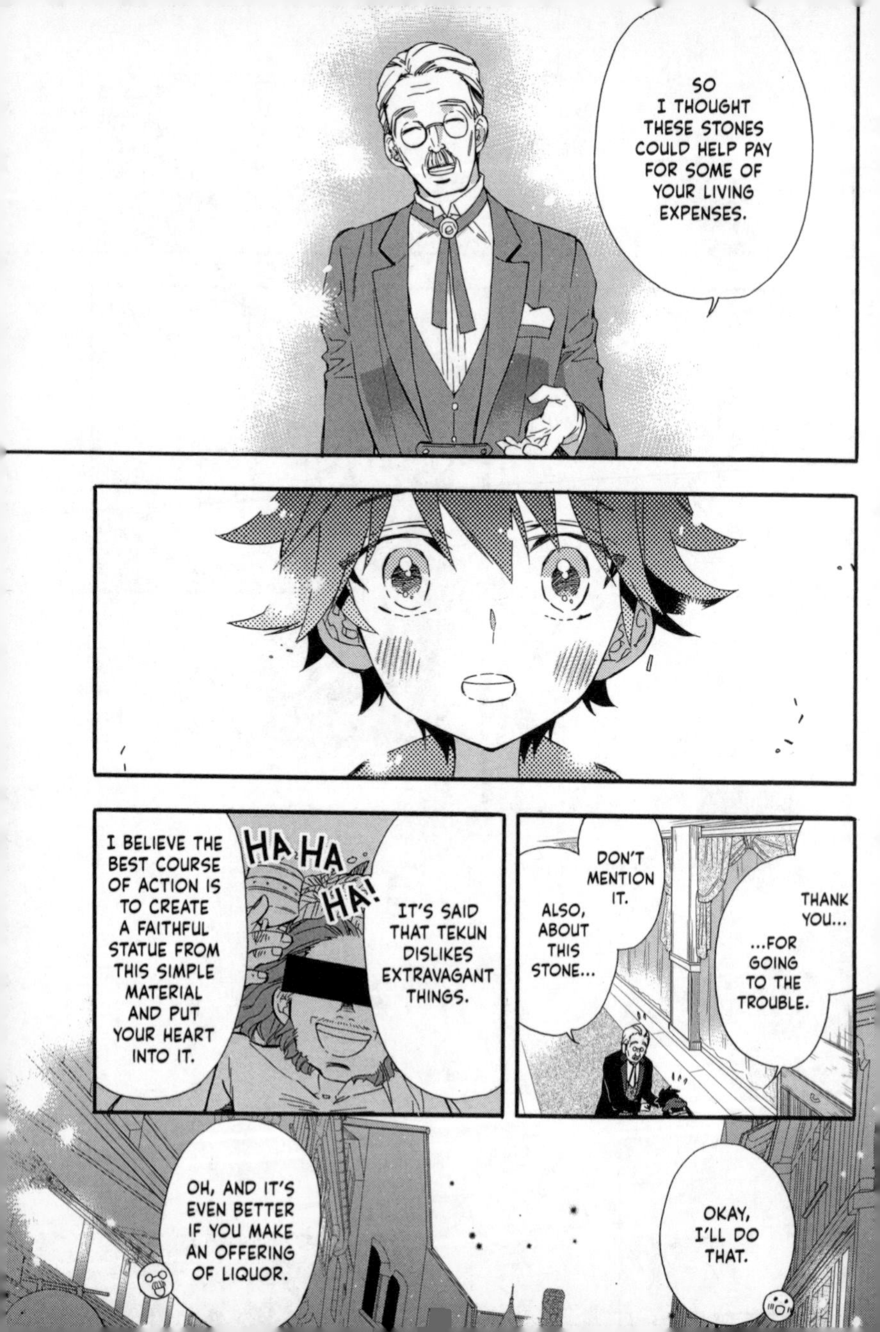
SO I THOUGHT THESE STONES COULD HELP PAY FOR SOME OF YOUR LIVING EXPENSES.
THANK YOU...
...FOR GOING TO THE TROUBLE.
DON'T MENTION IT.
ALSO, ABOUT THIS STONE...
IT'S SAID THAT TEKUN DISLIKES EXTRAVAGANT THINGS.
HA HA HA!
I BELIEVE THE BEST COURSE OF ACTION IS TO CREATE A FAITHFUL STATUE FROM THIS SIMPLE MATERIAL AND PUT YOUR HEART INTO IT.
OH, AND IT'S EVEN BETTER IF YOU MAKE AN OFFERING OF LIQUOR.
OKAY, I'LL DO THAT.

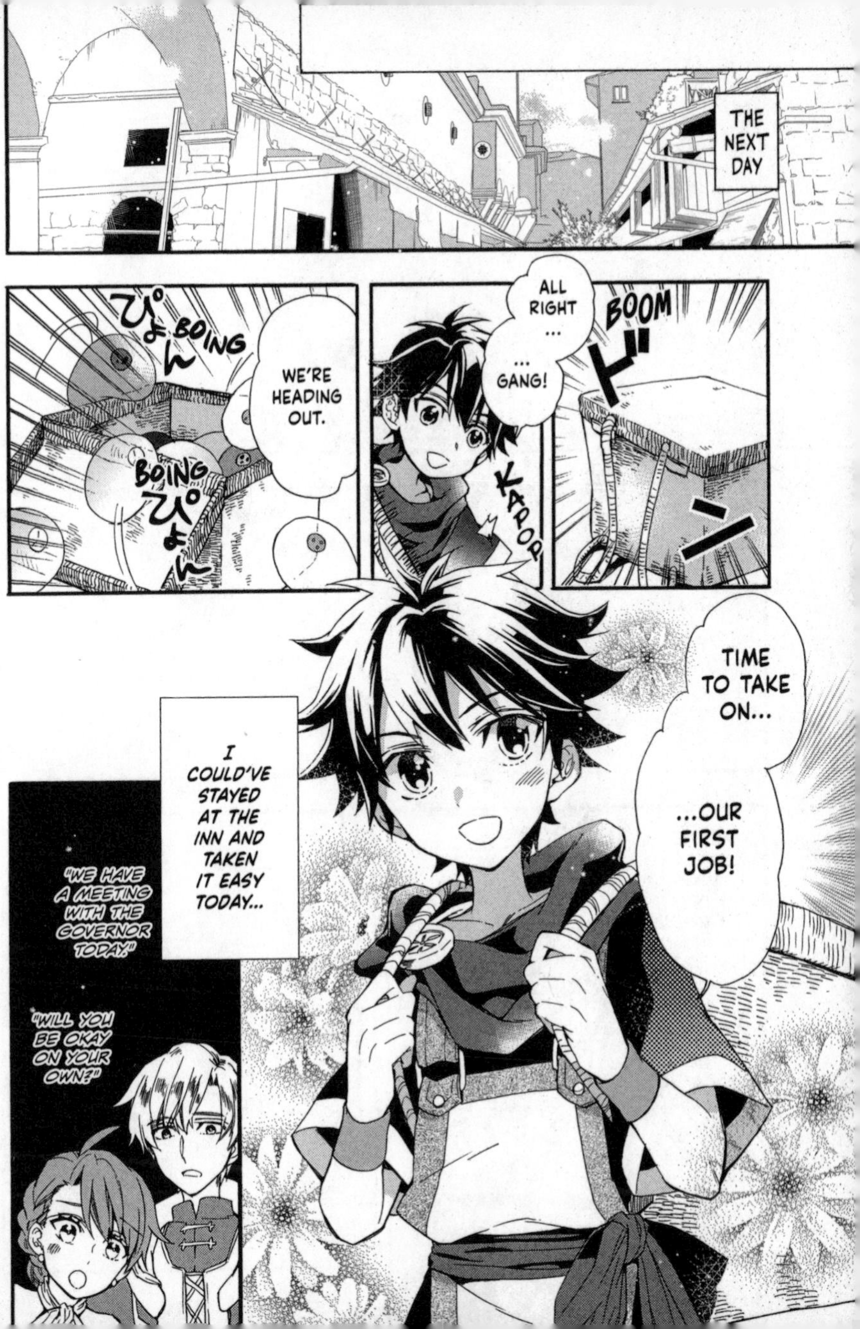
THE NEXT DAY
BOOM
ド
ン
ALL RIGHT ...
... GANG!
KAPOR
WE'RE HEADING OUT.
ぴょん BOING
BOING ぴょん
TIME TO TAKE ON...
...OUR FIRST JOB!
I COULD'VE STAYED AT THE INN AND TAKEN IT EASY TODAY...
"WE HAVE A MEETING WITH THE GOVERNOR TODAY."
"WILL YOU BE OKAY ON YOUR OWN?"

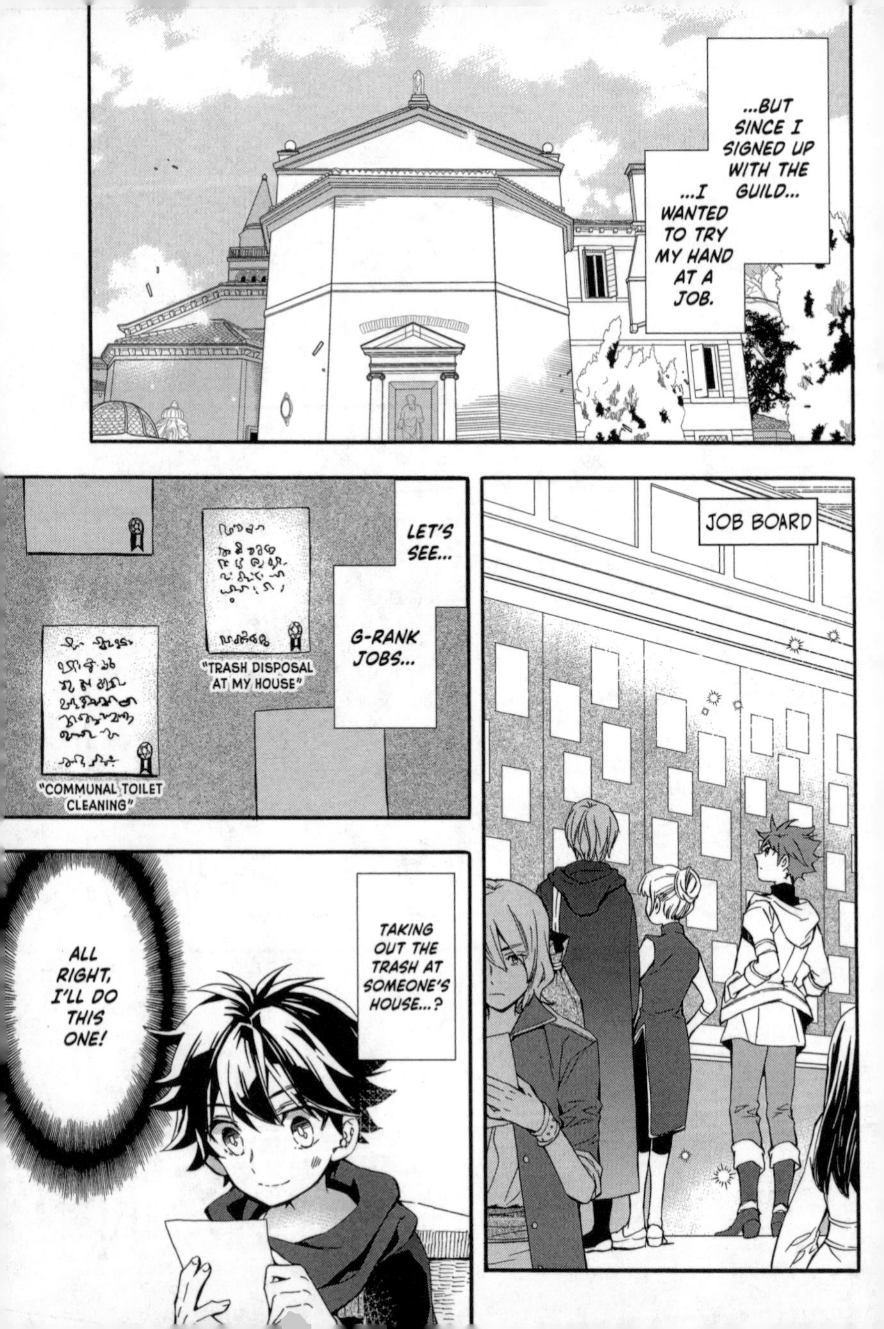
...BUT SINCE I SIGNED UP WITH THE GUILD...
...I WANTED TO TRY MY HAND AT A JOB.
JOB BOARD
LET'S SEE...
G-RANK JOBS...
"TRASH DISPOSAL AT MY HOUSE"
"COMMUNAL TOILET CLEANING"
TAKING OUT THE TRASH AT SOMEONE'S HOUSE...?
ALL RIGHT, I'LL DO THIS ONE!

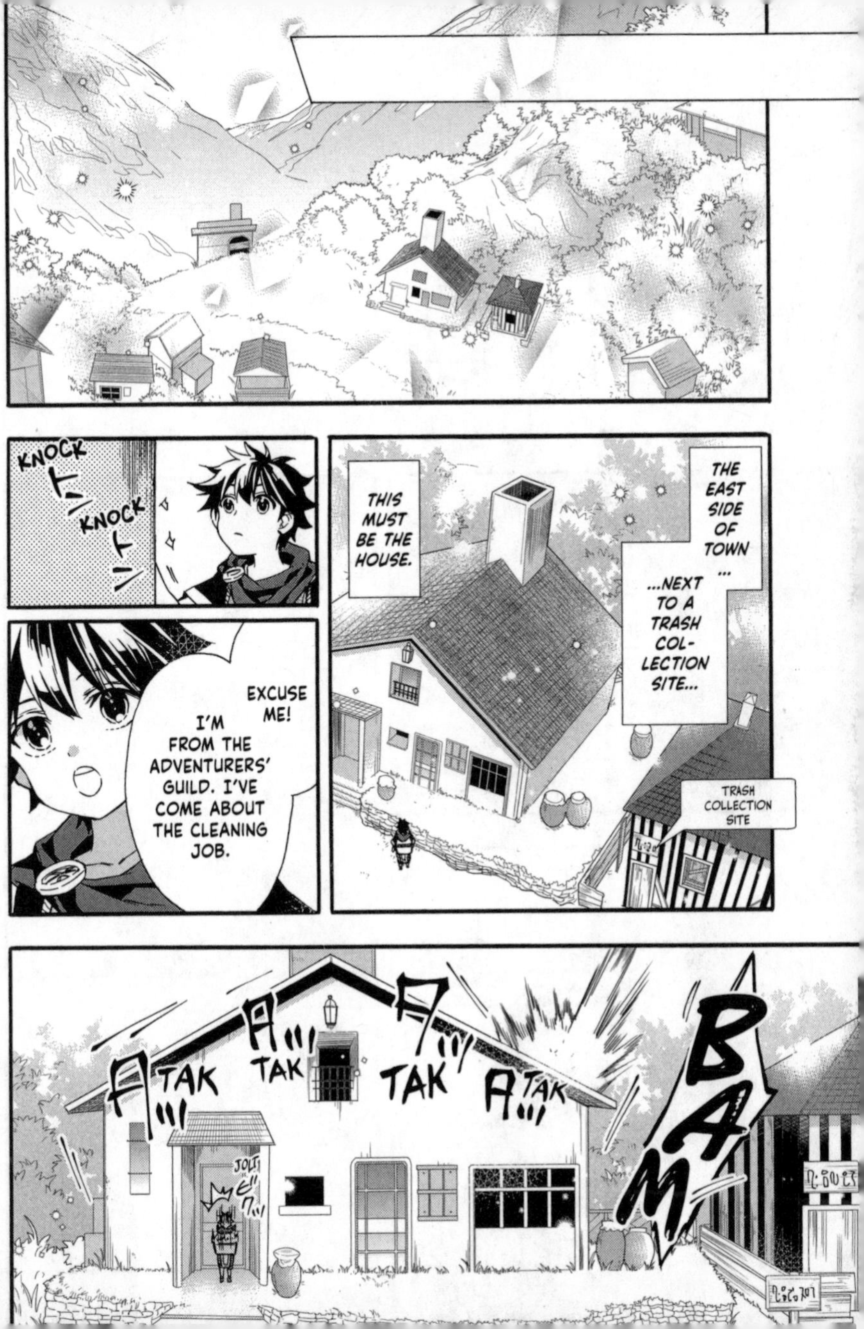

THE EAST SIDE OF TOWN...
...NEXT TO A TRASH COLLECTION SITE...
THIS MUST BE THE HOUSE.
TRASH COLLECTION SITE
KNOCK
KNOCK
EXCUSE ME!
I'M FROM THE ADVENTURERS' GUILD. I'VE COME ABOUT THE CLEANING JOB.
BAM
TAK
TAK
TAK
TAK
JOLT

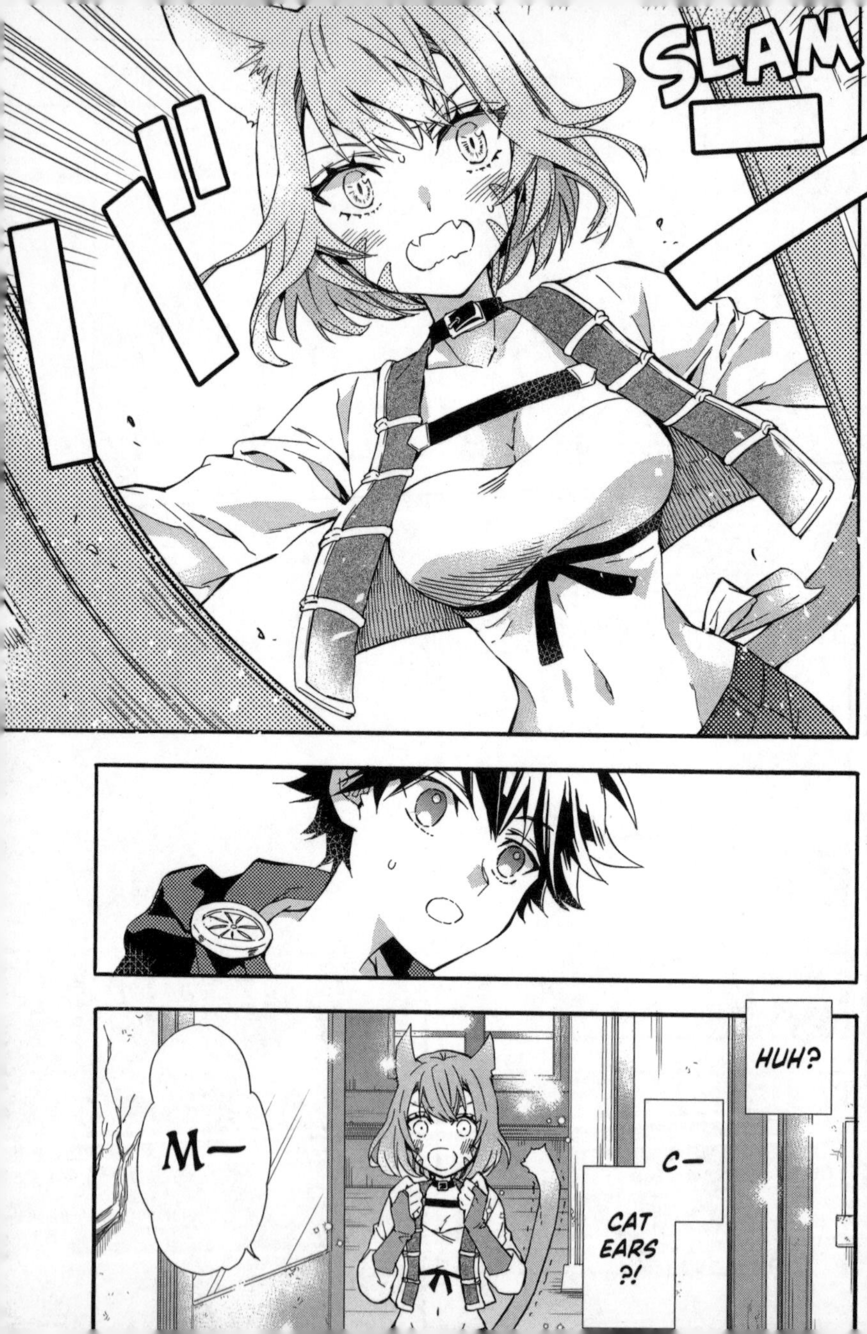
SLAM
HUH?
C—
CAT EARS?!
M—

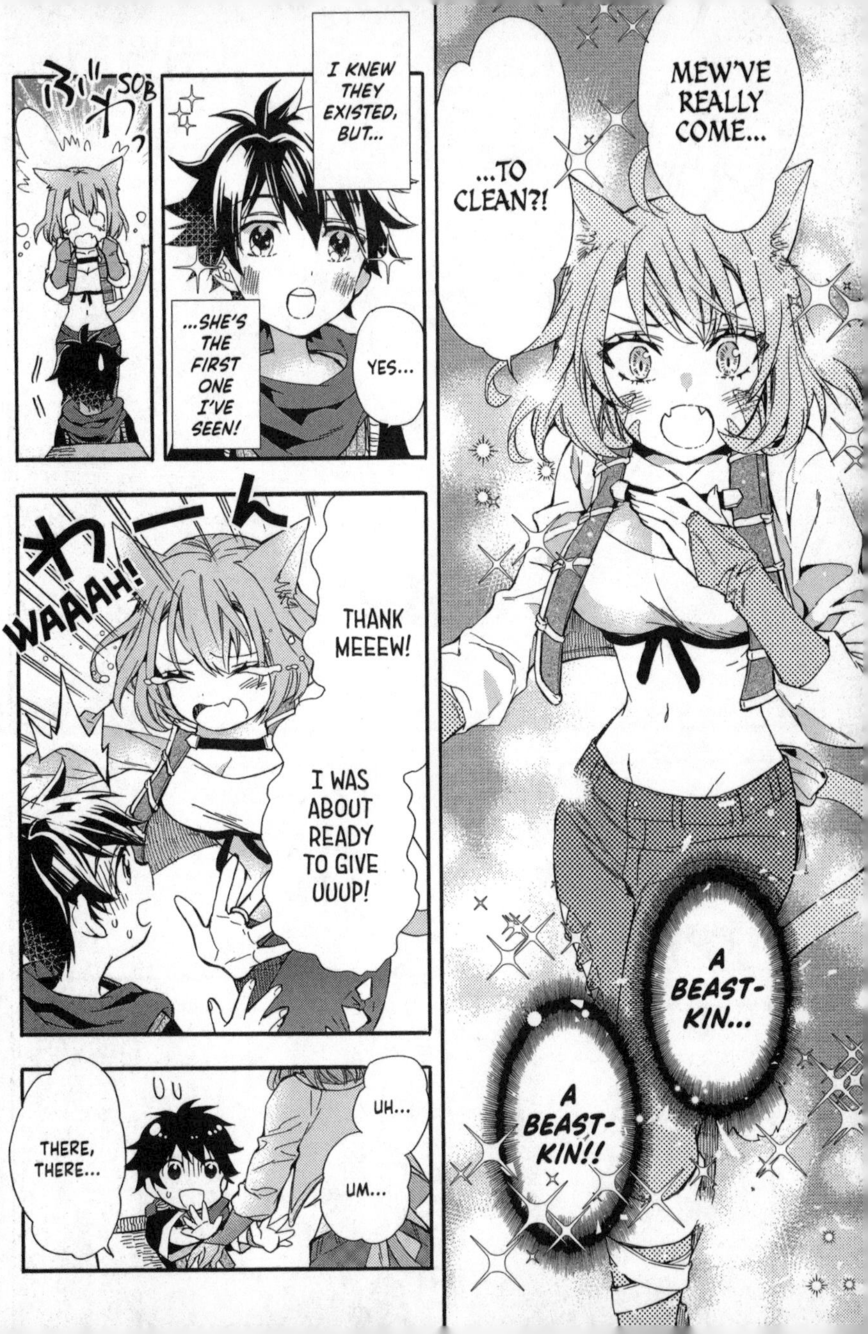

MEW'VE REALLY COME...
...TO CLEAN?!
A BEAST-KIN...
A BEAST-KIN!!
I KNEW THEY EXISTED, BUT...
...SHE'S THE FIRST ONE I'VE SEEN!
YES...
SOB
わーん
WAAAH!
THANK MEEEW!
I WAS ABOUT READY TO GIVE UUUP!
UH...
UM...
THERE, THERE...

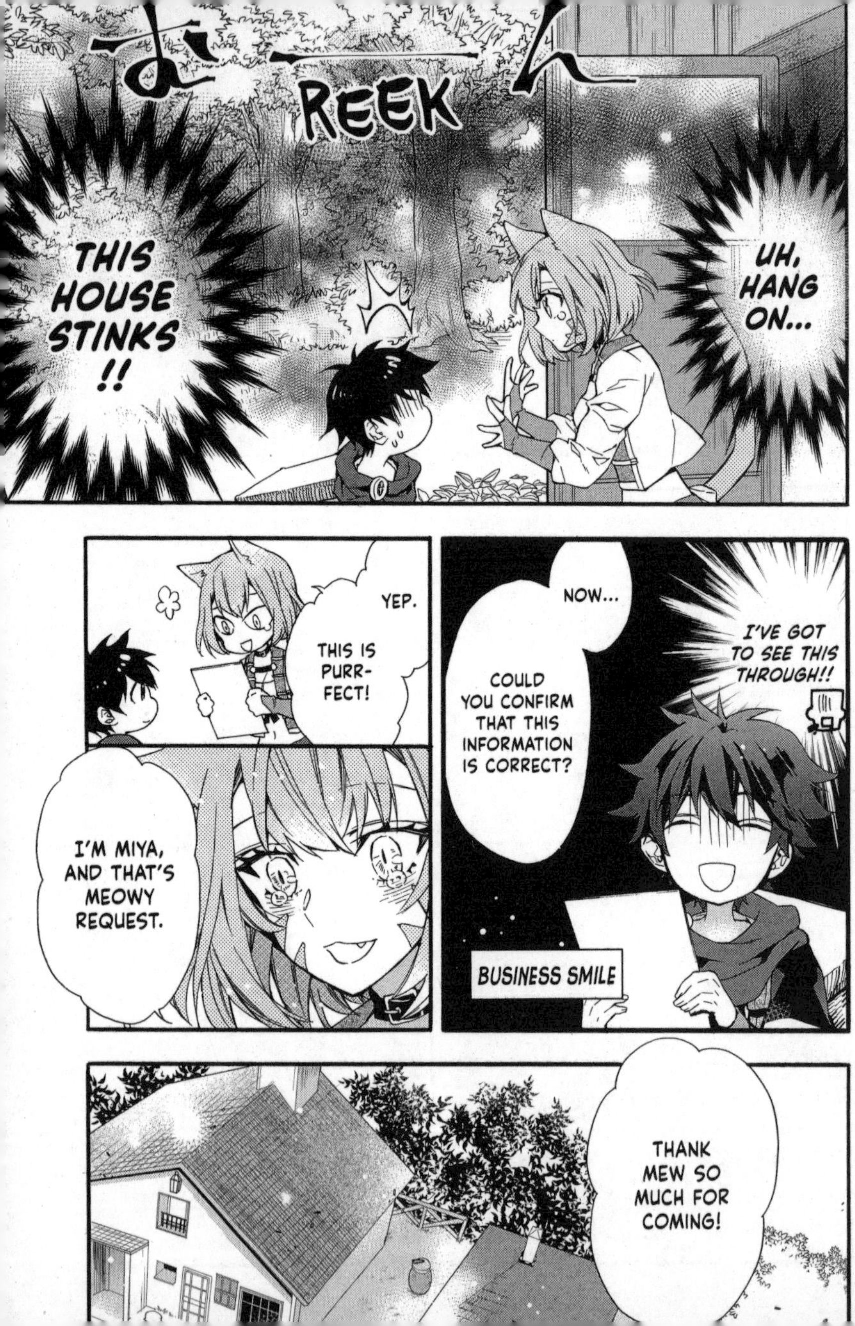
REEK
UH, HANG ON...
THIS HOUSE STINKS!!
I'VE GOT TO SEE THIS THROUGH!!
NOW...
COULD YOU CONFIRM THAT THIS INFORMATION IS CORRECT?
BUSINESS SMILE
YEP.
THIS IS PURR-FECT!
I'M MIYA, AND THAT'S MEOWY REQUEST.
THANK MEW SO MUCH FOR COMING!

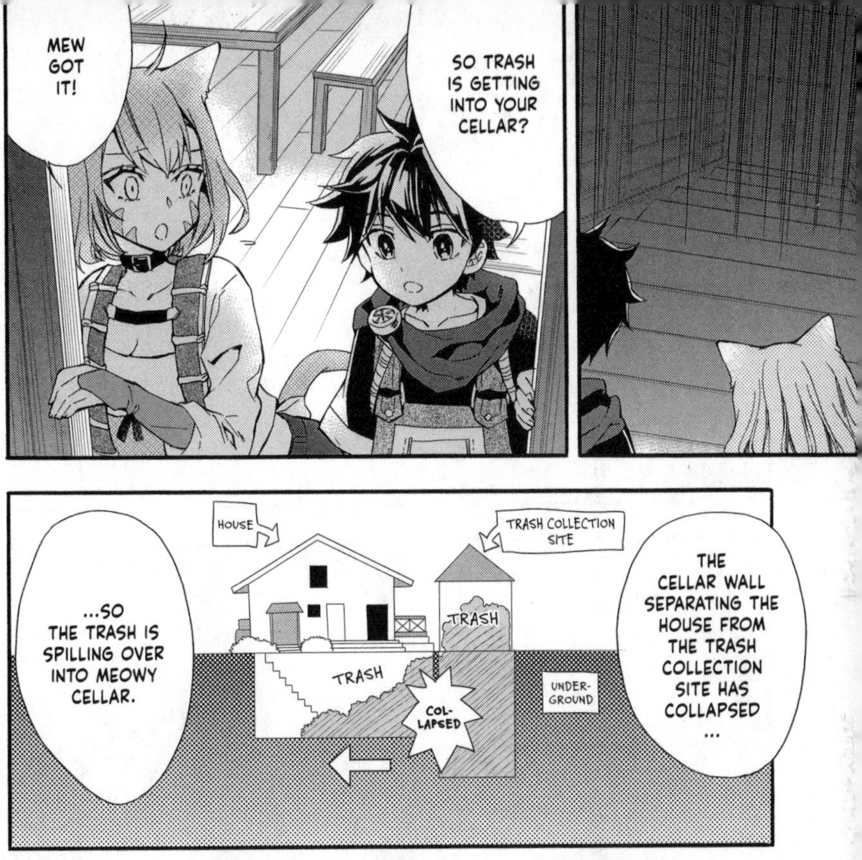
SO TRASH IS GETTING INTO YOUR CELLAR?
MEW GOT IT!
THE CELLAR WALL SEPARATING THE HOUSE FROM THE TRASH COLLECTION SITE HAS COLLAPSED ...
TRASH COLLECTION SITE
HOUSE
TRASH
TRASH
UNDER-GROUND
COL-LAPSED
...SO THE TRASH IS SPILLING OVER INTO MEOWY CELLAR.
UNDER-STOOD.
IS THERE ANYTHING OF VALUE IN THE CELLAR, MIYA?
NUH-UH.
I NEVER USED IT IN THE FURST PLACE.
IF I HAD, ANYTHING DOWN THERE WOULD'VE BEEN RUINED BY NOW, BURIED UNDER A MEOWNTAIN OF TRASH.

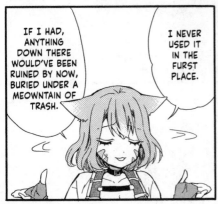

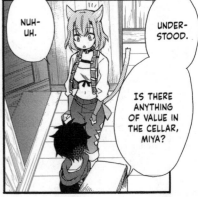

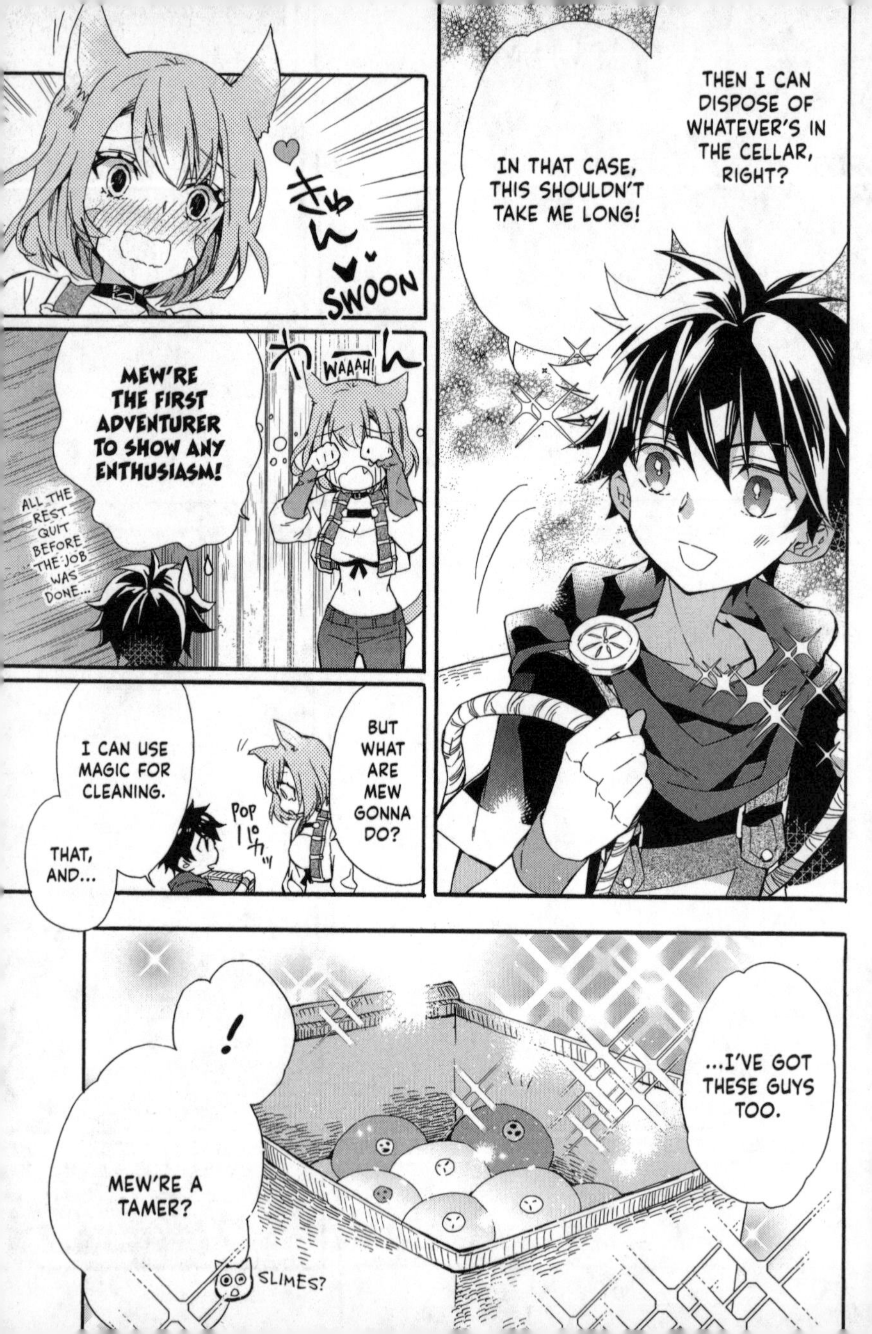
THEN I CAN DISPOSE OF WHATEVER'S IN THE CELLAR, RIGHT?
IN THAT CASE, THIS SHOULDN'T TAKE ME LONG!
きゅん
SWOON
MEW'RE THE FIRST ADVENTURER TO SHOW ANY ENTHUSIASM!
わーん
WAAAH!
ALL THE REST QUIT BEFORE THE JOB WAS DONE...
BUT WHAT ARE MEW GONNA DO?
I CAN USE MAGIC FOR CLEANING.
THAT, AND...
POP
パカッ
...I'VE GOT THESE GUYS TOO.
!
MEW'RE A TAMER?
SLIMES?

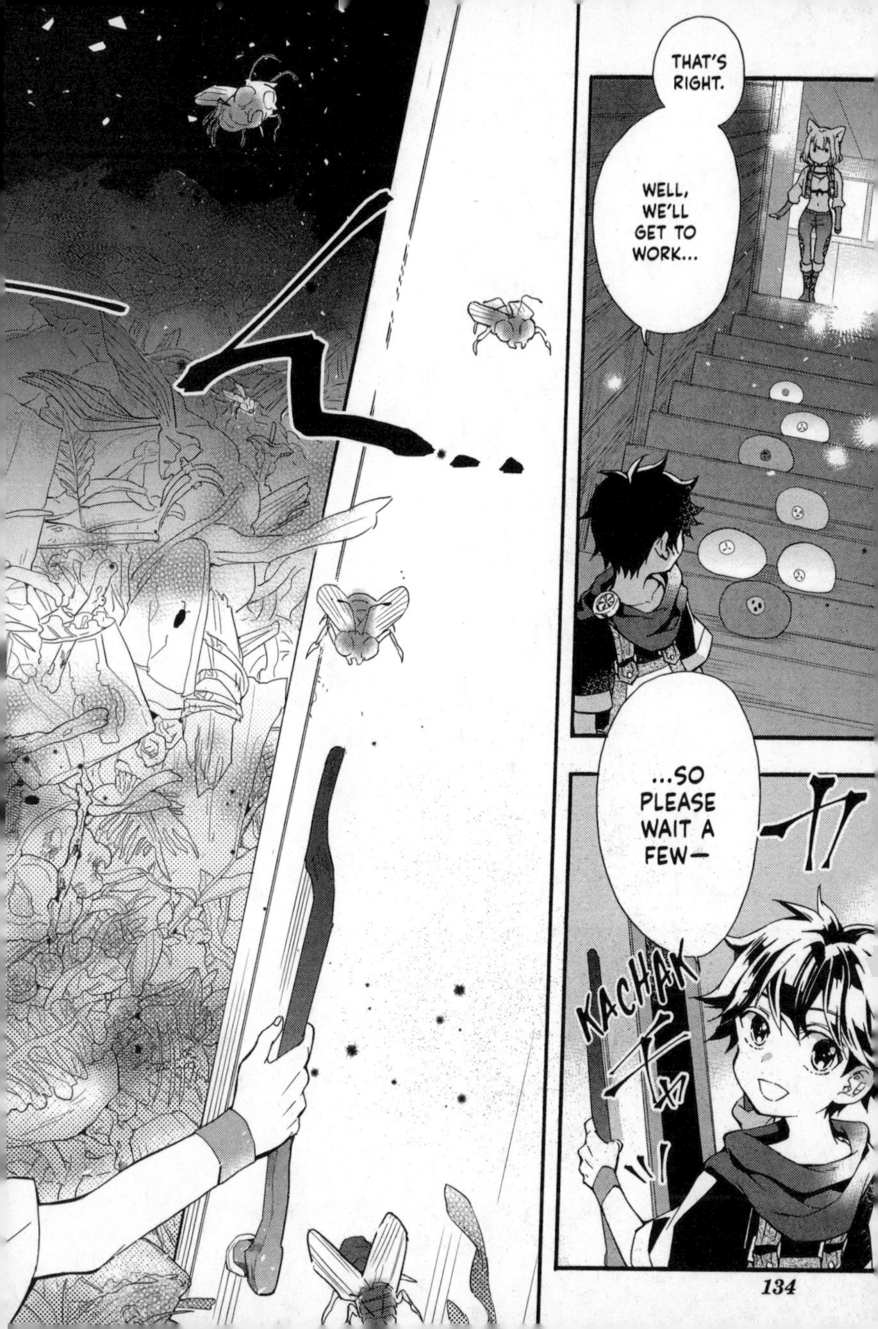
THAT'S RIGHT.
WELL, WE'LL GET TO WORK...
...SO PLEASE WAIT A FEW—
KACHAK

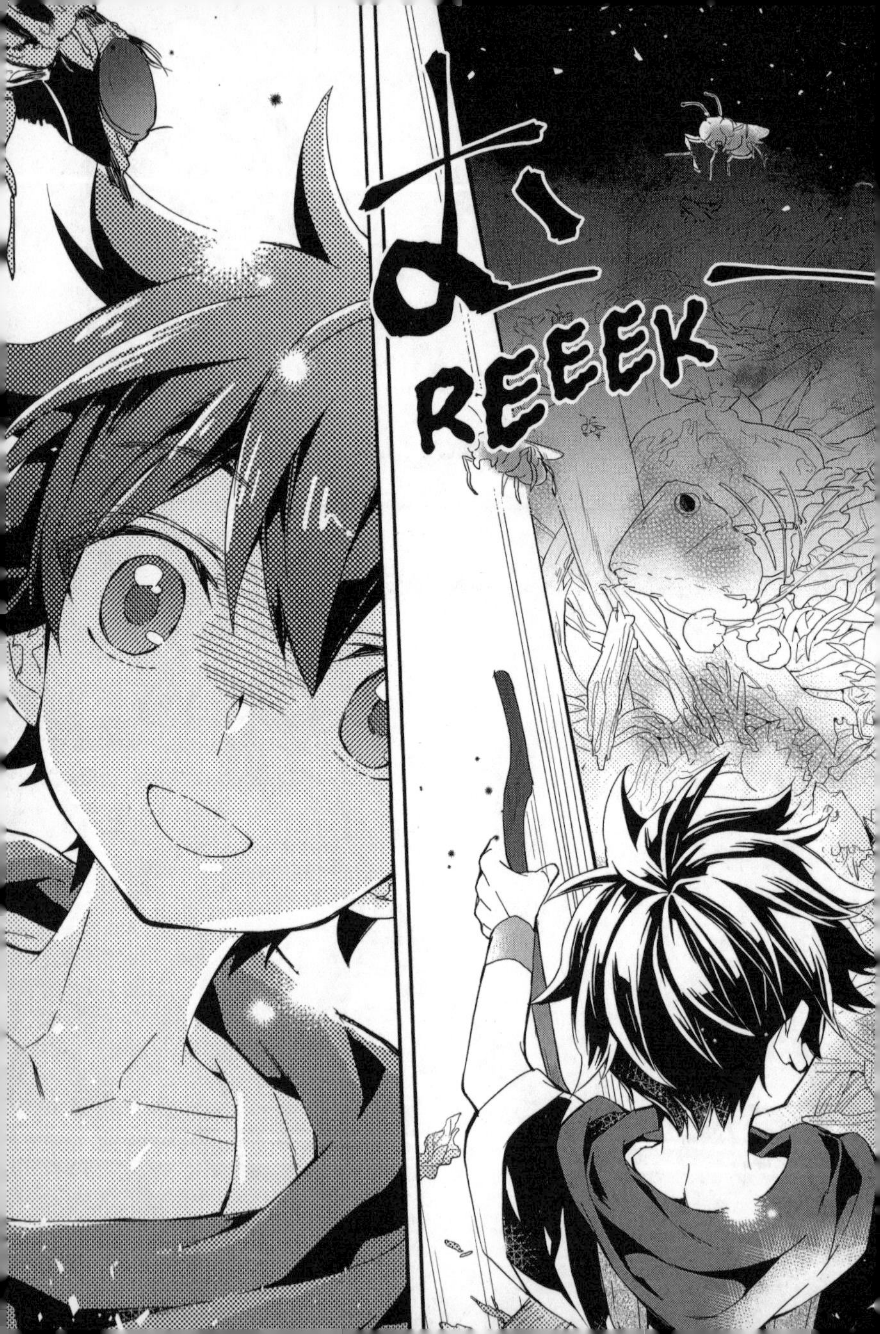
REEEK

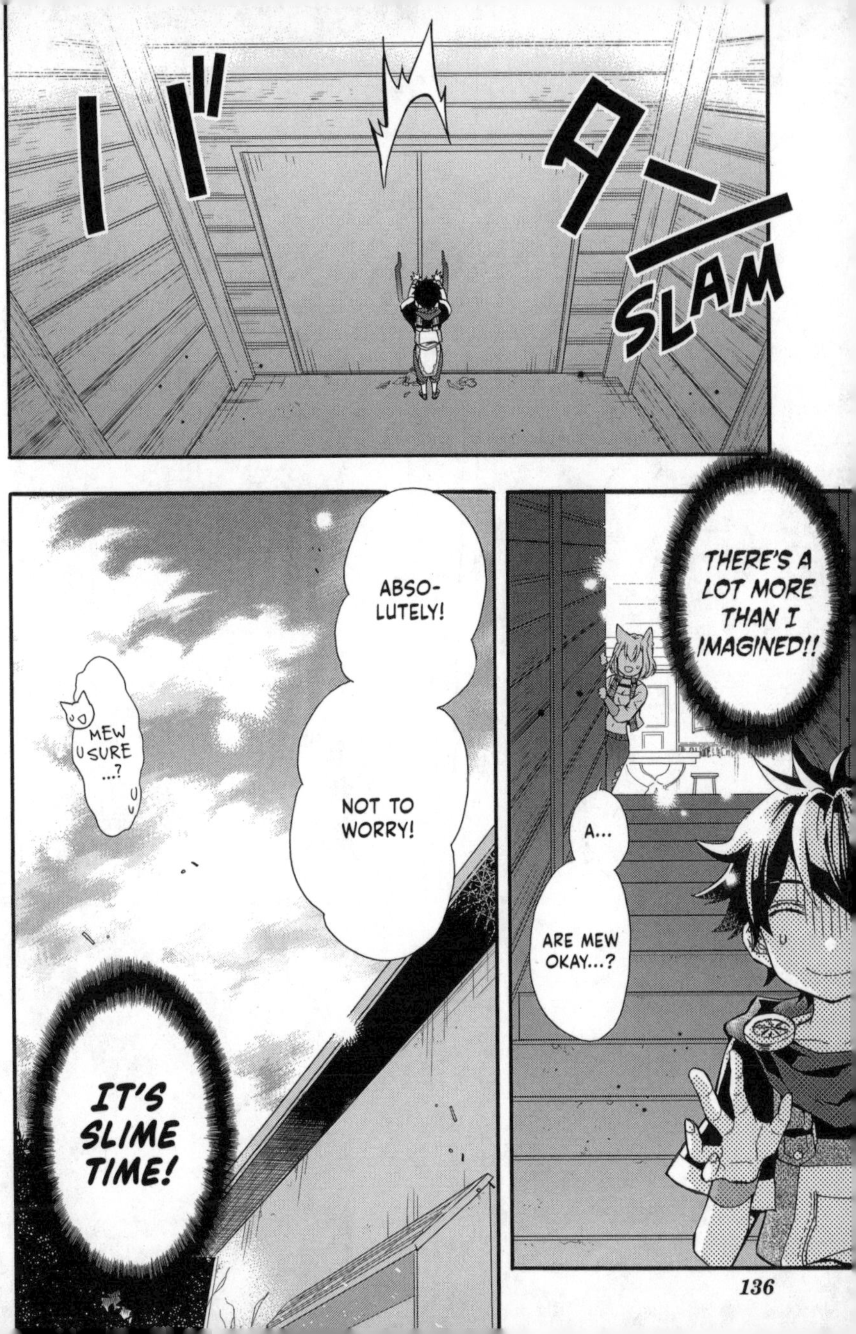
SLAM
THERE'S A LOT MORE THAN I IMAGINED!!
A...
ARE MEW OKAY...?
ABSO-LUTELY!
NOT TO WORRY!
MEW SURE ...?
IT'S SLIME TIME!

Chapter 9: First Job

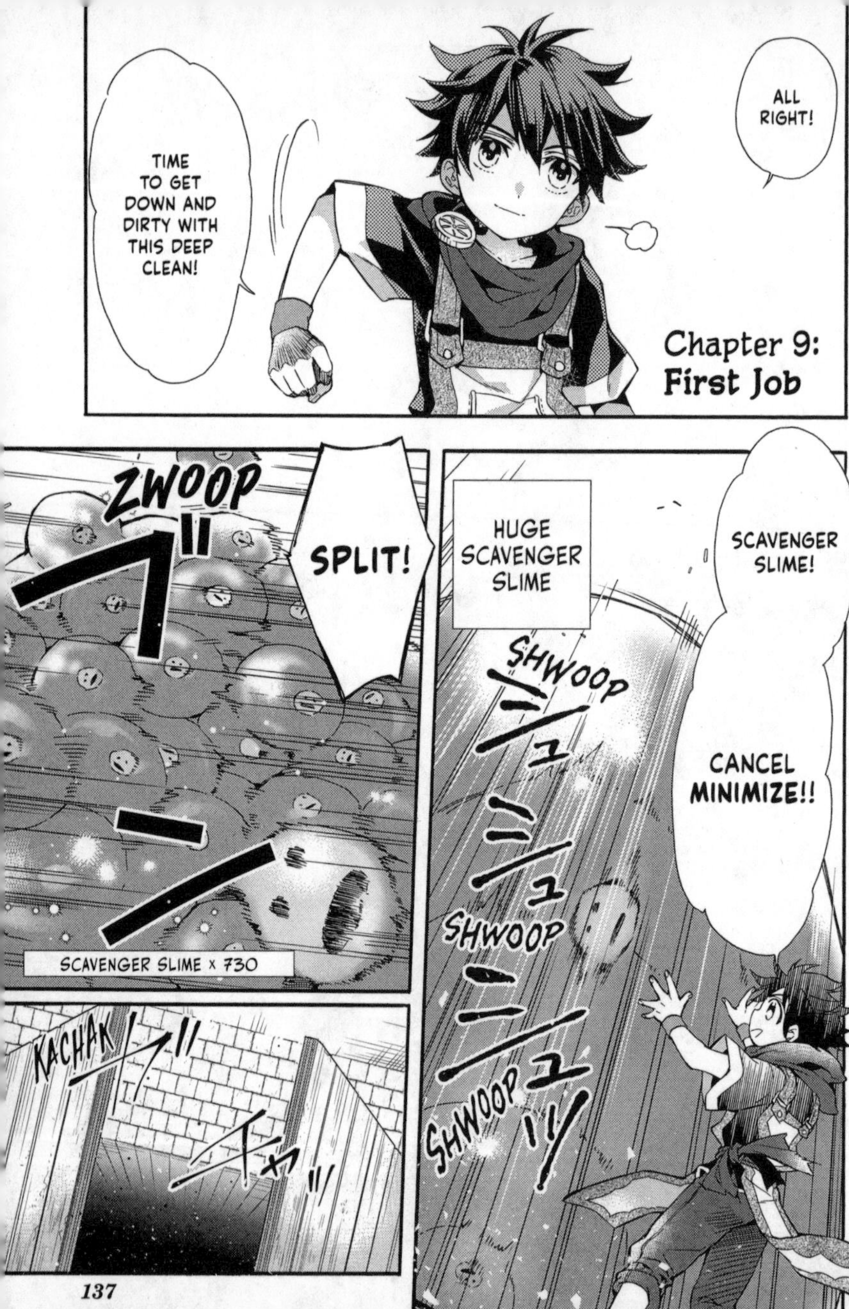
ALL RIGHT!
TIME TO GET DOWN AND DIRTY WITH THIS DEEP CLEAN!
Chapter 9: First Job
SCAVENGER SLIME!
CANCEL MINIMIZE!!
HUGE SCAVENGER SLIME
SHWOOP
SHWOOP
SHWOOP
SPLIT!
ZWOOP
SCAVENGER SLIME × 730
KACHAK

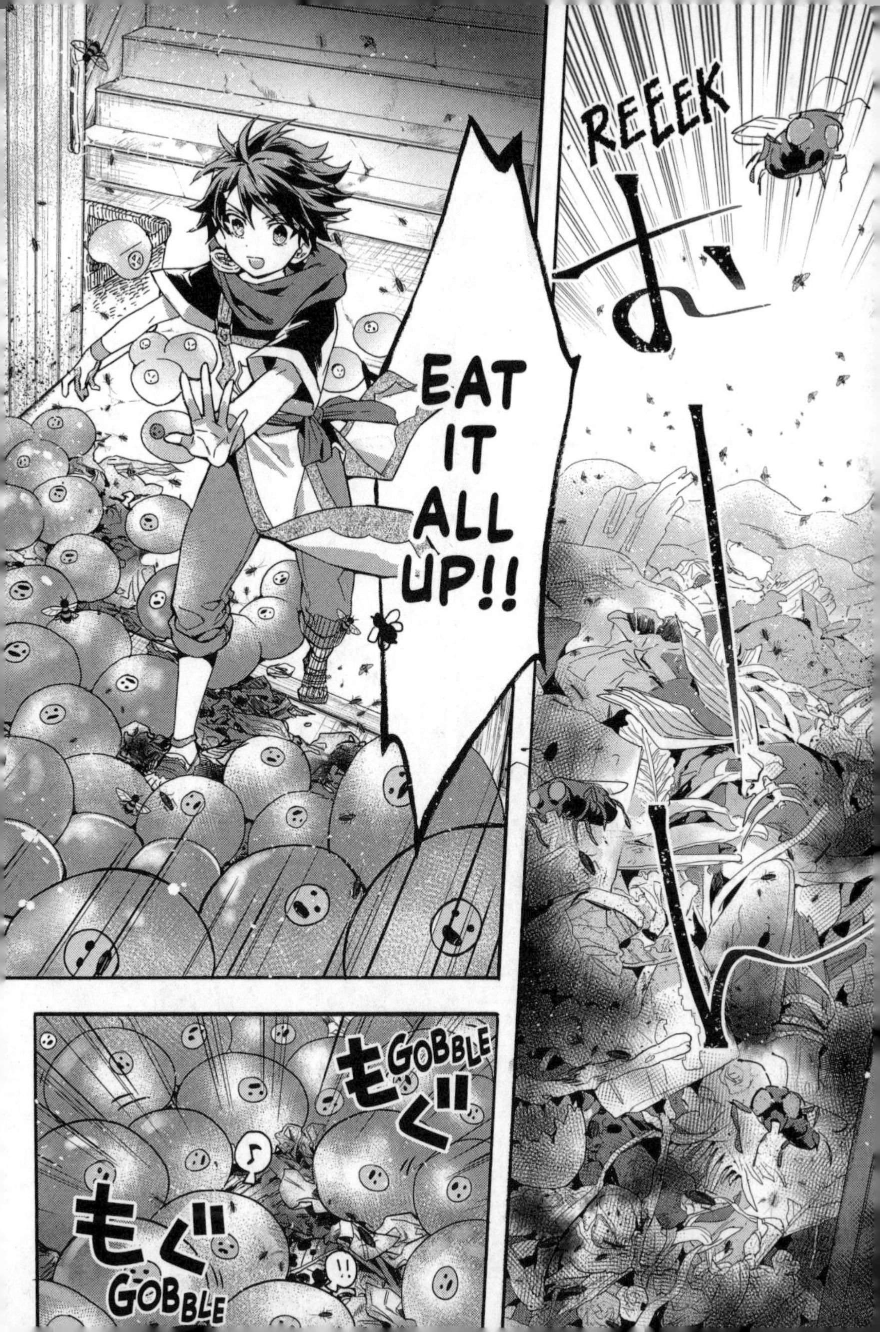
REEEK
EAT IT ALL UP!!
もぐ GOBBLE
もぐ GOBBLE

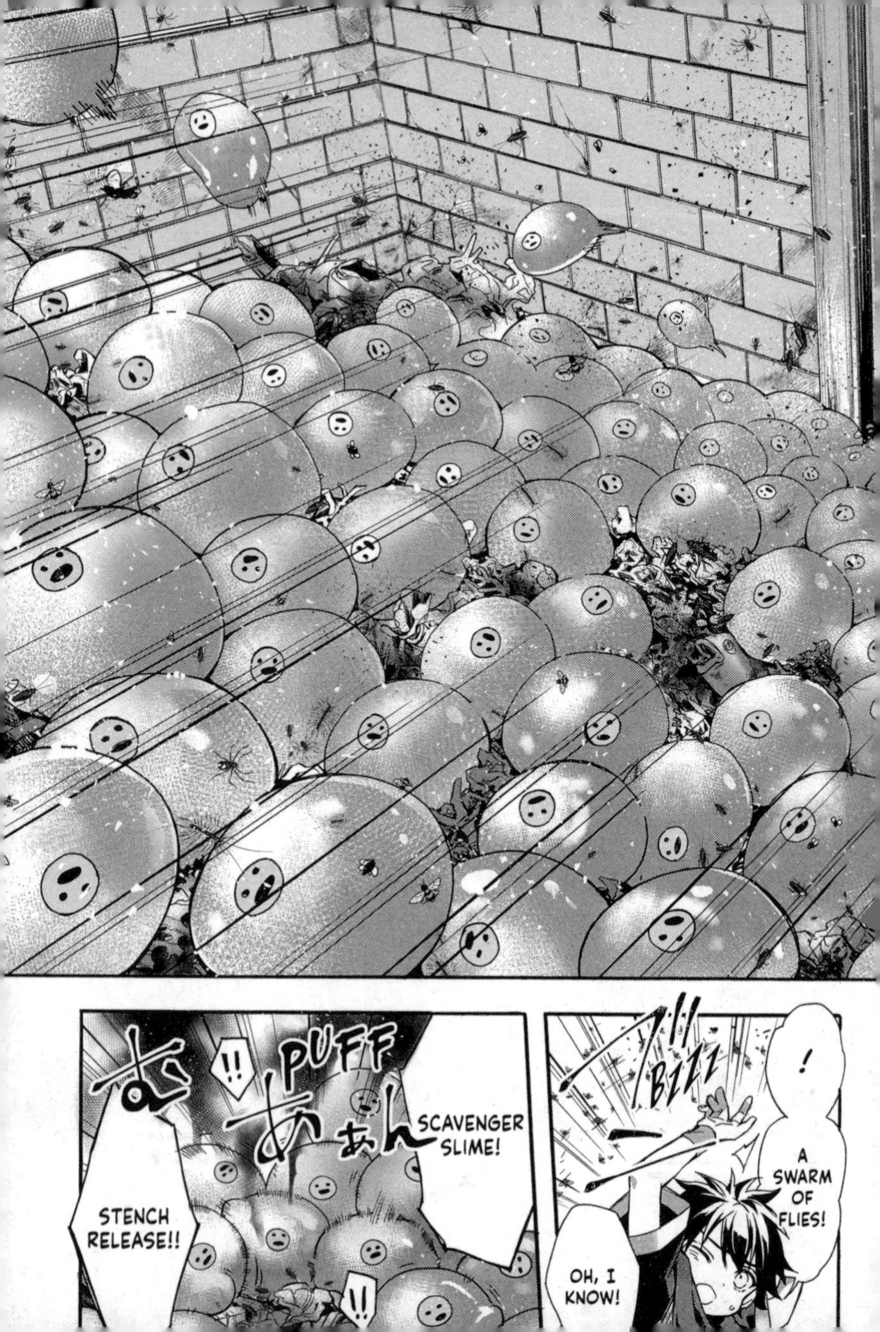
!
BZZZ
A SWARM OF FLIES!
OH, I KNOW!
SCAVENGER SLIME!
!!
PUFF
STENCH RELEASE!!
!!

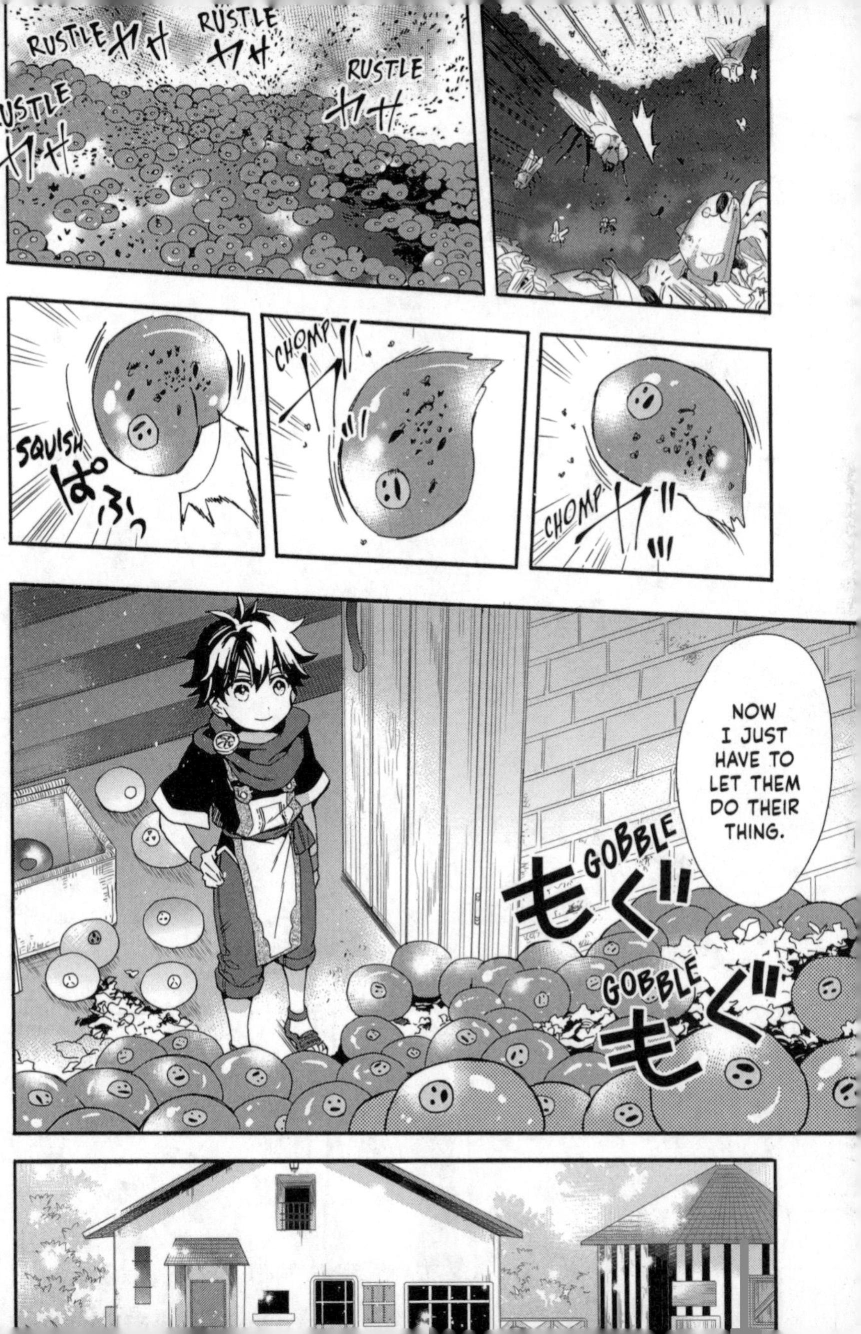
RUSTLE
RUSTLE
RUSTLE
RUSTLE
CHOMP
CHOMP
SQUISH
ぱふっ
NOW I JUST HAVE TO LET THEM DO THEIR THING.
GOBBLE
もぐ
GOBBLE
もぐ

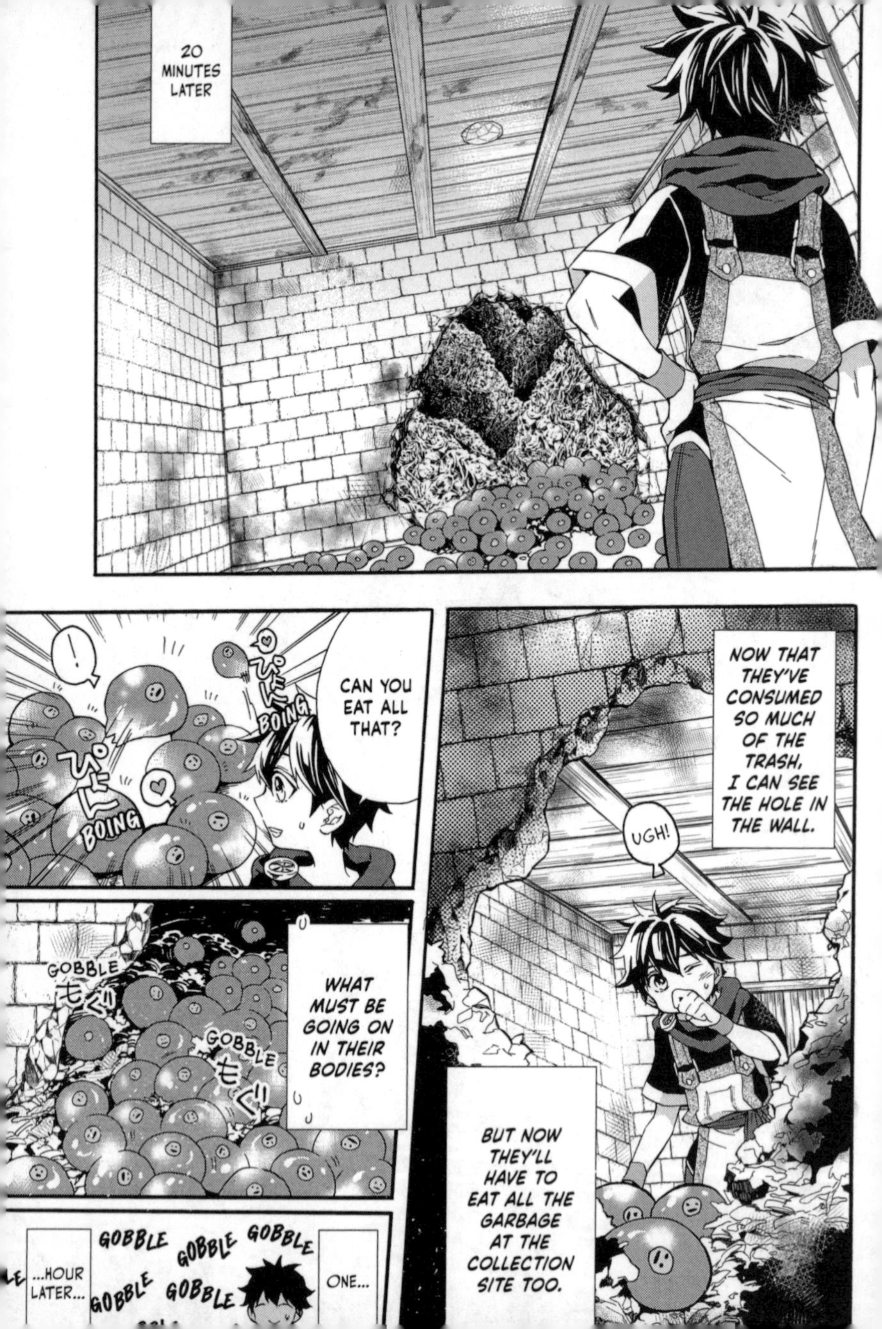
20 MINUTES LATER
NOW THAT THEY'VE CONSUMED SO MUCH OF THE TRASH, I CAN SEE THE HOLE IN THE WALL.
UGH!
BUT NOW THEY'LL HAVE TO EAT ALL THE GARBAGE AT THE COLLECTION SITE TOO.
CAN YOU EAT ALL THAT?
ぴょん BOING
!
ぴょん BOING
WHAT MUST BE GOING ON IN THEIR BODIES?
GOBBLE もぐ
GOBBLE もぐ
ONE...
GOBBLE GOBBLE GOBBLE
GOBBLE GOBBLE
...HOUR LATER...

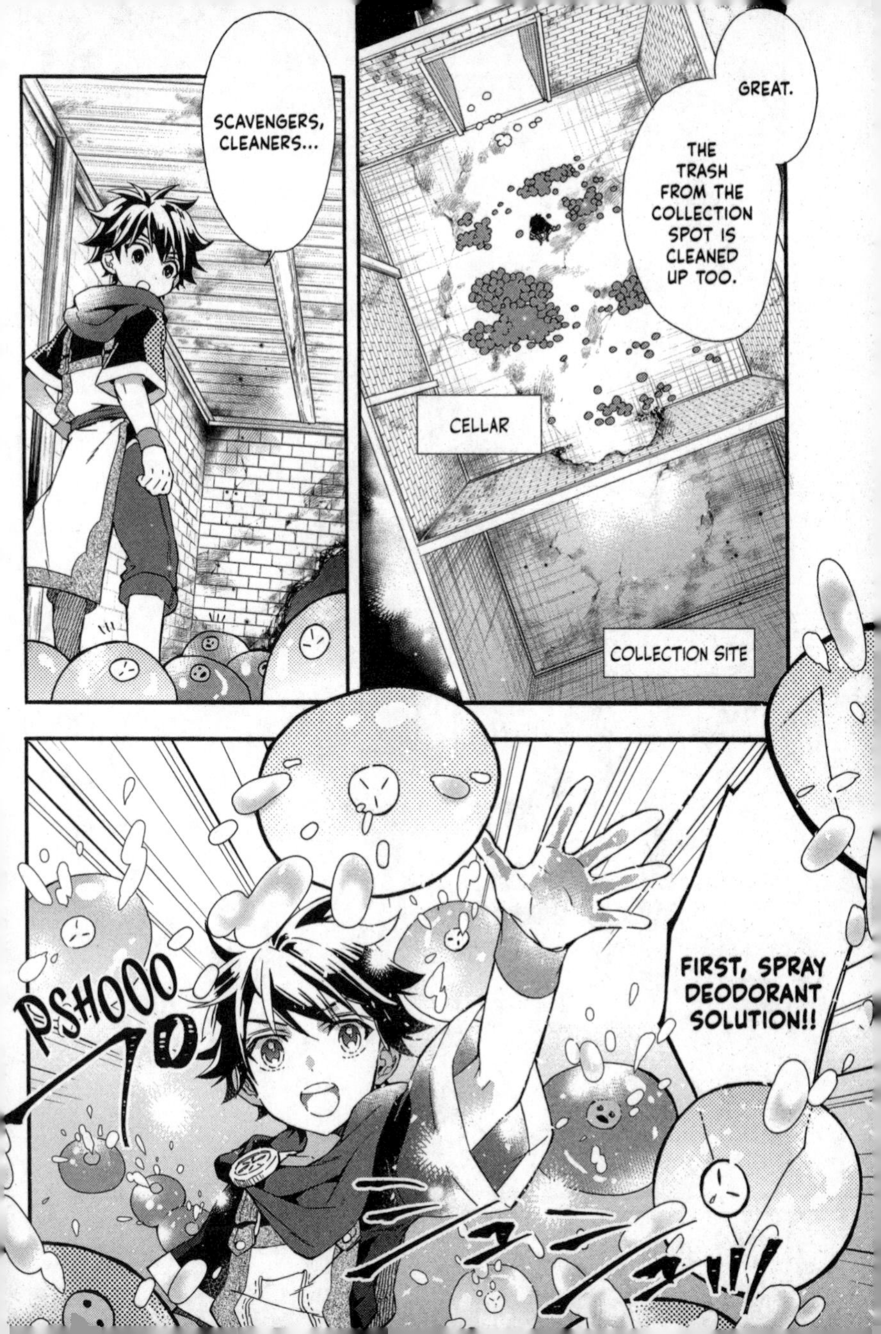
GREAT.
THE TRASH FROM THE COLLECTION SPOT IS CLEANED UP TOO.
CELLAR
COLLECTION SITE
SCAVENGERS, CLEANERS...
FIRST, SPRAY DEODORANT SOLUTION!!
PSHOOO

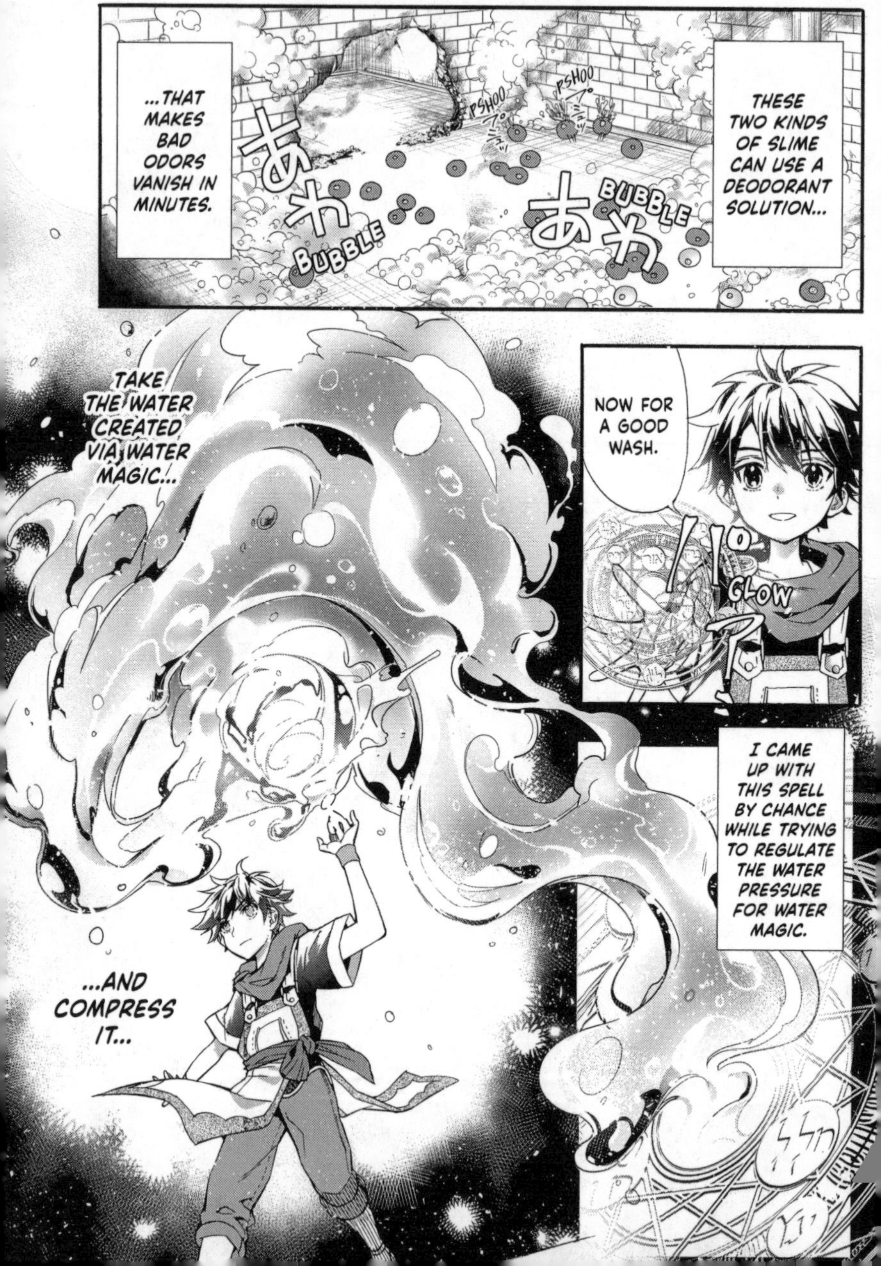
THESE TWO KINDS OF SLIME CAN USE A DEODORANT SOLUTION...
PSHOO
PSHOO
あわ
BUBBLE
あわ
BUBBLE
...THAT MAKES BAD ODORS VANISH IN MINUTES.
NOW FOR A GOOD WASH.
GLOW
I CAME UP WITH THIS SPELL BY CHANCE WHILE TRYING TO REGULATE THE WATER PRESSURE FOR WATER MAGIC.
TAKE THE WATER CREATED VIA WATER MAGIC...
...AND COMPRESS IT...

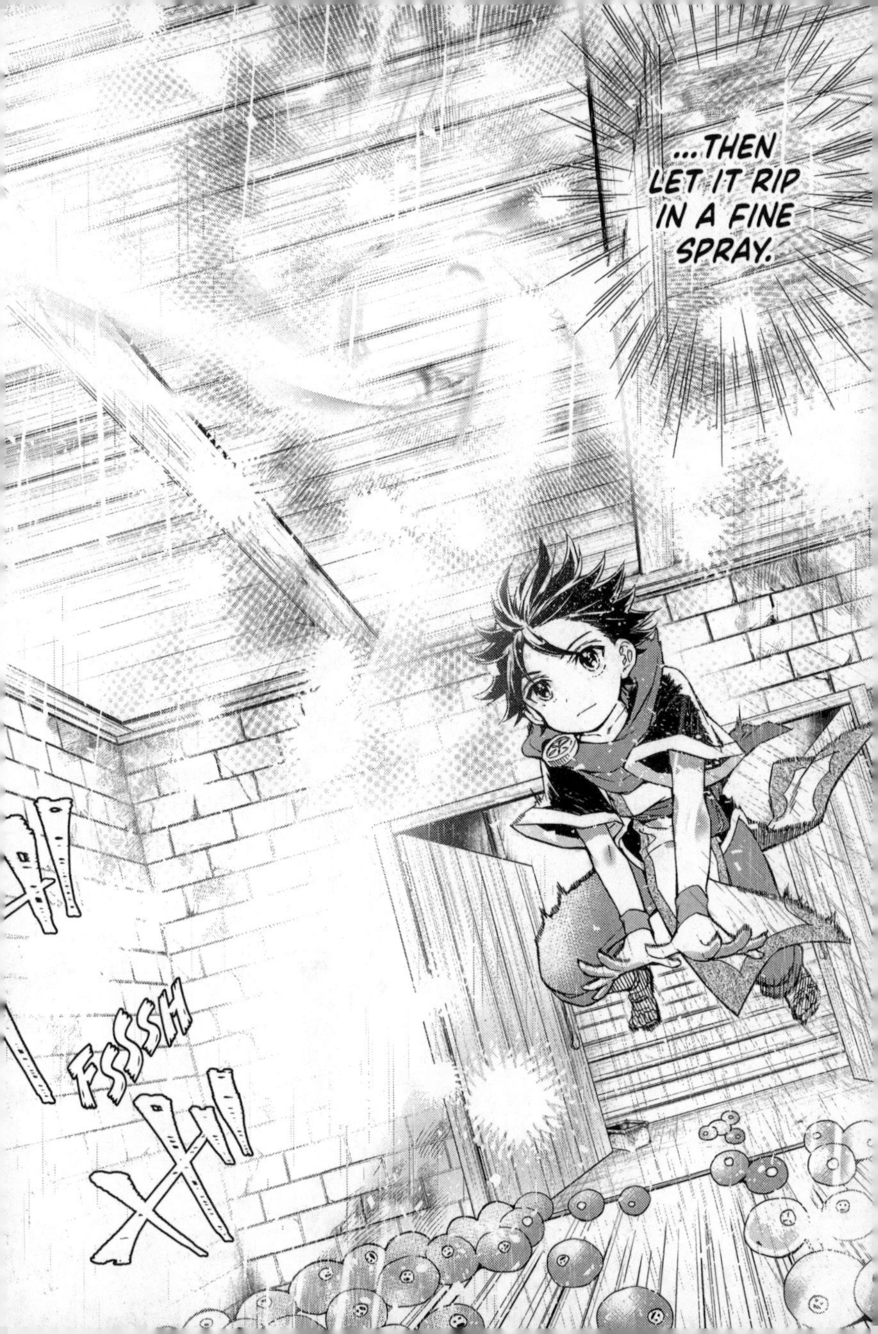
...THEN LET IT RIP IN A FINE SPRAY.
FSSSH

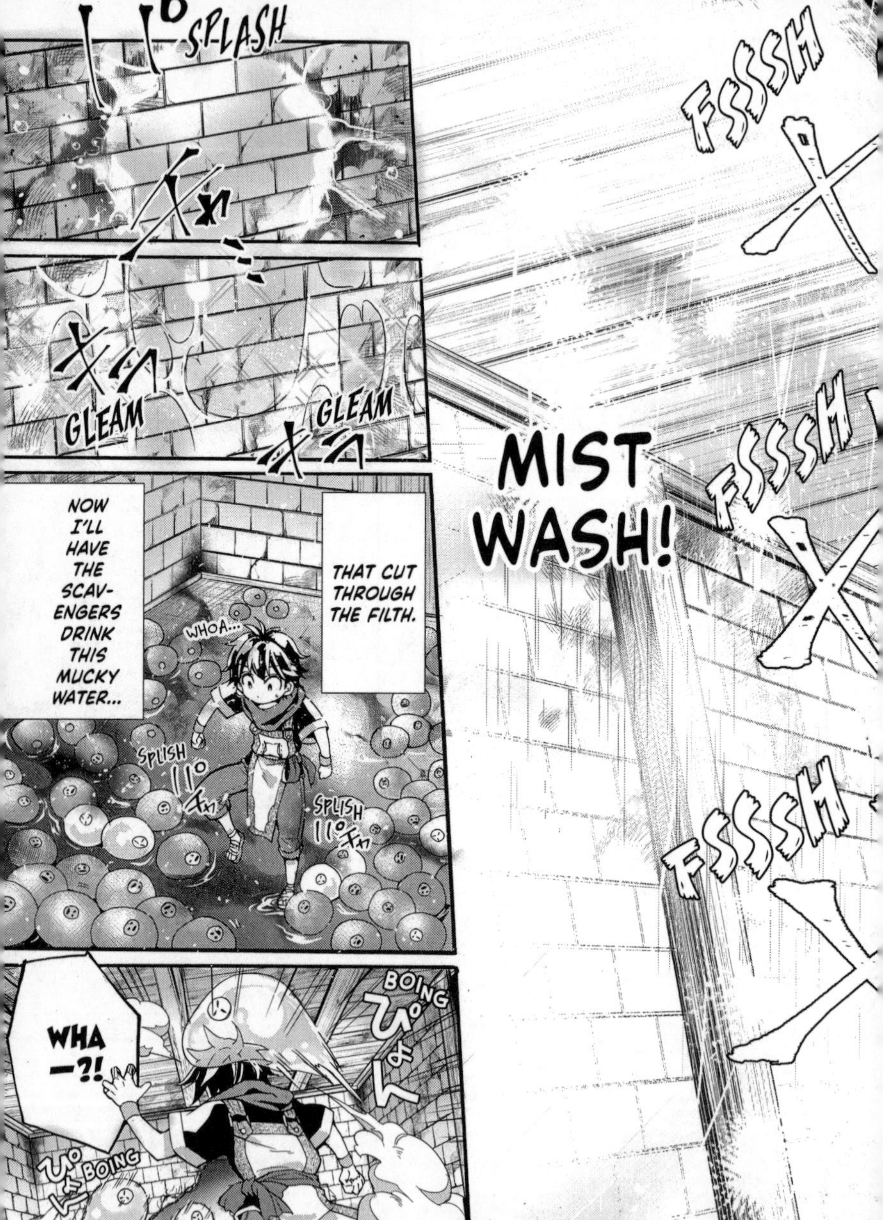
FSSSH
MIST WASH!
FSSSH
FSSSH
SPLASH
GLEAM
GLEAM
THAT CUT THROUGH THE FILTH.
NOW I'LL HAVE THE SCAV-ENGERS DRINK THIS MUCKY WATER...
WHOA...
SPLISH
SPLISH
BOING
WHA—?!
BOING

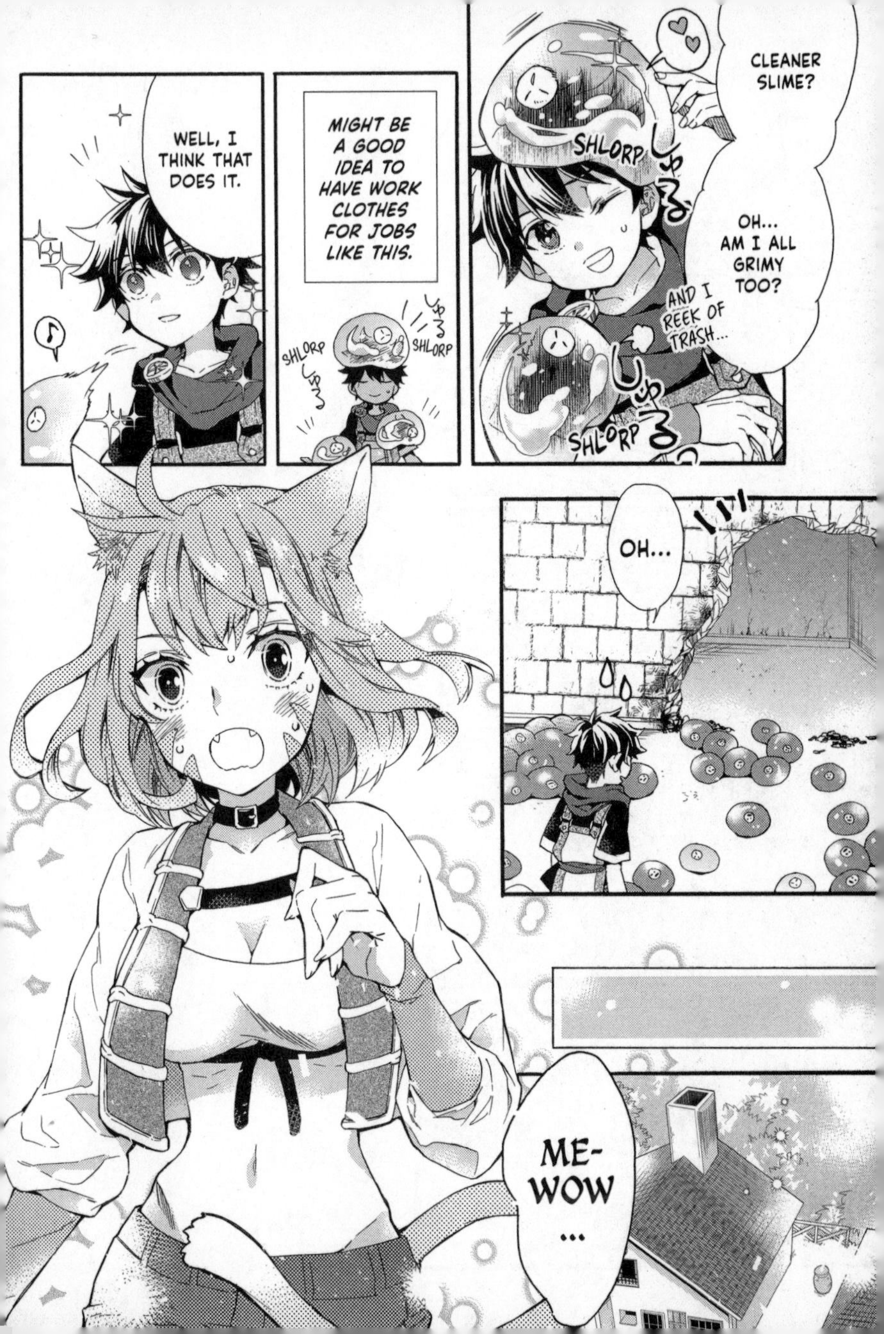
CLEANER SLIME?
SHLORP
OH... AM I ALL GRIMY TOO?
AND I REEK OF TRASH...
SHLORP
MIGHT BE A GOOD IDEA TO HAVE WORK CLOTHES FOR JOBS LIKE THIS.
SHLORP
SHLORP
WELL, I THINK THAT DOES IT.
OH...
ME-WOW...

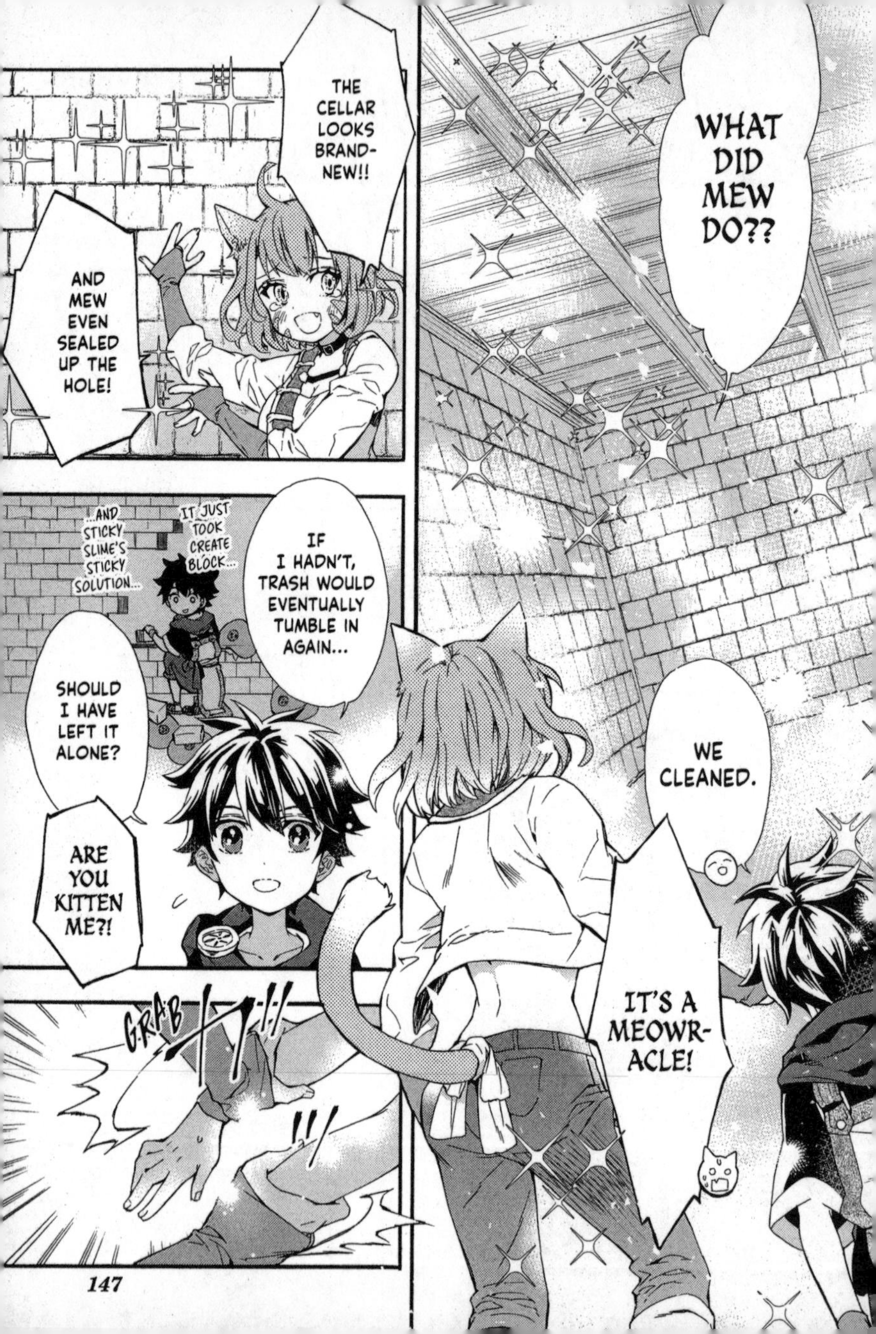
WHAT DID MEW DO??
WE CLEANED.
IT'S A MEOWR-ACLE!
THE CELLAR LOOKS BRAND-NEW!!
AND MEW EVEN SEALED UP THE HOLE!
IF I HADN'T, TRASH WOULD EVENTUALLY TUMBLE IN AGAIN...
IT JUST TOOK CREATE BLOCK...
...AND STICKY SLIME'S STICKY SOLUTION...
SHOULD I HAVE LEFT IT ALONE?
ARE YOU KITTEN ME?!
GRAB
!!

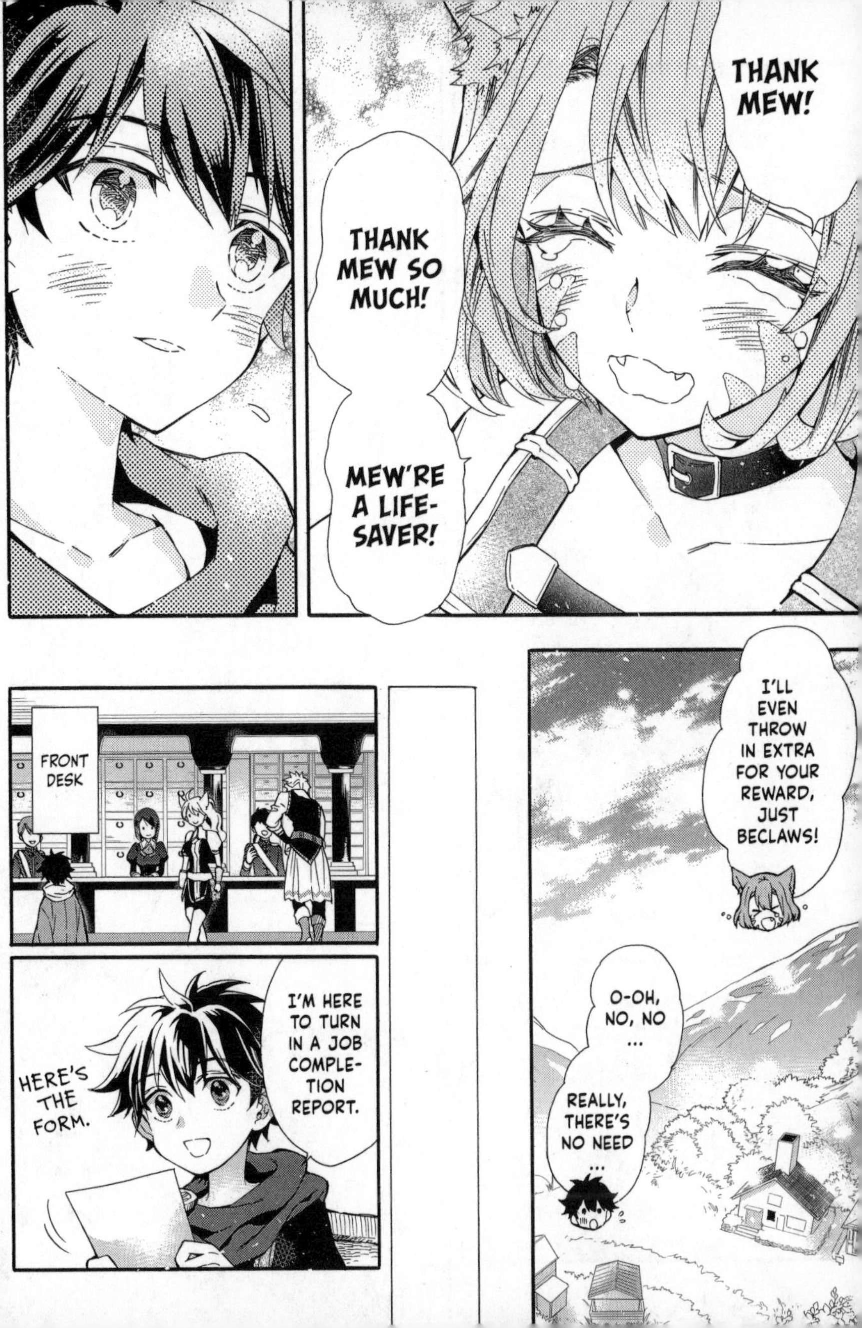
THANK MEW!
THANK MEW SO MUCH!
MEW'RE A LIFE-SAVER!
I'LL EVEN THROW IN EXTRA FOR YOUR REWARD, JUST BECLAWS!
O-OH, NO, NO ...
REALLY, THERE'S NO NEED ...
FRONT DESK
I'M HERE TO TURN IN A JOB COMPLETION REPORT.
HERE'S THE FORM.

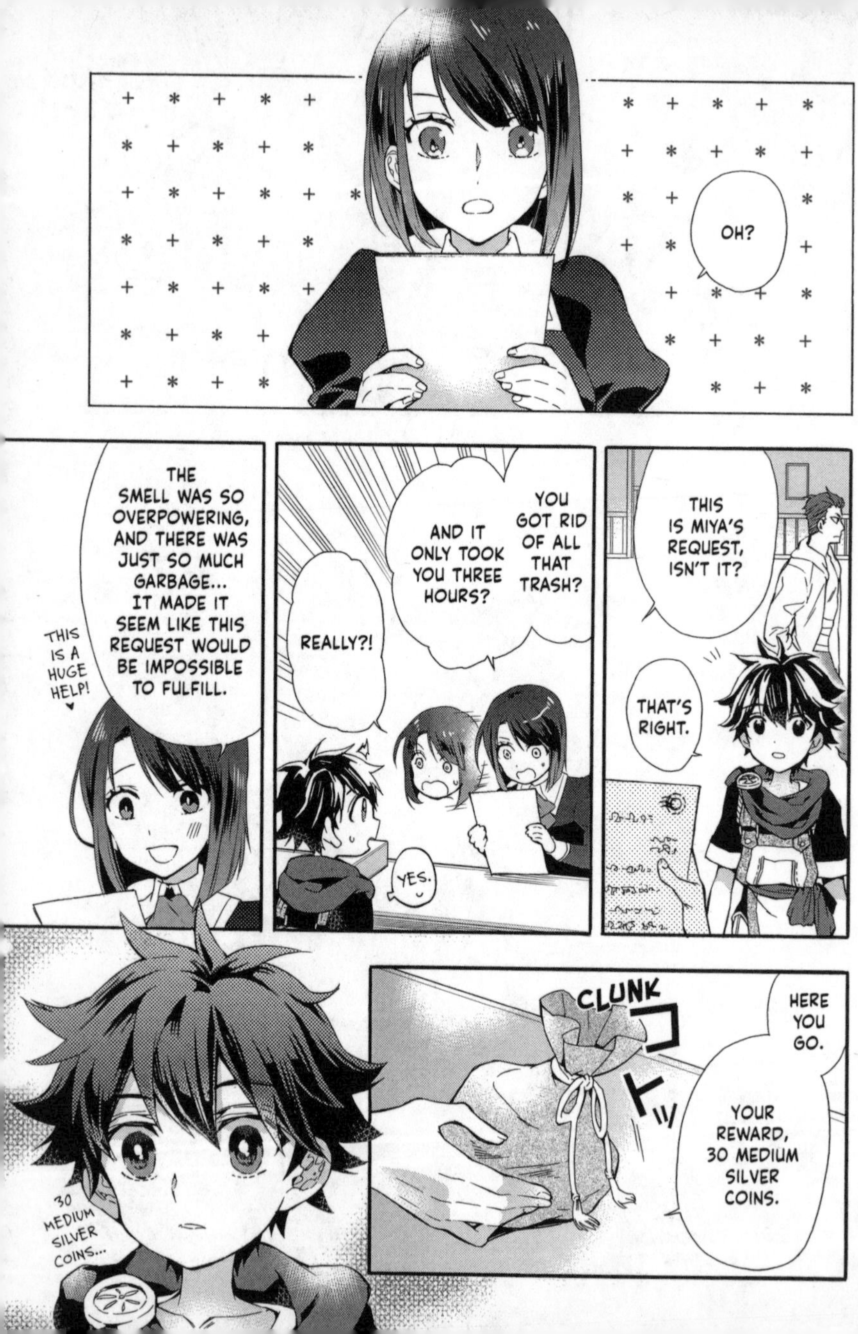
OH?
THIS IS MIYA'S REQUEST, ISN'T IT?
THAT'S RIGHT.
YOU GOT RID OF ALL THAT TRASH?
AND IT ONLY TOOK YOU THREE HOURS?
REALLY?!
YES.
THE SMELL WAS SO OVERPOWERING, AND THERE WAS JUST SO MUCH GARBAGE... IT MADE IT SEEM LIKE THIS REQUEST WOULD BE IMPOSSIBLE TO FULFILL.
THIS IS A HUGE HELP!
HERE YOU GO.
CLUNK
YOUR REWARD, 30 MEDIUM SILVER COINS.
30 MEDIUM SILVER COINS...

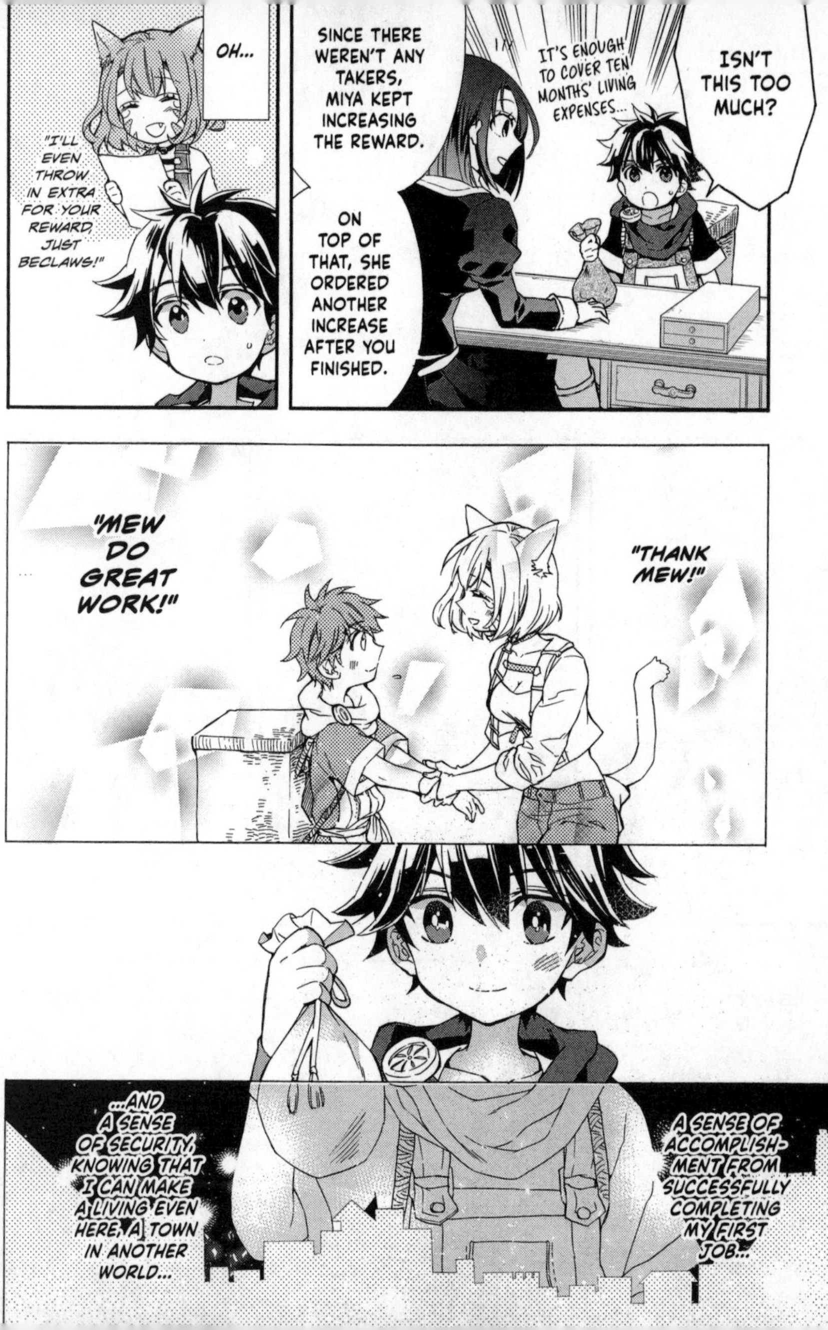
ISN'T THIS TOO MUCH?
IT'S ENOUGH TO COVER TEN MONTHS' LIVING EXPENSES...
SINCE THERE WEREN'T ANY TAKERS, MIYA KEPT INCREASING THE REWARD.
ON TOP OF THAT, SHE ORDERED ANOTHER INCREASE AFTER YOU FINISHED.
OH...
"I'LL EVEN THROW IN EXTRA FOR YOUR REWARD, JUST BECLAWS!"
"THANK MEW!"
"MEW DO GREAT WORK!"
A SENSE OF ACCOMPLISHMENT FROM SUCCESSFULLY COMPLETING MY FIRST JOB...
...AND A SENSE OF SECURITY, KNOWING THAT I CAN MAKE A LIVING EVEN HERE, A TOWN IN ANOTHER WORLD...

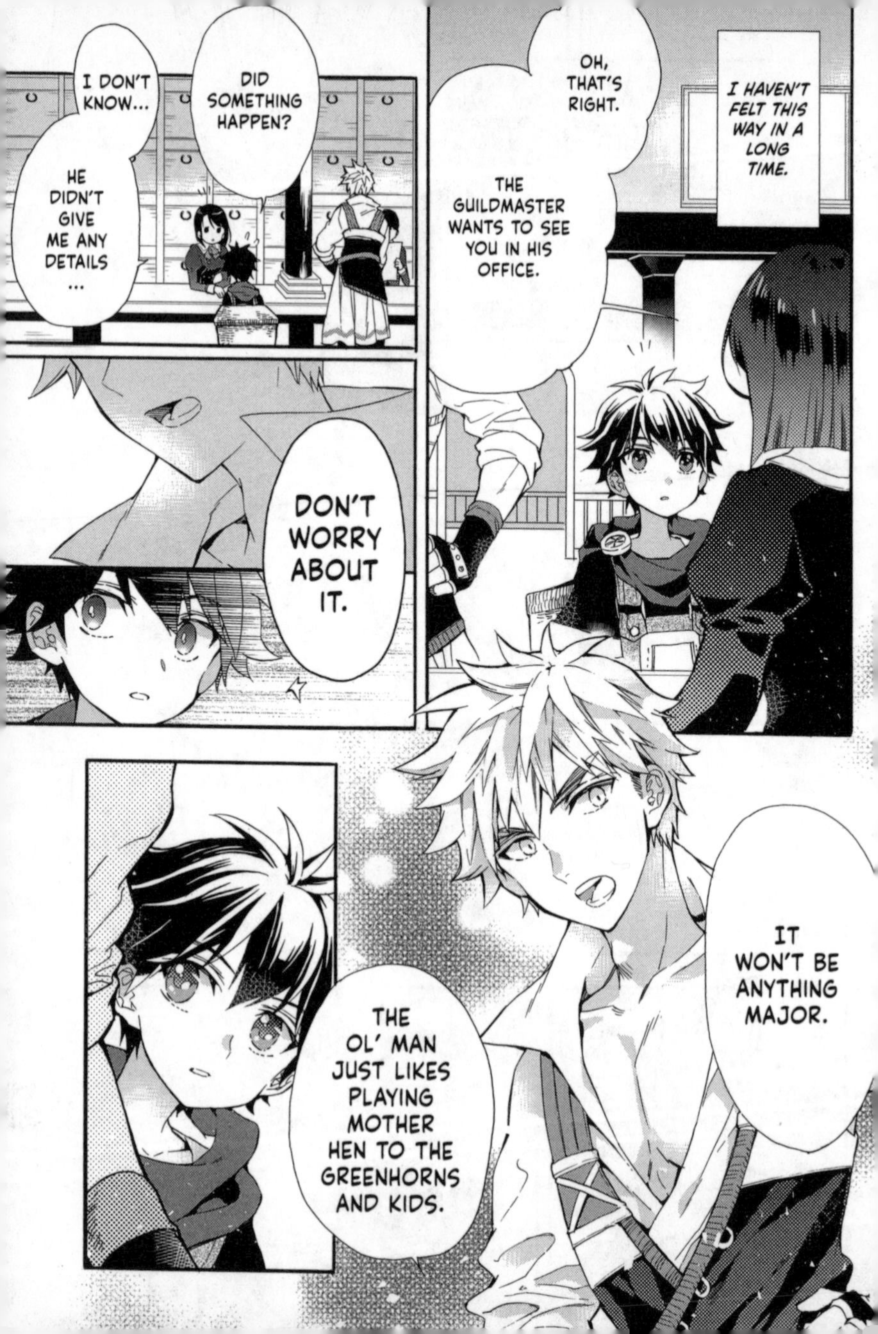
I HAVEN'T FELT THIS WAY IN A LONG TIME.
OH, THAT'S RIGHT.
THE GUILDMASTER WANTS TO SEE YOU IN HIS OFFICE.
DID SOMETHING HAPPEN?
I DON'T KNOW...
HE DIDN'T GIVE ME ANY DETAILS...
DON'T WORRY ABOUT IT.
IT WON'T BE ANYTHING MAJOR.
THE OL' MAN JUST LIKES PLAYING MOTHER HEN TO THE GREENHORNS AND KIDS.

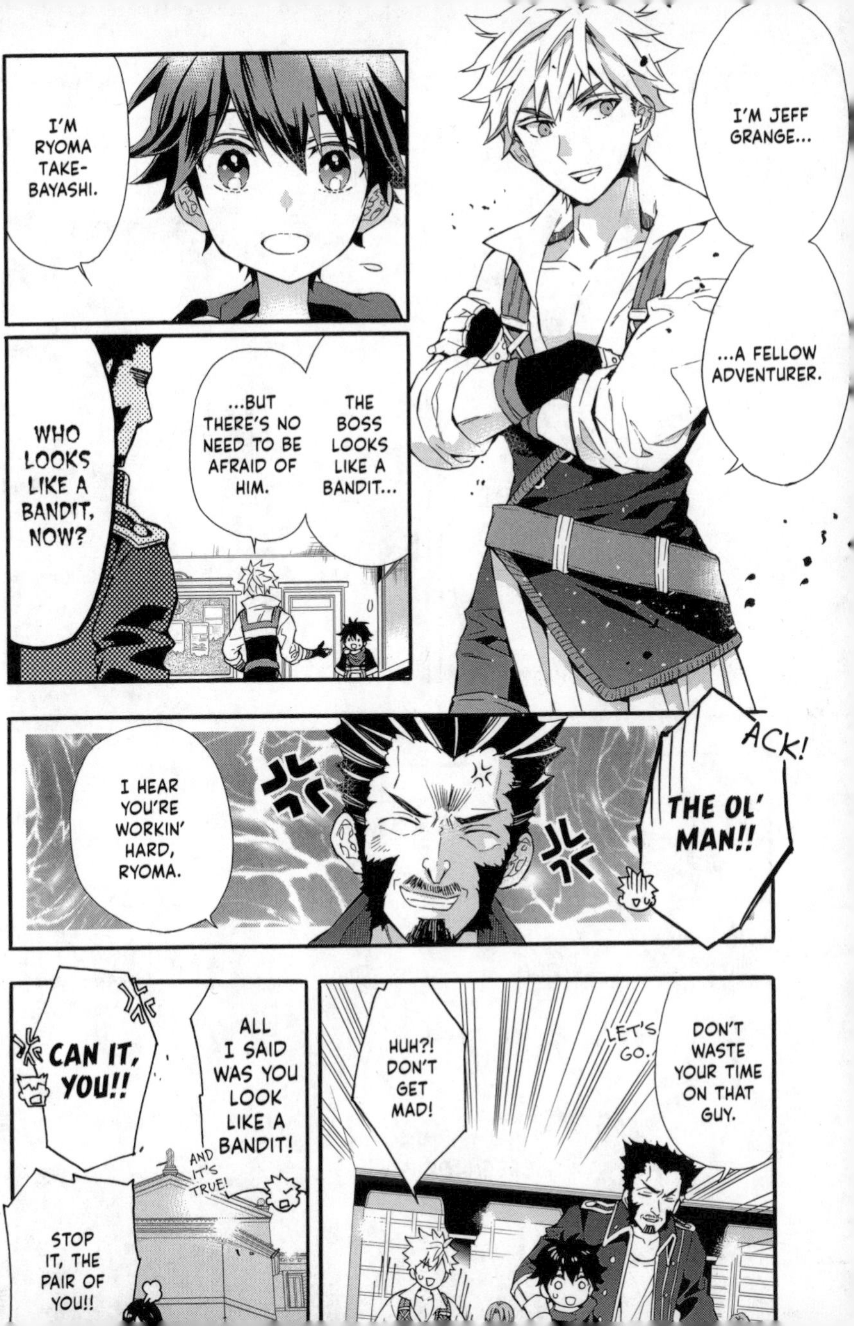
I'M JEFF GRANGE...
...A FELLOW ADVENTURER.
I'M RYOMA TAKE-BAYASHI.
THE BOSS LOOKS LIKE A BANDIT...
...BUT THERE'S NO NEED TO BE AFRAID OF HIM.
WHO LOOKS LIKE A BANDIT, NOW?
ACK!
THE OL' MAN!!
I HEAR YOU'RE WORKIN' HARD, RYOMA.
DON'T WASTE YOUR TIME ON THAT GUY.
LET'S GO...
HUH?! DON'T GET MAD!
ALL I SAID WAS YOU LOOK LIKE A BANDIT!
AND IT'S TRUE!
CAN IT, YOU!!
STOP IT, THE PAIR OF YOU!!

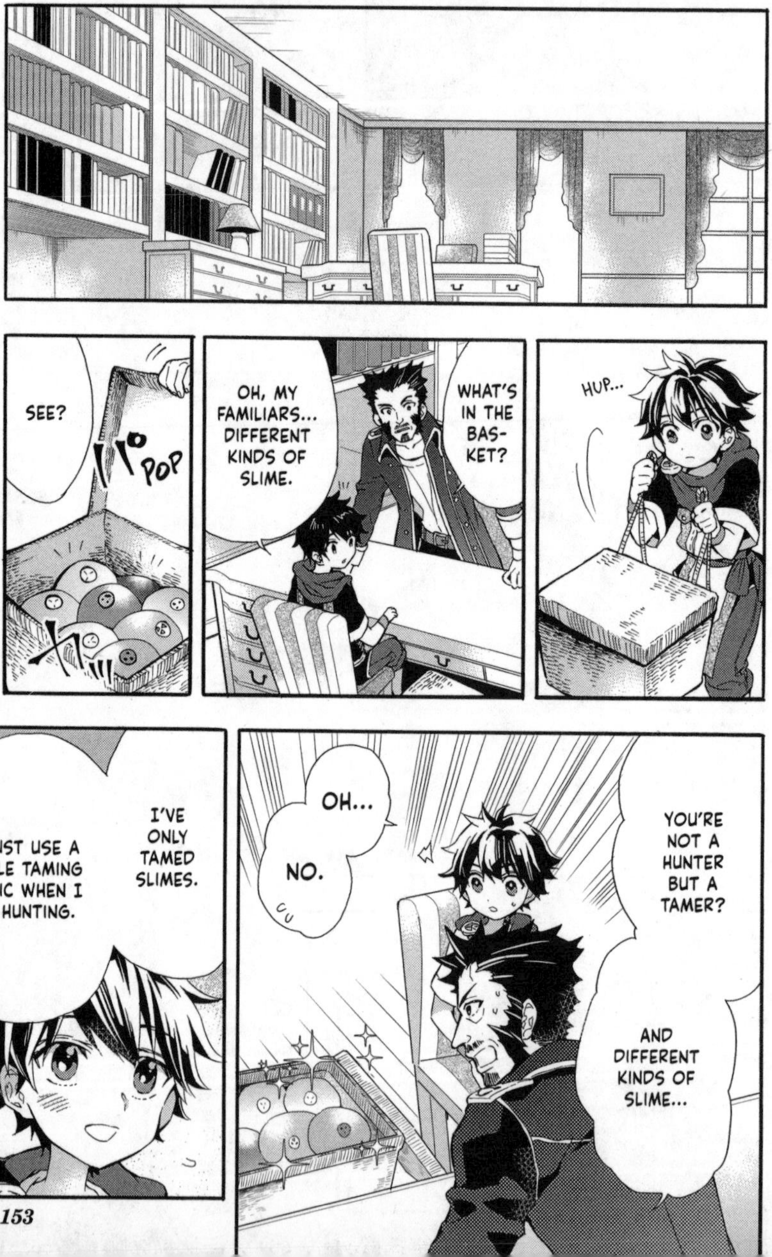
HUP...
WHAT'S IN THE BAS-KET?
OH, MY FAMILIARS... DIFFERENT KINDS OF SLIME.
SEE?
POP
YOU'RE NOT A HUNTER BUT A TAMER?
OH...
NO.
AND DIFFERENT KINDS OF SLIME...
I'VE ONLY TAMED SLIMES.
I JUST USE A LITTLE TAMING MAGIC WHEN I GO HUNTING.

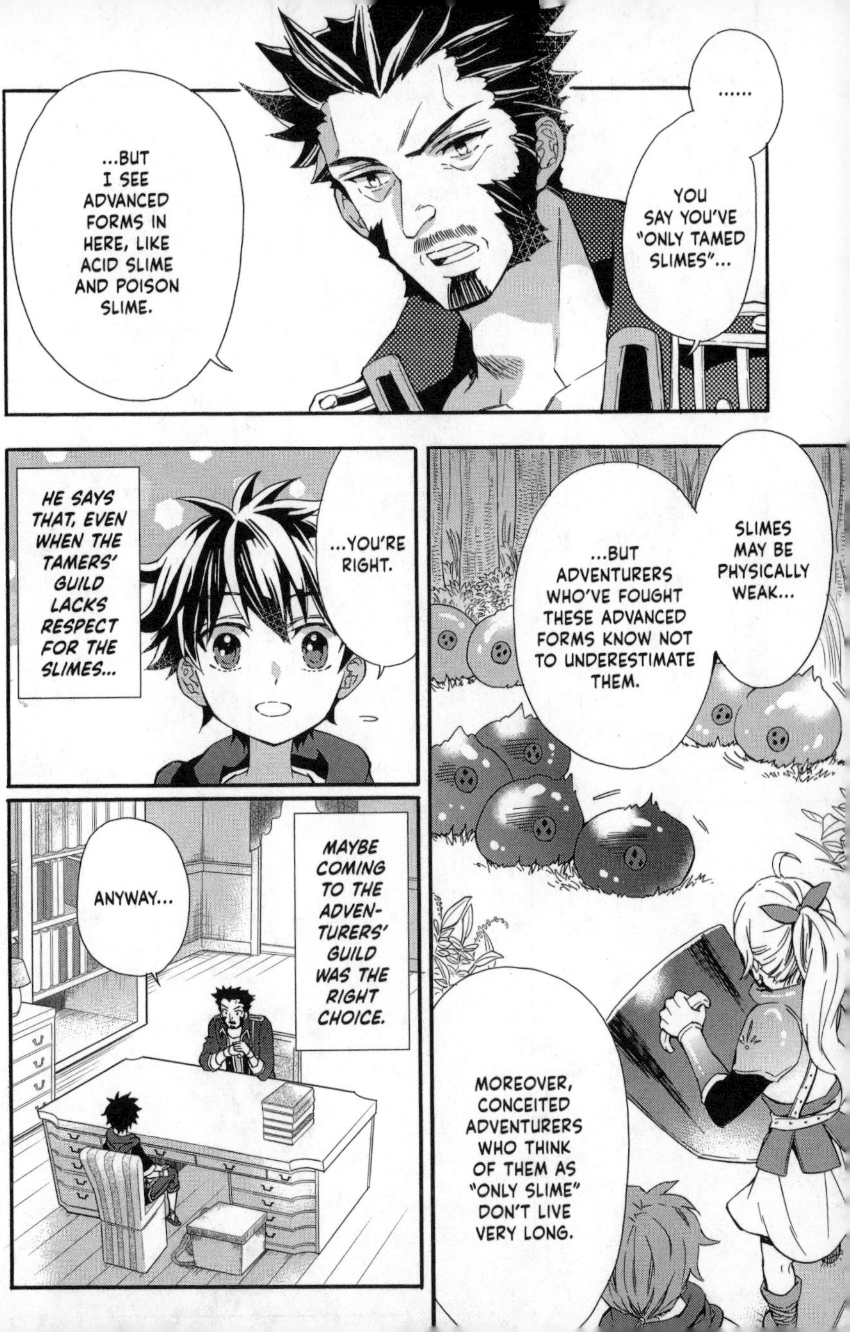
......
YOU SAY YOU'VE "ONLY TAMED SLIMES"...
...BUT I SEE ADVANCED FORMS IN HERE, LIKE ACID SLIME AND POISON SLIME.
SLIMES MAY BE PHYSICALLY WEAK...
...BUT ADVENTURERS WHO'VE FOUGHT THESE ADVANCED FORMS KNOW NOT TO UNDERESTIMATE THEM.
MOREOVER, CONCEITED ADVENTURERS WHO THINK OF THEM AS "ONLY SLIME" DON'T LIVE VERY LONG.
...YOU'RE RIGHT.
HE SAYS THAT, EVEN WHEN THE TAMERS' GUILD LACKS RESPECT FOR THE SLIMES...
MAYBE COMING TO THE ADVEN-TURERS' GUILD WAS THE RIGHT CHOICE.
ANYWAY...

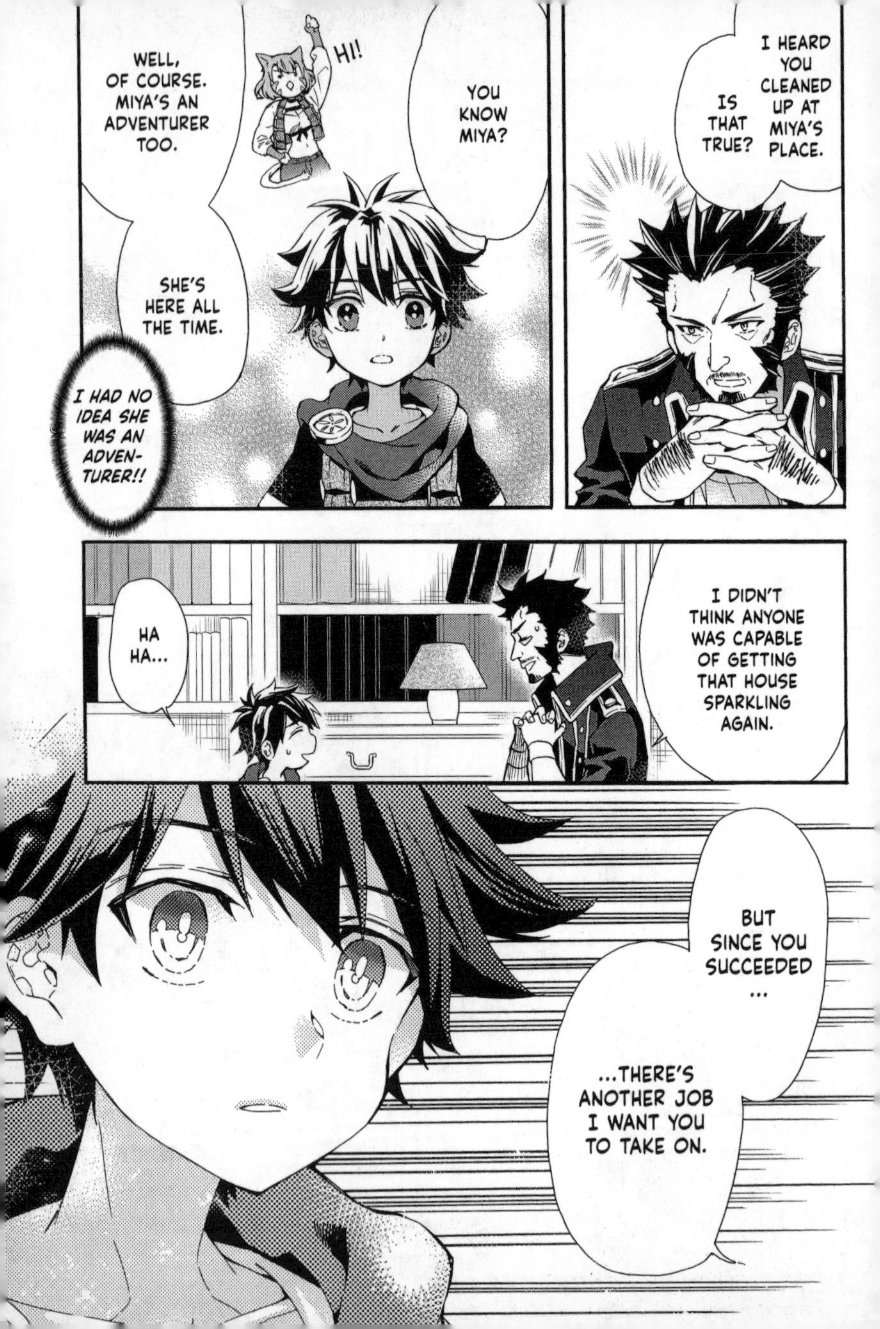
I HEARD YOU CLEANED UP AT MIYA'S PLACE.
IS THAT TRUE?
YOU KNOW MIYA?
WELL, OF COURSE. MIYA'S AN ADVENTURER TOO.
HI!
SHE'S HERE ALL THE TIME.
I HAD NO IDEA SHE WAS AN ADVEN-TURER!!
I DIDN'T THINK ANYONE WAS CAPABLE OF GETTING THAT HOUSE SPARKLING AGAIN.
HA HA...
BUT SINCE YOU SUCCEEDED...
...THERE'S ANOTHER JOB I WANT YOU TO TAKE ON.

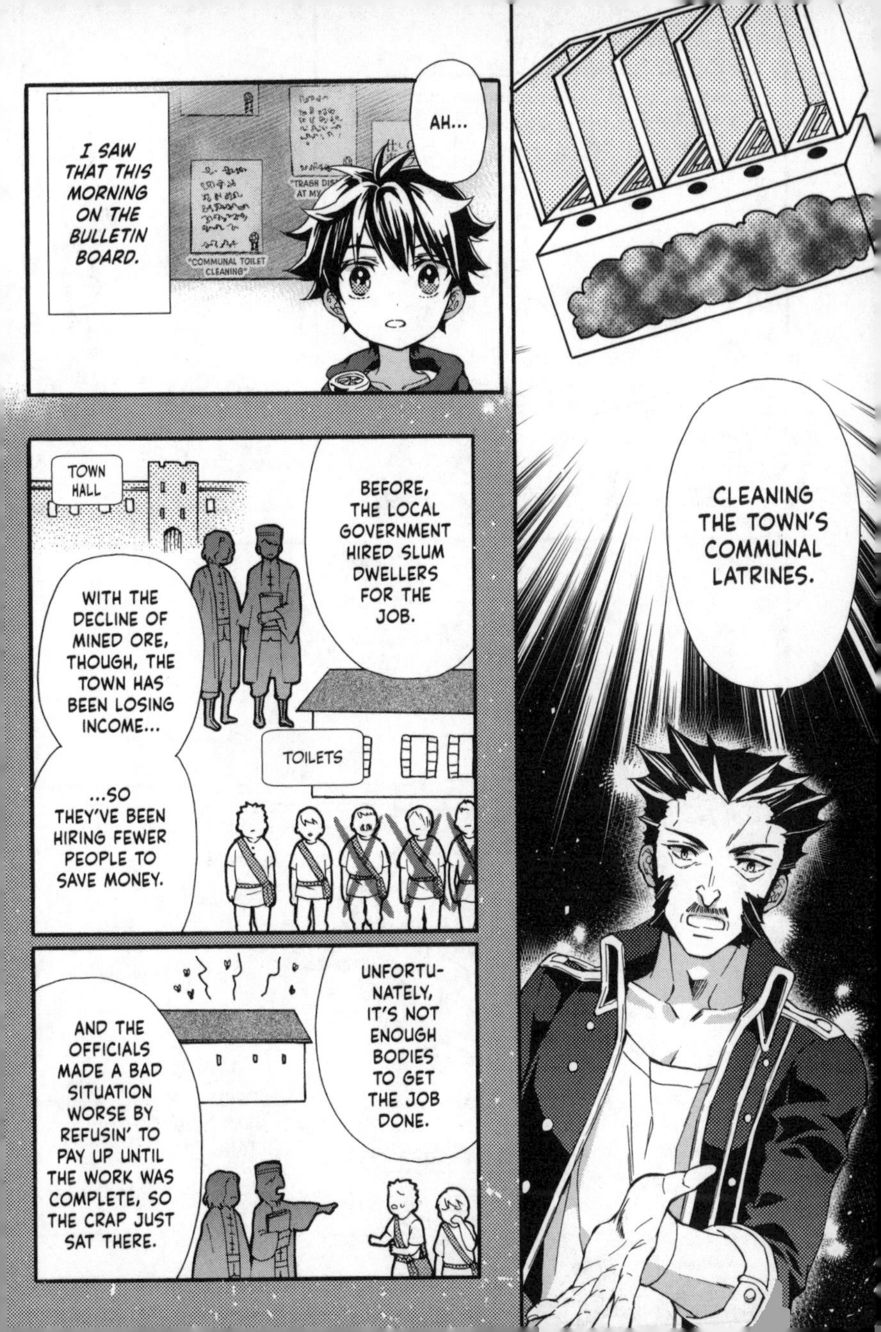
CLEANING THE TOWN'S COMMUNAL LATRINES.
AH...
I SAW THAT THIS MORNING ON THE BULLETIN BOARD.
"COMMUNAL TOILET CLEANING"
BEFORE, THE LOCAL GOVERNMENT HIRED SLUM DWELLERS FOR THE JOB.
TOWN HALL
WITH THE DECLINE OF MINED ORE, THOUGH, THE TOWN HAS BEEN LOSING INCOME...
TOILETS
...SO THEY'VE BEEN HIRING FEWER PEOPLE TO SAVE MONEY.
UNFORTU-NATELY, IT'S NOT ENOUGH BODIES TO GET THE JOB DONE.
AND THE OFFICIALS MADE A BAD SITUATION WORSE BY REFUSIN' TO PAY UP UNTIL THE WORK WAS COMPLETE, SO THE CRAP JUST SAT THERE.

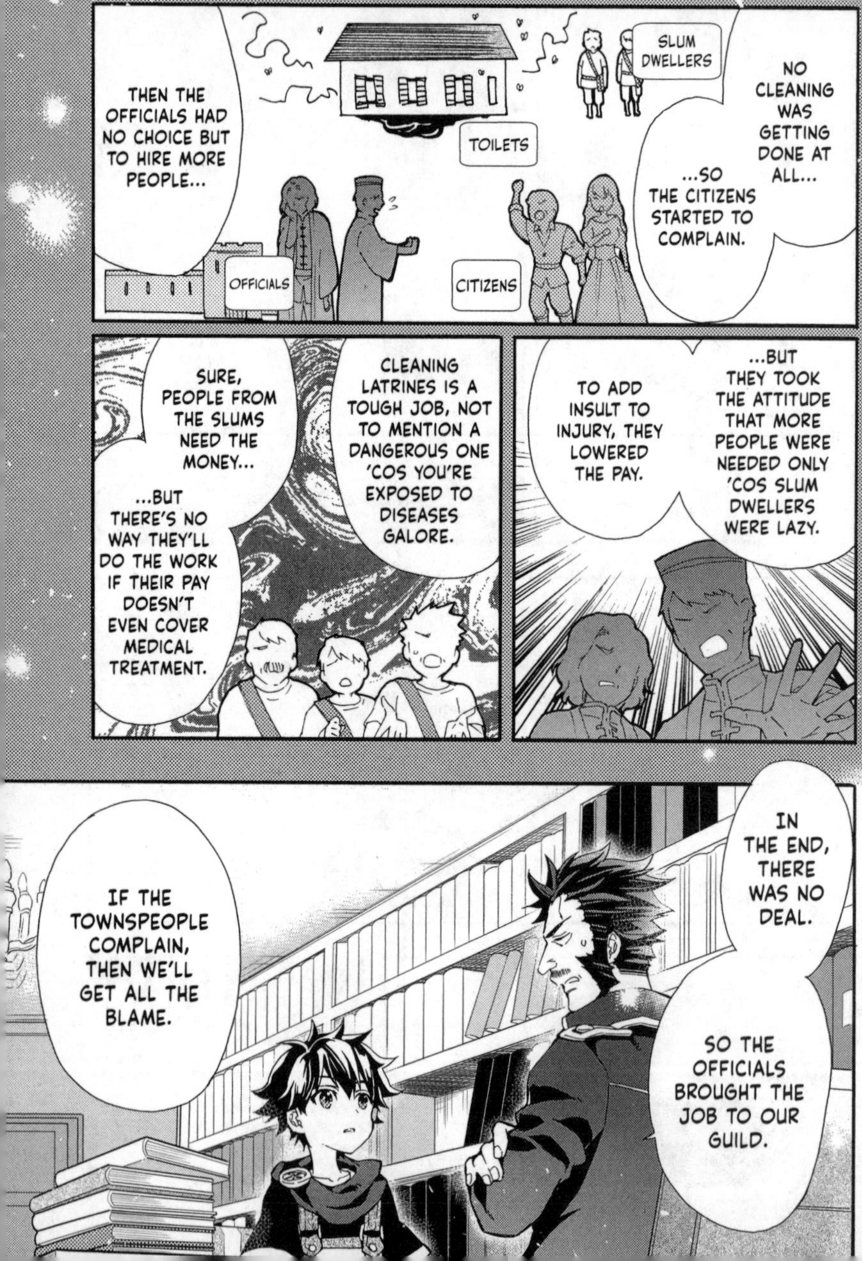
SLUM DWELLERS
NO CLEANING WAS GETTING DONE AT ALL...
...SO THE CITIZENS STARTED TO COMPLAIN.
TOILETS
THEN THE OFFICIALS HAD NO CHOICE BUT TO HIRE MORE PEOPLE...
CITIZENS
OFFICIALS
...BUT THEY TOOK THE ATTITUDE THAT MORE PEOPLE WERE NEEDED ONLY 'COS SLUM DWELLERS WERE LAZY.
TO ADD INSULT TO INJURY, THEY LOWERED THE PAY.
CLEANING LATRINES IS A TOUGH JOB, NOT TO MENTION A DANGEROUS ONE 'COS YOU'RE EXPOSED TO DISEASES GALORE.
SURE, PEOPLE FROM THE SLUMS NEED THE MONEY...
...BUT THERE'S NO WAY THEY'LL DO THE WORK IF THEIR PAY DOESN'T EVEN COVER MEDICAL TREATMENT.
IN THE END, THERE WAS NO DEAL.
SO THE OFFICIALS BROUGHT THE JOB TO OUR GUILD.
IF THE TOWNSPEOPLE COMPLAIN, THEN WE'LL GET ALL THE BLAME.

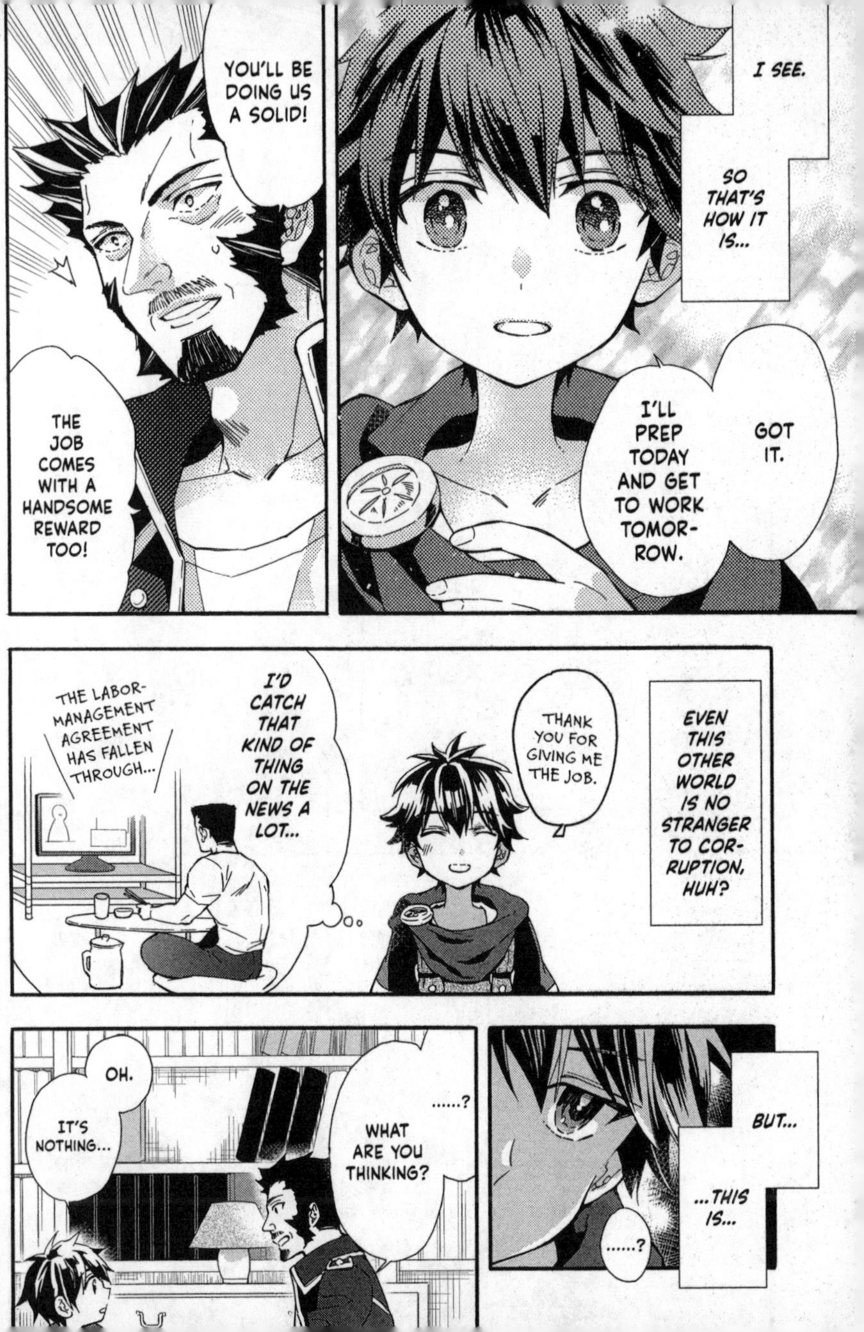
I SEE.
SO THAT'S HOW IT IS...
GOT IT.
I'LL PREP TODAY AND GET TO WORK TOMORROW.
YOU'LL BE DOING US A SOLID!
THE JOB COMES WITH A HANDSOME REWARD TOO!
EVEN THIS OTHER WORLD IS NO STRANGER TO CORRUPTION, HUH?
THANK YOU FOR GIVING ME THE JOB.
I'D CATCH THAT KIND OF THING ON THE NEWS A LOT...
THE LABOR-MANAGEMENT AGREEMENT HAS FALLEN THROUGH...
BUT...
...THIS IS...
......?
......?
WHAT ARE YOU THINKING?
OH.
IT'S NOTHING...

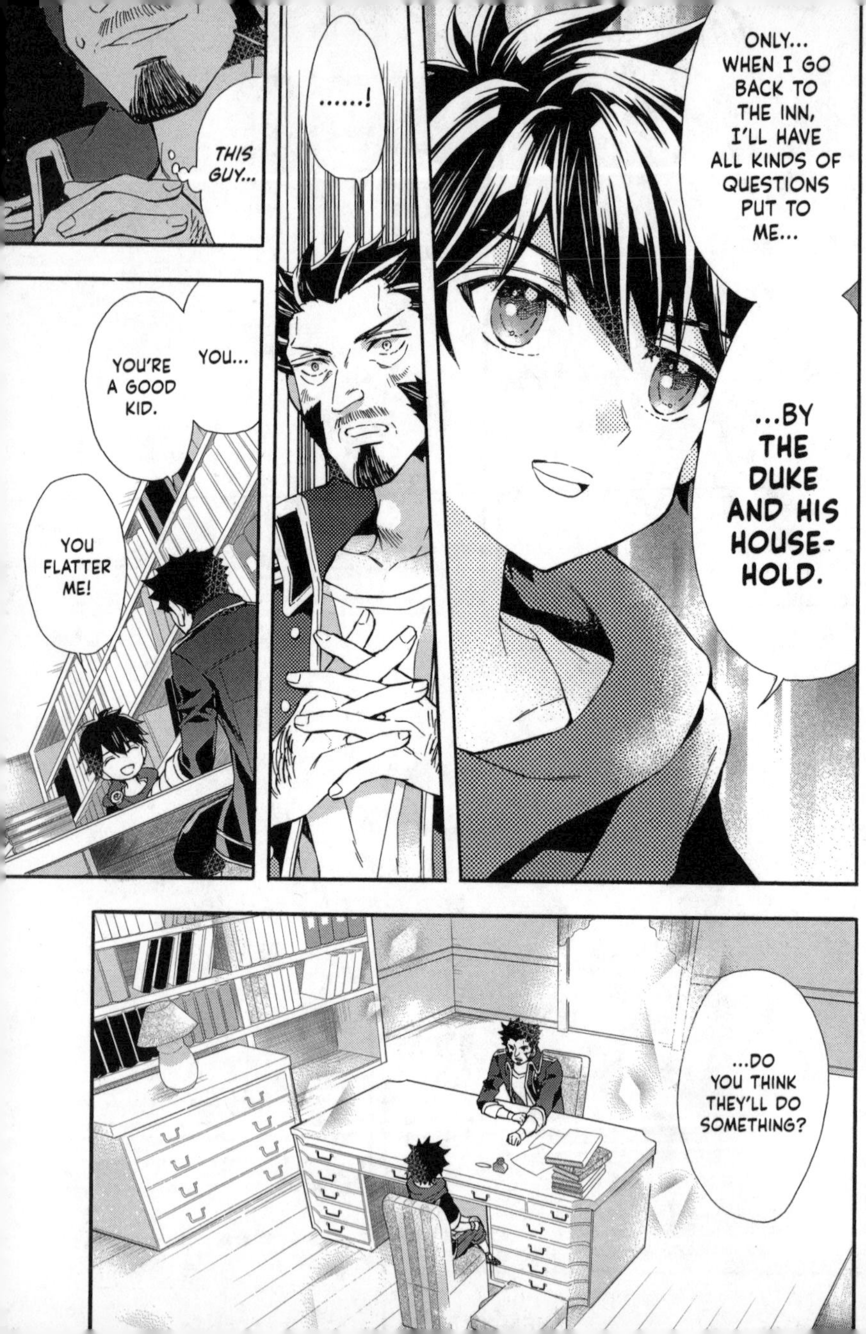
ONLY... WHEN I GO BACK TO THE INN, I'LL HAVE ALL KINDS OF QUESTIONS PUT TO ME...
...BY THE DUKE AND HIS HOUSE-HOLD.
......!
THIS GUY...
YOU...
YOU'RE A GOOD KID.
YOU FLATTER ME!
...DO YOU THINK THEY'LL DO SOMETHING?

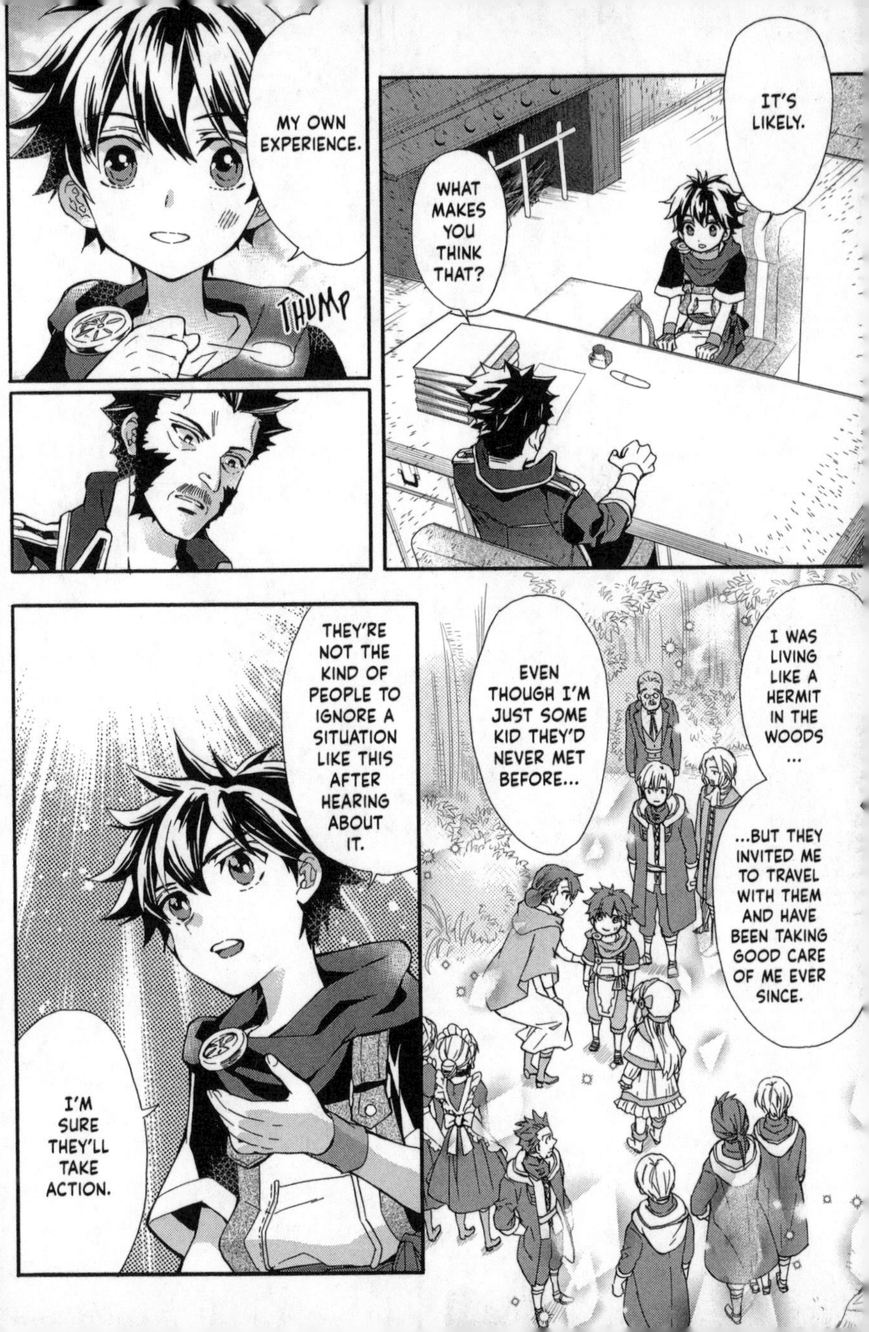
IT'S LIKELY.
WHAT MAKES YOU THINK THAT?
MY OWN EXPERIENCE.
THUMP
I WAS LIVING LIKE A HERMIT IN THE WOODS...
EVEN THOUGH I'M JUST SOME KID THEY'D NEVER MET BEFORE...
...BUT THEY INVITED ME TO TRAVEL WITH THEM AND HAVE BEEN TAKING GOOD CARE OF ME EVER SINCE.
THEY'RE NOT THE KIND OF PEOPLE TO IGNORE A SITUATION LIKE THIS AFTER HEARING ABOUT IT.
I'M SURE THEY'LL TAKE ACTION.

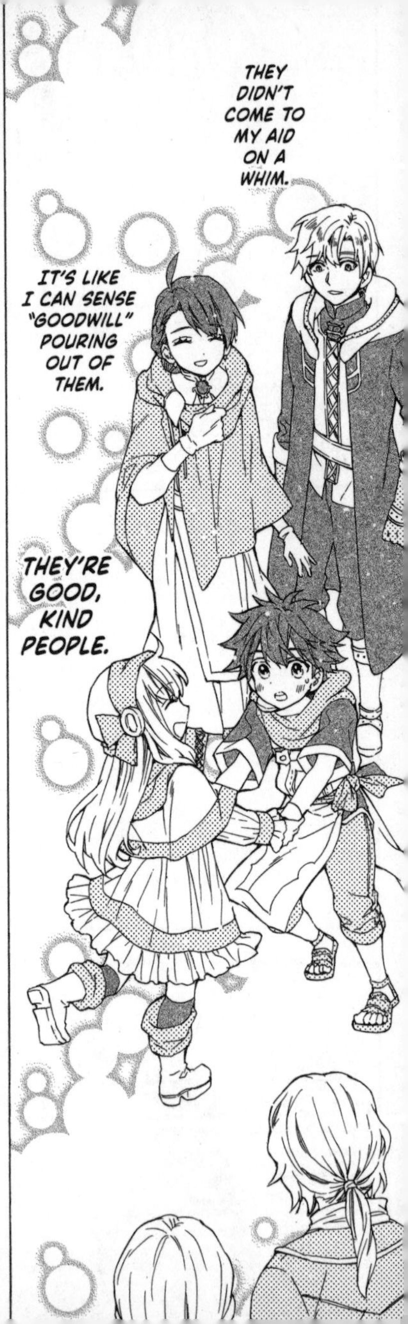
THEY DIDN'T COME TO MY AID ON A WHIM.
IT'S LIKE I CAN SENSE "GOODWILL" POURING OUT OF THEM.
THEY'RE GOOD, KIND PEOPLE.

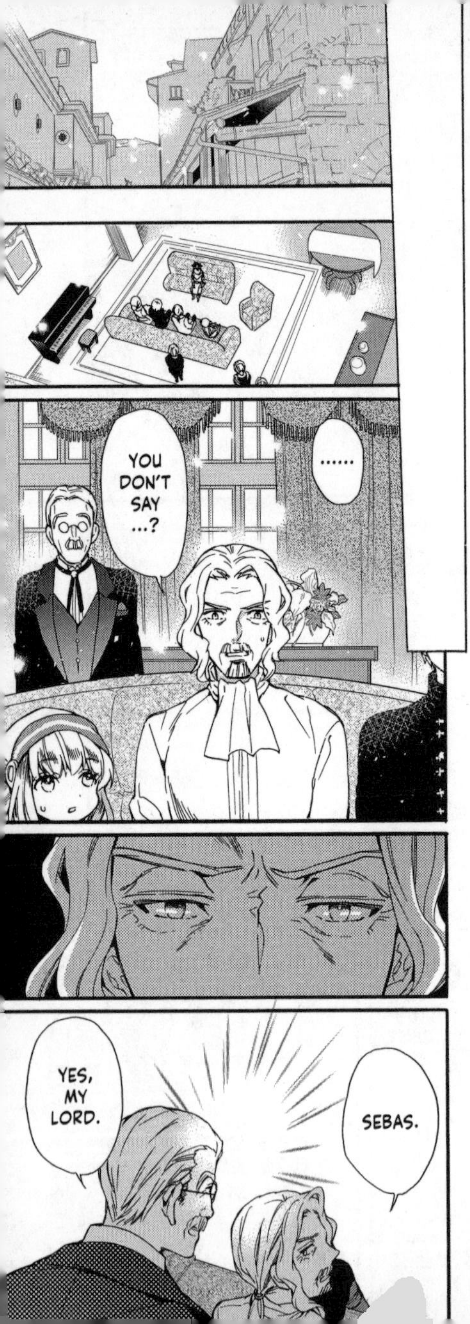
......
YOU DON'T SAY ...?
SEBAS.
YES, MY LORD.